BY THE EMPEROR'S HAND

BY THE EMPEROR'S HAND

Military Dress and Court Regalia in the later Romano–Byzantine Empire

TIMOTHY DAWSON

ILLUSTRATIONS BY
GRAHAM SUMNER

FRONTLINE BOOKS

BY THE EMPEROR'S HAND

This edition published in 2015 by Frontline Books,
an imprint of Pen & Sword Books Ltd,
47 Church Street, Barnsley, S. Yorkshire, S70 2AS

ISBN: 978-1-84832-589-0

CIP data records for this title are available from the British Library

For more information on our books, please visit
www.frontline-books.com, email info@frontline-books.com
or write to us at the above address.

Designed by David Rose

Printed and bound in Malta by Gutenberg Press Ltd

CONTENTS

PLATES

Between pages 66 and 67

INTRODUCTION

The study of the clothing of Rômania, or the Enduring Roman (or 'Byzantine') Empire, is an area which has been under-explored to date in serious scholarship.[1] Even in the area of court dress and regalia, for which there is a great deal more reliable source material than for the garb of common folk, the amount of study to date is quite scant. Much of the material that does exist on the subject is quite antiquated and all of it leaves a great deal of room for refinement.

The purpose of this volume is to trace as accurately as possible the evolution of clothing around the court and in the military from the sixth century to the end of the empire in 1453. Crucial to tracing this evolution will be the task of identifying wherever possible the precise form and defining characteristics of garments mentioned and depicted in the sources, for it is only with such clear identifications that changes in terminology can be distinguished from changes in the form of the physical items of dress, or changes in the manner of artistic representation. The principal sources will be in the first instance literary, corroborated where possible by pictures. The old paradigm which suggested that the art of Byzantion was unrelievedly formulaic[2] has come under significant challenge in recent years, and so it can be increasingly seen that pictorial sources can be accurate representations of their time and social context at least in some of their details.[3] Suitable middle and late Byzantine archaeological remains are scarce, but will make an indispensable contribution to the study, as will comparative material from Islamic and European realms. Other important inputs to this work are those of practical knowledge and practical application. The great majority of previous studies touching upon dress history in general, let alone that of Byzantion, even in the more popular realm, have manifestly been undertaken with little or no hands-on experience of the construction of clothing, and this has often led authors down blind alleys. Prior practical knowledge of this type proves to be especially invaluable in interpreting pictorial sources. In certain cases physical reconstruction has also proven to be very useful in testing and illustrating conclusions based upon academically conventional types of source material.

What will generally not be examined in much detail is the ritual and social significance of garments and ensembles. This is simply because the significance of formal court regalia is necessarily overt – it exists to advertise status in a specific and readily recognisable manner. There will, however, be some cases where there is an interrelation between the identity and nature of a garment and a signification projected across rank divisions, and then it will be discussed. Another caveat is that it is impossible to discuss all the permutations of garment, ensemble and use recorded in the sources.

A further area largely untouched here is that of religious regalia and vestments. This is not because I regard it as unimportant, nor because it is unconnected with the secular regalia, but rather because it merits dedicated study of its own.[4]

Clothing is often highly expressive, whether its wearers intend it to be or not. It can convey indications of gender, ethnicity, social class and status, occupation, identification with a subculture or, indeed, voluntary detachment from dominant social norms. The purpose of regalia is to make certain aspects of such expressiveness explicit, advertising rank and establishing a framework for the ritualistic enactment and validation of dominant social structures and the ideologies that underpin them. An essential characteristic of regalia is that it must differ from everyday dress and accessories in formally defined ways. The medieval Greek term used to denote regalia in our largest source, *allaxima*, embodies this, expressing the meaning of 'having been transformed from what commonly is'. This conceptual framework is fundamental to interpreting terminology that may use words which are also applied to more mundane situations and items.

The Principal Literary Sources

On the civilian side, the parameters of this study are based primarily upon three comparable works. The earliest is *On Powers or the Magistracies of the Roman State* written by the sixth-century courtier and literateur John Lydos. The second is a composite source comprising the brief so-called *Klêtôrologion* of Filotheos, and the encyclopaedic *Book of Ceremonies* which was based upon it. The latest is the *Treatise on the Offices* falsely attributed to Kodinos. These works are of a type called *taktikon* which originated in the Later Roman Empire, and were devoted to recording and systematising the hierarchy of the court.[5] More will be said about the nature of each of the works at the beginning of the chapters based upon them.

Another outstanding source for this project is the *Oneirokritikon* (Dream interpretation manual) of Achmet ben Sirin, believed to have been written in the tenth century. The importance of clothing in this social context is reflected by the large number of scenarios given in the work which hinge upon clothing. The exceptional value of many of these is that not only does the author give garment terminology, some of it unattested elsewhere, but the nature of the items discussed and their use and behaviour is often essential to the message to be drawn from the dream, and therefore the descriptions give unique insights into the character of the dress elements discussed.

It might well be said that the Roman Empire was not merely created and sustained by its military but defined by it. In keeping with this, it developed a rich tradition of military literature early in its history. There are military manuals attributed to the sixth century, but they contain little detail of use in this project.[6] The essential early source is the *Stratêgikon* attributed to Emperor Maurice from 602 CE. This work had enduring influence, for not only were manuscripts of it still being copied as late as the eleventh century, but Emperor Leo 'the Wise' incorporated much of it into his own manual, the *Taktika*,[7] around the turn of the tenth century; *Sullogê Taktikôn*, of the same period and sometimes associated with the same emperor, owes a similar debt to it. Two other major manuals largely conclude the tradition. The more important is the *Composition on Warfare* (traditionally known as *Praecepta Militaria*) newly written by General (later Emperor) Nikêforos (II) Fôkas around the middle of the tenth century. A little later, another General, Nikêforos Ouranos, produced a slightly reworked version of *Composition on Warfare*, once again under the title *Taktika*.[8] The incorporation of the *Stratêgikon* and the *Composition on Warfare* into later works has tempted some to suggest that this was a formulaic literature. The reverse, however, is true. We can rely on these sources because they reflect the normal nature of the military vocation – practical and pragmatic. For a soldier to be anything else carries the ultimate penalty, and for a commander to be otherwise may result in the death of the institution he serves. The sensitivity with which Leo and Ouranos adapt the earlier texts shows the characteristic which was fundamental to the empire's longevity – they knew how *not* to throw the baby out with the bath water.[9]

Since I embarked upon this project there has been one development which was of some help to me, and will be a great boon to many readers. It is an English translation of the *Book of Ceremonies* painstakingly prepared by Ann Moffat of the Australian National University. While my own theories and conclusions necessarily go beyond the established scholarship she could draw upon, I heartily recommend the work to anyone interested in the subject.

The limitations of the literary sources

Byzantine literary sources give us a copious terminology for clothing, but much more rarely do they give a clear indication of the nature of the item involved. This must often be deduced from subtle hints, gleaned sometimes from disparate sources, and sometimes corroborated by depiction in graphic arts. The very subtlety of such hints make interpretation, or even identification, of garments and accessories difficult, and often demands that some other bases of knowledge are needed to assist in illuminating them. Therein lie techniques which have as yet not been brought to bear to any great degree in this field. Previous scholars have certainly been highly knowledgeable in matters literary and artistic, and have done a great deal to elucidate matters in those disciplines. Yet, corroboration between the literary and artistic fields has often not been pursued as systematically as it might, and further significant advances can be made by forging links between the disciplines of textile history, the more embryonic field of costume history, and practical experience of textile craft.

Artistic sources

The traditional treatment of Byzantine art, whether in art history or in illustrating more general historiography, has done the field an enormous disservice in one respect. Again and again, a very narrow sampling of art works have been reproduced, at least in the more accessible published works. Those pictures may well be useful and representative of what they depict, but their endless re-iteration to the exclusion of so much other material misrepresents the entire culture. In choosing pictures for this volume, therefore, I have largely avoided the most widely reproduced pictures, however relevant, in favour of lesser-known pictures which could corroborate them or add new insights. Thus, it will assist a reader who wants to be able to look at more of the pictorial and 'minor' arts referred to in the following pages to have a Byzantine art book or two to hand, especially ones such as Helen Evans and William D. Wixom, *The Glory of Byzantium: Art and Culture of the Byzantine Era A.D. 843–1261* and Sarah T. Brooks (ed.), *Byzantium, Faith and Power (1261–1557): Perspectives on Late Byzantine Art and Culture.*

In pursuing a more extensive and systematic correlation of pictorial sources with the written ones, the difficulties with the artistic sources must be acknowledged. Despite the overall inaccuracy of Cyril Mango's summation of Byzantine art (see note 2), it does have a kernel of truth in the statement: 'Christ, the Apostles, the prophets appear in antique garb.' Iconographic stylisation does indeed rule the depiction of that narrow group of the dramatis personae of the biblical narratives. Furthermore, that stylisation does sometimes bleed outward from that core, influencing the representation of less-significant figures. Hence, a degree of sensitive discernment sometimes needs to be exercised in assessing the realism of what is shown, and, in that, a margin for error acknowledged. There is an array of good examples from the beginning of our period. The sixth century is often characterised as a time of religious apprehension, with many people expecting an imminent Second Coming. Yet, whether in spite of that or because of it, the major monuments of literary religious art of this time, the *Ashburnam Pentateuch*, *Rossano Gospels* and *Vienna Genesis*, show very limited stylisation, with many scenes dominated by a great deal of contemporary realism. After the first quarter of the seventh century we enter the so-called 'Dark Age of Byzantion'. The curtailment of artistic production is first caused by the effect of external threats. With the depredations of the Avars and Muslims diminishing, the potential for recovery was forestalled by the debate over the acceptability of the depiction of religious figures, the 'Iconoclast Controversy'. The Iconoclast Controversy was settled in favour of icons before the end of the ninth century, but artistic production was slow to recover, apparently taking more than a century to generate extensive results.[10] The eleventh century is quite well supplied, both in illuminated manuscripts and major monuments, while once again there are fewer in the twelfth century. Another dark age encompasses the thirteenth century in the wake of the atrocity of the Fourth Crusade and the hard fight back. The fourteenth century once again presents some good material, in contrast to the last half century before the Ottoman conquest, which has virtually none.

The nature of the art shows its own pattern of variance. As hitherto noted, the Late Antique artworks are usually highly realistic, even the religious scenes, even whilst being quite formal. Once source material begins again to be more prolific from the late tenth century onwards, the picture is much more mixed. Religious art tends to be much more stylised, yet that stylisation can vary from the hard-core antiquarianism which inspired Mango's comment, to a work such as the *Menologion of Basil II* (Vat. Gr. 1613), whose stylisation consists of quite realistic representations, but following fashions of two or three centuries earlier, rather than further back, and untainted by novelties and foreign influences. And yet, even works which treat the central religious figures in a hard-core antiquarian manner can still have realistic details in the margin or on peripheral figures (fig. 1). In the eleventh and twelfth centuries much more realistic pictorial material exists, although often with that subtle admixture of characteristics. The art of the Palaiologian period articulates a new paradigm, a greater dichotomy. The religious art is even more stylised than any prior period, and often in a way that is quite fantastical rather than antiquarian. The secular art consists almost entirely of donor portraits, and verges upon photo-realism. Through all this, even in the most realistic phases and examples of the art, however, there remained a sense that some things, however familiar in everyday life and well attested in the literature, were not suitable for inclusion in illustrations, either because they were trivial mundanities, or – particularly in the area of dress – seemingly because they were regarded as being 'not properly Roman'. A simple example of this last phenomenon is the turban. From literature we can see that turbans were common wear for men of Rômania from the ninth century, yet in a work of elite illumination such as the *Menologion of Basil II* they appear solely as a signifier for Arabs, and a generally negative one at that. Nevertheless, within these constraints the visual arts offer extensive and useful support to the written sources, and can help to explain much that is obscure.

FIG. 1. The marginal figures of even elite religious art may show points of realistic detail, like the way this man has an additional garment, most probably a coat, tied around his neck by the sleeves. Dionysiou Monastery, Athos, codex 587, f. 19v.

BELOW: FIG. 2. Vernacular art often embodies realistic details glossed over in more elite media, such as this depiction on a ceramic fragment of a coat gaping around its buttons. Archaeological Museum, Istanbul.

The traditional art history distinction between 'fine art' and the dismissively described 'minor arts' (ceramics, metalwork, stone and wood carving, and so on) has been another liability to scholarship. Images applied to them can be recognised as routinely more realistic than 'fine art' products (fig. 2).

Archaeology

Archaeological material relevant to this research is both rare and widely dispersed, but will make great contributions to our knowledge. It does have its own issues, however. Collections all around the world are replete with early clothing and textiles from the Near East. Unfortunately, most of these have been involved in an enormous commercial trade in such material, which commenced in the nineteenth century and continues to this day. This trade has always been commonly supplied by people and organisations whose motivation was purely monetary and quite often went as far as complete fakery.[11] Hence, an assertion of provenance or date must often be taken with some reservation, although the issue can be readily resolved in historical dress and textile studies as technological advances mean that carbon-14 dating can be done with smaller and smaller samples. That process has already yielded many surprises, and it seems very likely to go on doing so.[12] There has been a long tendency for almost any textile from the Near East which did not have modern archaeological stratigraphic data to be attributed to Late Antiquity (as well as 'probably Egypt'). Many such pieces might well be subject to major re-evaluation if tested by carbon-14, or, indeed, subjected to other forms of technical analysis.

Other inputs

The study of historical clothing and military equipment has often been an area that has been bedevilled by a lack of practical insight. Commentators on Byzantine sources were often certainly extremely fine historians and philologists, but without practical familiarity of how clothing, accessories, arms and armour were made and functioned, their conclusions could be quite wide of the mark, and even completely dysfunctional on occasion. Hence, another input which has made an important contribution to this volume is that of practical experience. The author has spent decades involved in practical historical reconstruction, combining the information gleaned using conventional scholarly methods with manual skills in tailoring, leatherwork and metalwork. The colour plates in this volume have had the most intensive input from this direction, with many of the garments and accessories being based upon reconstructions made by the author (fig. 3).[13] It must be acknowledged, however, that *uninformed* replication can be equally sterile, and this is especially evident in popular reproductions of Byzantine military equipment inspired by an uncritical acceptance of Byzantine art. A fusion of rigorous historical methods in amassing and assessing evidence with practical experience, and sometimes physical experimentation, is by far the best way to elucidate essentially practical subjects such as this one.

FIG. 3. The author (centre) and companions staying out of the rain at Deva: Chester Roman Festival, 2012. All clothing made by the author or under his supervision.

Conventions applied to the Greek terminology

The venerable academic tradition by which all foreign terms were Latinised may have made sense when the background of any educated person could be assumed to have included some study of classical Latin. That is no longer the case, and the Latin, Latin-derived and Latinised words which do occur in English are invariably pronounced in ways which bear no resemblance to historical practice. Hence, I see no virtue in persisting with that tradition, although names which have a familiar English form will not be restored to their original form. Where Greek terms are given out of specific context, they will normally be in the nominative singular, except where they relate to normally plural items such as footwear. Transliteration will be in phonetic form regarded as being contemporary with the sources. Medieval Greek pronunciation was already much like that of modern Greek by the beginning of our period. Thus, β will be v, η will be represented by ê but sounds like I and ω will be represented by ô but sounds like o and χ will be kh (not ch in order to make it clearly a fricative); υ will be u not y, and φ will be f not ph. In the latter part of the period the use of μπ to represent b was coming into use for foreign 'loan' words, yet there was still a significant quantity of terms, mostly earlier Latin borrowings, in which μπ was meant to be taken in the elementary sense. Hence, I have only transliterated μπ as b when I can be confident that that is what was intended.

TRIBULATION

LATE ANTIQUITY TO THE NINTH CENTURY

1

At the beginning of the sixth century, the court of the Roman Empire already had five centuries of accretion of ceremonial and regalia custom. Previous scholarship has theorised the existence of a Late Antique *taktikon* which might have recorded details of the structure, clothing and rituals of the court, but if such a thing had existed, it is now lost.[1] In the absence of that, more scattered evidence must be sought for the state of the court and its regalia through these periods. The situation regarding military clothing is only slightly more definite, despite recent adventurous views.[2] One major structural change at the top of the court in the early seventh century must be noted: Emperor Herakleios introduced the custom of crowning a son, or other designated heir, as junior co-emperor in order to stabilise dynastic continuity. This new position inherited the title *kaisar* (Hellenised phonetically from the Latin *Caesar*), while the supreme ruler became known either by the ancient Greek word for king, *vasileus*, or as *despotês*. Their consorts were known respectively as *kaisarissa* and *augousta* or *despoina*.

It is well known that white and purple were the two essential ceremonial colours from the Republican era, emblematically combined in the *toga praetexta* of noble Roman manhood with its purple stripe on a white background. The ceremonial supremacy of the colour white became institutionalised in the fourth century with the establishment of the corps of *candidati*.[3] A very important development at this time was the decree by Emperor Justinian prohibiting the sale of fabric in 'any colour resembling the imperial purple', and declaring the unauthorised possession of purple garments to be high treason.[4] Thus, purple in all forms was reserved for imperially sponsored court use. The controls on predominantly purple garments seem never to have been compromised, although about the turn of the tenth century, Leo VI 'the Wise' eased the prohibition by allowing the 'sale of small fragments and scraps of purple cloth, which afford means of ostentation to Our subjects'.[5]

Amongst pictorial sources for the sixth-century court the mosaics of the various churches at Ravenna must, of course, stand pre-eminent. The most famous ones were executed initially for the Ostrogothic king Theodoric, clearly by mosaicists brought in from Constantinople for the job, and then altered to depict Justinian, Theodôra and their court once Ravenna had come back under the suzerainty of Constantinople. Many of the features represented there are well corroborated by various other sources of the time. Firstly, the prevalence of plain colours, most often white, as the essential tinctures of the male court, in stark contrast to the vividly figured cloths worn by unranked men, even guards. The shoulder-fastened *khlamus* with its contrasting *tavlia* are familiar, and the courtiers' footwear are significant. Lest it be imagined that these mosaics are in way unusual, their details are amply corroborated by other pictures of the sixth century, such as those in the *Vienna Genesis*, *Ashburnham Pentateuch* and *Rossano Gospels* manuscripts (fig. 4).

FIG. 4. Constantine IV (668–85) and attendants. Church of St Apollinare in Classe, Ravenna.

Coming closest to being a *taktikon* for this era is John Lydos' *On Powers, or, The Magistracies of the Roman State*, written during the 540s.[6] This work is full of invaluable information, not merely for the sixth century, but for the middle Byzantine period of this study. John discusses the various permutations of the regalia of the ruler, that of the class of *patrikioi*, and of a couple of other ranks. The key sections of these are the definitions he gives of various garments and accessories which would continue into the central period of our study.

John Lydos is quite brief on the matter of the imperial regalia, presumably deeming it too well known to belabour. Most of the items he does discuss are presented in order to assert their antiquity. They are a jewelled coronet (*stefanos*), a sceptre surmounted by an eagle called *skipiô* (σκιπίω/σκιπίω) in Greek, transliterated directly from the Latin *scipio*,[7] the white and purple *toga praetexta*, and red footwear. To these he adds two items of military regalia: a spear and a crown crested in the manner of a helmet and called *iuba* in Latin, and *lofia* or *toufa* by others (Plate 12).[8]

Ceremonial Dress

Main Garments

The *Book of Ceremonies* attributes to this period the first step in the process that would rapidly transform the regalia of all the men of the court. It recounts that Emperor Anastasios I chose to be crowned in 491 wearing the *divêtêsion*, the first to do so. The copious surviving portraits of the middle Byzantine period show that a primary characteristic of the royal garment is full sleeves gathered into long, tight, decorated cuffs, a form which can be identified with what the tenth-century dream interpreter Achmet calls 'Persian-sleeves' (*persikomanikia*) by virtue of his description of their potential for coming unfastened and falling away from the wearer's arm (Plate 3, centre).[9] This sleeve style is already visibly established in the Roman Empire in the first half of the fifth century, illustrated on the arch of the Church of Saint Maria Maggiore in Rome, and on into the following century, though, remarkably, it is in women's clothing. At Maria Maggiore these sleeves are found on the dresses of the Holy Virgin and the Queen of Egypt, while in the sixth century they are familiar from the oft-reproduced mosaics of the Parade of Virgins in the Church of San Vitale at Ravenna. In all these examples, the garment is part of a style of outfit which clearly has Persian antecedents,[10] supporting the proposed derivation of *divêtêsion* from the Persian term *dibetsch*.[11] It is noteworthy that although they are dated later than the reign of Anastasios, this sleeve style does not appear in the Ravenna court scene which now depicts Justinian and his attendants. There are several possible explanations for this. The simplest once again derives from the fact that the mosaic was originally intended to depict Theodoric, and the Ostrogoths' willingness to imitate Byzantine court style probably did not go so far as to embrace what may still have been seen as an effeminate fashion. One thinks of the diatribes of a later Italian, Liutprand of Cremona, for whom the Byzantine custom of men wearing ankle-length tunics was enough to besmirch their masculinity. Another explanation could be that it would be unreasonable to expect such a change, which was challenging to both gender paradigms and Roman ethnic identity, to be accepted immediately, and Justinian is noted as something of a traditionalist. Finally, the attribution to Anastasios' coronation may not be correct. It cannot have been much later than that, however – although quite when in the century the change could be said to be irreversibly established in the royal regalia is uncertain, by the middle of the seventh century this sleeve form had already become well enough accepted as to have trickled down to be incorporated in garments of lesser members of the male court (fig. 5).[12]

FIG. 5. Madonna and child accompanied by saints in court dress, early seventh century. The volume of a 'Persian-sleeve' is clearly visible on the man to the right. Monastery of St Catherine, Sinai.

Another change which seems to directly accompany the spread of *persikomanikia* is in the lengthening of men's garments. Ankle-length tunics were already established in male clothing, particularly of a religious nature, prior to the beginning of this study, in contrast to the shorter garments of laymen. The early sources showing *persikomanikia* also show those court robes as being ankle-length. The assimilation of ankle-length garments with *persikomanikia* into the dress repertoire of high-status Roman men further illustrates a remarkable shift in the prevailing ideology of identity as these men were able to be seen in a style of dress which, in prior times, would have have been doubly excoriated as foreign and effeminate.

Late Antiquity was also a period in which the basic structure of main garments changed. Hitherto, tunics in the Roman Empire were usually made by a method which involved them being woven as a single piece on very large looms, already shaped with sleeves and with tapestry-woven decoration. The modern convention is to call this construction 'Coptic' due to the extensive finds in Egypt, although the likelihood is that the manufacture took place more widely across the empire than merely in Egypt, just as the art shows wide

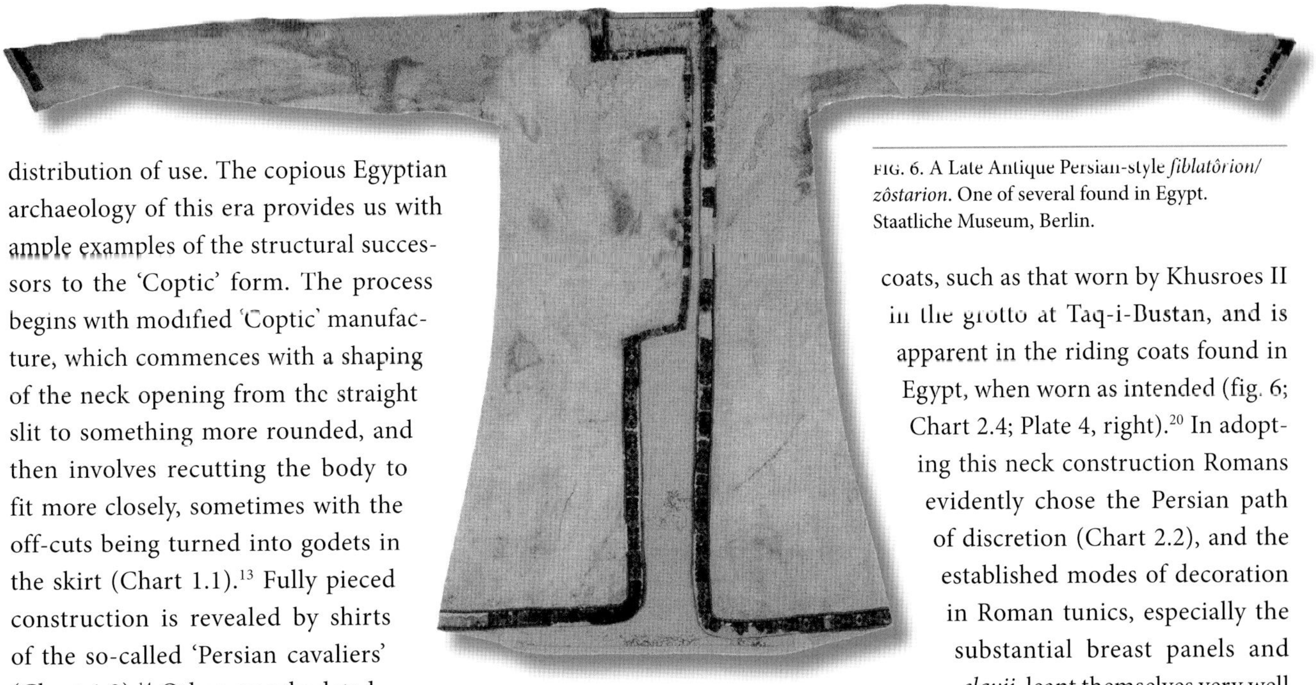

FIG. 6. A Late Antique Persian-style *fiblatôrion/zôstarion*. One of several found in Egypt. Staatliche Museum, Berlin.

distribution of use. The copious Egyptian archaeology of this era provides us with ample examples of the structural successors to the 'Coptic' form. The process begins with modified 'Coptic' manufacture, which commences with a shaping of the neck opening from the straight slit to something more rounded, and then involves recutting the body to fit more closely, sometimes with the off-cuts being turned into godets in the skirt (Chart 1.1).[13] Fully pieced construction is revealed by shirts of the so-called 'Persian cavaliers' (Chart 1.2).[14] Other, poorly dated, surviving examples show a pieced construction which may be in use by the ninth century (Chart 1.3).[15] This transition is also recorded in literature by Isidore of Seville in glossing the term *armelausa*. He says that the *armelausa* had splits in its skirt front and back, and says that it was named for the characteristic of having sleeves sewn on.[16] A continuing evolution in the arrangement of the neck opening also serves to determine the long-term form of Byzantine primary garments, and once again it involves a form which seems to derive from Persia. The shirts of the Persian cavaliers' ensembles have V necklines, which evidently had some currency for a while in the Roman Empire, for they are sporadically illustrated in later sources on people of both sexes.[17] The rounding of the neck opening mentioned above initially leaves vestiges of the primitive slit on the shoulder line in order that the opening can be widened enough to pass the head through. To begin with, the slit extended to both sides, as it did before reshaping, but then the practice arose of only leaving a slit on one shoulder, commonly the left (Chart 1.1). There are numerous Late Antique surviving examples which show these characteristics,[18] and the practice endured well into the medieval period.[19] At some point, the slit opening was moved to run vertically down from the neck hole. A construction with the slit on the left side of the neck hole is seen as early as the late second or early third century in carvings of men from Palmyra, where they are part of ensembles which are very conspicuously Persianate. The Palmyrenes were in the habit of making a feature of the slit by adding decorative trim, while the Persians themselves seem to have preferred to treat it so discretely that it all but disappears. The offset-to-the-left mode is, however, visible on Sassanian coats, such as that worn by Khusroes II in the grotto at Taq-i-Bustan, and is apparent in the riding coats found in Egypt, when worn as intended (fig. 6; Chart 2.4; Plate 4, right).[20] In adopting this neck construction Romans evidently chose the Persian path of discretion (Chart 2.2), and the established modes of decoration in Roman tunics, especially the substantial breast panels and *clavii*, leant themselves very well to concealing the opening (Plate 4, centre). One of the few places where such an offset opening is visible is the third-century funeral stele of a woman called Thalassia in the Istanbul Archaeological Museum (fig. 7). On the stele, the opening is not only distinctly visible, it is also on the right, two features which almost certainly signify conventional gender differences. Late survivals of the male mode of a left-side slit, one conspicuous and the other concealed amongst the decoration, are the tunic and alb of Roger II of Sicily, which were, of course, very much based on Byzantine precedent (fig. 19).

Paragôdês

The torso garment noted amongst the sixth-century regalia was the *paragôdês* or *paragaudês*. This tunic was another Persian import, according to John Lydos,[21] and existed in various styles. The base colour of the imperial *paragaudês* is not stated, probably because it was assumed to be purple ('how, indeed, not', as John Lydos comments of another purple imperial garment[22]), but it was decorated from top to toe and side to side with gold symbols such as the letter *gamma*. The *paragaudês* of the *eparkhos* of the *praitôrion* was an unadorned rich purple. That of the Patricians was white, and had purple edges decorated with spearhead symbols. John Lydos also says this tunic had *perikheiridai* (Gr: literally 'near, or around, the hand') or *manicae* (Lat: related to *manus*, hand). These terms are commonly translated today as 'sleeves', yet virtually all tunics of this time had sleeves extending to the wrist, so here they must mean something different. The key lies in the precise sense of the former term, 'around the hand' and the related expression given by Isidore of Seville, *kheirodutê*, 'put on the hand'.[23] The Persians are

FIG. 7. Funeral stele of Thalassia (third century) showing a dress with a vertical neck opening offset to the right. Istanbul Archaeological Museum.

well known to have had a fashion for sleeves rather longer than the wearer's arms. This feature is found most familiarly on coats, from those described by Xenofon[24] to the Late Antique surviving examples excavated in Egypt (fig. 6),[25] yet isolated pictorial sources also indicate that tunics could have the same feature.[26] Hence, it seems that the characteristic which sets this Persian garment apart from more prosaic Roman tunics was not its variable decoration, but very long sleeves. I have explained elsewhere that garments with very long sleeves were called *skaramangion* in the ninth and tenth centuries, and once again the advent of this term is attributed to Emperor Herakleios' Persian booty in the first quarter of the seventh century.[27] Such a reassignment of terminology would have freed *paragaudês*, or, as it subsequently became, *paragaudion*, to be applied to quite different garments in that later era.

Kôlovion

One notable reassignment of terminology had begun a couple of centuries earlier, but was not yet quite complete in John Lydos' time. It was in the meaning of *kôlovion*. The Latin *colobium* of the early Roman imperial period, from which this was derived, is well known to have been a long tunic without sleeves,[28] of a type well attested in archaeology, and depicted in early medieval art as the garment worn by Christ to his crucifixion,[29] which was used as a ritual vestment by early Christian functionaries.[30] The later sources reveal that, as time wore on, and as Christianity gained status as a state-sponsored religion, such a scanty garment ceased to be considered acceptable, and was supplanted by a sleeved garment which also went by the name *dalmatica*.[31] Epifanios, writing in the fourth century, confirms this equivalence, using the directly Hellenised form, 'and *dalmatikas*, that is to say *kôlovia*', and Church folklore came to associate this change with Pope Sylvester who served from 314 to 335. On the other hand, Dorotheos of Gaza could still give a very clear description of the older form, hence the change was not yet complete by the first half of the sixth century.[32] The anonymous author of *Concerning the Origins of Heresy*, sometimes attributed to John of Damascus, employs a term found elsewhere in the *Book of Ceremonies*: *delmatikion*, 'of the *delmatikia*, that is *kôlovia*'.[33] Thus, *kôlovion* was reassigned to mean the loose-sleeved *dalmatica* in male dress. *The Edict on Prices* of Diocletian confirms this explicitly, repeatedly distinguishing the prices 'for women's *delmatikai*' (*delmatikôn gunaikiôn*) from those 'for men's *delmatikai*, that is *kôlovia*' (*delmatikôn andreiôn êtoi kôlobiôn*).[34] In the succeeding centuries this distinction was further elaborated along gender lines until by the tenth century the term *delmatikion* was only applied to women's dresses.

Over-garments

John Lydos and the pictorial sources are in accord in showing that forms of mantle were the most conspicuous components of the court regalia of the sixth century. In view of the ritual imperative, noted in the preface, that an item of regalia must differ significantly and recognisably from mundane practice, it would seem strange to anyone familiar with Western medieval dress to find that mantles should be so central. What has to date gone unappreciated is that at the end of Late Antiquity in the eastern Roman Empire mantles had already been superseded in the everyday dress of men by a more 'modern' garment, the coat. This is illustrated most potently by two ivories. One is a plaque in the Bargello Museum, which explicitly contrasts the ceremonial use of the *khlamus* in the middle register with the mundane use of the coat in the lower frame (fig. 8).[35] That ivory is Lombardic, as can be inferred by the very un-Roman clothing worn by the common men, but it also shows the enthusiasm of the Lombardic elite for Roman social customs in terms of affirming their power and legitimacy. The other example, a pyxis held in the British Museum, again confronts the two garments, although without making the status distinction so recognisable. For more on coats, see below under military dress.

FIG. 8. Detail of one leaf of an ivory diptych attributed to Lombardic patronage but preserving Roman practice in contrasting the ceremonial use of the *khlamus* with the everyday employment of the *fiblatôrion/zôstarion*. Later fifth- or sixth-century. Bargello Museum, Florence.

Travea

One regalia item which Lydos does not discuss in any detail is the *travea* (Latin *trabea*), the long, originally white, drape wound about the body as a symbol in early times of royal authority, and later by members of the equestrian order. Presumably that was because he regarded it as too familiar and commonplace to be worth discussing. Well he might take this view: the considerable number of ivories that have survived do show it as an essential component of the consular regalia. Lydos does mention it in passing numerous times, generally as shorthand for holding public office.[36] The term Lydos uses is always 'belt' (*zônê*). When the office of consul was absorbed into that of emperor, the *travea* moved with it to become central to imperial iconography, just as it had been to consular dignity.[37] At some point in the 'Dark Age' it acquired the name *lôros*, cognate with the Latin *lorum*, a strap.

Khlamus

The premiere item of regalia across the court was the *khlamus*. This was a distinctly male garment. The only woman to wear it was the empress. The martial *khlamus* of the *kaisar* was 'double folded, red [*kokkos*], of first-grade silk and fastened on the shoulder with a golden, gemmed brooch' (fig. 9, right). His senatorial cloak was purple with square decorative panels (*sêmenta*) near the hem.[38] The patrician *khlamus* was 'double folded . . . from shoulder to shin, fastened by a golden brooch, of sooty colour, for which is called "*atravatika*", and had transverse purple marks at the middle' (fig. 9, left).[39] The description 'double folded' is explained by the surviving example from Antinoë which is oval with two rectangular panels across the long axis (the 'transverse purple marks at the middle' above) (Plate 3).[40] When worn, it was folded along that centre line, producing an almost semicircular shape, and then pinned on the shoulder. It was a defining characteristic of the *khlamus* that it was always worn fastened with a brooch on the right shoulder, according to a letter of Neilos of Ankara.[41] The statement of Isidore of Seville that a *khlamus* was 'put on from one side', unlike the *pallium* on the shoulders, implies the same thing.[42] It is evident that the white *khlamus* with purple *tavlia* seen in so many pictures of the sixth century was a fairly undistinguished garment in the context of court dress in that century, since John Lydos does not see fit to comment upon it.

FIG. 9. Saints Prokopios, Dêmetrios and Nestôr in court regalia. The saint on the left wears *tà atravatika*, 'the blacks'. Note the fine *maniakion* on the centre man. Monastery of St Catherine, Sinai.

FIG. 10. A typical example of a *manduas/mantion*. Monastery of St Panteleimon, Athos, codex 2, f. 243r.

Manduas

John Lydos draws a crucial distinction between the *khlamus* and another cape called the *manduas*. He asserts that this hung from the shoulders to no further than the knee (as distinct from the *khlamus* being almost ankle-length) and did not have *tavlia*. The *manduas*, or *manduê* or *mantion* as it was also called, was a single-layered, semicircular cape adopted from Persia.[43] Being hung from both shoulders, it was fastened at the centre of the chest, another variation from the *khlamus*. By the ninth century, it had become conflated with *sagion*, the old Latin *sagum*, a square military cape deriving from northern Europe.[44] Hesychios offers a basis for this merging of *manduas* with *sagion* by saying that the *manduas* is a 'type of garment of Persian soldiers' (fig. 10).[45] The distinction between the *manduas* and the *khlamus* can be seen to survive right up the middle of the eleventh century, after which the forms of decoration and methods of wearing are no longer differentiated.

Leg- and footwear

The emperor's footwear was second only to the crown in importance as regalia according to ancient custom.[46] Footwear coloured red to purple was a male imperial prerogative from the early fourth century,[47] and is positively proverbial in Byzantine literature all the way to the end of the empire. This time-honoured practice results in there being relatively little discussion of imperial footwear in our sources. Ibn Khordabeh, an Arab visitor to Constantinople in the middle of the ninth century, wrote of a development in this, saying that 'only the Heir Apparent wears one red shoe and one black one'.[48] No Roman source records this practice, although other authors writing in Arabic comment upon it into the eleventh century. Women were exempt from sumptuary rules, and one result of that is that red footwear was very popular with that gender. A statistical survey of a large sample of middle Byzantine manuscripts conducted by the author in the Vatican Library and elsewhere revealed that red footwear occurred more often on women than every other colour combined. This may be in part a contrivance of painters, but red is an easy tincture to obtain on leather, and red women's footwear is well represented in the archaeology (fig. 11, bottom). The popularity of the colour can be explained perhaps by it being an opulent indulgence that was not available to the average man.

FIG. 11. Examples of boots from the Late Antique cemeteries in Egypt. Top, male. Bottom, female.

The Patricians wore white leg coverings under their tunics, called *periskelides* by John Lydos. In the tenth century a neuter form of the term (*periskelismata*) appears in the *Oneirokritikon* of Achmet as breeches, which are accompanied by leggings called *touvia*. That John Lydos uses the term on its own suggests that in Late Antiquity it meant trousers that did not require any additional leg-wear. The leg-wear shown in the Ravenna mosaics is plainly fitted with feet, and footed trousers of this era have survived (Charts 4.2 and 4.3).[49]

John Lydos describes the sandals of the *patrikios* in detail thus: 'black footwear, wholly bare, enclosing the heel to the height of the ankle-bone and the tips of the toes, with laces from each side binding the ankle over the arch of the foot and allowing the hose to show through'.[50] The extremely close resemblance of this description to the footwear of the courtiers in the Ravenna mosaics and several other pictures of this period can readily be seen. These were known as *kampagia* after the old Roman military sandal, and this term, and evidently the footwear, persist into the eleventh century.[51] That even by the sixth century such *kampagia* were stylised ceremonial items is shown by the copious quantity of footwear taken from the Late Antique cemeteries of Egypt. Sandals do occur frequently in that corpus, but they are of much more familiar types, often corroborated by portraits of antique religious personages, and are nothing like those depicted at Ravenna. More commonly, much more modern-looking boots and shoes were in wide use (figs 11 and 12).

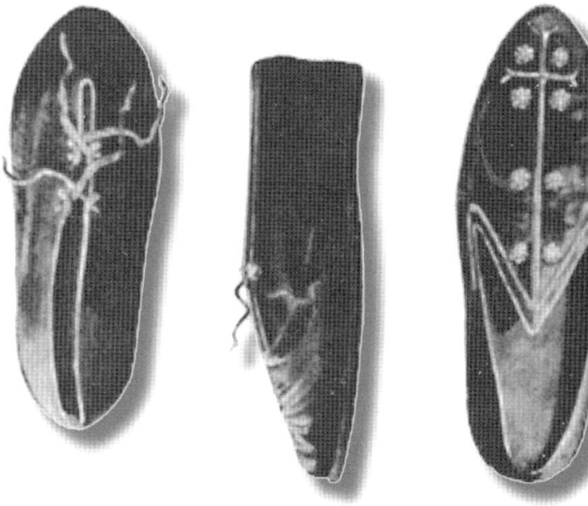

FIG. 12. Examples of shoes from the Late Antique cemeteries in Egypt.

Accessories

Two other items mentioned by John Lydos which continued in use are the torque (*streptos*, later *maniakion*), and a belt (*zôstêr*) of crimson leather. The *streptos* was a piece of military regalia which John has the commanders of the army place upon an incoming emperor to denote their acceptance of his fitness to command (fig. 9, centre), while the belt is another piece of the imperial ensemble.[52] The Ravenna mosaics indicate that the torque had already slipped from the elevated role that John attributed to it, being worn by Justinian's guards, and by the ninth century at least, the red belt has also rather slipped down the ranking.

Military Dress

The copious military literature of the Roman Empire is often quite parsimonious in its discussion of the clothing to be worn by its soldiers. One of the most detailed sources is the *Stratêgikon*, originally written at the very beginning of the seventh century, and remaining very influential through the middle Byzantine period. All the presently surviving copies date from the tenth and eleventh centuries, showing sporadic updating of the vocabulary. Where the earlier terminology is preserved, it embodies some developments in Roman clothing that were relatively recent to the time of its composition.[53]

Main garments

The tunic recommended for the infantry is called *armelausion*.[54] As discussed above, this means a tailored tunic, rather than one of the older, shapeless 'Coptic' style. Our source advises that this garment be 'short': that is, extending only to the knee, a paradigm for military garments that runs right through the middle Byzantine period, if not beyond. Isidore of Seville says that the *armelausa* (the Latin form of the term) had splits in its skirt front and back, although this is commonly regarded as being more of a cavalry style.[55] Examples of such short, split tunics can be seen in the lower register of the Bargello Ivory (fig. 8).

Outer garments

The *Stratêgikon* recommends a garment called *zôstarion* for both infantry and cavalry.[56] This is one of the various names current in this period for a coat. The earliest evidence for coats occur in Persia in Hellenistic antiquity.[57] Derived from a word for belt (*zôstêr*), *zôstarion* was used because in this period this garment was not fitted with buttons, and when worn as a coat (that is with the arms in the sleeves, rather than having it draped around the shoulders) it was held in place at the waist by a belt (Plate 4, right).[58] At the throat it was secured by a brooch (*fiboula*), both when worn as a coat and worn in the manner of a cape as it is shown in the Bargello Ivory (fig. 8) and other sources.[59] Surviving examples from Egypt corroborate the pictorial sources in showing no other fastening on these coats in Late Antiquity (fig. 6).[60] Hence, we find the terms *fiboulatôrion* and *fiblatôrion* used in the *Edict on Prices* and surviving right up to the composition of the *Klêtôrologion*.[61] The *Edict* lists *fiblatôria* that were said to come from a variety of different regions, and comparing the coats shown on the Bargello Ivory with the 'Persian riding coats' from Egypt confirms two permutations that the people of the time might have regarded as being regional. The Persian style has the outer straight edge descending from the left side of the neck (fig. 6), while the more widespread alternative embodies a central division (fig. 8). The *Stratêgikon* advises that cavalrymen have an Avar-style *zôstarion* which can cover the knees whilst riding, while the infantry were to have coats in the Gothic fashion just to the knee. The differences are functionally clear. An Avar *zôstarion* must have either a fuller skirt or a split or splits in the skirt at the rear to allow it to spread or divide over the saddle, otherwise the rider would have a large bundle of fabric under his buttocks, and that gathering would draw the skirts away from his thighs. Although the surviving 'Persian riding coats' do not appear to have this feature, the placement of the body seams in the back would allow two well-placed splits (Chart 5.1). In order to cover the knees while riding, this type of coat must also be quite long, down to the upper-calf when standing, as a garment always rides up in the mounted posture. A Gothic *zôstarion* would not only be shorter, but, like the coats from Egypt, would have no divisions in the skirt, thus affording greater warmth and protection.

A supplementary garment to be used by horsemen is the *gounion* or *noveronikion*. It is described as 'wide, made of quilted material with broad sleeves'.[62] Its skirt must have been very broad and quite long as it was intended to protect the strung bow-case and quiver, as well as any armour, from any precipitation. It seems likely that it would otherwise have been much like the *fiblatôrion* in being fastened at the neck but otherwise open down the front to allow access to the armament beneath it. Evidently it was assumed that the fabric of a *gounion* would be made of dark stuff for, besides weather protection, they were to serve as quasi-camouflage for scouts, concealing the shine of their armour from the enemy.

Foot- and leg-wear

The necessity for marching long distances means that the footwear of the infantry is one subject to which the manual writers do pay some attention. The *Stratêgikon* recommends simple, robust Gothic shoes with no more than two fastenings and a few small hobnails, (perhaps like fig. 12, left) and advises against boots and greaves as hampering easy travel.[63] There is no recommendation for the footwear of the cavalryman, but the Egyptian finds included numerous pairs of high boots (fig. 11), including some which must have been for riding as they have stiff flaps projecting up at the front clearly designed to protect the knee (Plate 4).[64]

Although Late Antique literature makes no mention of the leg-wear of common men and soldiers, once again archaeology and corroborating works of art come to our aid. Before the fall of the Western provinces the old Roman aversion to the barbarian trousers had long since vanished. Late Antique art shows that footed trousers of the type excavated at Thorsberg and Damendorf in Germany and Zenobia in Syria had become common across the empire,[65] alongside more robust open-bottom styles which were often finished with a wide decorated band around the hems (fig. 8, bottom).[66] Both the expansive Late Antique cemeteries of Egypt and a seventh-century archaeological site in Halabiye (Zenobia) in Syria yielded trousers with very sophisticated construction (see Chart 4).

Headgear

Hats seem not to have been a popular native Roman habit originally. The one Latin word for hat, *pileus*, was applied to a simple, close-fitting round cap (Plate 4, centre) that was worn at Pagan festivals and by ex-slaves, hence not everyday wear for free-born men. Thereafter, both the written references to hats and the art depicting them through Late Antiquity and onwards show one foreign import after another. The earliest written reference relevant to us is the recommendation of Vegetius that the soldiery wear a Pannonian hat in order to accustom themselves to having something substantial on their heads and so make wearing a helmet less of a strain.[67] This item is commonly identified with the cylindrical hat shown in funereal stelai of the early imperial centuries. The form continues to appear sporadically into the twelfth century, and better-quality pictures suggest that it might be made as a deep round-ended sleeve with the open end turned up outside to largely or entirely cover the dome, as well as the sewn pillbox found in archaeology (Plate 4, left; Chart 8.1).[68] Of the many influences from Persia which flowed into Roman use over the centuries, hats figure prominently. The earliest style to appear is a tall, rounded hat made not of formed felt, but sewn from heavy cloth in a manner much like the construction of some helmets of the time (Plate 4, right; Chart 8.2).[69]

Once tailored tunics and coats were fully established, military dress in Rômania had achieved a plateau of practicality which left limited room for improvement. Thus, the sole development that can be identified following the end of Late Antiquity is the advent of the button-and-loop fastening, apparently in the eighth century (Plate 4, left), and their application to the coat, thus rendering the brooch-and-belt fastening method irrelevant to the garment. After that, while the *fiblatôrion* survives for a while amongst the antiquarianism of court regalia, that word, along with *zôstarion,* disappear from speech and literature in favour of a diverse vocabulary for coat, ranging from a revival of the Hellenistic terms *kandus* and *kavadês*, to the medieval neuter *kavadion*, and for a while the fully Hellenised *diakoptês* ('fully divided').

WOMEN

John Lydos makes no reference to the women of the sixth-century court, nor do other literary sources offer much assistance through this era. Works of art and archaeology, however, do provide a great deal of assistance. For the immediate state of the women of the court the Ravenna mosaic depicting Empress Theodôra and her ladies is highly instructive, indicating that a certain amount of the regalia listed in the *Klêtôrologion* and *Book of Ceremonies* is already in place.

The *augousta*

An overall comparison of the regalia of Justinian and Theodôra reveals a significant paradigm which was to prevail in imperial regalia until the last quarter of the eleventh century – it is that the imperial regalia of both genders is essentially identical in its form, even in aspects where custom across the rest of society decreed significant gender difference. Here, both wear a main garment in plain white cloth with similarly extensive gold decoration (Plate 2). The contrast between Theodôra and her ladies in that alone is dramatic. As noted previously, the empress wears the shoulder-fastened *khlamus*, a male garment worn by no other woman. Furthermore, it is also in the quintessentially imperial colour scheme of murex purple adorned with gold. The crown of this empress also shows features which were to be characteristic of augoustal headgear right up to the final era of the empire. A central ornament is flanked by triangular peaks surmounted by a gem. The final item of note is the broad gemmed and pearled collar lying over the top of her *khlamus*. An example of such a collar from this period has survived and gives us an indication of its precise form.[70] It will be seen later that this accessory can be identified as the *stêthokarakallon* of the *Book of Ceremonies*.

A slightly earlier group of augoustal portraits should be noted here for important forward-looking features. Several ivories survive depicting Empress Ariadne (*c*.450–515) (fig. 13). Again the crown and collar are to be noted, but distinctively the *tavlion* of her *khlamus* exhibits an embroidered portrait of the the emperor. This convention, of an item of regalia bearing a picture of the wearer's hierarchical superior(s), will recur in art and on surviving items not only for the duration of the empire, but beyond into Orthodox religious regalia (figs 56, 58). The *Book of Ceremonies* will apply the term *opsimaros* to such a *khlamus* (see below).

The period from the early eighth century to the mid-ninth century saw a profound ideological conflict within the empire on the subject of whether it was valid to create images of beings of religious significance. This conflict spilled out of the religious sphere and for that period effectively forestalled even secular figural art. An early monument during the slow recovery after the defeat of the iconoclasts ('icon-breakers') was the *Homilies of Gregory of Nanzianzos*, made in the 880s. It is significant for this study in its portraits of Saint Helena (mother of Constantine I) and her attendants. While the New Testament scenes are costumed in conventionally antique garb, Helena and her courtiers are dressed in a more contemporary manner. Once again, the quasi-masculine mode of the empress' regalia is apparent, but her *khlamus* shows a significant point of evolution (fig. 14). The decoration makes it evident that it is no longer the oval of the Late Antique item, but that it has been cropped down the middle, and shaped at the centre of this new

FIG. 13 . At the beginning of our period, the regalia of the empress already embodied a feature which would endure until the late eleventh century – it was almost identical to that of the emperor. Empress Ariadne, ivory, Bargello Musuem, Florence.

straight edge to give it a smoother and more elegant neckline. It seems unlikely that only the cloak of the *augousta* would have been treated this way, and that the emperor's *khlamus* would show this development, although the process might not yet have affected the cloaks of the body of the court.

FIG. 14. Empress Saint Helena and attendants. *Homilies of Gregory of Nazianzos*, 880s. Bibliothèque Nationale, France, ms. Gr. 510.

Other women

The woman standing immediately to Theodôra's left in the mosaic panel at Ravenna is distinguished from her peers by her dress in a manner paralleling the distinction between male courtiers and common men. The fabric of her dress is quite plain, yet in the imperial colour. Furthermore, it is adorned with *stikhoi* or *potamoi,* full-length bands of decoration, a motif which had fallen out of fashion in everyday clothing. These characteristics show that this woman must have some formal status equivalent to the *zôstê patrikia* of the ninth to eleventh century. Indeed, in a slightly enigmatic passage Filotheos states that a *zôstê patrikia* was to give away 'her *stikharion*' to another courtier.

Other pictures at Ravenna, corroborated by some from a century earlier in Rome, show garments which were to become more significant in women's regalia in the later period, and which had already begun to influence male imperial regalia before the beginning of the sixth century. The Holy Virgin and Princess of Egypt depicted on the tympanum arch within the Church of St Maria Maggiore in Rome and the Parade of Virgins at Ravenna all wear very similar outfits derived from Persia. The largely hidden inner garment is important for the portion that is visible – loose sleeves which are gathered into long, highly decorated cuffs. It is unclear from either group of pictures whether this is a tailored feature, or whether the cuffs are separate and fastened over the fabric of the sleeve. These are what would later be called 'Persian-sleeve' (*persikomanikion*) which was to become the defining characteristic of male regalia garments into the twelfth century. As discussed above, this sleeve form began its transition into the male repertoire with Anastasios' use of the *divêtêsion* for his coronation in 491. Accompanying the 'Persian-sleeved' garments in these pictures, the women wear an ornate shawl draped from the left shoulder diagonally across to the right side. This item is seen again on one of the aristocratic holy women in an eighth-century frieze in the Church of Maria in Valle, Cividale (fig. 15, left). Again, another of these noble women wears a *stikharion* (fig. 15 centre). The dresses of these two aristocratic women show the next stage of development in the *delmatikê*, or, as it is now called, *delmatikion.* Its sleeves are still the mid-forearm length which characterised the antique *dalmatica*, but have widened dramatically at the cuff. It is evident that the adoption of Persian-sleeved garments into the male regalia has removed them from the female sphere (with the exception of the *augousta*) and so in its place the *delmatikion* has become an ubiquitous fashion for well-to-do women, with its ample sleeves providing both a display of conspicuous consumption and signalling such a woman's freedom from domestic labour. That fashion will endure until the end of the empire.

The literary and pictorial sources all show that an essential framework for the regalia of the court in Constantinople was already in place at the end of Late Antiquity. This basic framework would survive intact into the eleventh century, and only then disappear over the course of the next century and a half.

FIG. 15. Detail of pious noblewomen. Church St Maria in Valle, Cividale del Friuli. First half of the eighth century. The two on the left wear garments which will remain central to women's court regalia for centuries – *stikharion delmatikion* and *paragaudion*.

RESTORATION

THE *KLÊTÔROLOGION*

2

The *Taktikon Klêtôrologion* was compiled around 899 by a gentleman who, by his own account, held the rank of *prôtospatharios* and exercised the court function of *atriklinês*, whose job it was to ensure that the ranking (*taxis*) of the court was properly observed.[1] Filotheos' plainly written treatise was evidently intended primarily for the *Atriklinai* who were to come after him. He saw the need to record the revised state of court structure because 'many titles of ranks have disappeared with time, and all these novel distinctions of ranks have introduced some confusion into the precise understanding of them.'[2] The main source of this upheaval was presumably the changes introduced by Basil I,[3] the father of the emperors that Filotheos served, Leo VI and Alexander (fig. 16).[4]

FIG. 16. Emperor Alexander, one of the rulers who presided over the court practice recorded by Filotheos in the *Klêtôrologion*. Hagia Sofia.

The fact that no fewer than four *taktika* manuscripts are known from the period covering the mid-ninth century to the late tenth century does indeed show that the structure of the court was quite changeable. There is approximately sixty years from the first of these *taktika*, the so-called *Taktikon Uspenski*, to that of Filotheos, whereas intervals of approximately thirty years follow between the subsequent ones.[5] Change is to be expected from time to time, yet a detailed comparison indicates that the pace of change in the *taxis* of the court was accelerating, with offices being created more rapidly towards the end of the tenth century, and their sequence, especially in the lower orders, being substantially altered.

In view of this, there is an understandable element of self-preservation motivating Filotheos' enterprise, for he admitted himself with an admirable candour, which does much to establish his credibility: 'If from our actions some confusion were to happen to the imperial convocations, we ourselves would succumb to derision and uselessness of our office.'[6] However, there was a more fundamental and general issue at stake, which went to the heart of Constantinopolitan society. The ranks and their *taxis* were seen as being an essential part of the divinely ordained nature of the Enduring Roman Empire. Filotheos describes them as, 'The gifts of imperial honours given by the Grace of God, having received the imprimatur of God, at the magnificent and wondrous dais of the radiant Khrusotriklinos.'[7] Filotheos evidently believed that, as *atriklinês*, he had the task of ensuring that one modest portion of God's will was properly enacted on earth. In addition to this notional responsibility, a man in Filotheos' place was hardly in any position to initiate changes to the *taxis* or ceremonial. Any such novelty would have swiftly been noticed by his fellow courtiers, who must inevitably have been jealous of their relative position and privileges, and thus brought back into line. Even if he had presumed to exploit his editorial privilege in order to surreptitiously implement some change that would be enacted by a successor working from his book, it is no more likely to have passed unnoticed, whether by contemporary readers or the courtiers marshalled by the successor.

For these reasons alone, Filotheos' treatise can be accepted with a high degree of confidence, but there is a still more cogent reason. His work received an explicit imperial seal of approval. Not only was the text of it incorporated into Constantine Porfurogennêtos' encyclopaedic collation of court ceremonial records and prototypes, which might have been the work of some later editor or copyist, but it was cited in the text of the *Book of Ceremonies* as being a primary source for proper protocol.[8]

The *Klêtôrologion* is by far the most detailed of the *taktika* of this period. Whereas the others merely recorded the sequence of the ranks, Filotheos added one section of details of the regalia and some dress of the highest ranks, and descriptions of a number of ceremonies for important occasions, incorporating specifics of the customary dress and regalia of a wider range of the court. In this it was a prototype for the more extensive *Book of Ceremonies*, which was largely written in the second quarter of the tenth century.[9]

At this time the Roman Empire was well into a phase of consolidation after the period of upheaval sometimes called the 'Dark Age' of Byzantium. The geographical contraction occasioned by external assaults from several directions had been halted, and society had undergone radical transformation from the expansive and public cultural form of antiquity with its broad squares and large, colonnaded public buildings sheathed in marble, to the more circumscribed and private pattern of life in the Middle Ages. Recovery from that transformation had soon been inhibited by the trauma of the Iconoclast Controversy, which had riven the social fabric, had dramatically curtailed production in the visual arts, and occasioned the destruction of works of religious art.[10] Even with that issue settled, palace–Church relations, the stability of the court and the very legitimacy of Constantine VII Porfurogennêtos' birth and position were under a cloud after Leo VI's decision to take Constantine's mother as his fourth wife, contrary to ecclesiastical law.[11] The Byzantine court and society as a whole were desperately in need of some sense of stability and validation. Across many cultures, ritualistic public behaviour is a common response to social dislocation of that sort. In discussing the more recent innovation of an identity-affirming ritual among American Indians, Patricia Lerch defines the stages of the process as 'crisis, redressive action and re-integration'.[12] Due to the absence of detailed sources for the proceeding period it is impossible to make a full catalogue of the re-integrative ceremonial innovations of the half century prior to the *Klêtôrologion*, but some examples are plain. Most obviously, a ceremony had been introduced to celebrate the end of iconoclasm.[13] Other ceremonies had presumably been created to establish the new positions of *basileopatôr*, created by Leo VI,[14] and of *Sunkellos* of Constantinople. Doubtless the need for re-affirmation had also been answered by the revision of existing rituals to make them more imposing and theatrical. This process is clear enough in the half century between the *Klêtôrologion* and the *Book of Ceremonies*, as can be seen from a systematic comparison between the descriptions of what is to be observed for the various days of Christmas, for example.[15]

It has been noted previously that the structure of the court had evolved haphazardly over centuries. As a result of this erratic pattern of development there were three hierarchies in the non-female court, which were neither wholly distinct, nor consistent in attributing regalia. (I use the term 'non-female' because the Byzantines regarded eunuchs as a third gender.) The three realms were honorific ranks, official duties and a mixture of ranks and duties held by eunuchs. There seems to be customary practice that Filotheos does not record even for the men and eunuchs, and other sources reveal that there was a significant array of established practice within the female court which Filotheos completely ignores. Some guesses can be made regarding this from the *Klêtôrologion*, while more, though still evidently not all, is made explicit in the *Book of Ceremonies*.

The Ranks

The titles listed in the *Klêtôrologion* below the emperor and possessing regalia were thus, in order of seniority.[16] Offices, as distinct from honorific ranks, are underlined.

Male ranks	Eunuch ranks	Female ranks
kaisar		
nôvelêssimos		
kouropalatês		
		zôstê patrikia
magistros		
anthupatos		
patrikios	*patrikios*	
	<u>*praipositos*</u>	
prôtospatharios	*prôtospatharios*	
disupatos	<u>*primikêrios*</u>	
spatharokandidatos	<u>*ostiarios*</u>	
spatharios	*spatharokoubikoularios*	
hupatos	<u>*koubikoularios*</u>	<u>*koubikoularea*</u>
<u>*stratôr*</u>	<u>*nipsistratos*</u>	
kandidatos		
<u>*mandatôr*</u>		
<u>*vestitôr*</u>		
silentarios		

Although a couple of ranks are common to both lists, it should not be presumed that other ranks are in any way equivalent. There was normally only one *kaisar* at a time, while there could be more than one *nôvelêssimos*, *kouropalatês* and *zôstê patrikia*. The other ranks had many, and in some cases hundreds, of members. Similarly, the ranks below *prôtospatharios* in the male column should not be assumed to be equivalent to functions below *prôtospatharios* in the eunuch category.

The names of several of the titles suggest functions: *ostiarios* = doorkeeper (of the imperial apartments); *praipositos* = overseer (of court business); *primikêrios* = victualler (supervisor of the imperial table); *nipsistratos* = bath keeper; *stratôr* = groom; *vestitôr* = wardrobe attendant. However, it is not clear how many of these retained any specific functional role. Some, particularly *ostiarios* and *praipositos*, did have very conspicuous duties close to the throne in many of the ceremonies. It is clear that a man or eunuch was appointed to a functional office by virtue of already bearing an honorific rank – for example, *prôtospatharios* and *praipositos*. The *patrikioi* and *prôtospatharioi* were, so to speak, the general workforce of the top echelon of imperial administration, filling posts in the military and civil bureaucracy.

Male and female ranks

The rank of *nôvelêssimos* (from the Latin *nobelissimus*, 'most noble') was held at this time only by close members of the royal family.

Kouropalatês was an open rank of special distinction, the highest which could be obtained at this time by anyone not related to the emperor by blood.

Each empress appointed a *zôstê patrikia* as her personal chief lady-in-waiting. The appointment was for life, which is why there might be more than one at any one time. The *zôstê patrikia* was the lowest of the ranks which had a place at the imperial banquet table by right rather that by invitation.

The remaining ranks for 'entire' men (that is, non-eunuchs) formed the normal *cursus honorem* by which a man at court might progress either by service or favouritism. *Prôtospatharios*, *spatharokandidatos* and *spatharios* are, as their names indicate, distinguished by their right to bear a sword in the Emperor's presence (Latin *spatha*, Greek *spathê*, *spathion* means sword).

Eunuchs

Roman society had a very odd and ambivalent attitude to eunuchs. For one thing they were regarded as virtually a third gender. They were perceived as being indispensable to the running of the highest levels of court, at least in part because their inability to have heirs was deemed to make them less prone to ambition, yet they were also regarded as being by nature devious and malign.[17] For those ranks common to both eunuchs and men, the eunuchs had ceremonial precedence.

Listed regalia – men and women

These are the foremost ranks who are given their distinguishing regalia items 'by the Emperor's hand'.[18]

The *kaisar* is distinguished most by a coronet (*stefanos*) called *kaisarikion* which was made 'without the cross-shaped piece', according to Filotheos.[19] This sets it apart from the emperor's crown (*stemma*) in a manner which Filotheos does not explain, but which will become clearer when comparing the discussion in the body of the *Book of Ceremonies* with artworks.

The regalia of a *nôvelêssimos* was a murex purple tunic (*khitôn*) with gold decoration, a *khlamus* and *lôros*.

The regalia of a *kouropalatês* was a tunic (*khitôn*) of rich red embroidered with gold, a *khlamus* and *lôros*.

The emblem for the *zôstê patrikia* was an ivory diptych of the same type as carried by a *patrikios* (fig. 17). No regalia clothing is listed, but she certainly had some, for the name of this rank means 'patricienne of the "belt"', which in this source is *lôros*.[20]

The regalia of a *magistros* was a white tunic (*khitôn*) with gold decoration woven into it in various places, particularly as 'epaulettes', accompanied by a red leather belt set with precious stones called *valtidion*.

An *anthupatos* carried a sheaf of purple parchment inscribed in gold as his emblem.

One of the more populous ranks was that of *patrikios*. Their emblem consisted of an ivory diptych with inscribed leaves.

A still more populous rank was that of *prôtospatharios*. Their emblem was a gold torque (*kloios*) fitted with precious stones.

The emblem of a *disupatos* was an inscribed scroll (Plate 9, right).

The emblem of a *spatharokandidatos* was a gold torque (*maniakion*) set with a white semi-precious stone (fig. 18).

The emblem of a *spatharios* was a sword with gilded fittings.

The emblem of a *hupatos* was, like the *disupatos*, an inscribed scroll.

A *stratôr* (groom) had a gilded scourge (*fragellion*) with precious stones (Plate 9, centre).

The emblem of a *kandidatos* was a gold torque (*maniakion*) falling onto his chest with three ornaments (fig. 18).

A *mandatôr* (herald) carried a red-dyed baton (*ravdos*) as his badge of rank.

The regalia of a *vestêtôr* (gentleman of the wardrobe) was a *fiblatôrion*.

The emblem of a *silentarios* was a plain gilded baton (*ravdos*).

A provincial general (*stratêlatês*) received an inscribed scroll.

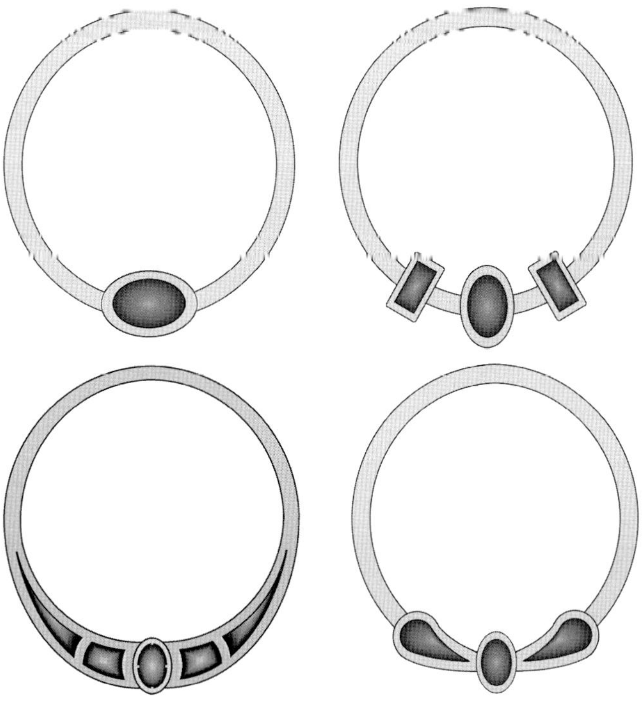

FIG. 18. Examples of forms of regalia collar (*kloios/maniakion/strepton*) from various works of art across the early and middle Byzantine eras.

Listed Regalia – eunuchs

A eunuch *patrikios* had an ivory diptych with inscribed leaves as his emblem. His regalia was identical to that of a *prôtospatharios*, except that he wore a *lôros*.

The emblem of a *praipositos* was an ivory diptych like that of a *patrikios* but without with inscribed leaves.

A eunuch *prôtospatharios* had a gilded torque (*maniakion*) with pearls and precious stones as his emblem, and his regalia was a white tunic (*khitôn*) 'like that of the emperor' (*divêtêsoidês*) adorned with gold, and a vivid red 'double-fold cloak' (*khlamus*) with gold panels (*tavlia*) woven into it.[21]

The regalia of a *primikêrios* was a white tunic (*khitôn*) with gold shoulder panels and stars woven into it.[22]

An *ostiarios* carried a gold baton with precious stones around the head.

The emblem of a *spatharokoubikoularios* was a sword with gilded fittings like that of the *spatharios*.

The regalia of a *koubikoularios*, or 'man of the imperial chambers', was a tunic (*kamision*) trimmed with silk, and a cape (*paragaudion*).

The regalia of a *nipsistratos* was a tunic (*kamision*) made of linen with silk woven into it in the shape of a yoke.

OPPOSITE: FIG. 17. Ivory diptych showing scenes from the life of Christ. Religious imagery notwithstanding, this may have been an item of court regalia for a *zôstê patrikia* or *patrikios*. Victoria and Albert Museum, London.

Ceremonial occasions

In the various ceremonies that follow, at times various attendees are required to attend 'in their regalia' (*allaxima*), while on other occasions they were to wear alternative garments. Sometimes this meant that the more eminent ranks were to wear a *kamision* rather than their usual *khitôn*, while on other occasions, another garment called *kontomanikion* (Chart 3.4; fig. 19), accompanied by an accessory called *thôrakion* (fig. 20), was substituted. For less-formal events, the *skaramangion* was the designated alternative to all primary regalia for every male and eunuch rank up to and including the emperor. Both the primary regalia and alternative garments are often accompanied by the specification 'with *khlamus*', or 'without *khlamus*' or 'alone', or sometimes with the specification for some other mantle, such as a *sagion*. On two occasions the *prôtospatharioi* were to wear a garment called a *spekion* with a russet *sagion*.[23] Likewise, there are just two mentions of the emperor's *divitision*, presumably because it is taken as read under most circumstances.[24] Certain foreigners from the north and east are said to habitually wear the *kavadion* – as previously noted, a form of coat.

THE GARMENTS

Filotheos' description of the garments is quite terse, and almost all these items will be found in much more detail in the *Book of Ceremonies*. In view of this, detailed discussion of those dress items will appear in the following chapter.

Tunics

In describing the main regalia garments of the listed ranks, the author uses some antique terms for their tunics: *khitôn* for the higher ranks and *kamision* (a Hellenisation of the old Latin *camisa*[25]) for those less elevated and less formal occasions. At this time these words had both been superseded in the vernacular as generic equivalents of 'tunic' by *roukhon*,[26] and by the compound which survives to the modern day, *hupokamis(i)on*.[27] Clearly, the older terms had been reallocated to a more technical significance as regalia items, evidently for varieties of the ankle-length tunic, with *persikomanikia*, which we saw established by the middle of the seventh century. Numerous other ranks and offices wore a garment called *kamision*, especially in the rituals described in the *Book of Ceremonies*, and it occurs with various forms of decoration, some of which are the same as garments to which the term *khitôn* is applied.

Stikharion

A garment called *stikharion* is associated with the *zôstê patrikia* in the *Klêtôrologion*. As previously noted, the name derives from a type of decoration rather than its form – two broad

FIG. 19. The alb of the regalia of the so-called 'Holy Roman Empire' is a *kontomanikion,* and shows the Persian-derived feature of the opening running down from the left side of the neck worked into the margin of a decorative panel.

stripes, called *clavii* in earlier Latin terminology and *stikhoi* or *potamoi* in Greek, running from shoulder to hem. This type of decoration had been very common in the earlier Roman imperial era, but had fallen out of fashion in everyday wear, being preserved by the ninth century only in certain forms of lay and religious regalia. The *Klêtôrologion* says that on her promotion she gives 'her *stikharion*' to the *praipositos* as a gift (all ranks celebrated their promotion with gifts to lower ranks, in several cases these being clothing or textiles) and it has been assumed to be her regalia.[28] It is not tenable, however, to imagine that she would be expected to give away the regalia for the rank to which she was being inducted. In a comparable case, an incoming *magistros* was to give 'his *kamision*' to the master of ceremonies (*ho tês katastaseôs*). Filotheos' list shows that this is certainly not his regalia as a *magistros,* but it would be the garment he would have worn in the rank he had just left, since it was the norm for a man to be promoted only one, or at most two, ranks at a time.[29] Furthermore, if the *stikharion* given away were the regalia garment of a *zôstê patrikia*, it could have no conceivable benefit or value for the *praipositos* or any woman with whom he might be connected. A solution to this conundrum lies in the observation made at the end of the last chapter that *potamoi* had continued as a form of decoration on the *delmatikia* of women of high status. Thus, the *stikharion* given away would be a *delmatikion* that could be worn by a 'woman of the chamber' (*koubikoularia,* about which much more is said in the *Book of Ceremonies*). It would then have been replaced by a new *stikharion delmatikion* of purple (as suggested by the Ravenna mosaic of Theodôra's closest lady), more befitting the *zôstê patrikia*'s unique position so close to the throne, and more in keeping with the regalia of the high male ranks with which she was associated at the imperial table.

Coats

The regalia garment of a *vestitôr*, the *fiblatôrion*, has been identified as a primitive form of coat, devoid of button fastenings, secured at the throat with a brooch (*fiboula*) and often worn slung around the shoulders in the manner of a cape. In common clothing it had been superseded when the advent of button and loop fastening in the eighth century turned the coat into a much more practical garment. The form preserved in the regalia to the turn of the tenth century can be confidently taken to be the one with very long vestigial sleeves. By the time of the composition of the *Book of Ceremonies* the *fiblatôrion* has disappeared, replaced, it seems, by the similar, though more elegant, *avdion*, a borrowing of the Arabic *abeyah*.

One of the newer terms for coat, *kavadion*, is also found in the *Klêtôrologion*; it was worn by various visitors. For Filotheos to observe that coats are the 'native garment' of Magyars and Khazars is entirely accurate, for these were originally Central Asian nomads known for such fashions from ancient times. Furthermore, that such people should be noted at court wearing their native dress is a testament to the enduring multiculturalism of the Roman imperial ethos.

Accessories

It is striking that what is said to distinguish various titles in Filotheos' list is not distinctive clothing, but sometimes quite mundane-seeming accessories. It may seem a little odd by modern standards that the accessory of one rank might seem to be a less-spectacular item than that of the rank below. An example being the *patrikios* with an ivory diptych compared to the *prôtospatharios* with his golden torque set with jewels. It must be realised, however, that relative value was more important than visual effect. The great wealth of the empire at this time was such that golden objects were not very unusual or costly, as highlighted by the many hundreds of items of Byzantine gold jewellery preserved in collections around the world. And while Byzantine ivories are also not rare objects, they were more valuable by virtue of the distances the raw materials had to travel, and the more specialised craftsmanship involved in their production. Amongst the ivories, the hierarchy was reflected in the amount of craftsmanship involved. The basic diptych of the office of *praipositos* simply had two inner faces carved with images, with the outer faces more or less plain, as in the surviving examples. The higher-ranking diptych of the patricians (men, women and eunuchs) had the other faces carved with text. The images carved into these diptyches *may* have been religious (fig. 17), but in view of their secular use, another possibility seems likely. It was noted earlier that there was already a long-established practice of regalia bearing a portrait of the owner's hierarchical superior. It would be very fitting if a regalia diptych were to carry a picture of the ruler(s) who had appointed the owner to his or her rank. Hence, the several surviving ivory panels showing rulers (figs 13, 24) may not have been passive pieces of imperial aggrandisement, but rather items of quite specific and frequent ceremonial use. The texts inscribed on the diptyches of the higher ranks can only be speculated upon because none have survived that can be definitively identified.

Regalia torques came in a variety of forms. The variations shown in art do reflect the descriptions in the *Klêtôrologion*. Some had distinct segments, while others were of a smoother profile (fig. 9, centre; figs 18, 29).

Two ranks carries scrolls as their emblems (Plate 9, right). Again, as apparently none have survived what would be written on them may remain a mystery, but the status distinction must have been very obvious. The lesser one was an ordinary piece of parchment, while the greater one was dyed in the imperial colour and written in gold. The purple codex of Rossano shows how striking that would appear.

The final diverse class of regalia accessory is that of batons. Filotheos is quite detailed on these. Although these were predominantly wood (*mandatôr*: Plate 9, left), but it is a natural conjecture that some ornamental fittings would have set them apart from a mundane stick – for example, a gold enamelled cap, which may well have been from just such a baton, has survived.[30] Others appear as though they would have been entirely sheathed in, if not made of, precious metal.

Colour, Fabrics and Applied Decoration

The dress and regalia stipulations of the *Klêtôrologion* are relatively simple. Filotheos' initial list only enumerates unique items for the highest sixteen ranks of the court, although he goes on to describe the most important religious festivals and the dress required to be worn by a much greater range of people of the court in observing them. The latter sections of the *Klêtôrologion* form the paradigm that the *Book of Ceremonies* elaborates at length and in detail. At first sight the dress requirements of the later compilation seem intricate and complex. On more systematic inspection, however, they are reduced to a modest number of consistent patterns. In discussing items mentioned in these sources it will be necessary at times to refer to later occurrences, especially in correlating the written sources with art; however, detailed discussion of such later occurrences will as much as possible be deferred to an appropriate point where any changes in the nature of the item or its pattern of use can be comprehensively considered.

Colour

There had been some sumptuary restrictions in place in the Roman Empire from very early times, although they were never very extensive. They were as much inspired by cultural protectionism, as by the aim of structuring society or publicising rank.[31] After the disappearance of the *toga praetexta*, the evidence suggests that restrictions were less focused on the actual garments to be worn by the various classes of society or of the court, than on the materials used, and especially the dyestuffs applied. Increasingly, from the time of Theodosius in the fourth century the most opulent purple dyes were restricted for imperial use.[32] Decrees of Justinian took this further, forbidding commoners not merely the use of Tyrian purple, but 'any colour resembling the Imperial purple', and stipulated death as the punishment for transgression.[33] Around the turn of the tenth century Leo VI dramatically eased those restrictions, issuing a decree which allowed the public 'sale of small fragments and scraps of purple cloth, which afford means of ostentation to Our subjects'.[34] Those rules applied to everyday life. In contrast, there was always the possibility of the restrictions being waived by imperial fiat for particular people and classes, and this is very evident in the Porfurogennêtan court.

The base colour of garments and accessories is by no means always stipulated in our sources. In fact, the occasions on which it is stated are in the minority. Nonetheless, it is clear that where no prescription is made the reason is not because the participants are left to their own preference, but rather because a custom is so well established that the colour does not need to be stated. Even for the emperor, the occasions on which he has a choice of what colour he wears, let alone what he wears, are so rare that they are stated on a scant handful of occasions, and then only once for any item other than the *stemma*.[35] Where base colour of the vestments is decreed in our sources, only two feature consistently – purple and white – with the multiplicity of terms used for them giving a deceptive impression of diversity at the first reading.

Whites

The most prevalent colour, both in aggregate and in most contexts, is white, designated by various terms. *Leukos* (λευκός) is by far the most used, followed by *aspros* (ἄσπρος) and *lampros* (λάμπρος). Whereas with the purples, some of the various terms can be taken in a technical sense to designate differing shades or qualities, the same cannot be confidently said for the whites. The rarer terms are indeed used exclusively for imperial items, and so may designate a particularly pure white, yet the very same imperial garments are just as often described with the mundane term *leukos*, which is by far the most dominant adjective – even for so pre-eminent an object as the 'Great White Crown'.[36]

The overwhelming predominance of white as a specified colour is of the utmost significance. It first became institutionalised as an important court colour in the fourth century with the establishment of the corps of *candidati*,[37] and by the tenth century had attained overwhelming importance. As will be discussed in more detail below, it is to be taken as the default colour for the majority of members of the court, and in some cases for imperial garments, on those many occasions where no colour is stated in the text (figs 22, 34) One indication of the importance of white is seen in ceremonies: the horse the Emperor rides is required to be white, as is the case during military triumphs.[38] This practice survived into the late eleventh century, when, during his tenure as *kaisar*, Nikêforos Bruennios states that white horses were reserved for imperial ceremonial use.[39]

Yet the pre-eminence of white is at the same time a curious phenomenon. The natural colour of linen, cotton and most wool is a whitish shade. Since every process performed upon a textile necessarily increases its cost, the most prevalent colour of the commonest garments throughout antiquity and the early Middle Ages was the natural off-white of those fibres. In the copious survivals of clothing said to be in the Coptic tradition, even highly ornate garments generally sported their decoration on a white base. Hence, for white to become such an important court colour seems at first somewhat contradictory. The contradiction is resolved when one appreciates the net effect of several observations. Prior to the development of chemical bleaches, obtaining a pure, sharp white was extremely difficult, requiring repeated treatments with weaker bleaches such as sodium compounds, or prolonged and repeated exposure to natural oxygen-generating processes,[40] or both. Such treatment is also harsh on the fibre and so tends to reduce the lifespan of the fabric, and of any garment made of it.[41] Furthermore, maintaining such a garment in its pristine state must have been quite impossible for anyone travelling on foot in the street, let alone engaged in any exertion or labour. Thus, purchasing court whites must have been very costly and such garments must have required frequent replacement to maintain a proper standard of presentation.

Purples

The less frequent colour is the familiar purple. *Tureos* (τύρεος), or 'Tyrian', the richest, most expensive and durable purple, derived from the shellfish *murex tinctoria*, is well known from ancient times.[42] Curiously, it is the least-often referred to in the work: once as the colour of the cloak (*khlamus*) of the patricians and of the senior staff of the imperial apartments (*hoi Arkhontes tou Kouboukleiou*)[43] and once for the additional colour for the cloaks of the *dêmarkhoi*.[44] The fact that Tyrian is never mentioned in the context of imperial garments seems curious at first sight. In fact, it is because it is the default tincture of purple for such use. The comment about why the *dêmarkhal klamudes* have this purple makes it explicit: 'as they are imperial cloaks'.

Another term that is rare in the *Book of Ceremonies*, *oxus* (ὀξύς), presents some difficulty of visualisation, albeit a difficulty shared with *porfureos* (πορφύρεος) in antiquity.[45] In common use, it can mean 'sharp', 'clear' or 'bold'. Vogt inconsistently translates it sometimes as 'red'[46] and otherwise as 'dark purple'.[47] The latter opinion is supported by Sophocles,[48] whereas Du Cange gives *violaceus*, which might suggest a lighter shade.[49] This expression is only ever used in describing imperial garments in the *Book of Ceremonies*, and so might be taken to be an opulent colour, whether light or dark. One entry indicates that it is synonymous with *tureos*.[50] A passage in Psellos' *Chronographie* goes far towards resolving the matter, saying that Emperor Basil II conducted his imperial business in a plain 'garment of dark purple' rather than 'the sharp purple'.[51]

In contrast with the raiment of the court, we find amongst those lesser-value garments to be given as gifts listed in the *Treatise on Imperial Military Expeditions* some that are 'false-purple', *pseudoxeos* (ψευδόξεος).[52] Chemical analyses of Byzantine silks in European collections have found that *pseudoxeos* dyes were mixtures of indigo and madder, and indigo and a lichen derivative.[53]

The most common terms for purple are *porfureos* and *alêthinos*, which occur with almost equal frequency, yet have strictly distinct usages. *Porfureos* is the word used for the rulers' clothing, while *alêthinos* is for the shade applied to the dress of courtiers.[54] This suggests that in this case there was certainly a technical distinction in quality and/or shade.

Other colours

Several other more mundane colours are mentioned much more rarely as the base tinctures for main garments: red (*kokkinos*, κόκκινος and *rouseos/rousios*, ῥούσεος/ῥούσιος); blue (*venetos*, βένετος); and green (*prasinos*, πράσινος). In the primary occurrences of *rousios* in the *Book of Ceremonies* it is very specifically a hue with military significance. It is the colour of the *divêtêsion* of the *nôvelêssimos*, who wears it with military leggings (*kampotouva*) and sandals (*kampagia*) at his elevation,[55] and it is decreed as the colour of the 'victory cape' of the tribune entrusted with the defence of the City while the emperor was away on campaign.[56] One of the four imperial crowns (*stemmata*) is also lined in red.[57] A reference to the imperial footwear establishes the equivalence of *kokkinos* and *rouseos*.[58]

Blue and green are still rarer, and commonly occur where one might expect. For example, they are the primary colours of the capes of the men representing the factions of the Blues and the Greens before the emperor.[59] It is reasonable to suppose that when the emperor is greeted on his return from a successful military campaign by the demarchs, each wearing his 'demotic tunic' and 'victory cape',[60] it does not imply that these garments were of some unique style, but that they were also in the deme colours. In addition to white and red, the other two *stemmata* are lined in green and blue.[61]

Russet

A colour commonly mentioned, but confined to capes (*sagia*), is one written as *rôeos* (ῥωέος) and just once as *roês* (ῥοῆς) in the *Klêtôrologion*, and by the latter term only in the *Book of Ceremonies*. While *rôeos* is declined in the normal Greek manner, *roês* is always undeclined, and is likely to be closer to the original form, a borrowing from Persian, as with many other terms which appear this way in our source.[62] The ancient tendency for the loss of intervocalic sigmas,[63] the mutability of vowels in Arabic, and the Late Antique and medieval contraction of the vowel paradigms in Greek,[64] make it almost certain that this term derives from *razîz*, the name of a dyer's herb common to both Arabic and Persian languages.[65] This plant may possibly have become rarely used even before natural dyes were supplanted by chemical dyestuffs, and it has proven to impossible to get any reliable impression of what shades it could produce. Commenting upon the rare Hellenised form *roêsios* (ῥοήσιος), Reiske advances the opinion that it was of some reddish shade,[66] a plausible suggestion in view of the Byzantines' manifest preference for colours of that sort as shown in art, and yet the rarity of the previously mentioned term for red (*rousios*) just mentioned.

Atravatikis

A more obscure term in the *Book of Ceremonies* is *atravatikis* (ἀτραβάτικις), the colour worn by various nobles on rare occasions. It is usually explicitly applied to cloaks (*khlanidia*),[67] but in a few places it is used in the form of a neuter plural noun, *tà atravatikia* (τὸ ἀτραβάτικια).[68] The latter seems to refer to an outfit rather than just a cloak. A clear impression of the colour has eluded modern authors. Sophocles translated this as 'dark brown' and Vogt described it in his commentary as 'a red tending towards black'. John Lydos describes *atravatikis* as *xêrampelinos* (ξεραμπέλινος), 'withered-dark', and also in the same passage derives the term from *atron* (ἄτρον), and equates it to *faios* (φαιός), which may mean 'grey', 'dun' or merely 'dusky', supporting those modern opinions.[69] Yet the use of precursor terms gives a clearer impression. The Latin *ater* may mean just 'dark', but it has a strong tendency to mean dense black.[70] It seems the middle Byzantine view was more in accord with that, for the *Suda* describes this colour rather more definitely as coal-black (μέλαν ἄτρον).[71] Some confirmation is given to this by an eleventh-century icon showing three saints well and truly garbed in the manner of the court (fig. 9), with Saint Prokopios on the left wearing a deep-black cloak with a lustrous gold *tavlion* over a tunic in the same colour scheme, surely a precise rendering of *tà atravatikia* – 'the blacks'.[72] The *atravatikion* is an almost unparalleled example of such a colour being worn by anyone other than monks[73] or widows.[74] Variations on the theme of wearing the black are proverbial in the writings of this period for entering a monastery.

Decorated fabrics and forms of applied decoration:

Previous scholarship has not been very successful in satisfactorily interpreting many of the terms relating to the nature of decoration on fabrics and garments described in our sources. Indeed, Vogt was of the opinion that it is not possible to know the precise nuances of the terminology.[75] The differences of the various scholars who have approached the subject apparently result from lack of knowledge of textile production and decoration techniques in use in that era, combined at times with a reluctance to accept the established antique senses of the component words of the adjectives employed. Once a study of historical textile decoration is brought to bear upon the terms, it becomes clear that the terminology has indeed preserved antique meanings, and displays considerable precision.

Double-colour terms

A number of colours occur in terms compounded with a prefix indicating double, *di-*, such as *diaspros* (δίασπρος), *dirodinos* (διρόδινος) and so on. It seems clear that these terms refer to damask fabrics, where variations in the weave create areas of contrasting texture which gives the impression of a subtle variation in colour.[76] Such fabrics are well known amongst Byzantine relics.[77]

Vlattion and its compounds

These terms have been the subject of some attention by past commentators, but with very mixed results. There is a general consensus that the basic form taken from Latin, *blatta*, referred originally to the related spectrum of richly coloured dyestuffs: purple to red.[78] This is explained comprehensively by John Lydos, who specifically equates the two colours and mentions both murex and kirmis dyestuffs, which produce purple and red respectively when properly processed.[79] Guilland proposed that it rapidly came to mean silk fabric without regard to colour, and that it is used in that way in the *Book of Ceremonies*.[80] There is a kernel of truth in Guilland's proposition. *Vlattion* (βλάττιον) is indeed used to denote fabric in sources around our period, but the evidence does not support the idea that it had been transferred comprehensively to the fibre. Had that been the case, one would expect to find some transference to other terms relating to silk fibre and fabric. In fact there is no such transference in evidence. Amongst the diverse and complex terminology for the Byzantine silk industry collected by Lopez, Muthesius and Shepard there is no mention of *vlattion* or compounds of it in connection with anything other than fully finished cloth.[81] In addition, Guilland himself accedes to a suggestion made by Goar, that *vlattion* may refer to cloth of a fibre other than silk.[82] Rather, the evidence suggests that the application of *vlattion* to cloth retains a strong element of its previous meaning, and that it means 'richly dyed cloth' with the emphasis still on strong but variable colouration rather than any particular fibre. In effect, this will have normally meant silk, simply because silk was the optimum fibre which would show a rich dye to best advantage, and was the preferred fibre for aristocratic clothing and furnishing, but its sense was still tied to colouration rather than composition. Guilland does refer to one instance of the phrase *leukon vlattion*, which might be seen to undermine this theory, but that comes from the *Treatise on the Offices*, and by the fourteenth century it is very likely that the evolving terminology has moved on to a point more in accord with his suggestion.

If it can thus be accepted that *vlattion* had come by the tenth century to mean 'richly coloured cloth', it will greatly assist in making more viable sense of its compounds, *divlattion* (διβλάττιον) and *trivlattion* (τριβλάττιον). In considering these terms Guilland does return to the matter of colour. He gives a highly significant passage from Peter Damian, the crucial part of which reads, 'from which a pallium which is seen to be of three colours is called *triblattion*'.[83] Guilland then offers two alternative explanations derived from Du Cange, which he says are both equally supported by Damian. They are that two and three colours are visible in the cloth or that the cloth is passed through the dye bath multiple times in order to deepen its colour. Guilland then considers each suggestion at some length and ultimately dismisses them both. The multiple dye bath opinion is the one most often accepted by authors following Du Cange, Reiske, Ebersolt and others, and yet, contrary to Guilland's assessment, it is the one which quite contradicts Damian's explanation. Guilland's arguments against this theory are quite persuasive in themselves, as he points out that *divlattion* and *trivlattion* by this interpretation would duplicate a group of well-attested terms, and that the visible difference between a twice-dipped and a thrice-dipped fabric would be scarcely discernible in many situations and certainly not enough to reliably support distinct terms. To Guilland's arguments I would add that it is very hard to grasp how it might be conceived that passing a cloth through a dye bath of a given colour three times can in any sense produce

FIG. 21. This ninth–tenth-century purple silk figured with lions in roundels (43–45 cm in diameter) is very likely to be the type of fabric of the *leukoleôn* cape mentioned in the *Book of Ceremonies*.
Museo Nationale, Ravenna.

three visible colours, as in Peter Damian's account. Even if the cloth were passed through three differently-coloured dye baths to dye evenly, the result still only produces one colour, whatever shade results from the fusion of the various tinctures. This much is familiar to anyone who has done any dyeing, and to anyone who has studied the processes of dyeing without practising them.[84]

Dismissing this suggestion returns us to the first alternative: that, in accord with Peter Damian's description, there are several colours visible in the single cloth. Again Guilland finds a problem with this theory, for reasons which will be discussed in detail below. Having disposed of this idea, Guilland presents yet a third theory to explain the *vlattion* compounds. Returning to the notion that *vlattion* means silk cloth, Guilland proposes that *divlattia* and *trivlattia* mean that a garment has two or three bands of silk applied to them as a decorative edging.[85] Guilland offers no actual evidence for this idea, but is apparently inspired by the repeated use of forms of *amphiennumi* with *divlattion* and *trivlattion* for garments carried amongst the gifts in the imperial baggage. This is an initially attractive notion, for the basic sense of *amphiennumi* is 'to put around' or 'to put on'. There is certainly ample physical evidence for the fact that strips of silk, usually highly ornamented, were applied to garments as decorative trim quite commonly from Late Antiquity through our period.[86] In this at least, Guilland is undoubtedly correct in respect of the garments of Constantine Porfurogennêtos' imperial baggage train, yet this very evidence casts the doubt upon the remainder of Guilland's theory. An extensive survey of extant clothing, both from publications and visits to major collections, reveals that nowhere amongst the surviving examples yielded by archaeology is there a garment with multiple applied bands. It is also notable that such silk trims are more commonly applied at the neck and cuffs, where they may most readily be seen, than applied at the hem. It might be countered that none of that evidence can be regarded as pertaining directly to tenth-century Constantinople, and this is entirely true. Yet even when we look at works of art which can be attributed to the court from the late ninth century through to the turn of the eleventh century, we again find no hint of garments decorated with multiple borders. In the light of the evidence we have, Guilland's multiple border theory should be dismissed, particularly in the light of a simpler solution.

No author to date has acknowledged that there is presently no recognised Greek terminology which could relate to the copious survivals of Byzantine polychrome figured fabrics (fig. 21). This would be a curious thing in view of the diverse, and evidently often very precise, technical terminology that exists on other aspects of textiles in historical sources. I propose that *divlattion* and *trivlattion* are the terms which filled that gap, precisely in accordance with Peter Damian's commentary. Guilland's objection to the idea of multicoloured cloth is founded upon the observation that on those occasions in the greater *Book of Ceremonies* when colours are enumerated for *divlattia* and *trivlattia* there are never as many listed as the prefix denotes. Compounding the question still further is the fact that, amongst surviving Byzantine brocades, as many as five distinct colours or shades were used, yet there is no trace of such terms as *tetravlattion* or *pentevlattion*. Countering both these issues, it is a questionable assumption that all the colours must necessarily have been enumerated or described to convey the essential information that the author of the *Book of Ceremonies* deemed it appropriate to impart. Looking at the surviving polychrome brocades, we may observe that at most one colour, the ground, is dominant and one, two or three colours define the main pattern elements on that ground, and thus determine the overall impression the fabric gives to the viewer. The other colour(s) appear much more sparsely, and in the case of four- and five-colour brocades, one colour is often employed very scantily for small highlights and details. Thus, *divlattion* with one colour specified, and *trivlattion* with two colours specified, might easily have supplied adequate descriptions for the *Book of Ceremonies* and gift lists of the *Treatise on Imperial Military Expeditions*. In the latter work, the patterns worked into the *divlattia* and *trivlattia* are also mentioned: eagles, basilisks and droplets. As observed above, Guilland's basic interpretation of the use of *amphiennumi* in this work to denote the application of a decorative band is undoubtedly correct, and that also points to the differing wording of the *Book of Ceremonies*, where it should be taken that certain garments of the emperor and *prôedros* are made entirely of *trivlattion* brocades.[87]

Khrusokentêtos

A well-recognised term for applied decoration is *khrusokentêtos*, 'embroidered with gold'.[88] Numerous examples of middle and late Byzantine embroidery survive, as well as European embroideries which were undoubtedly derived from Byzantine examples, most being samples of the precious-metal forms to which the *Book of Ceremonies* refers. The techniques employed in common threads were 'split-stitch', wherein the stitches run backwards to emerge passing through the previous stitch, and 'stem stitch', in which again the stitches run backwards but emerge beside the previous stitch to produce a wider line with a diagonal texture. Metal threads were routinely worked in 'underside couching', whereby gold or silver thread is secured to the surface with a non-precious binding thread which runs below the surface.[89]

Khrusosôlênokentêtos

A compound of the previous term is still more explicit, *khrusosôlênokentêtos*.[90] The classical word *sôlên* meant a pipe or channel,[91] a meaning which does not appear to have changed significantly in later usage.[92] Previous commentators have found this oddly problematic, yet even the most cursory study of surviving medieval embroidery would have settled the matter immediately.[93] The blue silk royal tunic of Roger II of Sicily, based very closely on Byzantine practices, and quite possibly manufactured by Byzantine artisans, has cuffs which employ the technique that the term *khrusosôlênokentêtos* describes so precisely. In a method closely related to later beadwork, minute tubes of gold are sewn to the garment in patterns bordered with small pearls in the typical Byzantine manner used both on textiles and in many other craft media, such as metalwork.[94]

Khrusoüfês and *khrusoüfantos*

Khrusoüfês and *khrusoüfantos* are terms upon which translators have disagreed, despite their inherent clarity.[95] They are clearly terms for gold threads woven into the fabric during the manufacturing process, rather than added in some way afterwards. The Byzantine brocade industry is another area that has been insufficiently explored by scholarship to date, whether by those commenting on the works being discussed here, and by textile specialists.[96] Considerable quantities of Byzantine brocades have survived, generally from having been used as reliquary linings or wrappings in the West, but unfortunately little bears any traces of metallic gold weaving.[97] Two main reasons are likely to explain that. Cloth of that quality was almost certainly on the list of restricted exports from Constantinople,[98] and when such material, and that embroidered with gold thread, was worn out, or was taken as booty, it was common practice to unpick the material or burn it for its metal content.

Khrusosêmentos

Khrusosêmentos is a term applied solely to some *kontomanikia* worn by tribunes and *vikarioi*.[99] The latter component (*sêmenton*) is derived from the Latin *segmentum*, traditionally meaning discrete panels of decoration at the shoulders and/or on the skirt, and so it could be rendered 'gold panelled'. Elsewhere, *kontomanikia* are *khrusa holosêmenta*, which is almost certainly the same thing, and, indeed, in view of the fifteen *kontomanikia* held in the imperial store, they are likely to be the very same garments.[100] In contrast, the imperial *kontomanikion* is said to be of gold brocade (*khrusoüfantos*).[101] Thus, while the royal *kontomanikion* was made of fabric with gold woven throughout, these lesser types had gold in specific areas, whether by weaving or embroidery.

Khrusoklavos

Khrusoklavos is a term applied only to some imperial *skaramangia*[102] and to the *spekia* of eunuch *prôtospatharioi*.[103] This is another term which ought to have presented previous scholars with less difficulty.[104] Looking at sources such as the portrait of Prôtospatharios Iôannês of the *Adrianople Gospels* (fig. 33), it must be suspected that they did not fully appreciate the precision of the terminology, and the persistence of forms. The Latin term *clavus* originally designated bands of decoration which might run the whole length of a garment vertically, but more usually meant a spur of decoration, often shaped much like a keyhole, which might project up from the hem of a garment or down the chest from beside the neck opening. Moving into Greek, the terminology became refined, with the full-length bands becoming known as *potamoi* or *stikhoi*. Through the same period fashions changed and the spurs running down from the shoulder ceased to be employed, thus leaving *klavos* to mean solely the bars running up from the hem. The tunic of Prôtospatharios Iôannês and many similar sources of this era show precisely this form of decoration (figs 22, 32, 46, 52) with royal portraits especially showing the keyhole shape (figs 24, 27, 39).

FIG. 22. St Bakkhos clad in regalia, possibly of a *spatharios*. A fine illustration of the primacy of white in regalia garments up to this date, and of forms of *fialion* and *klavoi*. Mosaic, Church of Nea Moni, Khios. *c.*1049.

Khrusofengês

The last of the gold compound adjectives is *khrusofengês*. It occurs just once for an imperial *khlamus*.[105] This word is truly vague in its basic sense. Its literal meaning is 'made bright, shining or lustrous with gold'.[106] This might well duplicate any of the adjectives discussed above; however, in view of the technical precision that can be observed in those, it is reasonable to hypothesise that this, too, has a specific technical meaning. I suggest that it denotes the direct application of gold leaf to the cloth of the cloak. Like tablet-weaving, fabric-gilding was a common technique throughout the region, although to date no specific evidence of it being used in Constantinople has come to light. The trousseau lists of the Cairo Geniza mention gilding as one of the most common forms of decoration for garments described.[107] The Metropolitan Museum of Art in

New York exhibits a particularly fine example of a cotton/silk *mulham* block-printed and gilded with lions, which is attributed to Persia in the tenth or eleventh century.[108] The convergence of arts and crafts between Persia and Byzantium makes it very unlikely that fabric gilding was not also done in Constantinople.

Fialion

Fialion is a term associated with some tunics. *Kamisia* and *raiktôrikia* are variously described as 'having a *fialion*',[109] as being 'under a *fialion*'[110] or as 'worked in silk with the figure of a *fialion*'.[111] This term is difficult in this context. The *fialê* from which it is derived meant 'a broad, flat bowl for drinking or pouring libations' in antiquity.[112] In our source, *fialê* has been adapted to designate an architectural feature (probably a semi-domed bay like the standard apse of a Byzantine church) of various localities in the palace precinct, especially in the *Trikonkhos*.[113] The diminutive is also used in a manner perhaps closer to the old meaning, as a bowl to catch the dripping wax from a candle, just as often as for garments.[114] In respect of its use for clothing, Reiske's suggestion that it is a hood[115] is in blatant conflict with the statement given in the text concerning the elevation of a *raiktôr* that among the regalia bestowed by the emperor is a hood or headscarf (*maforion*), which, like the main garment to which Reishe's hypothetical hood is supposed to be attached, the *raiktôrikion*, is also a carefully described and spectacular item. Wearing a hood over a headscarf, or vice versa would be very clumsy in both practical and aesthetic terms. Moffat proposes that the *fialion* is a separate collar laid on over the garment.[116] Such a type of accessory can be identified amongst the female regalia (see *stêthokarakallon* in the following chapter), but there is no evidence for observing it in male dress. In any case, the description of a tunic 'worked in silk with the figure of a *fialion*' is entirely sufficient to discredit this notion.

Being linked in the detailed description of the *raiktôrikion* with smaller portions extending towards the shoulders, the term *fialion* strongly suggests an extremely common form of decoration employed around the collars of Roman tunics from Late Antiquity. Viewed when laid out flat, it could be described as a 'double-ended keyhole'. When worn, however, the appearance is quite different, yet both views might indeed form visual analogies to the profiles of double-handled bowls well known from antique and Hellenistic eras.[117] Such pottery forms and others closely related survived in use over long periods of time, and many original pieces must have been excavated in our period as foundations for new buildings were dug, just as they are today. In addition, these forms were echoed in contemporary items such as the various double-handled goblets and bowls now held in the treasury of Saint Mark's Cathedral in Venice. In its earlier form the description 'double-ended keyhole' was particularly apt for this form of tunic decoration, as earlier *both* of the 'epaulettes' and later just the left 'epaulette' contained an opening to allow the head to pass through. Despite the fact that such a placement of neck opening had been superseded in most Byzantine male dress before our era, the exigencies of weaving such a garment in one piece in the time-honoured manner – which our source implies for both the *raiktôrikion* and the 'linen *kamision* with the figure of a *fialion* woven with silk' – would also require the continuation of the line-of-shoulder neck opening as the most easily executed and least intrusive to the decorative scheme.

Conclusions regarding colour and decoration

The *Klêtôrologion* and *Book of Ceremonies* make it very clear that the chromatic character of the ninth- and tenth-century court was overwhelmingly monochrome. The dominant base colour of the majority of regalia garments was white, with varying degrees and styles of gold decoration applied to them. A few ranks, such as *prôtospatharios*, had the privilege of wearing tunics in colours, most often purples, on certain occasions. The assorted cloaks and capes provided some variety from time to time, some being patterned, and others in unusual shades, such as the dark *atravatikis*.

That this chromatic scheme was artificial and antiquated is shown by a range of evidence from both within our source and beyond. On occasion courtiers would change out of their formal wear into *skaramangia*, which were of diverse colours, and could also be made of brocade, as those of the emperor more often were.[118] A further indication of just how far the monochromy of court regalia lagged behind what was available has already been seen in the mosaics of Ravenna, where the courtiers in their formal whites stand in stark contrast to the guardsmen and women in the their unregulated dress of luxuriously figured cloths.

The plain white or purple ground of the court garments were set off by various sorts of applied decoration in gold: the yoke with shoulder-tabs of the *fialion*; bands running down the length of the garment, or *potamoi*; discs or squares, *sêmenta*; hem band; and spurs running up from the hem band, or *klavoi*. These were often woven in, *khrusoüfantos*, but might be embroidered by various techniques, *khrusokentêtos*/*khrusosôlênokenêtos*, or by applying gold leaf directly to the cloth, *khrusofengês*.

Mantles of plain cloth might similarly be gold edged, *khrusoperikleistos*, or have gold or purple panels, *khrusotavlos* or *oxeotavlos*.

STABILITY

THE *BOOK OF CEREMONIES* ONWARDS

3

There are reasons enough to take the *Klêtôrologion* at face value as having a high degree of accuracy. The same question needs to be asked of the *Book of Ceremonies*. Past scholarly discussion largely concludes that it can be taken so. While observing how Constantine Porfurogennêtos' antiquarianism introduced major distortions into some of the other works he wrote or edited dealing with matters beyond the palace and the City, Arnold Toynbee accepted this work as being essentially accurate.[1] More recently Averil Cameron came to a similar conclusion, adding some interesting observations.[2] Michael McCormick implies a similar position while discussing how the accounts of the ceremonies should be read for their layers of accretion and acknowledging that they were a repertoire which was drawn upon selectively and with adaptation by court masters of ceremony.[3] As I have observed above, there are clear, evolving continuities between the *Klêtôrologion* and the *Book of Ceremonies*. Needless to say, no one was better placed to initiate such developments and see them implemented than Constantine as emperor, acting upon his expressed concern about the state of court ritual. He could, and did, not merely revive old ceremonies but also 'invent traditions', which the court then enacted.[4] Some recent scholarship has dubbed this sort of behaviour that is consciously re-affirmative of tradition 'traditionalist', as distinct from merely passively traditional, and has been disposed to view it as typical of the medieval era generally.[5] We can indeed accept the accuracy of the contents of the *Book of Ceremonies* with a high degree of confidence as being representative of the conduct of the court in the middle of the tenth century. The simplest reason for this is that, as Constantine pursued the task of recording and systematising court ceremonial anew, it is inconceivable that he would not have demanded that observance conform to his paradigms as much as possible. In addition, the *Book of Ceremonies* records events which had actually happened, and is not entirely a wish-list. Our confidence in the specific subject matter to be covered by this book is even higher, for while Constantine Porfurogennêtos may have composed new and more elaborate ceremonies, there is no reason to suggest that he invented garments or other material items unfamiliar to Byzantine society. On the contrary, it has already become evident in looking at the *Klêtôrologion* that it and the *Book of Ceremonies* are indeed somewhat antiquarian in their treatment of dress, not merely in preserving fashions which had become rare on the street, but also in preserving terminology for garments still in use which had been superseded in common speech.

In compiling the *Book of Ceremonies* Emperor Constantine VII Porfurogennêtos took his model from the *Klêtôrologion*. In doing so, he did not feel the need to compile a new list of the ranks, rather simply interpolating the one new rank which had arisen, the *prôedros*. This stability in the structure of the court is supported by the *Taktikon Beneseviç* of 934–44.

The *Book of Ceremonies* was not compiled as a single work according to a unitary scheme. The earlier part is relatively coherent, expanding upon the latter section of the *Klêtôrologion* by discussing the major religious festivals and what should be worn by the participants in them. The later part is more erratic, setting paradigms for various secular occasions, ranging from the wedding of the emperor to the promotion of some quite lowly ranks, and collecting some accounts of past events as exemplars of suitable ceremonial conduct, as well as reproducing the text of the *Klêtôrologion*.[6] The second part also contains some interpolations which post-date Constantine Porfurogennêtos himself. This diffuse structure makes extracting a concise summary of the default regalia along with that used on special occasions a delicate task. Fortunately, in addition to the text itself, numerous other sources help to clarify the subject.

REGALIA ITEMS COMMON TO VARIOUS MALE RANKS AND FUNCTIONS

Many ranks in the court had a number of garments and accessories in common, both as main and supplementary regalia.

Headgear

The headwear of the mass of the male court is a subject about which the main sources are somewhat uninformative. Evidently, this was not because there was none, but rather because there was a convention so deeply embedded in ancient practice that our authors did not think to mention it. Our insight into this comes from a tenth-century visitor to Constantinople, Liutprand of Cremona, who tells us that the custom was that no man might go hatted (*pileatus*) in the presence of the emperor. Instead, Liutprand was instructed to wear something he called a *teristrum*. To this, he retorted, 'Amongst us, women wear the *tiarae* and *teristra*, while men wear hats [*pilei*].'[7] In the account of an earlier voyage to the City he had referred to a *teristrum Graecorum* worn by Emperor Rômanos I.[8] Liutprand's employment of these terms is not entirely in accord with dominant medieval Latin usage as is commonly recorded in literary sources which have survived. In keeping with his reply, *teristrum* or *theristrum* does commonly mean a woman's mantle (*pallium*) or shawl (*palliolum*),[9] with all the imprecision of those terms. In contrast, *tiara* is most commonly used for the mitre of higher religious functionaries.[10]

Vêlarion

As part of the Brumalia celebrations the emperor gives a sum of money and a fine silk (*khasdion*[11]) *vêlarion*, or an *avdion*, to each *magistros*, and money and a half-silk (*molkhamion*, *mulham*[12]) *vêlarion*, or an *avdion*, to each *prôtospatharios*. It appears to be derived from the Latin *velarium*, most commonly meaning an awning.[13] In Achmet's *Oneirokritikon*, *vêlarion* does indeed occur in a chapter concerning various hangings and floor coverings, and may well be an awning as Oberhelman chooses to translate it.[14] There are several places in the *Book of Ceremonies* where it unmistakably means 'awning' or 'curtain',[15] but it would be entirely contrary to the pattern of gift-giving set out in that work, and in the *Treatise on Imperial Military Expeditions*, for the Brumalia gifts to be furnishings. The normal practice was that textile gifts were items of clothing, and the fact that the alternative to a *vêlarion* was a garment supports this. In the other occurrences of this word in middle Byzantium it is still less likely to be equivalent to 'awning'. In the will of Kalê Pakourianê, set down in the last quarter of the eleventh century, the testatrix gave away no less than twenty-nine *vêlaria* to her serving women, in groups of two or three. Many of these are significantly also made of the type of silk called *khasdion*, or an even more exotic cotton.[16] Both in the testament and in the *Book of Ceremonies* it is much more likely that *vêlarion* is headgear than an awning or a curtain (*rideau*), as the editors of the will would have it.[17] Such a usage for *vêlarion* would closely parallel the ways in which *kamelaukion* and *kalumma* are employed for awnings, furnishing textiles and headgear in different sources.

Maforion

There is one item of secular male headgear appearing prominently in the *Book of Ceremonies* which offers a very ready identification with Liutprand's *teristrum Graecorum*. It is the *maforion*, derived from an obscure item referred to in Latin as *mafors*.[18] Early citations suggest no more than that it is a woman's head covering. The *Edict on Prices* of Emperor Diocletian is more informative, making repeated mention of '*delmatikê* with *mafors*' (*dalmatikomafertion*), strongly suggesting that the *mafors* was a type of hood.[19] Hooded tunics survive in the copious Late Antique archaeology of clothing from Egypt. A plain white *maforion* is employed during the promotion of a eunuch to the role of *koubikoularios*.[20] A complication in the terminology concerns the rather more ornate *maforion* which plays a prominent role in the creation of a *raiktôr* (see below under that rank), yet that complication has direct parallels in the evolution of the use of *felônion*.

Felônion

Felônia are well known as religious regalia and certainly appear as such in our present source.[21] Yet the term also appears in connection with *patrikioi*, *taxaiôtai* and particularly with the *eparkhos* of the City.[22] The first two groups wear these as a matter of course, while the *eparkhos* is vested with it as part of his elevation. The *felônion* is universally acknowledged to be derived via *fainôlês* from the Latin *paenula*, originally a type of cloak, often hooded, for heavy weather.[23] The orthographical conflation of 'p' and 'f' continues in our source as we find *penolion* used interchangeably with *fenolion*. *Paenulae* had been common dress in the earlier Roman Empire. They began the transition to regalia status in the Senate with the Theodosian code in the late fourth century, and it is evidently from that institution that they are standard wear for *patrikioi*, who were the mainstay of the Senate.[24] The latter-day ecclesiastical *fenôlion* preserved the early hoodless form, and was identical with the Western chasuble, a closed conical mantle sometimes reaching down close to the ankle. Previous commentators have assumed that the lay *fenôlion* must be the same. There are reasons for doubting this assumption based upon the investiture of the *eparkhos*. A *lôros* also figures amongst the regalia of the *eparkhos*, and, at the end of the ceremony of eparkhial elevation, the patriarch wears both a *fenôlion* and *lôros*. This is a remarkable and unique case of the patriarch wearing such a piece of secular regalia as a *lôros*. In the first of these cases the *fenôlion* is mentioned before the *lôros*, while in the latter, the order is reversed, so no guess can be made on that basis as to which item is put on before the other. Despite this, both cases present practical problems, which suggests that the secular *fenôlion* cannot be identical to the ecclesiastical one. If the *lôros* were under a voluminous *fenôlion*, its presence would be almost completely obscured, rendering it null as an insignium. In contrast, if the *lôros* were placed over an ecclesiastical style *fenôlion*, the volume of the mantle would make the result quite bulky and clumsy, as indeed it is shown to be on Late Antique diptychs (fig. 23).[25]

These problems can be obviated by the proposition that in the transition from a mundane garment to regalia the lay and ecclesiastical *fenôlia* evolved divergent forms. In church use, the *paenula* held its old form as an all-enveloping garment, while as lay regalia the hooded form shrank until it was

FIG. 23. Detail of an ivory plaque depicting the early sixth-century Constantinopolitan Consul Flavius, illustrating the brief fashion for wrapping a *trevenna/lôros* over a *fainôlês*.

no more than a hood. In many social contexts it was imperative to create a visible distinction between secular vocations and functions and religious ones. Such a divergent evolution would serve very well to create that distinction. In addition to dispelling the difficulties of combining a large *fenôlion* with a *lôros*, this conclusion is supported by eleventh- and twelfth-century pictures of *eparkhoi*, which are confirmed in detail by contemporary literary evidence, and can be seen to preserve the stipulations of the *Book of Ceremonies*. These *eparkhoi* do indeed both wear a hood, in one case red and in the other white, but decorated identically with a ring of small circles around a large circle in black.

Thus, the lay *fenôlion* worn by *patrikioi*, *taxaiôtai* and the *eparkhos* of the City should be recognised to be not another type of mantle,[26] but a form of hood in company with *vêlarion* and *maforion*. The recognition of these three terms as designating forms of ceremonial hood or headscarf reveals that the majority of the ranks of the upper court, *magistros*, *patrikios*, *prôtospatharios* and *koubikoularios*, all wore such head coverings at times, and puts into context the significance of the account of Liutprand of Cremona in writing of *teristrum Graecorum*.

Main Garments

Kamision

The regalia tunic worn by the most ranks is that called a *kamision*. As with so much else, there are few surviving pictures of non-imperial regalia tunics between the seventh century and the eleventh century. Those few, however, do show the same sleeve form as the imperial tunic, identified previously as 'Persian-sleeves' (*persikomanikia*) (figs 5 and 9; Chart 3.3). The tenth-century dream interpreter Achmet states that, when worn by a man of non-royal rank, 'Persian-sleeves' symbolise the economy of his household. Thus, it seems that *kamision* was the catch-all term for all those tunics which possessed 'Persian-sleeves' but lacked adornment or whose decoration had not conferred upon them a particular name, such as *divêtêsion*, *spekion* or *stikharion*, discussed below, but which might sometimes have a certain identity, as in the *eparkhikon kamision*.

Khitôn

The *Book of Ceremonies* persists with the use of *khitôn* for some regalia tunics. As discussed in the previous chapter, this ancient term must have had a new and more specific meaning conferred upon it. It is often applied to regalia tunics which are more eminent than the *kamision* and which elsewhere have some of the more unique titles just mentioned.

Kôlovion

As established in chapter 1, by the end of Late Antiquity the *kôlovion* had become a tunic with full-length, loose sleeves (Chart 3.2). On the single occasion when the whole court wears the *kôlovion*, their garment is designated by the compound term, *esôforokôlovion*.[27] Other such compounds employed in the *Book of Ceremonies* denote a set of two separate but related items: for example, *sellokalinon*, a set of saddle and bridle,[28] and *khartokalamaria*, scrolls and pen-cases.[29] From such precedents it has been suggested that *esôforokôlovion* refers to an *esôforion* and a *kôlovion*.[30] There are sound practical reasons for doubting this proposition. Primarily, in the sense of *esôforion* being an under-tunic, it was normal for any person of some affluence to wear one routinely, as we can see illustrated in many sources.[31] There is, therefore, no sensible reason to specify that an *esôforion* should be worn with the *kôlovion* on this occasion, when no similar statement is ever made in respect of any other garment. Rather more likely is that *esôforion* has the usual sense of a light garment more commonly worn indoors, and describes the *kôlovion* itself. The fact that *esôforokôlovia* were to be worn on the afternoon during open days at the palace, which were to take place at Easter when the weather is likely to be warm, is further reason for thinking that this type of *kôlovion* was a lightweight garment (Plate 15, left). For more on the *esôforion*, see below.

Kontomanikion

The *kontomanikion* was an occasional regalia garment which was not specific to any rank or office. The imperial store contained a variety of *kontomanikia* which were issued to various courtiers and some quite lowly special guests (painters and craftsmen)[32] when occasion demanded.[33] The very name of the *kontomanikion* is descriptive – the 'short-sleeved' garment (Chart 3.4). A surviving example exists in the alb of Roger II of Sicily, now in the Kaiserliche Schatzkammer, Vienna (fig. 19).

More information is given about its form in the *Book of Ceremonies*, showing that *kontomanikia* came in various forms and decorations, yet were always ultimately defined by this characteristic of having elbow-length sleeves.[34] This adds to the picture starting to be sketched out that in this era garments used as regalia were distinguished from each other in the first instance by the form of their sleeves, and then by other factors such as decoration. Tunics with sleeves to the elbow occur in the most antiquarian of middle Byzantine art, as well as such sporadically realistic sources close to our period as the *Menologion of Basil II*.[35]

The *kontomanikia* in the imperial store are highly ornate, being purple (*oxus*), crimson-shot (*alêthinaeros khroakos*), woven with gold (*khrusoüfantos*), and crimson-shot with silver embroidery (*argurokentêtos alêthinaeros*). Of particular interest is a group of *kontomanikia* worn by tribunes and *vêgarioi* which were apparently not kept in the imperial store. They are as lavish as the others, coming in all four old deme colours, blue, white, green and red with gold panels (*khrusosêmentos*), but what makes them more noteworthy is that, unlike the others, they are *diakoptos*, 'split in twain'. The verb *diakoptô* has the sense of a full sundering, rather than a partial division indicated by the adjective *diskhistos* that we find applied to tunics in the literature. Hence, while *diskhistos* should be taken to mean that the garments had divisions in the skirt (Chart 2.7), for which there is ample artistic evidence in men's clothing around our period,[36] *diakoptos* must mean that these *kontomanikia* are completely split, and so are coats in modern terms, just like the nominal form found in the empress' wardrobe, *diakoptês* (Chart 2.3).[37] In middle Byzantine art, short-sleeved garments usually occur in archaising contexts, but the late twelfth-century donor portrait of Theodore Lêmniotês in the Church of Hagioi Anarguroi at Kastoria gives a fine example of a *diakopton kontomanikion*.[38]

Mantles

Khlamus/khlanidion

The *khlamus* remains the most prevalent garment common across ranks. The form that was still worn by default by virtually all ranks and functions was white with purple *tavlia*. The common alternative for more special occasions was a white *khlamus* with gold *tavlia*. Filotheos seems to suggest that the gold *tavlia* alone of such a cloak cost twenty-four nomismata.[39] Also worn by all ranks on rare occasions was the black *khlamus* called the *atravatikion*, which harks back to John Lydos' account of the Late Antique regalia. While that author suggests that the *atravatikis khlamus* had purple *tavlia*, an eleventh-century icon showing three saints garbed in the manner of the court includes Saint Prokopios on the left wearing a deep-black cloak with a lustrous gold *tavlia* (fig. 9).[40] It seems likely that the gold-panelled form was characteristic of this period, in keeping with the greater prevalence of gold in the middle Byzantine era, and its much greater visual effect. The *khlamus* worn by a range of officers is *foundatos*.[41] Other sources of the time use this word to mean 'tasselled'.[42] Tasselled mantles do occur in the mildly archaising art of this period, but only on women.[43] In male use, therefore, *foundatos* can be taken to derive from the Latin *fundatus*, meaning gold-bordered, fully in agreement with many of the pictorial sources.[44] The development of gold-bordered *khlamudes* is almost certainly bound up with a change in the shape of the garment. The *Klêtôrologion* continues to speak of 'doubled' cloaks, yet the art of this period clearly indicates *khlamudes* which have been cut down to a semi-oval, probably also with a further notch cut out for the neck, to eliminate the inelegant bundle of fabric that arises with a straight edge. One of the clearest illustrations of that is in the cloak of Saint Helena in the Paris *Homilies of Gregory of Nazianzos* manuscript (fig. 14). There, the semi-oval shape is indicated not only by the gold border all the way around, which is wider at the neck, but even more so by the pearl drops along the straight edge. This evidence shows that the process of simplification from oval to semi-oval was already underway before the end of the ninth century, but was probably not applied to all *khlamudes* until the ancient white ones were finally abandoned in the eleventh century.

Confirming the paradigm, defined in a previous chapter, of the *khlamus* normally being fastened on the right shoulder, there are a couple of references to it being worn in the style of a *sagion*: that is, 'in a frontal manner'.[45] This very much looks forward to the courtiers shown in the Paris *Homilies of John Chrysostom* manuscript (Coislin 79) with the gold *tavlia* panels a feature on their centrally-fastened cloaks.

Various other colours are mentioned in the *Book of Ceremonies*, specific to ranks or functions. Each *dêmarkhos* wore a *khlamus* in his deme colour, while men of the imperial chambers (*koubikoularioi*) had several unique types. These will be discussed further under the respective titles.

Sagion

The *sagion* originated as the coarse military *sagum* of the early Roman era.[46] In its primitive form it was a rectangular woollen cloth which could double as mantle or blanket. By this time it was much changed and gentrified, and our source indicates that the court version had been conflated with the *mantion*, a semicircular cape of Persian origin (fig. 10).[47] It did nevertheless retain its military associations, as we can readily see from art, for there is hardly a portrait of a military saint in the annals of Byzantine art that does not depict him wearing a short cape fastened on the centre of his chest. One of the finest examples is the oft-reproduced triumphal portrait of Basil II in the frontispiece of his Psalter in the Bibliotheca Marciana. The military parade *sagion* was evidently a little different from the court version, and will be discussed under military dress. Two varieties of *sagion* are common to virtually all the court. The more frequent is *alêthinon* ('true') purple, while the other was the russet colour, *roês* (Plate 9, right). The emperor and *kaisar* had unique varieties, further discussed below.

Paragaudion

Two high functionaries, *ostiarios* and master of ceremonies (*ho tês Katasteôs*), occasionally wear a garment called a *paragaudion*, and Filotheos declares it to be part of the regalia of a *koubikoularios*. In the tenth century, it is evidently not the tunic that had borne the name in Late Antiquity, for it is frequently paired with a *kamision*.[48] Another thing which sets it apart from the earlier item is the colour. The tenth-century *paragaudion* is gold. A natural conclusion is that in this era the *paragaudion* was a cape. In view of the eminent roles of the wearers, this is probably a lower-status version of the imperial golden *sagion*, in a similar manner seen with the *khlamus* of a *koubikoularios*.

Other capes

Capes made of patterned fabrics were designated by titles which evidently reflect the motifs worked into them – *aetos* (eagle), *leontarion* (little lion), *leukoleôn* (white lion), *taôn* (peacock) and *thalassa* (sea). The different sorts were all worn on the same occasions by numerous ranks, making a very definite contrast to the carefully monochrome presentation of the normal court outfits. Such patterned fabrics have survived in considerable quantity from around this period. Their consistent style refutes Reiske's suggestion that the *leukoleôn* had lions on a white field, because the colour scheme for beast-bearing brocades is always for a strongly-coloured background, usually with the design in a lighter colour.[49]

One or other of two surviving fabrics of the ninth or tenth century may be the *leukoleôn* or *leontarion* of which the *Book of Ceremonies* speaks. One is covered with white lions in roundels on a purple background (fig. 21).[50] The other has the lions standing alone on a purple field.[51] In addition to a discrete item appearing amongst a list of capes, some *skaramangia* are also made of this fabric.[52] Without more evidence it is impossible to conclude whether *leukoleôn* and *leontarion* were synonymous, or perhaps referred to the pattern variants in the surviving examples.

Aetos (eagle) and *thalassa* (sea) are somewhat less certain. The *aetos* is known as a variety of ancient military mantle, and Theofanês Continuatus states that *thalassa* is identical to it. Yet these two are mentioned separately in the same passage of the *Book of Ceremonies*: an indication that they were not the same thing in the tenth-century court.[53]

The *aetoi* of the *Book of Ceremonies* are 'green-red' (*prasinorodinos*) or, more significantly, 'many circled' (*poluguros*). The second description denotes a very common patterning of figured cloths made both within the eastern Roman Empire and in adjacent countries of this era, which was covered with a tessellation of circles or polygons containing vegetation, beasts or birds. Hence, we can confidently conclude that the *aetos* was so called because its many circles contained depictions of eagles, which, like lions, are one of the most popular motifs in Byzantine brocade production.[54]

One explanation offered for *thalassa* – suggesting that the lightness of the garment causes it to ripple like waves – is not very plausible.[55] It is much more likely that it refers to a light effect on the cloth, such as is visible with sea-wool or shot silk as Haldon theorises.[56] Alternatively it might be *ikat* cloth, which was produced in Yemen in the tenth century and earlier, and traded extensively in the Levant. *Ikat* at this time was made of cotton dyed shades of blue, brown and white in quite random distribution, which could certainly look like sea waves.[57]

There is, alas, little data in the *Book of Ceremonies* which would indicate the overall form of these patterned capes or how they were worn. Pictorial sources across the whole period sporadically show patterned mantles following both the

FIG. 24. Coronation ivory of Constantine Porfurogennêtos showing the distinctive type of *lôros* associated with him, and the *modiolos/kaisarikion* form of lesser crown. Tenth century. Pushkin Museum, Moscow.

khlamus and *sagion/mantion* paradigms (see, for example, figs 5, 46, 52). One passage hints that the *leontarion*, at least, was comparable to a *khlamus* – it was *khrusotavlon*, having gold panels. This may imply that it was also worn fastened on the right shoulder like a *khlamus*.

Lôros

It has been observed that the *lôros* is descended from the old Roman consular *trabea*, originally associated with the military triumphs which were normally a feature of consulship in Late Antique Rome, and itself descended from the ancient *toga* (fig. 23).[58] However by the tenth century its ceremonial use and symbolism had changed dramatically. When the *lôros* is worn on the Sunday of Holy Week, the *Book of Ceremonies* asserts that, in that context at least, it symbolises the shroud of Christ.[59] In surviving art, the *lôros* is almost exclusively associated with the rulers, yet the *Book of Ceremonies* tells us that on that occasion and some others it was worn by other ranks of the court, specifically *magistroi* and *anthupatoi*.[60] These *lôroi* were 'gold-woven' (*khrusoüfantos*) and fifteen of them were held in the imperial regalia store attached to the Church of Saint Stephen of Dafnê.[61] A *lôros* was part of the regalia of the *zôstê patrikia* and *Eparkhos tês Poleôs* (Governor of Constantinople). The forms of the *lôros* at the time of the composition of our source were twofold. The long-established type, wrapped in the manner apparently descended from the *toga* (Chart 6.1 and shown from the rear on Plate 5, right) and a simplified form associated with Constantine Porfurogennêtos (fig. 24; Chart 6.3). The width of the *lôros* seems somewhat variable according to the art, but the generic type is five metres long, while the Porfurogennêtan form is approximately three and a half metres in length.[62]

Footwear

On frequent occasions the court was to wear *kampagia* or *kaligia*.[63] As noted above, it seems that the conservatism of the court and the stylisation of the regalia meant that these preserved something like the sandals shown in the Ravenna mosaics.[64] The term also virtually defines the Senate – 'the *kampagia*-shod Senate' (*ho hupo kampagin sunklêtos*)[65] – indicating that there were probably their standard wear when discharging their formal duties, not just when explicitly specified by our source.

Accessory – *thôrakion*

As noted in the last chapter, much of the court, including the emperor, occasionally wore the *thôrakion*. This item is commonly associated with the *lôros*, but would also be worn with a *skaramangion*, *kamision* or *kontomanikion*.[66] Past attention to this item has misguidedly focused on it purely as part of the empress' regalia, to exclusion of the emperor and the rest of the court. Ebersolt originated the misconception that it was the tear-drop shaped piece on the lower part of the empress' costume as depicted in the eleventh century,[67] which de Jerphanion more correctly identified as part of a garment,[68] and which is, in fact, the tail of the empress' *lôros*.

The use of the term *thôrakion* elsewhere in medieval Greek is of some assistance in identifying this item. Its precursor, *thorax*, refers to the upper part of the torso or chest, and other uses of *thôrakion* flow on logically from this – the fighting platforms or towers mounted on the backs of elephants; projecting towers or other forward lines of defence in fortifications, directly equivalent to the English expression 'breastwork'; or a bandage around the chest.[69] This last seems at first most promising, for a band of cloth tied around the chest does appear in middle Byzantine pictorial sources. Almost always this is on soldiers,[70] and on rare occasions on civilian men,[71] although there are instances of it appearing on women.[72] Yet this possibility is undermined by the fact that, while the *Klêtôrologion* mentions gold, there is never any specification of colour for the *thôrakion* in the *Book of Ceremonies*, which would be expected for an item of cloth, especially in view of the varying colours that are represented in the pictorial sources. One answer to this question might be that in an item as unlikely to appear in everyday dress, colour has no bearing on its distinctiveness. Such an answer, although possible, does not readily accommodate the high level of importance that is attached to colour in the *Book of Ceremonies*. In addition to this reservation, our source includes another word which can be applied to a cloth chest band with much less doubt: *pektorarion*.

Another much more attractive possibility occurs. Amongst jewellery found in Late Antique and medieval archaeological sites is an object consisting of two metal discs joined with four lengths of chain or chains of discs attaching at cardinal points. A very finely preserved complete example dated to the ninth century is held in the British Museum (fig. 20), and another in the Museum of Byzantine Art in Berlin.[73] This arrangement immediately suggests the item being worn with two of the chains running over the shoulders, and the other two passing around the body. This would result in the roundels lying in the centre of the chest and the centre of the back. Being metal and fastened around the body in such a way, the *thôrakion* might also then symbolically refer back to the item to which its precursor word, *thôrax*, most often refers, a cuirass of armour. Filotheos' two references to *thôrakia* being gold support this connection.[74] Cloth of gold is certainly mentioned often enough in our sources; however, with the improbability that a *thôrakion* was made of cloth discussed above, this tincture should be taken as further support for the notion of this item being jewellery. With the *thôrakion* worn over the *lôros*, such jewellery might be contrived to have the roundel lying very attractively in the intersection of the *lôros* (Plate 17, left), an arrangement which would be very reminiscent of the regalia depicted upon Sassanian royal portraits.[75] This notion has already gained some acceptance amongst recent scholarship.[76]

It seems very likely that *katakoilion*, an ornament worn by the *prôedros* of the Senate, is another term for *thôrakion*.[77]

Non-regalia garments common to various male ranks and functions

Esôforion

The *esôforion* is mentioned twice in the description of court ceremonial. In the first instance it was worn by the Macedonian Guard on the occasion of a reception by Constantine Porfurogennêtos and Rômanos I for prisoners of war released from Tarsos on 31 May 946.[78] Otherwise each of the *anthupatoi* and *patrikioi* are given one made wholly of silk and striped in the Saracen manner at the Brumalia celebrations.[79]

The meaning of *esôforion* can be taken to be either 'worn-within'[80] or 'worn-underneath', that is, as either an indoor garment or an undergarment. It would be mistaken to try to decide that it meant exclusively one or the other, for we can see in many another era and culture, including our own, that a light and fine garment can serve both of these functions at different times, and might even serve as a primary garment outdoors in hot weather – conditions we can guess prevailed in early summer at the time of the imperial reception mentioned above. Thus, *esôforion* can be seen to be directly equivalent to our 'shirt'.

They were evidently highly regarded as gifts, for they are recommended in the *Treatise on Imperial Expeditions*,[81] and form a significant part of the cargo sent to King Hugh of Italy,[82] and of the stores of the Cretan Expedition.[83] One reason for this is likely to be that the long-established and more sophisticated workshops of Constantinople were able to produce finer and softer fabrics than were available in provincial areas. Another possibility is that *esôforia* could be made of cotton, as is recorded in documents of the following century from Byzantine territories in Italy.[84] Cotton is by nature softer than any linen but also wears better. Such qualities would be very welcome in garments worn against the skin.

From the *Homilies of Gregory of Nazianzos* dated 880,[85] through the *Menologion of Basil II* around the turn of the eleventh century[86] and the Madrid Skylitzes near the mid-twelfth century,[87] to a Bodleian Library manuscript attributed to the late twelfth century,[88] and in numerous other sources,[89] both men and women are shown wearing undergarments of fine, white or generally pastel-coloured cloth. The more contemporaneously realistic of these sources show an important

FIG. 25. A surviving linen *esôforion*, carbon-dated to the early thirteenth century, but showing features dating back to the tenth or eleventh century: an applied breast panel and low standing collar. Karaman Museum, Tashkale Province, Turkey.

point of detail which separates Byzantine dress of this period from all of its neighbours and from what had gone before. These *esôforia* have a distinct collar band which extends some distance up the wearer's throat. Figure 25 shows an *esôforion* which was removed from a chamber with a Greek inscription in the Manazan Caves in eastern Anatolia, and which is on display in the museum of Karaman. This garment is now known from carbon-14 dating to be of the early thirteenth century, but shows characteristics which can be traced back into the tenth century.[90] The basic construction layout of this shirt appears in Chart 1.4.

Esôforia sent to Italy as gifts to King Hugh are described as *alêthinos*, *lôrôtos* and *oktalios*. The first is a familiar colour, 'true purple'. The second adjective has been rendered elsewhere as 'striped'.[91] This can be accepted without hesitation, for, in addition to the derivation of the word, there are reliable depictions of striped garments, particularly undergarments, in Byzantine art,[92] as well as their being a staple of fashion in the Islamic world, as indicated by the description of those given to the *anthupatoi* and *patrikioi* at the Brumalia celebrations.[93] The last term, which might be rendered as 'eightfold', is more mysterious. It might reasonably be inferred from the accompanying adjectives to be a form of decoration, however no ready theory comes forward as to what it might be.[94] The waters are further muddied by the fact that *esôforia* for the Cretan Expedition included not only *oktalios*, but also *dekalios* and *heptalios* forms, with matching stockings (*touvia*) for each type.[95]

Skaramangion

The *skaramangion* was a garment characterised by very long sleeves, which had been called *paragôdês* in Late Antiquity.[96] Achmet routinely refers to the *skaramangion* as a *kavadion*, although all the surviving pictures of this period (relatively few as they are) show it as a pull-over garment (fig. 26). It was universally worn by any man attending an imperial banquet, and to less formal ceremonies. As usual, white was frequent, and other plain colours are mentioned, as are occasions of patterned cloths, though evidently colour was often a matter of choice for the wearer.

Regalia Specific to Certain Male Ranks

The Emperor and *Kaisar*

It is no surprise to find that the imperial regalia is the most changeable – the rulers can be expected to have the largest wardrobe, and the conspicuous display of its range and quality was essential to exhibiting their majesty, wealth and power. The emperor and *kaisar* had much in common in this respect. The variations are discussed below.

Pictorial sources for the rulers are, again, unsurprisingly, the most common. They are also generally very accurate to

FIG. 26. This mourner at the raising of Lazarus muffles his nose from the charnel stench with the long sleeve of his *skaramangion* tunic. Dionysiou Monastery, Mount Athos, codex 587, f. 44v.

the literary material, with one notable exception. The orb surmounted by the cross is a conspicuous feature of royal portraits on coins and seals. It is, in contrast, strikingly absent from pictures in more elite media, and there is nothing in any of the literature which can be identified with it. The pattern of evidence is clear enough in supporting the suggestion that the *sfaira staurofora* (*globus crucifer* in Latin) was in Byzantium purely a graphical device and never existed as a physical object.[97]

Headgear

The head is necessarily the focus of the most attention and this is reflected in the diversity of headgear the emperor wore. This array had its own hierarchy and occasion-specific items.

Stemma

The pre-eminent piece of imperial headgear was the *stemma*, worn by the emperor but not the *kaisar*. This crown was made of gold and set with precious stones and multitudes of pearls. The band encircling the head was surmounted by two low crossing arches which supported a lining – the 'cross-shaped piece' which Filotheos told us that the coronet of the *kaisar* lacked. This framework is rarely shown in earlier works of art, but it is clearly visible in the crown being presented to Basil II by Christ in his Psalter portrait, and on the crown being placed upon the head of Rômanos on the ivory in the Cabinet des Médailles, Paris (fig. 27). Furthermore, one was added to the woman's coronet which was sent to Hungary late in the eleventh century. Filotheos' remark about the *kaisarikion*, combined with the pictorial sources, conclusively debunks Anna Komnênê's claim that her father 'invented' the crown with the cruciform superstructure, although he may well have modified it, as will be discussed later.[98] There were four *stemmata*, each lined in a different colour. The primary crown was the 'great white *stemma*', while the others had linings in green, red and blue. When the artistic convention changed in the eleventh century, we begin to see the superstructure and white lining of the *stemma* becoming visible. The lesser *stemmata* were often used in excursions outside the ceremonial core of the palace, with a frequent practice being that one colour was worn in the morning when going out, and another colour when returning in the afternoon.

Kaisarikion

As its name signals, this was the normal headgear of the *kaisar*. In addition to that, when celebrating a triumph,[99] or if he chose not to stand upon full formality when viewed by certain foreigners on palace open days,[100] the emperor might wear a *kaisarikion* in place of the *stemma*. The dominant convention in tenth-century art was to show emperors wearing this coronet, rather than the great crown (*stemma*), as we can see from the ivory portrait of the author of the *Book of Ceremonies* (fig. 24). This coronet was also called *diadêma* and *modiolos*.[101] Pictures of this era show that this crown was surmounted at the front by a small cross made of tear-drop pearls or something of the same shape. Hence, the assertion by Filotheos that the *kaisarikion* lacked a 'cross-shaped piece' must refer to another component of a crown as noted above; again the pictorial sources come to our aid by showing that the *modiolos* was not enclosed above and allows the wearer's hair to be seen.

IC XC
ΡΩΜΑΝΟϹ ΒΑϹΙΛΕΥϹ ΡΩΜΑΙΩΝ
ΕΥΔΟΚΙΑ ΒΑϹΙΛΙϹ ΡΩΜΑΙΩΝ

OPPOSITE: FIG. 27. Emperor Rômanos IV Diogenês and Empress Evdokia Makrembolitissa. Evdokia was the last empress to wear the *divitision* as her primary regalia garment throughout her reign. Close inspection of Rômanos' crown shows the domed superstructure of a *stemma* under Christ's hand. Cabinet des Medailles, Bibliothèque Nationale, Paris.

Toufa

The crested crown in use in Late Antiquity and subsequently called *lofia* or *toufa* continued in use in this period. It was still called *toufa*, but also in the tenth century it was referred to as a *toga* or *tiara*.[102] Although this retained its military associations, it was also used in other ceremonies, such as at Easter if the emperor so chose.[103] Allegorical figures representing Rome and Constantinople each present a *toufa* to Emperor Basil II on a textile now in Bamberg Cathedral (fig. 28). The exceptional detail of the Bamberg Tapestry shows that the *toufa* also has a gemmed and pearled cross-shaped superstructure like the *stemma*. Zonaras reaffirms the synonymity of *toufa* and *tiara* in writing of Basil II's triumph over the Bulgarians.[104] This crown was, like the *kaisarikion*, common to both emperor and *kaisar* on occasions such as Easter.

FIG. 28. Detail of a *toufa* from the 'Bamberg Tapestry' depicting Emperor Basil II in triumph. Note the crossing arches, one supporting the crest.

Praipendoulia

The primary crowns were fitted with *praipendoulia*, two pendant ornaments framing the face. Illustrations throughout the life of the empire from this period onwards show these as being a remarkably stable item composed of a string of large pearls terminating in tear-drop pearls, often in a triplet (figs 13, 14, 16, 24, 27, 43, 45, 47, 59, 63). The lack of representations of the *toufa* in use prevents certainty as to whether that crown was also fitted with *praipendoulia*.

FIG. 29. Detail of the cuff of what was possibly the last *divêtêsion* ever made. Created in Sicily for the 'Holy Roman' emperor, Frederick II, in 1225. Taken from his tomb but now lost.

Tzitzakion

On a very few special occasions the emperor and *kaisar* were to wear a *tzitzakion*, an item adopted from the Khazars in honour of a Khazarian *augousta* whose native name had been Chichak ('Flower'). The *Book of Ceremonies* is entirely silent on the nature of this piece of regalia, nor has past scholarship offered any proposals as to what it might have been. The likelihood that this was a form of headgear comes about by a process of elimination. The clothes and accessories that it accompanied leave little option for it to be something worn about the body, yet it is never mentioned as being worn with any type of headgear, which is quite contrary to the normal paradigms in our source. Unfortunately, there is no extraneous hint, either from Constantinople or Khazaria, as to just what the *tzitzakion* may have looked like.

Main garments

Divêtêsion

The premiere garment of the emperor was the *divêtêsion* (also written *divitision*, but phonetically identical at this time), which was also called *divikion*[105] and *diaitêsion*.[106] It is almost confined to imperial use, and strongly associated with coronation. George the Monk, an author of unknown identity writing in the third quarter of the ninth century, depicts the process of investment with the *divêtêsion* as one of the crucial moments in the coronation of a new emperor, along with the donning of the imperial red boots or *tzangia*.[107] Unfortunately, the crucial passage of the *Book of Ceremonies* which ought to have given explicit corroboration of the coronation process – Book II, chapter 17: 'The inauguration of Rômanos *Porfurogennêtos*, son of Emperor Constantine' listed in the contents – is absent from the manuscripts.[108] Not confined to use in religious observances and coronations, the *divêtêsion* also features in Constantine Porfurogennêtos' ideal model of a military triumph, attributed to Emperor Theofilos.[109]

Pictorial sources are unanimous is showing that this was a tunic with ample sleeves gathered into long, ornate, close-fitting buttoned cuffs (figs 16, 24, 27, 45). A surviving example of such a cuff made in the first decade of the thirteenth century was found in the tomb of Frederick II of Sicily (fig. 29).[110] The Norman kings of Sicily habitually imitated Constantinople in their royal art and regalia. As has been previously noted, the tenth-century dream interpreter Achmet calls this form of sleeve 'Persian-sleeves' (*persikomanikion*).[111] He asserts that, for the emperor, the cuff symbolises the military state of the empire. If it should become unfastened and fall away from the arm, it indicates disarray in the state of the army, and if the fastening should be torn apart, then likewise the army would be destroyed.

The typical imperial *divêtêsion* of this era was either the royal purple most commonly or white. At an imperial triumph the emperor might wear a *divêtêsion* of figured cloth.[112] One imperial *divêtêsion* apparently worn at the coronation, was *stikharin*: that is, decorated with vertical bands down its length. This was the precedent attributed to Emperor Anastasios, as noted in chapter 1, and continued or revived by Nikêforos Fôkas, who inserted it into our source. The illustrations of *divitêsia* give no indication of the broad construction of the garment – usually, of course, because the body is largely covered by a *khlamus or lôros* – but any of the three fully pieced constructions shown on chart 1 are viable. One imperial *divêtêsion* was 'rustic' (*paganon*), and could be worn with a 'rustic' *khlamus*. This means that they were short – just to the knees, like the tunic of a common country dweller or soldier, rather than to the ankle, like the normal aristocratic garments (Chart 2.2; fig. 30).[113]

FIG. 30. Gentlemen wearing regalia in the 'rustic' (*paganos*) style of short tunics and cloaks. British Library, Add. 19352, f. 19v.

Kôlovion

The emperor's main ceremonial alternative to the *divêtêsion*, though worn much less often, was the *kôlovion*.[114] The process by which this Hellenised version of the Latin *colobium* had been transferred from an antique sleeveless sack to the wide-sleeved *dalmatica* has been discussed in chapter 1.

Two imperial *kôlovia* are mentioned. One is called the 'bunch' or 'cluster' (*votrus*), and is extremely ornate, being made of figured silk, with tubular gold embroidery, gems and pearls.[115] The other is called 'the rams' (*hoi krioi*).[116] It is not described, but it seems reasonable to imagine that it, too, was a figured cloth depicting this animal.

Over-garments

Lôros

The emperor's most pre-eminent over-garment, so familiar from imperial portraits, was the *lôros*. A long narrow strip of densely decorated fabric, the imperial *lôros* was usually only worn on the most august occasions of imperial pomp within the precincts of the palace.

Khlamus

When not wearing a *lôros* the emperor, like most of the court, wore a *khlamus*. The paradigm that we have seen already existing in the sixth century still held of the premiere imperial *khlamus* being rich purple with gold *tavlia*. Numismatic evidence in particular shows one change which had been introduced in the intervening period. The imperial cloak now shows a gold edging all the way around, a phenomenon which had been visible in the empress' *khlamus* since Late Antiquity. This form of *khlamus* is designated by the term *foundatos* in our source.[117] If this *khlamus* is still oval, this feature would belie a significant change in the decorative scheme, with a gold band running along the long axis of the garment. It is more likely to indicate the simplification of the *khlamus* to a semi-oval, a process which was certainly complete by the middle of the eleventh century. The basic imperial *khlamus* was purple (*porfureos*),[118] while other plain-coloured ones were lustrous white (*lampros*),[119] and gold.[120]

One imperial *khlamus* is described as *opsimaros*.[121] Previous scholarship has attempted to interpret this as a colour, deriving it from *opse/opsia* with the sense of evening, yet with no certain interpretation for the latter part.[122] None of these arguments is very convincing, and they collapse completely in the face of other sources. The *Paschal Chronicle* mentions a client king being vested with a cloak bearing the picture of Emperor Justin on the *tavlion*,[123] and two early ivories depicting empresses show them each wearing a *khlamus* with a bust portrait of the emperor clasping a sceptre and *akakia* worked upon the *tavlion* (fig. 13).[124] In the light of this it makes far more sense to derive the first part of *opsimaros* from *opsis*, meaning the countenance or visage. The second part remains less certain, and may be a rather more convoluted derivation through vernacular usages.[125]

Another imperial *khlamus* was patterned with an octagonal tessellation (*oktogônos*).[126] Such patterning is well represented in surviving Near Eastern textiles of this era.

Sagion

The *lôros* and *khlamus* were the emperor's two most august over-garments, and either could be worn with the *stemma* and *divêtêsion*. The next level down in formality was the *sagion*. As noted previously, the court *sagion* was a semicircular cape falling to the knee and fastened at the centre of the chest.

This cape scarcely constituted regalia for the emperor, as it did for lower ranks, for he most often wore it with the non-regalia formal wear garment, the *skaramangion*. The emperor had three *sagia* – 'gold-bordered' (*khrusoperikleiston*, presumably on a purple field), entirely gold (*khrusoun*) and a russet (*roês*) *sagion*, apparently the same as one worn by much of the court. The *sagion* was invariably of a plain colour, aside from any edging. Similar capes made of figured cloth were given distinctive names, as we have seen.

One cloth of gold *sagion*, worn solely by the junior ruler, shared the name *kaisarikion* with the coronet.[127] It may have been the same as the golden *sagion* worn by the emperor, which he wore, like the coronet, when dressing with lesser formality, although the *kaisar*'s cape was edged with pearls.

Accessories

Footwear

Almost as significant to the imperial regalia as the crown, and certainly as ancient, was the emperor's footwear. As part of his highest regalia he wore calf-length boots, called *tzangia*, or low boots or shoes, called *hupodêmata*, dyed red.[128] Numerous accounts focus upon the wearing of red footwear – more than any other item of regalia – as the sign of usurpation.

Custom was so deeply entrenched and familiar that only deviation from established practice needed to be mentioned. Several Arabic accounts shed important light upon imperial footwear practice in this period. Ibn Khordabeh, writing in the middle of the ninth century, says that 'only the Heir Apparent wears one red shoe and one black one.'[129] Harun Ibn Yahya also saw a royal person wearing this combination of footwear during his visit to Constantinople in first quarter of the tenth century.[130] Ibn Yahya believed that man to be the emperor, but Jenkins has argued persuasively enough that it was, in fact, Kaisar Alexander.[131] Ibn Yahya's error would be easy enough for a native Byzantine to have made, given how little systematic difference the *Klêtôrologion* and *Book of Ceremonies* record there being between the regalia of the emperor and the *kaisar*. This curious practice of multicoloured footwear is never mentioned or depicted in East Roman sources, yet can be seen to be persistent, for it is again mentioned by an Arab traveller in the later eleventh century. The symbolism of this distinctive colour system obviously relates to the position of the *kaisar* being halfway from the populace to the throne, so to speak.

On rare occasions the rulers would join the other courtiers in wearing a version of the ancient sandals noted in chapter 1, generally called *kaligia* or *kampagia*. It appears that the imperial sandals were also called *strikta*,[132] and *pedila*,[133] and that the latter, at least, were gilded, a treatment known from Late Antique surviving examples.[134] Close inspection of the Rômanos ivory (fig. 27) shows that the structure of the imperial sandals had not changed since the time of Justinian, with a toe-cap edged with pearls linked with pearled straps crossing the instep.

Leg-wear

With the *kampagia* the emperor's leg-wear was visible, and so needs to be mentioned in our source. These are called *touvia* and *kampotouva*, with the terms being used in a slightly antiquated way compared to other sources of the era. *Touvia* were footed hose, doubtless much like those shown on the Ravenna mosaics.[135] These may still have been fabricated of woven cloth, as they were in Europe up to the sixteenth century, yet from Late Antiquity in the Near East we find a steadily developing trend for socks (*podôrtia*)[136] and hose to be made by varieties of knitting.[137] *Kampotouva*, or 'field-hose', were open tubes of fairly heavy cloth, which could be padded in everyday use, just as in military use.[138] These leggings had originated near the end of Late Antiquity as protection for horsemen against the chafing of stirrup leathers against their shins,[139] and are known in surviving examples from Egypt.[140] Perhaps predictably, *kampotouva* were worn by the rulers with the *strikta*.

Leg bindings are commonly illustrated in middle Byzantine religious art. They are usually a conventional component of antique bucolic dress, such as on the biblical shepherds. They can also be seen on some more antiquarian warrior saints in military dress or armour. In that context their nature as a stylised artistic convention is often unmistakeable, as they are shown as being arranged in ways which could never be functional.[141] Easter is a time in which ceremonial practice imitated art in this area. The *Book of Ceremonies* says that the emperor binds his legs with linen and wears gilded *pedila*.[142] The linen bindings, with their resemblance to a corpse's winding sheet (fig. 26, right) symbolise mortality, while the gold of the footwear (and the *lôros* which is also part of this outfit) symbolises the splendour of resurrection.

Thôrakion

The rulers wore the *thôrakion* with the *lôros*, as did other courtiers. There is nothing to suggest that this accessory differed for them from the common one.

Sceptres

Sceptres and staves have been the quintessential symbols of royal authority since distant antiquity. This being so, it is to be expected that various forms of staff had a major role in court ceremonies since long before the commencement point of this study. They had a similar prominence in the Abbasid court.[143]

Amongst the consular regalia of the Later Roman Empire was a staff called *skipiô*, which is well illustrated in consular diptyches.[144] It appears then to have been approximately a metre long and earlier forms of this staff were surmounted by an eagle (fig. 23). With the increasingly entrenched Christianisation of the empire, the eagle on the head of the *skipiô* began to be replaced with a cross. The same era also saw the ascendancy of Greek over Latin as the dominant language of the empire. With that, the terminology of so much Roman impedimenta was also increasingly Hellenised. Thus, *skipiô*, already partially Hellenised by transliteration from Latin to Greek script, became *skêpiôn*, and with the assimilation of consular regalia into imperial regalia, the cross-headed *skêpiôn* became a distinctly royal symbol (fig. 31.1). This evolution is well reflected in the *Book of Ceremonies*. Our source traces the term back to the illustrious Roman general, Scipio Africanus, saying that these staves carry on his good name.[145] Further, while any of the other staves referred to in the *Book of Ceremonies*, even that called *skêptron*, might be carried by junior ranks, the *skêpiôn* is only recorded as either being held by the emperor, or being amongst uniquely imperial symbols.[146] Finally, the *Book of Ceremonies* confirms the equivalence of the *skêpiôn* with the cross. This correlation is often implied by the fact that both terms are applied to the object the emperor holds in his left hand while he brandishes the *akakia*, a pouch of earth symbolising mortality, in his right.[147] The account of the Hippodrome festivities staged in honour of Muslim 'friends' in 946 makes it explicit. Contrasting the regalia of the occasion, our source says that the emperor wore a *lôros* and held the cross and the *akakia*, while the *magistroi* and *anthupatoi* wore *lôroi* but did not have *skêpiônes* and *akakiai*.[148] Both the cross and the *skêpiôn* are said to be gilded with gems and pearls, as, indeed, one would anticipate even if these were not the very same object.[149] Pictorial sources supply us with ample detail of imperial *skêpiônes*, including one which is likely be that of Constantine Porfurogennêtos himself.[150]

One unique staff, used on rare, highly religious occasions, is attributed to Moses.[151] Although our source gives no information as to what sets this apart, early Christian iconography

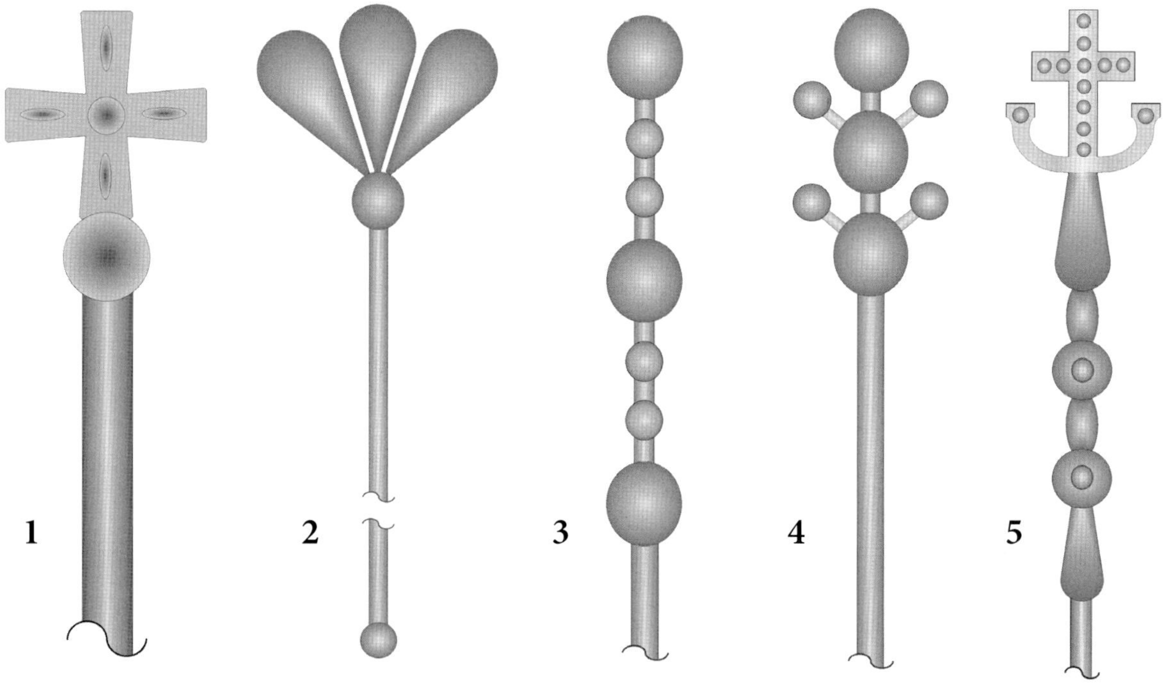

FIG. 31. Imperial sceptres, sixth to fifteenth centuries. 1. *Skêpiôn*; 2. *vergion triklônon*; 3. sceptre of Empress Zôê; 4. *khusoun vaion* or 'golden bough'; 5. *skêpiôn* of Empress Maria of Alania. Not to common scale.

frequently shows Moses striking the rock, and very consistently the object he uses is a very light wand with a slight curve, rather than the solid stick one would normally associate with the term 'staff'.[152] The wand that is quite often shown in the hands of Christ as he raises Lazarus also bears a strong resemblance to that used by Moses.[153] Most interestingly, the Topkapi Treasury in Istanbul contains an item also said to be the staff of Moses, which is of very similar light form. It seems highly likely that the 'Staff of Moses' of the tenth century was also a light wand consistent with these examples.

The most frequently illustrated imperial staff is the *lavaron* (from Latin *labarum*) (fig. 49).[154] This was originally a square or rectangular military banner hung from a cross bar, but when it was re-introduced in the ninth century after a period of disuse, it seems to have become a smaller panel, of more-solid material, gilded and set with gems and pearls, and often with pendants of pearls and/or gems hanging from the top corners, which bore an image of Christ or the Virgin. It retains its military and triumphal associations throughout the middle Byzantine period and commonly appears on coinage.

It has been suggested that the object called *fengion* (φέγγιον), which is carried by some of the common attendees at the imperial balls in the *Khrusotriklinos*, refers to a staff surmounted by a crescent.[155] While not impossible, this suggestion requires an unnecessary stretch of the analogy from the earlier *fengos*. It is more likely to mean a particular type of torch or lamp, an alternative term for the device named *fatlion* (φάτλιον) mentioned frequently in religious, ceremonial and military contexts.[156] In the lead-in to the ball, the moving lights would produce an even more spectacular effect than the relatively static illumination of the *polukandela* one may infer were installed in that chamber.

Nôvelêssimos

In the *Klêtôrologion* the regalia tunic of the *nôvelêssimos* was said to be a murex-purple *khitôn* with gold decoration (fig. 32). In the *Book of Ceremonies* it is recorded as a red (*rousion*) *divêtêsion*.[157] The change of colour from purple to red is paralleled by the reverse change from red to purple in the rank below it, *kouropalatês*. The reason for this change may lie in the cloak. Between the two manuals this rank seems to have acquired the most distinctive *khlamus* in the whole court. It is risky to attribute contemporary, or perhaps idiosyncratic, aesthetics to the past, but the base colour of the *nôvelêssimos*' new cloak, green, might be seen to clash with the purple of the old tunic, while the red of the new *khitôn* would be striking but less offensive to the eye.

The *khlamus* of the *nôvelêssimos* was set apart from the rest of the court by more than just its unique colour, for it was also not plain. The green field was worked with golden roses, and like other cloaks it sported gold *tavlia*.[158]

Nôvelêssimos was one of the ranks which wore a *lôros* as a matter of course. This would presumably be less ornate than those of the emperor and *kaisar* – still heavily embroidered with gold, no doubt, but perhaps with less in the way of pearls and precious stones.

Kouropalatês

As noted above, the tunic of the *kouropalatês* has changed colour between the *Klêtôrologion* and the *Book of Ceremonies*. From being red previously, it had become a 'true purple' *divêtêsion*, although undoubtedly still embroidered with gold as Filotheos had recorded. This rank has no other distinctive regalia, and so would wear the standard range of cloaks and capes that the entire court shared.

Magistros

The *Klêtôrologion* had described the regalia tunic of a *magistros* as a white tunic (*khitôn*) with gold decoration woven into it, particularly as 'epaulettes'. Panels of decoration on the shoulders are a commonplace of Roman tunics going back into antiquity. They were commonly linked to a collar, but could be discrete. On this tunic they were probably discrete, for a specific term can be found for a motif of a collar with extension onto the shoulders, *fialion*. Filotheos' use of the term *khitôn* for this indicates that it shares with the *divêtêsion* and the tunic of the *prôtospatharios* and *patrikios* the characteristic of having 'Persian-sleeves'. The *Book of Ceremonies* adds further to our knowledge of the appearance of this garment by calling it a *stikharion* in the account of the magistral elevation ceremony.[159] The description of the regalia created for the rank of *raiktôr*, which had not had any in the *Klêtôrologion*, adds yet more detail, for it declares that the tunic of the *raiktôr* lacks the *gonateia*, or knee-patches, that the *stikharion* tunics of the eunuch *prôtospatharioi* and *magistroi* possess.[160] Patches of decoration at knee level are another common feature of earlier tunics and often found in company with *stikhoi*. All these pieces of information make the magistral *stikharion* a garment that can be visualised in detail with confidence.

Magistroi continued to wear the *valtidion*, the red leather belt set with precious stones, as noted in the *Klêtôrologion*, along with the standard *khlamudes*, *sagia* and patterned capes.

FIG. 32. A *nôvellissimos* in his regalia of a red *divitision* and purple *khlamus*, with the addition of a *maniakion* bearing a large red gem. British Library, Add. 19352, f. 33v.

Raiktôr

The *raiktôr* (Latin, *rector*) apparently did not have any regalia at the time the *Klêtôrologion* was written. Sometime afterwards this rank received an elevation in status which did not actually change its position in the hierarchy, but which did gain it a spectacular set of regalia. Being new, this needed more detailed definition than that of other ranks.

The tunic of the *raiktôr* was considered so unique that it was named accordingly *raiktôrikion*. It is described as being 'pure white, having a magnificent, gold-woven *fialion*, as much as four fingers wide, and some small things extending out towards the shoulders, also with magnificent gold-woven cuffs and gold-woven hems. It does not have emblems at the knees (*gonateia*), as do the *stikharia* of the eunuch *prôtospatharioi* and *magistroi*.'[161] As discussed in the section on colour and decoration, *fialion* denotes a broad yoke around the neck opening of the garment (Plate 15, left).

The *raiktôr* also has a *maforion* that was special to him. It also has a particular name, *loupênariôn*, and is rather more ornate than the others alluded to in our source, being rich purple, all covered with roses embroidered in gold. This accessory is doubly remarkable for reasons beyond its colour and decoration. We are told that he wears it just once at his promotion ceremony and never again. It is also described as 'put on from his head so as to cover his entire body'. This strongly suggests that this particular *maforion* is a full-sized vestige of the ancient hooded *paenula*.

In a modest deviation from common practice, the primary over-garment for a *raiktôr* was not a *khlamus*, but a gold-bordered (*khrusoperikleiston*) *mantion*. This term is normally only used for the capes worn by women and religious functionaries, but we are told elsewhere that *mantion* and *sagion* are synonymous, and hence was a knee-length, semicircular cape fastened at the centre of the chest.[162] We are not informed of the base colour of the *mantion*. Perhaps it did not matter and was left to personal preference, with the mere fact of its gold border being enough to set it apart.

Prôtospatharios

Whereas in the *Klêtôrologion* there had been a substantial difference in the regalia of the bearded *prôtospatharioi* and that of the eunuchs, this division seems to have broken down by the time of the composition of the main body of the *Book of Ceremonies*. In the later source the regalia of the *prôtospatharioi* is called *spekion*, and described as *alêthinon auroklavon* – true purple with gold hem ornaments. This colour scheme would still make it '*divisition*-like' (*divitisioidês*), as the *Klêtôrologion* had described the tunics of the eunuch *prôtospatharioi*, despite the difference in fabric tincture. The outstanding donor portrait of Prôtospatharios Iôvannês in the *Adrianople Gospels* of 1007 offers a very accurate rendering of a 'true purple, gold-barred *spekion*', but for the yellow serving as a substitute for applied gold on a manuscript of modest value (fig. 33; compare fig. 53) Grotowski has proposed that the presence of *klavoi* should alone be sufficient to identify a garment as a *spekion*.[163] If that were true, then virtually every man of status shown in middle Byzantine art is wearing one, and some of the women also! The clearest evidence for the untenability of this theory is the presence of *klavoi* on imperial tunics manifestly meant to be *divêtêsia* (figs 24, 27). *Klavoi* were merely one of the most popular motifs for decorating an opulent garment, and more is required to distinguish a *spekion* from other tunics which might be so adorned. It is the complete combination of golden hem and *klavoi* applied onto purple silk in a tunic with *persikomanikia* which sets the *spekion* apart from other garments; for example, the *kamision*, which had 'Persian-sleeves' and golden hem and *klavoi* on a white ground (fig. 22). On some designated occasions *prôtospatharioi* would wear the *stikharion*, and on others, perhaps deemed to be less significant, the more mundane *kamision*.

FIG. 33. Prôtospatharios Iôannês wears triumphal regalia of a *spekion khrusoklavon paganon* and gilded *klivanion*, 1007. Note also his light turban. *Adrianople Gospels*, St Lazarus Monastery, Venice.

In addition to the usual *khlamudes* and *sagion*, *prôtospatharioi* had another secondary mantle called a *savanion*. This term is otherwise found in reference to items made of fine linen or cotton, such as towels and headscarves, suggesting it was a lighter garment than the primary mantles. Alas, there is no indication in the source of colour or decoration for this cape. The donor portraits of Vatican Urb. Gr. 1, a manuscript contemporaneous with the composition of the *Book of Ceremonies*, may shed some light on this. Two of the donors, Constantine, *prôtospatharios*, and his brother Leo, *patrikios*, *praipositos* and *sakellarios*, and evidently a eunuch, both wear identical fine red capes with scrolled golden edging and paired fastenings. The *Klêtôrologion* asserted that the regalia of these two eunuch ranks was almost identical, and we have seen that a higher rank (in this case, *patrikios*) may 'borrow' regalia items from a lower rank (*prôtospatharios*). So it seems very likely that these pictures show examples of the male regalia *savanion*.

Spatharokandidatos

The *Book of Ceremonies* makes it clear that nothing has changed with the regalia of this rank since the composition of the *Klêtôrologion*. Its one truly distinctive piece of regalia remains a torque (*maniakion*) which was decorated with a white semi-precious stone.[164] In some ceremonies he was to carry a single-bladed axe (*distralion monopelukon*) and shield (*skoutarion*).[165]

Kandidatos

The description of the regalia torque with which a *kandidatos* was invested, gold with three ornaments and falling onto the chest, is a form strongly reminiscent of the collars depicted on the seventh-century icon of Saints George and Theodore from the Monastery of Saint Catherine at Mount Sinai (fig. 5), or that of an eleventh-century Sinai icon of Saint Dêmêtrios in the company of two other saints.[166]

When holding a military rank, a prospective *kandidatos* approached his elevation wearing a red *pektorarion*, along with the standard white *khlamus*.[167] This term is evidently derived from the Latin *pectus*, the chest, but neither the Greek, nor a direct Latin precursor, occurs in any of the available lexica. Its derivation and its appearance in a specifically military context immediately suggest the band of cloth that is often seen tied around the chest of soldiers in armour, and unarmoured men performing what would commonly be official military functions right up to the end of the empire (Plate 8, right and Plate 13, right).[168] In pictures executed in polychrome media, the *pektorarion* is most often white, but other colours do occur, predominantly red and blue in common with the great majority of textiles in Byzantine art, and with the two most common dyestuffs of the region, kirmis and indigo. That a *kandidatos* should wear a red *pektorarion* is readily explicable. His *kamision* was the standard court white and over that he was to wear the ubiquitous white *khlamus*. A white *pektorarion* in keeping with the majority of the pictorial sources would be indistinct between those garments, while one in the properly martial red created a striking contrast. For further discussion of this item see below, under military dress.

Regalia According to Eunuch Rank or Function

Koubikoularios

Koubikoularios (attendant of the imperial apartments) was one of the various ranks which wore the ceremonial hood called a *maforion*. Perhaps reflecting the eunuch's non-male status, his *maforion* was plain white, like that of female ranks.

Members of this rank also had a *khlamus* in an unusual colour. As a token of their proximity to the rulers, they wore a cloak of Tyrian purple, although evidently without the sort of gold ornamentation which would make it truly imperial. As noted above, a eunuch *koubikoularios* also had a *paragaudion*, a gold cape, as an alternative to that *khlamus*.

Miscellaneous Functionaries

Eparkhos

The *eparkhos* or *Huparkhos tês Poleôs* (Latin: *Praefectus Urbis*) was the Governor of Constantinople. He was responsible for all facets of urban administration, including the regulation of trade and law enforcement. In the latter capacity, at least, he enacted power which could be seen to flow down from the throne, and, indeed, beyond. Perhaps on account of that, his suite of regalia is extensive, and includes quasi-imperial elements.

Kamision

The *eparkhos* wore a particular form of *kamision*.[169] What set this tunic apart from the basic *kamision* is not stated in the *Book of Ceremonies*, but pictorial and literary sources of the first half of the next century agree that it was white with cuffs and hem of unrelieved black – a most unusual style (fig. 34). Its colour scheme is mentioned in a verse written by Christopher of Mitylênê in the first half of the eleventh century celebrating the appointment of a friend to the post:

This tunic at once white and black
Naturally underwrites the twofold character of the decrees,
Of those decrees, for which the coils of Justice
You rightly hew. The axe of judges,
Casts a black stain upon those who fall short,
While bearing white to those triumphing in law.[170]

Given the stability of the regalia, discussed further below, this was undoubtedly already the case in the tenth century.

Fenôlion

Another item formally vested upon the *eparkhos* at his elevation was the *fenôlion* or *felônion*, noted above as being a type of hood. Once again, the most explicit evidence for this item occurs in the first half of the eleventh century, but it seems apparent for many ranks that little had changed then from the time of the composition of the *Book of Ceremonies*. Hence, we can be confident that the eparkhal *fenôlion* was a hood bearing circular decoration on the crown, most often a large disc surrounded by smaller discs all in black on a white, or less often red, field. The *Book of Ceremonies* also mentions that the judicial staff (*taxaiôtai*) also wore *felônia*.[171] This explains the

FIG. 34. Pontius Pilate garbed in the regalia of the *eparkhos* of Constantinople, largely corroborating the *Book of Ceremonies.* Eleventh century. Dionysiou Monastery, Athos, codex 587, f. 113r.

appearance of a considerable number of pictures of mature men in civilian dress, and even a woman,[172] wearing white headdresses with circular ornamentation in eleventh- and twelfth-century manuscripts, and the practice in the same period of showing the centurion at the Crucifixion clad in just such headgear (fig. 56; Plates 13 and 14).

Lôros

The eparkhal regalia is completed by a *lôros*. While no specific further information is forthcoming from the tenth century, illustrations from the following century indicate that this differs from the imperial *lôros* and those worn by other high courtiers only in being somewhat less ornate, perhaps even just a strip of modestly figured cloth.

Footwear

As a high court functionary, the governor routinely wore *kampagia*. This is something that would change in the following century.

Droungarios of the watch

In processions and on palace open days, the *droungarios tês viglas* (chief of the city watch) is instructed to wear a sword whilst carrying a whip (*manklavion*) in his right hand, and an axe called *tzikourion* sloped on his left shoulder.[173] This array of armament is symbolic of his position as the chief of the city watch, which involved the day-to-day policing of Constantinople.

There are two terms for whips in use in this era, and it seems likely that one must be a single-strap whip and the other a scourge, or 'cat-o'-nine-tails', both of which are illustrated in middle Byzantine art. Achmet uses the term *kharzanion* for another type which he suggests is an inferior implement of punishment to the *maglavion*.[174] The term *kharzanion* also occurs in the *Taktika* of Leo the Wise[175] as a practice weapon in mock battles, and elsewhere in the *Book of Ceremonies* as a head ornament of ladies-in-waiting shown in later sources as a three-stranded pendant. On balance, it seems that the *maglavion* is a single-stranded whip, rather than a scourge.

Tzikourion is an adaptation from the Latin *securis*, which is noted as being, at least at times, synonymous with *bipennis*, a double-bladed axe.[176] Double-bladed axes are illustrated sporadically in art close to the time of these sources, and always in military use.[177] Leo's *Taktika* lists various forms of *tzikouria,* some having two identical blades, also shown in pictorial sources, and some with disparate blades (Plate 10, left).[178] The carriage of a *tzikourion* calls to mind the image of the 'axe of judges' referred to by Christopher of Mitylênê in his poem about the position of *eparkhos* quoted above.[179]

The *Book of Ceremonies* mentions no clothing in relation to the *droungarios* of the watch, yet it is virtually certain that he, too, probably along with the watch officers who served under him, wore a *felônion* like the judicial staff (*taxaiôtai*) (fig. 56). The evidence for this will be discussed in more detail in the following chapter.

Dêmarkhos

The cultural and sporting life of Constantinople's population was organised through the *dêmoi*, the factions of old. By the tenth century the four old factions had reduced to two, the Greens and Blues, each of which had absorbed one of the others. Each *dêmos* had a head who represented it in ceremonies, and who went through a formal elevation ceremony.[180] The incumbent was a man of court rank and appointed by the emperor, but popular agitation could influence the choice.[181] The primary regalia of the *dêmarkhos* consisted of a particular *kamision* and a *khlamus*.[182] The particular characteristics of the *kamision* is unspecified, however the use of the term *kamision* indicates that it was a 'Persian-sleeved' tunic, and it almost certain that they were in the colours of their *dêmos*, that is, blue or green. This is recorded explicitly in the case of the *khlamus* of each *dêmarkhos*.[183] On one occasion the book says that the *khlamudes* of the *dêmarkhoi*, are in the deme colour 'and Tyrian (purple), as they are imperial cloaks'.[184] It seems a reasonable assumption that this means they had a purple edging around the deme tincture. At the ceremony that marked the end of a session of chariot racing, the *dêmarkhos* of the deme that had taken overall honours was to wear a *sagion* in place of his *khlamus*, and that was appropriately to be entirely of Tyrian purple.

During the lay festivities for the elevation of a *patrikios*, the *dêmarkhoi* were to wear an *avdion* in place of their *sagion* (Plate 16).[185] *Avdia* are also one option for gifts to *prôtospatharioi* and *spatharokandidatoi* at Brumalia, and are among the recommended stock of gifts to be taken on imperial military expeditions.[186] The repeated appearance of *avdion* in our sources is somewhat surprising. Previous scholars have accepted it as the Arabic *aba* or *abeyah*,[187] and, while it is by no means rare that items come into mainstream Byzantine use from abroad, it is unusual from that quarter. Its appearance in imperial ceremonies would be still more unexpected if *abeyah* were always thick garments of wool as those authors suggest. In fact there are numerous survivals of substantially complete *abeyahs* from close to our period which are extremely fine cloths of various fibres with bands of intricate decoration in silk. The best known is the so-called 'Veil of Saint Anne' in the Cathedral of Apt in southern France, said to have been brought back by members of the First Crusade, which has silk bands on a base of linen.[188] The Metropolitan Museum in New York also has several less-complete pieces of similar quality which were almost certainly *abeyahs*.[189]

Other men

Charioteers

Chariot racing was the celebrity sport of the Roman Republic and Empire, and remained so in the tenth century. It, too, had a great accretion of custom and ritual of its own, which is described in a lengthy chapter in the *Book of Ceremonies*. A victorious charioteer was awarded a distinctive garment, called the *aurigarion* along with a silvered helmet and a belt.[190] Precisely what set the *aurigarion* apart remains unknown, although it might be conjectured that, as the garment was to be presented by the emperor and was regarded as being 'of the people' or 'of the state', it may well have been a 'Persian-sleeved' garment (*kamision*) and, like the regalia of the *dêmarkhoi*, in the colour of the *dêmos* whose driver had gained the victory (Plate 8, right). The distinctive character of the belt is also mysterious. A likely possibility is that it was set apart by particular metal fittings.

'Saracen friends'

On special occasions the designated 'Saracen friends', who were either aristocratic refugees or noble hostages from Muslim nations, were to be presented to the emperor, they wore the type of tunic called *spekion* – 'not their own,' the book tells us, 'but more beautiful and appropriate' – and, along with those, torques (*maniakia*) decorated with gems and large pearls.[191] These are presumably from amongst the stock held in the Chapel of Saint Theodôros attached to the throne room, the Khrusotriklinos, which includes collars of forms worn by *prôtospatharioi* and *spatharokandidatoi*, as well as some gilded silver *maniakia* of unspecified use.[192]

Military Clothing and Equipment

The basic practicalities of military clothing had been established at the end of Late Antiquity and fundamentally nothing would change up to the end of the empire. The copious military literature of the tenth century does no more than repeat, often verbatim, the recommendations of the *Stratêgikon* that main garments (tunics and coats) should be no longer than to the knee for infantry, and long enough to cover the knees when mounted for cavalry, and that footwear should be modest, well made and with just a few hobnails (fig. 35).

One very striking omission from the military manuals is any mention of rank insignia. It may just have been that a soldier would quickly learn to recognise his immediate superior officers, and that would be all he would need in most situations. Yet the appearance of sashes tied around the chests of the great majority of military saints, and the red chest-sash (*pektorarion*) worn by a military *kandidatos* at his promotion suggests the persistence of a customary practice known from early Roman times.[193] These sashes come in a variety of colours in the pictures, predominantly white, red and blue in descending order of frequency, but also green and purple on occasion. It would be tempting to speculate that rank might be thereby colour coded, but the evidence offers no clear support for that idea. In more idealising art the *pektorarion* is shown tied horizontally around the upper chest. The experience of living-history practitioners (including the author) is that it soon succumbs to gravity that way, and a few pictures do show *pektoraria* descending towards the waist. Some pictures show more realistic functionality, with the sash being tied diagonally over one shoulder (the

TOP: FIG. 35. These light cavalry warriors wear a very light turban over a padded, pointed cap and a *peristêthidion* (arming coat) with elbow-length sleeves and skirts almost to the knee over a tunic with a low collar. Victoria and Albert Museum, London.

ABOVE: FIG. 36. Soldiers in padded arming garments with heavy longitudinal quilting. Details of eleventh-century frescos in Tokali Kilese Church, Kappadokhia.

left, where it will not interfere with the baldric of the sword), or else, with still greater stability, over the right shoulder with a free end being drawn forward around the the right side and tied again at the centre of the chest in a diagonal T shape.[194]

A few developments *are* discernible in the literature, although they are as much matters of terminology as of substance. The substantive change was the increasing availability of cotton – (βάμβαξ) *vamvax* and later (*βαμβάκιον*) *vamvakion* – for use as padding; this resulted in an even more extensive use of padded garments as the primary protection for several troop types.[195] With this, the terminology shifted, and initially became more specific. The term *zava*, which at the end of Late Antiquity meant a complete protective garment made either of padding or of mail, was relegated to referring to a mail facing or a supplementary armour piece,[196] while *kavadion* came to denote a stand-alone arming garment. *Epilôrikion* was at first a surcoat worn over more solid armour, as its name suggests. The initial use in the *Sullogê Taktikôn* of *epanoklivanon*, which ought to mean the same thing and certainly did so later, was as a stand-alone protective garment for cavalry. Art shows less-extensive padded arming garments than the description in the manuals suggest, sometimes shorter but always with short sleeves, both under solid armour and as sole protection (fig. 36). *Peristêthidion* is used for these in the literature. The observation that *vamvakion*, the word for cotton as a raw material, entered medieval Latin and French in garbled form as *wambasium* and *gambison* respectively has been interpreted as indicating that it may have been used in the vernacular for a garment.[197] Yet the Arabic word for cotton, *al-qutun*, did the same thing, becoming *akheton*, likewise without corroborating evidence of it being used by Arab speakers for a garment. The reassignment of titles as they pass from one language to another is a far-from-rare phenomenon, so in the absence of specific evidence there is no basis for believing that *vamvakion* or *al-qutun* were used for garments in their original languages.

The descriptions of the sleeve arrangements given for the *kavadion* and *epilôrikion* have important ramifications for later periods. *Sullogê Taktikôn* explicitly states that they are to be the full length of the arm, and advises that opening for the arms be made at the elbows (fig. 37, left) with the loose lower portion being folded up and fastened back to the shoulder, while Nikêforos Fôkas recommends that the openings be in the armpits (fig. 37, right), again with the empty sleeve being fastened back to the shoulder, once more implying that they must be longer than to the elbow.[198] This was intended to allow the soldiers freedom of arm movement. The latter form can be seen to go back to garments of Late Antiquity, and both these forms were to migrate back into civilian dress over the next two centuries, and, as we shall see later, even make it to the status of high regalia.

FIG. 37. Two illustrations of Richard I of England travelling back from the Levant, clad in a *gounion* represented with both sleeve variants copied from Roman military practice. *Liber ad Honorem Augusti* of Peter of Eboli, *c*.1225.

The other substantive development of the later tenth century was the attribution of more substantial footwear to the infantry by Nikêforos Fôkas. We have seen that the earlier evidence associated calf-length boots with horsemen and low shoes with foot soldiers. Fôkas recommended thigh-high boots which could be folded down for ease of marching as protection for an infantryman's legs.[199] Yet, once again, the erratic treatment of realistic middle Byzantine pictures of foot soldiers mean we only see such high boots depicted on riders, or on military saints, who may be shown on foot, but whose inherently superior status will always presume them to be of the elite service, the cavalry.

One item relatively new to men's dress at the commencement of the tenth century was the turban (*fakeolion*). The suggestions that it came from the Medes via the Persians[200] or was 'a concession to Turkish fashion'[201] are both incorrect, for amongst both those peoples men traditionally in antiquity and the earlier Middle Ages wore hats, while turbans were women's wear. Both the Persians and later the Turks only adopted the turban to a limited degree under the influence of Islam, in which that headgear has great status deriving from association with the Prophet.[202] Turbans are most likely to to have been introduced to Rômania and Armenia by Christian Arabs fleeing Islamic expansion. When wrapped over a thick cap, a turban became a reasonably effective substitute for a helmet (figs 35, 38).[203] The caps may have been felt, but were evidently more normally quilted, as 'cap stitchers' were among the personnel a besieged commander was urged to take care to retain by a tenth-century manual on siege defence.[204]

FIG. 38. A padded turban cap from Syria very much like some shown in Byzantine sources. Cleveland Museum of Art, Ohio.

Dress used in military ceremonies

Gounion

The group of related terms *gauna*, *gouna* and *gounion* had always had a more general use for ample, heavy-weather over-garments beyond the military. Dispersed evidence suggests that as such they often also had the sort of sleeve arrangements described for military garments in the tenth century (split at the armpit or elbow) and could be hooded (fig. 37). Previous commentators have interpreted the word as denoting fur or fur-lined garments,[205] which may be true for those worn primarily for warmth, but in the military context it makes more sense to regard them as quilted protective garments in the manner described in tenth-century military manuals.[206] This garment appears once in the *Book of Ceremonies*, worn by 'Gothic' (a vague term for anyone from northern Europe) mercenaries carrying shields and staves (Plate 10, right).[207] They are to wear the *gounia* 'inside out'. That would certainly be striking if they were fur-lined, but also makes very sound sense if they were normal padded military garments as well, for turning them inside out would bring a cleaner and less worn face to the outside, thus making for a better ceremonial show. This practice was employed in more-recent European military practice from the fifteenth to the nineteenth centuries.

Esôforion

On one occasion, the Macedonian Hetaireia was ordered to turn out for a parade just in their shirts (*esôforia*).[208] This is unusual, but may be explained by being a way for them to blend into the dominant white mode of the basic forms of court regalia (Plate 10, centre; fig. 25).

Military equipment used in ceremonies

In their roles as commander-in-chief and deputy, so to speak, it was not unusual for the emperor and the *kaisar* to wear or carry items with military connotations even in ceremonies which were not primarily of a military nature. As noted above, the foremost such item was the triumphal crown, or *toufa*. In addition to outfits which are discussed in detail there is a 'royal panoply' (*vasilika armata*) which is used on occasion.[209] The only components of this that are explicitly mentioned are a spear and a shield, harking back the classical hoplite paradigm. The spear may be one of the silver-gilt pair which are stored amongst the equipment of the Chapel of Saint Theodore in the Khrusotriklinos,[210] while a suitable candidate for the royal shield was held in the same imperial store, gilded and decorated with enamels, pearls and precious stones.[211] We can be

FIG. 39. The so-called 'Crown of Constantine Monomakhos' was not headgear, but a ceremonial arm-ring presented to a general serving that emperor when the officer celebrated a formal triumph.

FIG. 40. Saint Orestês in triumphal military dress. The band on his right arm may be intended to be the triumphal *stephanos* presented to a victorious commander as he entered the City. Church of Nea Moni, Khios. *c.*1049

confident that this shield was round, for round shields were those carried by the elite arm, the cavalry (infantry carried tear-drop shaped or oblong shields), and such shields are much more often illustrated than infantry types.[212]

Triumphal parades naturally had their own variants on the regalia. There was another ornament which the *Book of Ceremonies* calls a 'crown' (*stephanos*) employed on the occasion of military triumphs. It was not destined for the head, rather it was presented by the *Eparkhos tês Poleôs* as the triumphal leader entered the City at the Golden Gate. He then wore it on his right arm for the remainder of the parade.[213] One example of such an object survives in the so-called 'Crown of Constantine Monomakhos', made for a eunuch *prôtospatharios* who had been delegated to suppress a rebellion (fig. 39).[214] The armband shown on the early eleventh-century mosaic of Saint Orestês in the Church of Nea Moni which shows the saint in what is probably meant to be triumphal regalia (gilded *klivanion* over a dark-blue or purple *khitôn paganon* with *kaligia* and *kampotouva*) may well be intended to be such a *stefanos* (fig. 40). Without any other survivals or pictorial sources for the item, it is impossible to know if either example is in any way typical. One would imagine, however, that a triumphal armband made for an emperor or *kaisar* would be more ornate than these, and, we may conclude with more confidence, that any central images would be Christ accompanied by angels or saints.

An addendum to the *Book of Ceremonies* records the details of two imperial triumphs as exemplars (Plate 12). They vary significantly in the regalia worn by both rulers, although in both cases it is the *kaisar* who is more heavily laden, perhaps simply because he was the younger man. In the both cases, the emperor wore the *toufa*, an *epilôrikion* called *rodovotrun* and a belt-hung sword. The *kaisar* on both occasions wore a belt-hung sword like the emperor, a corselet of gilded lamellar armour (*klivanion*) and gilded greaves, and carried a gilded spear. His headgear differs in the two accounts. In the first he wore a turban, while in the second he wore a helm with a gilded brow band (Plate 12, left).

In these parades the rulers were accompanied by an honour guard of officers, notably *prôtospatharioi*, clad in short versions of their usual *spekion*, each with a gilded *klivanion* (Plate 12, left; figs 33, 41).

Rodovotrun

The most visible piece of the emperor's triumphal regalia was the *epilôrikion* called the 'rose-cluster' (*rodovotrun*).[215] The description of this garment is quite detailed – 'wholly gold-woven in a trellis pattern with pearls, and in the borders adorned with perfect pearls'. The detail given in the passage precludes the possibility suggested by this name that the garment was adorned with representations of the flower, hence 'rose' should be taken to indicate the colour of the *epilôrikion*. Modern associations take 'rose' as a pale shade, yet pictures of flowers from around this period consistently show the same predilection for strong colours, as can be seen in surviving textiles, as well as in other aspects of painting.[216]

FIG. 41. The author's reproduction of the prôtospathariate triumphal parade ensemble based primarily on the donor portrait of the *Adrianople Gospels*, comprising a *spekion paganon*, gilded *klivanion*, military *sagion* and the gilded *spathion* that was part of the *prôtospatharios*' everyday regalia. All manufactured by the author.

Therefore the tincture of the *rodovotrun* should be seen as a rich red, a properly martial hue. The phrase 'gold-woven in a trellis pattern' can easily be seen to relate to what would be the main quilting pattern on a functional military *epilôrikion*. One of the quilting patterns most commonly illustrated on military garments has diamond hatching with a figure within each partition, such as a cross, a circle or a circle with rays.[217] The 'cluster' of the title must consequently refer to the arrangement of pearls. A cluster of pearls would make a spectacular substitute for the stitched figure in the centre of each compartment. It seems likely that the Nikêforian form of the *epilôrikion* was the one used for the *rodovotrun*, as its sleeves would hang more elegantly behind the emperor's shoulders, and may even have been lengthened in the manner of a *skaramangion* to heighten that effect (fig. 42).

FIG. 42. An ornate *epilôrikion* with very long sleeves hanging loose behind shown on a pottery fragment. The striations on the upper arms represent splinted armoured sleeves. Probably somewhat earlier than the twelfth–fourteenth-century date attributed by the Victoria and Albert Museum.

Klivanion

While the tenth century is not so forthcoming, the eleventh and twelfth centuries provide such a sufficient array of depictions of *klivania* that details of methods of construction can be traced.[218] Two pictures of the first decade of the eleventh century are likely to embody survivals of the prior century. The donor portrait of Iôannes, a *prôtospatharios* at the court of Basil II, shows him dressed for a triumph (figs 33, 41). Although gilded, the construction of his *klivanion* is clearly of a standard battlefield form, corroborated by other pictures. Complementing this is the triumphal portrait of Emperor Basil II from his Psalter (now in Saint Mark's Library, Venice) showing an imperial-dress *klivanion*. It is manifestly a purpose-made parade armour since this method of construction would produce a virtually rigid structure which would be somewhat encumbering in combat; it is unique and radically different from any other depiction of middle Byzantine lamellar.

Turban

Another unusual feature of the triumphal dress of the *kaisar* in one account is the presence of a white turban (*fakeolion*) embroidered with gold. This turban is described as 'said to be like a *propolôma*'. Haldon proposed that this interpolation was drawing an analogy with the headdress worn by women, and indeed it is so, yet there is more implied.[219] The *propolôma* was a sizeable hat (see the following discussion of women's dress), and so comparing this *fakeolion* to a *propolôma* at least suggests that it was a more substantial item than, for example, the light turban worn by Prôtospatharios Iôannês from the *Adrianople Gospels*. This comparison probably indicates that, like turbans manufactured in various parts of the Islamic world at this time, and which later became typical of the Ottoman Turks, it was made up in a fixed shape and put on like a hat, rather than wrapped on at each wearing.[220]

Sagion

In everyday military use all forms of mantle had been comprehensively superseded in Late Antiquity by the much more practical coat. Although absent from the literary material in this context, it is clear from numerous artworks that the *sagion* had retained a place in military ceremonial, just as it had at court. While the court *sagion* had been conflated with the semicircular, and often more ornate, Persian *manduas* (fig. 10), the military parade *sagion* had evidently preserved the primordial form of the *sagum* from which it was derived, as a plain rectangle, but perhaps now made of silk, rather than wool. The finest depiction of a *sagion* in military parade use is the often-reproduced portrait of Emperor Basil II in his Psalter in St Mark's Library, while the cape of Prôtospatharios Iôannês is less conspicuous, yet showing the interesting feature of distinct knobs at the corners (fig. 33).

Swords

The rulers had three types of swords, a standard *spathion*, a *spathion* hung from a belt (*spathion zôstikion*) and a sabre or *paramêrion*. It seems they had these in both ceremonial and functional varieties. The imperial ceremonial swords were, it need hardly be said, gilded and bedecked with precious stones. The term *spathion* is derived from the Latin *spatha*, adopted with the long, straight, slashing swords which came into Roman use through the fourth century.[221] The Roman army adapted this weapon to its established habits, first fitting the long, narrow straight blade with a handle in the same pattern as their native *gladius* and suspending it from a baldric over the shoulder connected to the opposite sides of the ring encircling the scabbard near the mouth so that it hung close to vertical. This style survived through to this era, although more substantial hilts had also come into use. The belt-hung *spathion* began as a Persian style, well represented by surviving examples and illustrated on Sassanian silverware.[222] It was also straight and double-edged, but the scabbard had two suspension points on the same edge, one near the mouth and one further down from which straps ran to the belt, thereby causing it to hang near to horizontal.[223] The term *paramêrion* literally means 'beside the thigh'. Apparently the *paramêrion* could be suspended by either method used on the *spathion*, a baldric or a belt, with the scabbard suspension mounts on the inside curve, but in either case it hung the same way, at a shallow slant next to the wearer's leg, much like the *spathion zôstikion*. The *paramêrion* is rarely mentioned in connection with any ceremonies, while a *spathion* was added to the emperor's ensemble at some civilian events.[224]

Various officers were also at times required to wear or carry a sword (*spathion*). Indeed, as was noted in the previous chapter, several ranks are named for this very characteristic: *spatharios*, *spatharokandidatos*, *spatharokoubikoularios* and *prôtospatharios* (figs 14, 22).[225] As is to be expected, they were borne by lower ranks of military function on the sparse instances that such men were represented.[226] The swords of lesser men would have been whatever was generally available for combat use, but for the ranks of *spatharios* upwards the ceremonial arms had gilded fittings (fig. 41).

Verbs employed in relation to swords in the *Book of Ceremonies* on occasion are *vallô*,[227] *perivallô*[228] and *hupalassô*,[229] all with the simple meaning 'put on' in the same sense as a garment. Much more often used is *ferô*, which in common parlance can equally mean 'wear' or 'carry'. In this work it is usually apparent that 'wear' is the standard meaning, for it is frequently used for the sword and a garment conjointly,[230] and sword-bearers are very often also carrying an axe (*distralion* or *tzikourion*) or a mace (*spathovaklion*) in their right hand, and sometimes a shield (*skoutarion*) in their left hand. The terms used in respect of these other items is consistent with this distinction – *katekhô*, 'hold fast',[231] and *krateô*, 'lay hold of',[232] and most frequently *vastazô*, 'hold up' or 'carry in the hands'.[233]

When a man was required to carry a sword, rather than wear it, pictorial sources show us that the proper ceremonial method throughout the period covered by this volume was that it was scabbarded and held sloped on the shoulder with the hilt beside or above the head.[234]

Mace

Another weapon carried in ceremonies by sword-wearers is the *spathovaklion*. This term is strikingly absent from the extensive contemporary military literature, but the Grottaferrata *Digenês*

Akritas employs a very similar expression, *spathoravdion* which is evidently another term for this weapon.[235] The significance of these compounds of 'sword' and 'staff" is open to divergent interpretation. The possibility of it being a collative compound, 'a sword and a mace', is immediately dispelled by the fact that these men are already said to be wearing swords, and also the observation that they are often carrying a shield, which would make carrying two weapons virtually impossible. Another possibility is a combination of a sword-like blade attached to a staff for a handle as suggested by Reiske.[236] Weapons of that sort were in medieval European use some centuries later,[237] but the only comparable item attested in Roman use at this time is the *lonkhodrepanon*, which was part of the equipment of a dromond.[238] That combination of the words for spear (*lonkhê*) and scythe or pruning hook (*drepanon*) immediately suggests an implement like the so-called 'English bill' of the later Middle Ages, and just such are depicted in late Byzantine art. That tool would be very useful in the naval context for cutting rigging, but neither resembles a sword, nor seems a likely item for high-status, land-based courtiers to be carrying in a parade. Grotowski has suggested that the staves held by various warrior saints in some eleventh-century pictures are *spathovaklia*, but offers no argument why these implements, which do not look at all like weapons, should be so identified, rather than being examples of the ceremonial batons which might accompany the court dress in which those saints are clad.[239]

A term which does occur in military manuals of the tenth century provides a plausible parallel. It is *sideroravdion* or 'iron staff'. Al-Tartusi confirmed in the twelfth century that maces made entirely of iron were used by the Byzantines.[240] Taking a cue from this, it appears that *spathovaklion* is a descriptive compound, a 'sword-like staff', hence a variety of mace which, unlike the common form of a metal head on a wooden shaft, was made all of iron and had a handle with features similar to a sword hilt: that is, some sort of guard and pommel. Later medieval maces used in Europe developed just such an all-iron construction and hilt features.[241] The *spathovaklia* of the eunuch *prôtospatharioi* are gilded and with precious stones,[242] which is again a practice well known with all-iron maces with hilts in later medieval Eastern Europe.[243]

Axes

When the principal sword-bearing ranks have occasion to wear their swords, they often also carry another weapon. Again, as in the Abbasid court, axes feature prominently.[244] The *distralion* is one such weapon. This antique term preserved its meaning as a light, single-handed axe from the time it was adopted into Greek from the Latin *dextralis*.[245] Once, a *distralion* bore the tautological qualification, *monopelukon*,[246] while later the word stood alone as the term for a single-bladed axe, distinct from a *tzikourion*.[247] In addition to the *droungarios* of the watch (see above), soldiers the Macedonian Hetaireia carry a *tzikourion* when parading garbed in *esôforia*.[248] Leo is quite specific about the forms of a *tzikourion* – two differing blades, one of them like a sword (Plate 10, left).[249]

Spear

A spear (*doru*) is an element of the 'imperial panoply' which was carried by imperial *spatharioi*.[250] As noted above, these are almost certainly the silver-gilt pair in the regalia store attached to the Chapel of Saint Theodôros. The spear held by Basil II in the portrait in his Psalter is evidently a more prosaic item than those, for it is unadorned wood and steel without a hint of gold. The accompanying poem refers to it by the ancient term very frequently used for this weapon in *koinê* literary sources, *romfaia*.[251] Unsurprisingly, more mundane spears (*kontaria*) are carried by cavalrymen escorting a triumphal commander (fig. 40).[252]

Shields

Men bearing arms would also commonly carry a shield, or *skoutarion*, a diminutive adaptation of the Latin *scutum*. Although illustrated often in antiquarian art of the ninth to eleventh centuries, the oval *scutum* used by later Roman armies was quite outmoded by this period.[253] It had been replaced in part by the more adaptable and easily-used round shield, gripped in the centre, that was used by all manner of warrior, or, for infantry, by the *thureos*, a revival of the old rectangular *scutum*,[254] or an innovation of the ninth century, the tear-drop-shaped shield, soon to gain popularity in continental Europe (Plate 10, right).[255] The *skoutarion* of the *Book of Ceremonies* was undoubtedly the round sort, possibly of the distinctively Byzantine conical section often shown in tenth- and eleventh-century art (fig. 56).[256]

When substantial numbers of the capital's garrison turned out on parade, the majority of the *skoutaria* employed in imperial ceremonial were fairly mundane items. Perhaps newly made in order to present the best appearance, but not much different from those carried into battle (Plate 10, right and Plate 11). Members of the Macedonian Hetaireia, however, were at times to bear shields which must have been purpose-made for ceremonials. They included entirely gilded shields (Plate 10, left) and bronze *skoutaria* with gilding, along with less-exotic polished iron shields.[257] Another matter again were the two *skoutaria* kept in the imperial regalia store. Both were gilded, one with enamels and pearl work, the other adding precious stones to those embellishments.[258] There is no indication when these shields were to be used, but we may reasonably conjecture that they were carried by the *kaisar* and emperor respectively during military parades, and perhaps held by *prôtospatharioi* flanking the throne in the manner shown in the depiction of the Judgement of Solomon in the ninth-century Paris manuscript of the *Homilies of Gregory of Nazianzos*.[259]

When Constantine Porfurogennêtos received the ambassadors from Lesser Armenia, he was accompanied by a large and diverse contingent of troops, including marines (*ploimoi*), *toulmatzoi* and Rus who paraded wearing swords and carrying *dorkas*.[260] This word is otherwise unknown in surviving literature. David Nicolle suggests that it may be a light shield made of leather, presumably from the earlier use of *dorkas* for various sorts of deer.[261] This suggestion is pragmatically viable here, one reason being the common pairing of weapon and shield, a connection reinforced by several direct parallels. The main body of the *toulmatzoi* carried *dorkas* and banners (*flammoula*) and wore swords and bow cases. The supernumerary *toulmatzoi* had *skoutaria*, banners and swords (Plate 11), likewise 'the rest of the marines' and the baptised Rus. It does indeed appear that *dorkas* and *skoutaria* were equivalent pieces of equipment. The proposition is viable from another point of view also. A smaller, lighter shield would have been much more suitable for shipboard use for many reasons – in terms of stowage, as lesser encumbrance should the user fall overboard, and due to the fact that their primary use would have been for deflecting missiles rather than prolonged hand-to-hand combat.

WOMEN

The *Book of Ceremonies* somewhat redresses the lacuna in the *Klêtôrologion* in dealing with the women of the court more widely and in more detail. Even so, it is evidently far from complete, for it rarely discusses when women, even the *augousta* and *kaisarissa*, participated in ceremonies. That the empress, at least, must have done so often is beyond doubt. The importance of the part played in the ritual life of the court by the *augousta* was such that it was deemed necessary for Leo VI to crown his daughter, Anna, as a stand-in after his second wife Zôê died around the turn of 899–900.[262] The emperor asserted that in the absence of an empress it was not possible to celebrate the festivities of the court in accordance with proper established custom.[263] Even the censorious Patriarch Nikholas was willing to concede that this necessity excused an otherwise debatable third marriage by Emperor Leo VI when Anna was married away to a Frankish king.[264] Despite this, precise details of the participation of the *auguosta*, let alone her dress when she was present, remain curiously sketchy. The suggestion that amongst the roles of the *auguosta* was the management of the women's quarter of the palace, supervising the education of the children and receiving wives and children of visiting dignitaries is hardly questionable, yet with her own suite of staff at her command, more is very likely.[265] Arabic sources suggest a very active role for the empress. Al-Marvazî states that the *augousta* was normally present at throne-room receptions and other royal councils, and even accompanied the emperor on military expeditions, although there is some doubt about how direct his sources of information were.[266] Theofanês records that Maria, wife of Leo III, attended the baptism of their son, Constantine, in Hagia Sofia separately from her husband, processing there and back in public and distributing alms as she returned to the palace. It is evident from the treatment of this incident that the author regards it as unusual, but whether it was because she went alone or because she did it so publicly is not apparent.[267] Undoubtedly more normal was the arrival of Irênê, the fiancée of Kaisar Leo (later Leo IV), from Greece. She was met by *arkhontes* accompanied by their wives, who escorted her from the port to the palace.[268]

The specifications for rituals in the *Book of Ceremonies* rarely yield conclusive evidence of whether the *augousta* was even present at any given occasion, let alone what she should have been wearing if she were present. While often the work states that the emperor (*vasileus*) acts alone in a given ritual,[269] the work otherwise normally refers to 'the rulers' (*hoi despotai*). This phrase may denote the emperor and *kaisar*, or emperor and *augousta*, or the whole group of the emperor, *kaisar* and their consorts, and so further internal evidence must be sought that may shed some light upon what this phrase signifies. It seems likely that an occurrence of 'the rulers together with the *kaisares*', all in the plural, must indicate that, in this case at least, both genders were to be present.[270] As it was an appointment usually in the hands of the empress, it would seem natural that 'the rulers' who attend the promotion of a *zôstê patrikia* should include the *augousta*,[271] and that she must surely be among 'the rulers' attending the baptism of a new imperial son, as may be implied by Theofanês in his account of the royal baptism given above. The lack of specificity would be appropriate if the normal practice was that the empress travelled there in the company of the emperor.[272] In contrast to this, the cropping of the son's hair is purely a matter for the emperor alone, and we may infer only the male members of the ranks specified were present.[273] We may contrast the promotion of a *zôstê patrikia*, where the composition of the imperial party is never mentioned in a long and complex ceremony, with the elevation of a *koubikoularea*.[274] In this latter case, the candidate is collected from the bed chamber of the *augousta* by a small party of male officers to be inducted and robed in a chapel off the Khrusotriklinos. From there, she passes out to be acknowledged by the emperor enthroned in the Khrusoriklinos and then to be received again by the empress in her bed chamber. The separation of the rulers in this case is both appropriate and symbolically important. Whereas *zôstê patrikiai* were high-ranking members of the public court and had to be publicly acknowledged as such, an incoming *koubikoularea* was about to become privy to intimate aspects of the empress' private life, thus it was only fitting that she should be welcomed into the augustal apartments by the *augousta* herself. One might conjecture that 'the rulers' only refers to the males when it is said that they wear, or change into, *skaramangia*, for the *skaramangion* is a purely masculine garment.[275] Yet even that inference would be risky, for it is clear from both pictorial and other literary material that the variations in middle Byzantine women's dress, as well as the regalia in our source, were notably less that those of men,[276] and so it may have been that women were present, but that their dress did not need to be dictated since there was little room for change from one phase of the ritual to another.

Beyond this, the position and participation of women of all the other ranks in court ceremony remains even more vexed. The prevailing wisdom is that in the Porfurogennêtan era the court was rigidly segregated into the male realm and 'the court of women' whose activities hardly ever coincided.[277] Certainly it is clear that the empress had her own full suite of staff, a *prôtovestiarissa* (wardrobe mistress), *primikêrissa* (catering manageress) and *koitônissai* (tent staff) are mentioned, who were all women.[278] Furthermore, there were some ceremonies confined to one sex or the other beyond those already discussed. The *Book of Ceremonies* does record that two separate banquets were held on Sunday 18 October 958 for visiting Russian royalty, and this has been taken as evidence of the segregation of the male and female realms of the court.[279] However, a more distinctive feature of this occasion is likely to have been the presence at the women's banquet of the children of both the Byzantine and Russian rulers and other nobles, an occurrence which was surely rather more unusual. In fact, the evidence for the proposition of largely complete separation has been overstated. In the first place, the expression employed in the *Book of Ceremonies* that has been translated as 'the court of women' (*to sekreton tôn gunaikôn*)[280] could be much better rendered as 'the privy chamber of women' for it manifestly refers to a location in the Great Palace, and is directly paralleled by 'the privy chamber of the *patrikioi*' (*to sekreton tôn patrikiôn*),[281] 'the privy chamber of the Senate' (*to sekreton tôn sunklêtikôn*)[282] and various other *sekreta* dedicated to other ranks, functions and individuals. The news that the 'the privy chamber of women' and other venues in the palace[283] sometimes hosted ceremonies restricted to women does not, in fact, give us any definite information about what happened on other occasions, even by implication.

One purpose of the *Book of Ceremonies* was certainly to record and to set norms of court life. That the work records these events as happening during the reign of Constantine Porfurogennêtos without any of the clear qualifications which might have been given to indicate that they were being done according to established paradigms suggests that they were actually innovations. In attempting to represent these events as norms, Constantine may have been acting to increase the gender segregation of court ritual for reasons which can only be speculated about. Without further evidence, it is just as likely to have been in order to enhance the prominence of the *augousta* as for any other reason. Aside from these notable occasions, the *Klêtôrologion* places the *zôstê patrikia* amongst members of those exalted ranks who were never summoned to the imperial table by name, implying that their presence was routine at formal banquets.

The non-imperial women of the court in fact partook of two parallel hierarchies. One was unique to the women and only partially intersected with the other. The uniquely female hierarchy appears to have consisted of just three divisions: *zôstai patrikiai*, *koubikoulareai* and the rest. The other was based upon the attributed rank of their husbands. In the women's ceremonies the ranks were called in order just as in the male court: 1. *zôstai*; 2. *magistrissai*; 3. *patrikiai*; 4. official *prôtospathareai*; 5. other *prôtospathareai*; 6. *spatharokadidatissai*; 7. *spathareai*, *stratêotissai* and *kandidatissai*, and finally all the other *arkhontissai*.[284] The absence of *koubikoulareai* from these lists is conspicuous, so we are left with the conclusion that this was a position which was unrelated to this hierarchy. This leaves two possibilities for the role and placement of the *koubikoulareai*. The less likely one is that they would have been scattered through the other divisions according to their marital rank. It seems more probable that, as their title, 'lady of the chamber', implies, they would already have been standing in attendance upon the empress in her apartments prior to the commencement of any ceremony.

The weight of the evidence in the *Book of Ceremonies* suggests that, in fact, female participation in the life of the court was the norm, with segregation of the genders only taking place when some symbolic or social significance made it desirable. This practice would be consistent with the indications from the wider society that middle Byzantine Rômania was characterised by a significantly lower degree of gender inequality than virtually any Western society before the modern era.

The Empress

In terms of what is mentioned in our source, the empress almost seems to have an even greater array of regalia that the emperor himself, yet there is almost no indication of when or how she used many of the pieces. For a whole group of items we are only told that on an occasion they were hung around the palace, and there is no way of knowing whether that was their only use, or whether they were worn at other times.

Headgear

The *Book of Ceremonies* does not tell us anything detailed about the form of the crown of the empress. Particularly lacking from all the sources is any definite indication that there was a division in rank and usage paralleling that of the men between a grand crown worn by the *augousta* when standing upon her highest dignity, and a lesser coronet worn routinely by the *kaisarissa* and by the empress when 'dressing down', yet art sources from the ninth into the twelfth century do suggest that it was so (Chart 7).

The indications given by art prior to and during this era suggest that there were long-established forms for the empress' headgear. Coinage and artworks consistently show that from the fifth century right through our period the distinguishing characteristic of empresses' crowns was a number of triangular points projecting above the band, and commonly arranged about a small, central cross.[285] Portraits of Saint Helena in the Paris *Homilies of Gregory of Nazianzos* manuscript (BNF Gr. 510) from 886 CE show one crown consistently, which incorporates the upward projections as well as the unique feature of a central downward projection. The exact rendering of this crown varies across the manuscript, some showing it as a parallel-sided cylinder (fig. 14), while most show the characteristic commonly seen on portraits of empresses through to the very end of the empire: it becomes wider towards the top (Chart 7.2). The tenth century has left us only a few major artworks showing empresses. Amongst them is an inlaid marble portrait of Saint Evdokia, found in the ruins of Lips Monastery dated to *c*.905, showing the crown as a straight cylinder with points (fig. 43).[286] Another example is an ivory of Constantine the Great and Helena ascribed to the end of the tenth century, in the Staatliche Museum, Berlin. It shows the man wearing a *kaisarikion*, in keeping with the other ivories of this century, along with the unique 'Porfurogennêtan' form of the *lôros*, all factors that confirm its dating. The coronet of the empress has the expected arrangement of a small cross at the centre flanked by a series of triangular peaks with knobs at the tops, while the narrow breadth, straight sides and details of the decoration of the body is identical to the *diadêma* of the emperor. These pieces of evidence suggest that the tenth-century convention of depicting the emperor in the *diadêma* rather than the *stemma* applied also to the empress.

FIG. 43. Inlaid marble icon of Saint Evdokia depicted in the regalia of an empress from the Lips Monastery, tenth century. Istanbul Archaeological Museum.

FIG. 44. Helen of Troy in the guise of a tenth- or eleventh-century noblewoman. St Mark's Library, Venice, ms Z454 (822) f. 1v.

Pendants

Amongst the items hung from the lamp array (*polukandêlon*) of the Khrusotriklinos are 'the two augustal *kataseista*'. The term means 'the things shaken down', and, as noted by Reiske,[287] is almost certain to refer to the *praipendoulia* of the empress' crowns, which the account of the coronation ceremony tells us are not fixed to the crown but are blessed separately and then attached after the crown is placed upon the empress' head.[288] The terminology for the *praipendoulia* is evidently quite flexible, for Achmet calls them *kremastaria*.[289] The *praipendoulia* on the tenth-century ivories previously discussed are a single chain of pearls terminating in three tear-drop pearls at the end, a pattern replicated in both ivories and coinage. This example does indicate that the items hung about the palace were things which were worn by the empress at other times.

Main garments

Art works of this era continue to show that the empress' primary regalia was virtually identical to that of the emperor. Thus, her main tunic, which the *Book of Ceremonies* calls the *stikharion vasilikon*,[290] was a *divêtêsion*, the one continuation of 'Persian-sleeves' in female use following their co-option into the male regalia in the sixth century.

Coats

Amongst those garments which are recorded as being displayed in the palace are an ordinary *diakoptês* and a bridal *diakoptês*. This is a name derived from *diakoptos*, and, as noted above under *kontomanikion*, *diakoptos* means 'fully divided' and indicates that the garment was a coat. Curiously, as with the marriage belts that the *augousta* also owns, the bridal *diakoptês* is conspicuously absent from the account of the imperial wedding festivities.[291] This may suggest that it had fallen out of use, as the marriage belts also may have done, but it is more likely to have been the survival of such a deeply entrenched custom that it did not bear mentioning. In the earlier Roman Empire, wealthier women wore a reddish mantle, called *flammeum*, to indicate their newly married status.[292] A similar practice existed in Islamic countries at the time: a newly married person wore a particular sort of red garment for a month after the wedding.[293]

Over-garments

Lôros

As significant in representing the position of the *augousta* as the crown was the *lôros*. Curiously, the *Book of Ceremonies* makes no mention of the empress' *lôros* at all, so we are again left to draw such conclusions as we may from art. The relatively few representations of empresses in this period often show them in the *khlamus*. Three pictures, the Lips Monastery marble of Saint Evdokia (fig. 43), the Kappadokhian frescos of Nikêforos Fôkas and Theofano,[294] and the ivory of the Theofanu who married the German king Otto II,[295] all show *lôroi* of the T pattern, which seems to be typical of the mid- to late tenth century (Chart 6.3). The Kappadokhian fresco is indistinct in its lower portion and so the full form of Theofano's *lôros* is not discernible. The other two are entirely different in their lower details. Theofanu is shown wearing a *lôros* of the simplest form, without any of the train visible at the front in any of the usual manners. This is probably due to its context of production, and not a reliable guide to practice in Byzantium. Certainly the so-called *lôros* of the Hoard of Mainz associated with the Ottonian court bears little resemblance to a familiar Byzantine precursor, suggesting that Theofanu did not take such an item with her, and so the artist of the ivory worked from memory or another picture.[296] The Lips Monastery marble is much more significant for it shows the saint wearing a *lôros* with an inverted tear-drop-shaped piece secured to the lower front. This practice has been mistakenly called *thôrakion* in the past, and described as some sort of separate item, but more recent scholarship has gradually come to recognise it as part of a garment, then as part of the *lôros*, brought around and up to be pinned to the belt.[297] It must be stiffened and deliberately shaped to create such an outline, for if it were simply left square and pinned to the waist at a single point, the fabric would fall awkwardly and not produce the elegant tear-drop shape shown in the pictorial sources. It was also earlier suggested to be a characteristic of eleventh-century iconography, yet the Lips marble indicates that it was established early in this period, if not at the beginning of it.[298]

Khlamus

The *khlamus* with which the *augousta* is vested at her coronation is unique to her, but unfortunately neither of the references to it in the *Book of Ceremonies* give any further detail.[299] We can be confident that it was very similar to one of those belonging to the emperor, which were variously lustrous white,[300] gold,[301] purple,[302] bearing a portrait (*opsimaros*)[303] and patterned with an octagonal tessellation.[304] Alas, we cannot even be completely sure which of these possibilities was the one deemed to be 'imperial' (*vasilikôs*), although purple with a gold *tavlion* seems most likely, preserving the style worn by Empress Theodôra in the Ravenna mosaic and Helena in the Paris *Homilies of Gregory of Nazianzos* manuscript. Furthermore, in view of the conservatism of court practice, we may look to the portraits of empresses wearing the *opsimaros* cloak, and hypothesise that the *augoustikon khlanidion* was purple with a portrait of the reigning emperor on a bejewelled gold *tavlion*.

Other Capes

As part of the 'set dressing' of the palace for special occasions, a remarkable array of mantles were taken from the imperial wardrobes to be hung in various locations. Amongst those listed for this purpose are even some belonging to the *despotês* which do not appear to be mentioned in relation to any described ceremony, and this is also true for those of the *augousta*.

An alternative to her *khlamus* there is the empress' *mandion*, called the 'peacock' (*taôn*),[305] or the 'little peacock' (*taônion*).[306] *Mandion* is but one version of possibly the most mutable garment name in Byzantine literature. Other forms are *manduas*, *manduê*, *manduon* and *mantion*. Early authors inform us that it was a garment adopted from the Persians, indicating that *manduas* was the form closest to the Persian word.[307] The prevalent references to this in the literature are as an item of ecclesiastical regalia for both sexes.[308] It has been noted previously that in male use, this cape had been conflated with *sagion*, and was a semicircle, secured not on the right shoulder like a *khlamus*, but rather with the straight edges falling down the centre and fastened high on the breast, often with one or two circular or diamond-shaped brooches. Art further shows that the female form could often have rounded corners, the form associated in art with Persians since Late Antiquity.[309]

There are a couple of strong possibilities for identifying the distinctive characteristic of the empress' cape called 'peacock'. Archaeological sites across the Levant, and reliquaries in western Europe preserve numerous fragments of a style of silk brocade which was produced in both Byzantium and Persia. This brocade was patterned in abutting roundels containing birds or beasts (figs 18, 19), amongst which peacocks feature prominently, commonly in confronted or addorsed pairs.[310] An alternative is that this refers to brocade woven with a pattern of adjacent waves commonly filled with stylised foliage which could itself look like the 'eyes' clustered on a peacock's tail. Such cloth is represented on tenth-century Iranian pictures of clothing, and survives in Byzantine fabrics of the following century.[311]

Evidently less eminent than that *mandion* was another called the 'little eagle' (*aetarion*). Comparison with the 'eagle' (*aetos*) worn by male courtiers makes an identification as a brocade much more certain. The diminutive form is less likely to indicate that the eagle pattern on the cloth was smaller in size than to denote its lesser status as a woman's *mandion* in contrast to the male *aetos*, which was probably worn fastened on the left shoulder in the manner of a *khlamus*.

One mantle used for set dressing that not only does not figure in a ceremony, but does not even appear anywhere else in surviving Greek literature is the *hêplêsion*.[312] Moffat suggested that it was a version of *hippêlasion*, a riding cloak.[313] That the imperial mantle that is hung in the same chamber as the *hêplêsion* is an equestrian garment makes this a viable idea. As a riding cape, it was very probably shorter than her other *mandia*, but beyond that there is nothing that can be said of it.

Accessories

As well as the two coats (*diakoptai*) and the crown pendants (*kataseista*) discussed above, a number of the empress' accessories were also hung about the palace at times. Treated thus were her choker (*pniktarion*), her *hêplêsion*, her two *stêthokarakalla* and her two 'wedding belts'.[314] Art confirms that the collar was definitely also worn at other times, and it seems likely that the others were also.

The augoustal choker, or *pniktarion*, is well illustrated in pictorial sources, at least during the richer period of the eleventh century onwards (fig. 47).[315] It is evidently a rather stiff item of cloth covering the full length of the neck and presumably fastened at the back, bedecked with the usual array of gold embroidery and pearls.

The *stêthokarakallon* is also somewhat obscure. Reiske confessed incomprehension, pointing out that the component words are contradictory in terms of classical languages.[316] The first component of this compound, *stêthos* has the straightforward meaning of 'breast' or 'heart', while the second part, *karakallon* is given in modern dictionaries with divergent meanings. In dictionaries of the earlier period the meaning is given as 'hood',[317] whereas in the later period it is 'a type of mantle'.[318] Its earlier Latin form, *caracalla*, is given as *capa* or *scapular* by early medieval authors,[319] going back to a coarse, hooded cloak adopted from the Gauls in the earlier Roman imperial period.[320] If the meaning more prevalent in later Latin applies to the Greek, *stêthos* may qualify *caracalla* meaningfully to mean a '*scapular* covering only the upper part of the chest'. Hence this word probably applies to the jewelled yoke seen on portraits of empresses which were discussed in chapter 1 (fig. 4). The material from which this yoke was normally made is a matter of conjecture. The pictures suggest a base of cloth, yet a complete collar of metal showing the same characteristics as the pictures survives from the early seventh century.[321]

The 'wedding belts' hung about the palace are a quite uncomplicated matter, for several survive. They are belts of embossed gold discs clasped with two larger discs showing Christ joining the married couple and bearing an inscription invoking health during the owner's married life. The surviving examples are all Late Antique, yet in view of the cross-over that has been pointed out between imperial commemorative practice in Rome,[322] and the conservatism of the court, it is highly likely that the practice continued in the old style, even while marriage customs were changing in the wider society. Those described in the *Book of Ceremonies* are, not surprisingly, very much more ornate than the survivals, being 'decorated with gems and pearls'.[323]

Unlike the emperor, the empress had no regalia footwear. This is not very surprising given how little her shoes would be seen under long, voluminous skirts. In so far as art shows women's footwear, it is worth noting that red, the colour forbidden to common men, is the most prevalent for all classes, appearing as often as all other shades combined.[324]

Sceptre

There is no readily identifiable reference in the *Book of Ceremonies* to the empress bearing a sceptre, however pictorial sources suggest that such was, in fact, the case. Coinage is the most copious source of these representations. In the eighth and ninth centuries empresses can be seen holding the cruciform *skêpiôn* (see above and fig. 31.1), which has been shown to be a real item, contrary to the view of Grierson.[325] There is less specific evidence for the tenth century, but in view of the clear illustrations which are again frequent in the eleventh century it seems unlikely that there was a complete hiatus in the practice in the tenth century. In addition to carrying the *skêpiôn* at times, there may already have been a distinct form of sceptre for the empress. Grierson notes one borne by Evdokia Ingerina, the wife of Basil I (867–886), which resembles a three-lobed form known from mid-eleventh-century coins and described in later literature (fig. 31.2).[326]

Ranking women

Zôstê Patrikia

After the *augousta* there are but two other ranks held by women in their own right which are explicitly mentioned in the *Book of Ceremonies*. Foremost of these was the *zôstê patrikia* (Plate 17, left). In all the *taktika* of the ninth and tenth centuries this position remained a stable feature of the highest levels of the court. In the middle of the ninth century the *Taktikon Uspenski* records her as fifth of the listed ranks after the patriarch, the *kaisar*, the *nôvelêssimos* and the *kouropalatês*.[327] In the late ninth century Leo VI created the position of *vasileopatôr*, ranking above the *zôstê patrikia*. By the time of the compilation of the *Taktikon Beneseviç* between 934 and 944, the rank of *proedros* was introduced above the *zôstê patrikia*, and *papas rômês* above the patriarch,[328] but shortly afterwards in the *Escorial Taktikon* (971–5) the *papas rômês* was eliminated and the *proedros* demoted to the rank below *zôstê*, thus restoring the sequence given by Filotheos.[329]

The *zôstê patrikia* was amongst members of those exalted ranks who were never summoned to the imperial table by name, implying that their presence was routine at the formal banquets. It has been said that each empress appointed a *zôstê patrikia* to be the first amongst her attendant ladies, with the appointment being for life.[330] A *zôstê patrikia* might well outlive the term of the empress who appointed her, and emperors did create *zôstai patrikiai ex gratia*, so there must usually have been a number of *zôstai patrikiai* at any given time, a fact acknowledged by the *Book of Ceremonies*.[331] In the *Book of Ceremonies* the regalia vested upon a *zôstê patrikia* consists of a white hood (*maforion*), *propolôma*, a *delmatikion*, a *thôrakion* and *lôros*, in addition to the ivory diptych referred to in the *Klêtôrologion*, which is mentioned several times in the course of the elevation ceremony.

Headgear

The *maforion* has been discussed previously in connection with several male ranks and identified as a form of head cloth or hood, and representations have been cited. Headscarves are very commonly illustrated in middle Byzantine art as one of the most essential items of women's everyday dress, yet the imperatives of ritual and regalia demand something distinct from daily mundanity. Hence the regalia *maforion* must be in some way different from the common dress item, probably more so than the male version, which was so far from everyday male dress practice. There unfortunately appear to be no illuminations surviving from the ninth to eleventh centuries showing non-imperial women of the court wearing anything which might be taken to be regalia, but moving on to the twelfth century we do find something which might plausibly explain the stylised form of the tenth-century regalia *maforion*. Illustrations to an *epithalamion* for a French princess show her being received by two parties of women.[332] One party looking on wear more common clothing and the generic unshaped headscarf that is characteristic of common Byzantine women. The other party, who greet the princess and prepare her for her marriage, are dressed in opulent dresses and fan-shaped hats normally seen on noble women of the eleventh and twelfth centuries. These women can only be a group of *koubikoulareai*, and may even include a *zôstê patrikia*. In addition to the garb mentioned, all of these women wear a hood-like affair which falls from under their hats, framing their faces, fanning stiffly out to the points of their shoulders and evidently fastened under the chin, yet without actually meeting there (see fig. 57, bottom right). Significantly, the princess, when robed in Byzantine style and enthroned, does not adopt this accessory. In this miniature we therefore have a pattern of usage for this head covering which precisely matches that specified for the feminine *maforion* in the *Book of Ceremonies*. Its stiffness and shaping are suitably different from the soft draping of a common cloth headscarf to effectively set it apart for regalia purposes. The *maforion* of the *zôstê patrikia* is simply described as white like those of the *koubikoularea* and *koubikoularios*.[333]

Propolôma is a term which appears to be unique to the *Book of Ceremonies*. The *zôstai patrikiai* share its use with *koubikoulareai* and the common *patrikiai*.[334] It must be assumed that in accordance with the listed *taxis*, the same is true of *magistrissai* also, for they are a group listed second in the 'entries', between the *zôstai* and the common *patrikiai*.[335] Numerous unpersuasive attempts have been made to identify this item, ranging from a coronet,[336] some sort of grandiose hairstyle,[337] to something like a turban.[338] More recently, Melita Emmanuel speculated that the large, flaring hat, commonly white and occasionally detailed with some decoration, that is frequently illustrated on aristocrat ladies across the tenth to twelfth centuries could be identified with this term, a proposition which can be readily accepted, especially in the light of Emmanuel's observation that it would be impossible to make a prostration in such a hat, just as the *Book of Ceremonies* says regarding the elevation of a *zôstê patrikia*.[339]

None of the pictorial sources show these hats from any identifiable angle other than full face or a slight angle, so it is impossible to say precisely what its form was. However, the simplest and most effective way to form the shape shown, especially considering the distribution of the diverse decoration shown, is as an inverted truncated cone with the open wide end pressed closed (Plate 17; Chart 8.6–7).

Main garment

While it is far from certain that the *stikharion* mentioned in the *Klêtôrologion* was the regalia garment of the *zôstê patrikia*, in the *Book of Ceremonies* there is no confusion. It is a *delmatikion* received from the hands of the emperor.[340] The overall form of this garment has previously been established as a dress with flaring sleeves. There is no detailed information given regarding the *delmatikion* with which the *zôstê* is vested, yet something must set it apart from the *delmatikia* worn mundanely by aristocratic women. In view of the distinction visible in the Ravenna mosaics, and clearly still in force in the tenth century, between the austere monochromatism of the regalia and the ornate patterning of the non-regalia garments, it is reasonable to suppose that the *delmatikion* of the *zôstê patrikia* was a plain colour, either the essential court white, or perhaps a purple due to her exalted position. It may have been a *stikharion*, as Filotheos mentioned, but that remains implausible if she is to give it away.

Over-garment

The *zôstê patrikia* was the sole woman other than the *augousta* accorded the privilege of wearing a *lôros*. Indeed, it has been suggested that her title was derived from this very fact.[341] It is an idea which gains support from Achmet, who refers to the *lôros* as a 'belt' (*zônê*).[342] We can be confident that the *lôros* of the *zôstê* was less ornate than that of the empress. Without pictorial evidence, however, is impossible to say whether it followed the form of that of the empress, with the tail drawn around to be fastened at the waist, or retained the older style of the tail being carried draped over the left arm.

Accessory

Again with her eminence and quasi-male status, the *zôstê patrikia* wore a *thôrakion*, like the royalty and senior male courtiers (fig. 20). Unlike with those men, however, it plays a prominent place in her ceremony of elevation.

Koubikoularea

The last named rank of honour for a woman was that of 'lady of the empress' chamber', or *koubikoularea*. This rank cannot have been a simple attributed equivalent of *koubikoularios* in the manner that a *prôtospatharea* was the wife of a *prôtospatharios* for the very simple reason that *koubikoularios* was at this time a rank confined to eunuchs. However, *koubikoularea* was the direct equivalent of *koubikoularios* in terms of function, and that is very specifically reflected in her regalia. The regalia with which a *koubikoularea* is invested consists of a white *maforion* and a garment called the 'golden *paragaudion*', the same as a *koubikoularios*, with a *propolôma* and a *kharzanion*. Before the ceremony these items are all placed on the *vêma* screens of the chapel of Saint Theodore adjacent to the Khrusotriklinos. What the woman is wearing as she enters the ceremony is not specified, so we must infer that they were her ordinary garments. A *koubikoularea* is most likely to have been appointed from within the ranks of *magistrissai* and *patrikia*, and so would already be entitled to wear the *propolôma*, and would otherwise be likely to be wearing the common style of *delmatikion*.

Headgear

The major part of the investiture of a *koubikoularea* involves dressing her with three items of headgear, first a *maforion*, then a *kharzanion* and finally a *propolôma*. As noted above, it is almost certain that the incoming *koubikoularea* would have already been of a rank entitled to wear a *propolôma*, yet there is one waiting with the other regalia. It must be inferred from this that the candidate enters the ceremony bareheaded to undergo the sequence described in the *Book of Ceremonies*.[343]

The nature of the regalia *maforion* has been discussed above under the *zôstê patrikia* section. The placing of a stiff hood upon the lady's head presents no difficulty.

The *maforion* is followed with a white *kharzanion*. *Kharzanion* is found elsewhere in the literature of this era meaning strap or thong.[344] The *Interpretation of Dreams* of Achmet tells us that it is inferior as an instrument of corporal punishment to the implement called *manklavion*, a single-strand whip.[345] The sequence of the robing clearly implies that the *kharzanion* lies between the *maforion* and *propolôma*. The image that this evokes is of a ribbon laid over the candidate's head from side to side, hanging down onto her shoulders and held in place by the hat. As such, it would be the ancestor of the much-elaborated pendants hanging from the headgear of the ladies in the *Eisitêrioi for Agnes of France* (fig. 57).

The *propolôma* has been discussed previously amongst the regalia of the *zôstê patrikia*. The identification proposed then, as a large hat, rather than as a turban, is further strengthened by the details of the investiture ceremony of the *koubikoularea*. Whereas it is merely said that the *zôstê patrikia* 'wears' a *propolôma*,[346] the *koubikoularea* has one placed upon her during the ceremony by *praipositoi*.[347] The winding of a turban is a lengthy and delicate operation prone to mishap. Far simpler, and ritualistically reliable, would be the placing of a solid hat.

The golden *himation* and *zônarion*

The major piece of regalia a *koubikoularea* is vested with is described as a 'golden *himation* in the fashion of a *paragaudion*'.[348] This garment is placed upon her and then belted by the *praipositoi*. *Himation* is a rather vague term, which tends to refer to a variety of cape or cloak, but may also refer to a tailored garment. *Paragaudion* as a man's garment has changed its meaning over time, from a type of tunic in Late Antiquity to a variety of cape in the *Book of Ceremonies* (see under *paragaudion* above). Although it is not stated that the belt is put on over this 'golden *himation*', we must nevertheless accept the implication that this is the case, for if this garment were a cape, we are presented with the awkward image of the *praipositoi* delving under swathes of fabric to fasten the belt around the lady's waist. Such a scene would be quite clumsy and would have detracted from the quality of the ritual. Similarly, had this item been a mantle like the male *paragaudion*, surely the author would have simply said so, rather than using a circuitous phrase. Art offers a possibility which can reconcile these otherwise seemingly contradictory tendencies. Beginning with the pictures of the Holy Virgin and the Princess of Egypt in the fifth-century Church of Saint Maria Maggiore in Rome, then the Saintly Virgins of Saint Appolinaire Nuovo, Ravenna and two of the saints of the Church of Saint Maria in Valle, we have seen women wearing a *himation epômis*, a shawl draped from the left shoulder to right hip (fig. 15, left; Plate 7, right). The 'golden *himation* in the fashion of a *paragaudion*' should be recognised as a survival of this shawl, and can be said to be like a *paragaudion* because it has the same scheme of colour and decoration as that cape: cloth of gold with purple borders.

The great majority of pictures of the *himation epômis* are girded with a broad jewelled or pearled belt with a roundel in the centre. Lest it be thought that such belts may have disappeared after the sixth century, it should be noted that an identical example appears on the Bamberg Silk, while versions without the roundel commonly appear in works of the eleventh century like the crown of Constantine Monomakhos and the often-reproduced picture of the Dance of Miriam and the Israelite women in Vat. Gr. Ms. 752.[349] The *zônarion* with which the *praipositos* girds the new *koubikoularea* was therefore certainly of this type.

Other Women

The presence at court ceremonies of women of other ranks was touched upon in the introduction of this section. The mosaics of Ravenna show that in the sixth century women were very much at liberty to wear what they pleased at court while the men were constrained to their regalia. Despite the existence of regalia-clad women's ranks by this time that were not visible in the earlier sources, there is no reason to think that this practice had changed by tenth century. Hence, those with no specified regalia were presumably wearing some version of their usual attire – a non-regalia *delmatikion*, the ubiquitous *mantion*, and *propolôma* for those entitled to wear it.

Later Tenth Century

Constantine Porfurogennêtos, author of the *Book of Ceremonies*, died in 959. Most of the next two decades were an unsettled period of short reigns, whose incumbents were more focused on matters other than palace administration. As a result, as far as can be ascertained, the customs of the court generally remained settled in the patterns established previously. Some exceptions to this were interpolated into the manuscript of the *Book of Ceremonies* on behalf of Emperor Nikêforos II Fôkas between 963 and 969.

One of the interpolations is an account of Nikêforos' coronation.[350] The exact significance of this is hard to assess, for the chapter on coronation is absent from the original book. It is quite likely that the ceremony had been done in a largely traditional manner, drawing on the reservoir of oral transmission or lesser records which evidently existed, and then the record added to remedy the lacuna which had been noted in the manual. In any case, in terms of regalia there is nothing out of the ordinary in the ceremony. The crucial insignia of the *stemma* and red footwear hold the expected pride of place, with the standard *divêtêsion* accompanied by the familiar *kampagia* and *kampotouva* appearing later in the ritual, followed by the *tzitzakion*.

Prôedros of the Senate

A definite change instituted by Nikêforos was the elevation of the hitherto functionary position of *prôedros* (chairman or president) of the Senate into an honorific rank with regalia.[351] In doing this he seems to have crystallised a process initiated by Constantine Porfurogennêtos some decades earlier. Constantine evidently wished to re-integrate the Senate, which had become somewhat marginal, into the ceremonial of the court. He did this not only by having the Senate attend more ceremonies and do so more prominently, but also by promoting the *prôedros* of the Senate to a court rank above that of *zôstê patrikia*, where it is listed in the *Taktikon Beneseviç* compiled between 934 and 944. In the *Beneseviç* ranking it would have been something of a contradiction to have a man of the relatively lowly rank of *patrikios* (which was the most usual rank for a senator) in his rather undistinguished regalia set amongst the highest handful of ranks. So Nikêforos remedied this by appointing a favoured eunuch, Basil the Parakoimomenos, as *prôedros* of the Senate in 963 and instituting suitably spectacular regalia. The contradictions were further ameliorated by the *prôedros* being demoted to a rank immediately below the *zôstê patrikia*, where it is recorded as such in the *Escorial Taktikon* of *c*.975.

The regalia instituted for the elevated position of *prôedros* of the Senate comprised a remarkably opulent suite of garments and accessories. His primary outfit consisted of a 'Persian-sleeved' tunic (*khitôn*/*stikharion*) of red damask with gold decoration, a purple belt with gems and a white damask *khlamus* with gold decoration (probably an edging) and gold *tavlia* worked with small ivy leaves.[352] This was accompanied on feast days by purple *kampotouva* and *kampagia*.[353] His undress outfit comprised a *skaramangion* of five-colour brocade on which purple and green predominated, a russet (*roês*) *sagion* with gold frogs[354] and gold decoration (again, probably an edging) with small ivy leaves like his *khlamus*, and an ornament called *katakoilion*, which is most likely to be another term for *thôrakion*.

Continuity into the Eleventh Century

The unsettled times of the third quarter of the tenth century were brought to an end by the accession of Basil II in 976. The half century of Basil's reign were characterised by austerity and conservatism, attested by both literature and art, but it brought internal stability and external victories. In 985 Emperor Basil II deposed Parakoimomenos Basil, for whom the rank of *prôedros* of the Senate had been created, and exiled him from the court.[355] It appears that the emperor held such rancour towards the eunuch that he discontinued the rank. Thus the norms of the *Book of Ceremonies* were reasserted, and seem to have prevailed to the end of Basil's life and somewhat beyond. As was noted earlier, one spectacular illustration of this continuity is to be found in the donor protrait of a copy of the gospels created in Adrianople in 1007 for one Iôannês, an Armenian *prôtospatharios* in Basil's court.[356] A more extensive suite of sources giving evidence of continuity, also touched upon earlier, are artworks dealing with the *eparkhos* of the City. Four secular illuminations of men of known rank other than emperors, which clearly show 'Persian-sleeved' tunics, are all pictures of *eparkhoi*. Two represent Pilate in biblical manuscripts,[357] the third depicts the *eparkhos* of Kapadokhian Kaisaria,[358] and the fourth a historical *eparkhos* of the city.[359] One of the pictures of Pilate is in a codex with a recorded date of 1059 (fig. 34), the other three are attributed to the twelfth century, although the Madrid Skylitzes, which contains the historical governor of the City, is traceable to later eleventh-century prototypes, with some influences from the contemporary experiences of the painters in the first half of the twelfth century; there must also be some doubt as to the dating of one of the others on account of its detail. Despite their disparate sources, all have striking similarities and points of detail which tend to support their credibility. Three of the four wear *lôroi.* The two pictures of Pilate show him seated in formal session wearing very similar hoods, bearing the same pattern of black dots around a black disc. The other two pictures show the *eparkhoi* wearing the white dome hats which had begin to appear in court contexts in the later eleventh century. The *kamision* is also very consistent across these pictures. In all cases the base colour is white, as we would expect if there were continuity from the common colour scheme set out in the *Book of Ceremonies.* The dated eleventh-century example is depicted with black cuffs and hem band, while the garments of the Governor of Kaisaria and the two scenes of the *eparkhos* in the Madrid Skylitzes are identical in having a dark hem band but white cuffs.

The remaining depiction of Pilate (Athens codex 93, f. 138) shows his *kamision* as being entirely white. However, it must be noted that his *lôros* is also sketchily rendered and devoid of detail, and so it should be accepted that in this case the artist has merely illustrated the figure in the traditional manner with the minimum of detail essential to identify his position. These sources indicate that up to the middle of the eleventh century the bulk of the regalia of the *eparkhos* changed little from the forms defined in the *Book of Ceremonies.* One discernible change from the tenth century is, however, visible in the sources. The *eparkhos* now has designated regalia footwear, which Christopher of Mitylênê describes as 'tawny-orange, stridently bright in colour',[360] which the pictures do attempt to represent. This is a significant development which presages trends into the twelfth century. Hitherto, only the emperor and the *kaisar* were entitled to footwear of a designated colour.

ROBING THE EMPRESS: SIXTH CENTURY I

The woman on the left continues the time-honoured form of clothing for Roman women. In the Greek terminology, which had supplanted Latin from the fourth century, a garment with full-length decorative bands was called a *stikharion*. This *stikharion*, with gold woven into a purple ground, continued to be associated with the empress' chief lady-in-waiting up to the eleventh century, yet the close-fitting sleeves as yet show no sign of the developments which will characterise aristocratic women's dress in following centuries. This lady holds another quasi-masculine element of the empress' regalia, the imperial *khlamus* of Tyrian purple worked with gold.

The lady on the right represents some of the most formative influences on Roman court dress in Late Antiquity. Her outfit was imported from Persia and adopted by royal Roman women in the first half of the fifth century, if not earlier. The most significant elements of the outfit are the cloth of gold shawl draped from her left shoulder, a garment which would endure into the tenth century under the name *paragaudion*, and the sleeve style with a loose tube gathered into long, close-fitting cuffs. Her burden is the jewelled yoke, later called *sthêthokarokallon*.

PLATE

2

Robing the Empress: Sixth Century II

The *augousta*'s dress shows the merging of Roman and imported elements. It also represents a paradigm which will prevail until the late eleventh century – that the regalia of the empress should be virtually identical to that of the emperor and incorporate distinctly male elements. Thus, its decoration of *sêmenta* on the shoulders and knees and *klavoi* projecting up from the hem are in accord with venerable Roman custom, although more typical of male dress, while in contrast, the sleeves are of the Persian form, which at this point had not made the full transition into male court clothing. She holds the older form of crown, the *diadêma*, which would remain the staple for royal portraits for centuries, even after it was supplanted for the most eminent use by the *stemma*.

ROBING THE EMPEROR: SIXTH CENTURY

The end of Late Antiquity was a cusp for the empire in many ways, not least for the regalia of the court. Crucial to the transformation was the increasing assimilation of Eastern influences. In the sixth century most of the dress of the court retained traditional forms, main garments with tapestry-woven decoration in the form of *klavoi* (Latin *clavii*), *sêmenta* (Latin *segmenta*) and *fialion* (yoke), the oval *khlamus* with contrasting *tavlia* across the long axis upon which it was folded, and stylised sandals, which would continue to be called *kaligai* or *kampagia* until they fell out of use in the eleventh century. In the metropolis, main garments were increasingly being tailored, rather than woven in a piece by the method nowadays associated with the Egyptian Copts. The development of tailoring facilitated a crucial change, beginning with the imperial regalia tunic. It is said that for his investiture in 491 Anastasios I adopted the *divitision*, a garment of Persian provenance, characterised by very full sleeves gathered into long, close-fitting cuffs. This development was curious for another reason – the *divitision* had been worn by royal women in the Roman Empire for a century of so at that point.

PLATE

4

SOLDIERS, 650–900

The period from the fifth to the eight centuries saw dramatic changes in common men's clothing. The most significant change was that by the beginning of the sixth century all forms of the cloak or cape had been abandoned in everyday dress in favour of the coat, one of the many imports from Persia. Although the term *kandus* is used as early as Xenofon, coats were known in Rômania in Late Antiquity as *fiblatôrion* ('brooched garment') or as *zôstarion* ('belted garment'). These names were used because before the advent of buttons, such coats were only fastened by a brooch at the throat supplemented by a belt (right figure). Buttons seem to have become established during the eighth century, accompanied by a change in the terminology to *kavadion* (left). The practice of passing the arms through openings in the armpits was to continue until the end of the empire, as was the motif of sleeves significantly longer than the wearer's arms. Other Persian influences were swords hung from a waist belt rather than a shoulder strap (*spathion zôstikion*, right), the use of hose over light breeches (centre) and a proliferation of hats. The already venerable round cap (*pilos*) continued in use (centre) as did the cylindrical hat traditionally identified as the 'Pannonian' mentioned by Vegetius (left). Alongside these, the Persian *kalansuwa* was adopted (right). These could be felted to shape as other hats were, but both art and archaeology show they could be sewn from woven fabrics to get a more colourful effect. The Late Antique cemeteries of Egypt have shown that by the sixth century the old Roman sandals had been almost entirely replaced with a very wide variety of increasingly sophisticated footwear, ranging from low slip-on or lace-up shoes to tall boots, some clearly intended for riding (left).

COURTIER AND OFFICER *C.* 650–900

The period of the later sixth to mid-seventh centuries was to establish forms of dress, both in the everyday clothing of better-off men and in regalia, which were to endure with much less alteration into the eleventh century.

The left figure embodies a full suite of Persian imports: *kalansuwa* hat, long-sleeved *skaramangion* tunic and *mantion* cape. With the establishment of the principle that no man might wear a hat in the presence of the emperor, the court use of the *kalansuwa* – or as it becamc known in Greek, *kausia* – lags far behind the garments in its representation at court.

The right-hand man was probably the most powerful man in the empire after the emperor himself, the *Eparkhos tês Poleôs*, the Governor of Constantinople. He had a regalia tunic embodying a simplified form of the antique decoration and a *felonion* or ceremonial hood, with distinctive patterning. He is the only man beside the rulers who wore the *lôros* as a routine element of his regalia. The antique *kampagia* footwear remained a staple of the regalia of the senatorial class (effectively the majority of the court) into the early eleventh century.

PLATE

6

Courtier and servant

Left, a courtier, seventh century. Although his tunic bears the traditional forms of decoration, it embodies the 'Persian-sleeve' now percolating down from its adoption as imperial regalia. The use of patterned fabric in a *khlamus* is unusual and did not become general practice. The date of and reason for the adoption of the ceremonial hood or headscarf (*maforian*/*felonion*) for men remains something of a mystery, lost in the so-called Dark Age.

Unsurprisingly, the clothing of common and poor women were slow to take up new fashions, retaining simple, frugal forms through the duration of the empire.

Ladies of the Court, *c.*650–900

In the fifth century the 'Persian-sleeve' had been a signifier of high status amongst women. With its assimilation into the male regalia (Plate 3, centre) it could no longer serve that function, and, indeed, seems to have been taken out of the female realm almost entirely. Hence, a new status signifier was needed in women's dress. This was achieved by taking the *delmatikê* (Latin, *dalmatica*) – originally a tunic with loose, but square sleeves – and widening its cuffs. Hence, a status contrast was drawn not only between quality of fabric and decoration, but also with the common close-fitting sleeve (Plate 6, right). At first the widening was modest, but the fashion was to persist to the end of the empire with the sleeves becoming progressively larger. Along the way, the fashion influenced Western clothing in the eleventh and twelfth centuries. The common medieval Greek linguistic trend turned the name of this garment into *delmatikion*.

Other Persian fashions which had accompanied the Persian-sleeved dress continued in use and were assimilated into women's court regalia. Foremost of these was the ornate diagonal shawl (right). This came to be known by the term which had been attributed to several Persian-derived items, *paragavdês* and *paragavdion*.

MOBILISATION!

There is increasing evidence that the place of women in early and middle-Byzantine Rômania was freer and more equal than any western society in modern times; and in unusual circumstances might even have strayed into challenging male areas. Theofanês tells of a female espionage agent and Bishop Evstathios writes with a hint of approval of the active participation of women in the defence of Thessaloniki in the twelth century, saying that they made turbans and padded protective garments for themselves in the manner of regular soldiers (left); and took to the walls to shoot and cast stones at the attackers. (See also Plate 14.)

The basic clothing of common men and soldiers had not changed much for centuries. The carouser's tunic (centre) shows the long-established slit opening down from the left side of the neck, here untidily unbuttoned.

With the end of the last of the Classical arena games in the early seventh century, chariot racing took on pre-eminence, not only as the premiere mass entertainment for the populace of Constantinople, but also, being run by the demes, a primary way of organising and managing the community and its activities. Charioteers thereby became the sporting superstars of the day, and appear also to have taken social and ceremonial roles. This charioteer (right) won the last round of racing and, in order to enhance his authority as he aids the mobilisation, he wears the regalia awarded to him for his victory: a silvered helm, a special belt and *aurgarion* tunic.

JUNIOR COURTIERS, NINTH TO EARLY ELEVENTH CENTURIES

The junior ranks and functions of the middle-Byzantine-era court were often distinguished not by their clothing, but by accessories which could represent their rank or symbolise their actual or notional function. Thus, a *stratôr* (centre) carried an ornamental whip to represent his office in the imperial stables. The task of a *mandatôr* (left) was to relay imperial decrees or military orders, and he carried a red-dyed swagger stick. These lowly functions were commonly discharged by men of such ranks as *patrikios* or *Prôtospatharios* who might also be eunuchs (left). The rank emblem of a *disupatos* (right) was an inscribed scroll. The men all wear the most basic regalia tunic, a plain white *kamision*, while the *khrusotavlê* (gold-panelled) *khlamus* (left), *oxeotavlê* (purple-panelled) *khlamus* (centre) and *roês* (russet) *sagion* (right) were common to virtually all ranks, though worn on different occasions as set out in the *Book of Ceremonies*.

PLATE

10

SOLDIERS ON PARADE, TENTH CENTURY I

Soldiers of the standing units based in the capital often had to do parade duties attached to court ceremonies. The *Book of Ceremonies* specifies the presentation of some of them in varying degrees of detail. Right, one of the 'Gothic' mercenaries (the term was applied to anyone from Northern or Eastern Europe who was not considered to be Orthodox Christian) wearing a hooded overcoat called a *gouna* and armed only with a cudgel.

The Great Macedonian Hetaireia had a particularly prominent role in some ceremonies (left). On such occasions each was to turn out clad in a shirt (*esôforion*), probably to bring them into the dominant white colour scheme of the court for this occasion, wearing belt-hung swords with silvered and gilded fittings. This individual, left, carries a *tzikourion* (double-bladed battle axe) and a gilded shield, while other men of the unit taking part in the same ceremony could carry other types of battle axe, and shields which were either bronze with gilding, or plain, presumably polished, iron.

PLATE

11

SOLDIERS ON PARADE, TENTH CENTURY II

The navy of the Enduring Roman Empire was the first to have a standing marine (*ploïmos*) contingent. In one ceremonial prototype they were to parade along with some ethnic units each wearing a sword (in this case a *paramêrion*, but the source does not specify type) and carrying a hide shield and banner. No clothing is specified, so here the man wears everyday dress including the type of tunic with a long central opening, just to the waist, called *sfinktourion* in this era, and *makhlamion* later.

PLATE

12

Hail to the Rulers! Triumphal Regalia, Tenth–Eleventh Centuries

As with other areas of court life, detailed protocols existed to guide the rulers in ways of celebrating the empire's victories. This plate is based upon those recorded by Constantine Porfurogênnetos in the tenth century. On his head the emperor (centre) wears the 'triumphal crown' (*toufa*) surmounted by a spray of semi-precious stones in a manner which recalls helmet crests of earlier Roman soldiers. His parade surcoat (*epilôrikion*) was called the 'rose-cluster' after its colour and pearl decoration. The ceremonial armband was presented to him by the Governor of the City as the parade entered the Golden Gate.

The *kaisar* (right) is clad in gilded items of armour and carries a gilded spear. His curious combination of one black boot and one red symbolises his position halfway between the populace and the throne.

On the left the parade helm of the *kaisar* is brought by a man of the populous rank of *prôtospatharios*, clad as one of the select party to accompany the rulers as they rode into the City. He wears a short version of his usual regalia tunic (*spekion*) and a gilded *klivanion* like the *kaisar*.

PLATE

13

JUDICIAL OFFICERS, TENTH–ELEVENTH CENTURIES I

As an ancient civil society, the Roman Empire of the tenth century had sophisticated laws and law enforcement systems. The *Eparkhos tês Poleôs*, or City Governor (Plate 5), had an extensive staff to underpin his position as chief judicial officer. These included magistrates of various grades (left) and the *vigla*, or watch (centre and right). To show that they acted upon his behalf, these people wore the *felonion* (hood) just as the governor did, marked, as his was, with distinctive concentric decoration shown in these and other slight variants in eleventh-century pictures.

The gold-hilted sword and *pektorarion* show that the man on the right is the *droungarios tês viglas* (chief of police) in his everyday garb. Pictures indicate that his full dress replaced the common boots with *kampagia* and *kampotouva* (padded leggings) and added a sky-blue cloak with gold *tavlion*.

PLATE

14

Judicial officers, tenth–eleventh centuries II

There is increasing evidence that Rômania during this era was one of the most gender-integrated societies in recorded history. Women not only had distinct areas of life dictated by biology; some physical spaces were restricted for their use. Hence, the need for comprehensive law enforcement demanded female agents. Although not hinted at in literary material, art indicates that there were female watch officers. Just as with the men, their main clothing has nothing to set it apart from everyday wear (here a *diakoptês/kavadion* and *manduas*), but their role is indicated by the presence of the distinctively marked white hood or headscarf.

COURTIERS AND OFFICERS TO *C.*1050 I

The evidence suggests that the regalia described in the *Book of Ceremonies* remained fairly stable into the eleventh century, beginning a gradual process of change after the end of the reign of Basil II. From time to time, the regular presentation of court with its predominance of white and other plain colours was varied.

Left: the regalia did not exist in a vacuum. As a concession to summer weather, some rituals were enacted with the participants clad in shirts (*esôforia*) rather than heavier outer garments. In this case the shirt has the form called *kôlovion* on account of its loose sleeves, and so is named *esôforokolovion*. Striped *esôforia* are mentioned in tenth-century sources and begin to be illustrated in eleventh-century pictures. Two developments of the eleventh century were the replacement of the old *kapagia* sandals with contemporary footwear, and the acceptance of hats in court contexts.

Right: the tunic of the *raiktôr*, called, appropriately, *raiktorikion*, is one of the most comprehensively described in the ceremony book. It is defined as having a gold yoke with broad shoulder spurs, gold cuffs and a gold hem band but without certain additional decoration found on certain other court garments. Here, he wears not the more common version of the regalia where the gold is applied to a white base, but the rarely used alternative black, accompanied by a cloak of the same style. This combination is referred to as 'the blacks' (*ta atravatikia*) and would be worn by much of the court on those rare occasions. Otherwise, it is almost unheard of for black to appear in lay clothing in Byzantion.

PLATE

16

COURTIERS AND OFFICERS TO *C.*1050 II

The Dêmes, the old circus factions, were each presided over by a courtier appointed by the Emperor. The *Dêmarkhoi* had various regalia items. For more formal occasions they had a tunic and *khlamus* in their deme colour (blue or green) trimmed with purple, but were presented with an *avdion* (the Arabic *abeyah*) as part of their annual bonus, and were required to wear it at some ceremonies. Here he wears it with everyday dress, a *sfinktourion* and turban over a padded cap.

THE MOST EMINENT LADIES OF THE COURT, TENTH–ELEVENTH CENTURIES

The clothing of women in Constantinople generally shows less change over time than that of men, and it tended to be even more stable in the court. The *zôstê patrikia*, or chief lady-in-waiting, (left) is the one whose regalia is described in most detail. The white *propolôma* (hat) was common to all women of court status, and the stylised hood (*maforion*) was also worn by *koubikoularaia*, the general ladies-in-waiting, although the *zôstê patrikia* had the addition of the *kharzanion*, a band terminating in triple ornaments of pearls and gems draped over the head under the *propolôma*. As the *zôstê* part of the title indicates, she was the only non-imperial woman entitled to wear the *lôros* as a routine part of her regalia, and it was often accompanied by a 'golden *thôrakion*', a chain harness surviving from ancient fashion.

The woman on the right shows the fashion for wide ornate lapels and falling collar which prevailed in the eleventh century. That she must be a member of the extended royal family is shown not only by the costly brocade of her *delmatikion*, but the fact that her *propolôma* is purple, rather than the white of other women. A wide, decorated textile belt, called *zônarion*, was a common feature of women's dress throughout this period.

PLATE

18

WOMEN OF THE COURT, ELEVENTH–TWELFTH CENTURIES

Not all the women seen at court were noble. Professional dancers are well attested in middle Byzantine society, even at court, and the art of the period shows that they had a particular style of stage costume. Right: this is the more risqué form, with the arms bare. More modest dancers would also wear a fine, decorated *esôforion* (chemise) under their main dress. The flounced skirt anticipates much later fashion.

Women's clothing at court had always been much less regulated than that of men, and we have seen that from as early as the Ravenna mosaics the mass of more affluent court women could be wearing opulently decorated fabrics. With the greater availability of brocades in the eleventh century this phenomenon was not only more extensive, but also became more formalised, with a suite of set patterns established in the twelfth century for court use. It also appears that the diverse application of decorative bands to the earlier *propolôma* has now been formalised into a system representing a more complex hierarchy than had existed amongst tenth-century court ladies, with horizontal bands indicating a higher status than diagonal bands and three bands ranking higher than two.

EMPEROR AND COURTIERS, LATE TWELFTH CENTURY

The major change in the regalia that developed through the middle half of the eleventh century was the adoption of figured fabrics. The ancient chromatic paradigm of the court dressed formally, predominantly clad in white with highlights of purple, crimson and gold, was swept away for senior ranks and replaced with cloths decorated with motifs already in use in lay clothing of the previous century: droplets, stylised palm trees and ivy leaves. Hats became more prominent, with senior male courtiers adopting an extravagant variant of the women's *propolôma* (left) around the end of the eleventh century. Emperor Iôannês Komnênos (right) was a successful military commander. He gave away this surcoat when a courtier remarked that the fact that it was dyed with the 'bloody bile' of the murex shellfish made it an unlucky omen. Three-quarters of the way through the twelfth century saw another cusp in the transformation of the regalia, when the 'Persian-sleeve' was abandoned in favour of a simpler construction for some garments, while the *kôlovion* sleeve became more widely used for others.

PLATE

20

SOLDIERY, PALAIOLOGIAN ERA

The military suffered no less that other areas from the lasting damage done to Rômania by the Fourth Crusade. One of the technological losses was the lamellar armour that had been such a feature of the middle Byzantine era and so copiously depicted in icons of military saints. Icon painters continued to try to copy those precedents, using lamellaresque patterning in forms which show their lack of understanding of it. The most common radial patterning of armours on Palaiologian military saints suggests that the so-called 'mirror armours' (Persian *char-aina*) were in use (front figure). Thus, once again, Rômiosi soldiery must have looked very 'Turkish', as we might think of it now – yet looking so perhaps well before the Turks did themselves.

Another proto-Turkish feature was the junior *skaranikon*, the origin of the fez, worn here (left) by one of the small ceremonial guard unit called *romfaiokratores*, characterised by their gilded *romfaia* spears and shields bearing a portrait of the mounted emperor.

The sleeveless coat worn as part military regalia was descended from the middle Byzantine surcoat and still called *epilôrikion*. The surcoat of the *logothete* (chief financial officer) of the cavalry (right) is made of one of the regulation brocades woven for court use. He carries his *skiadion*, which is the occasional alternative to the turban which normally accompanied an *epilôrikion*.

Senior courtiers, Palaiologian era

Senior members of the Palaiologian court had a suite of very colourful, yet very similar, brocades to choose from for their outfits, which are very well represented in art.

Sevastokratôr (left) was one of the very highest ranks, normally restricted to men related by blood to the Emperor. Thus, his primary regalia garment was the tunic with tight cuffs (*roukhon*) rather than a coat, and his *tabarion* (as the old khlamus was now called) is much more ornate. The most eminent version of the *skaranikon* (hat) could be domical or a truncated cone, but either way highly decorated with portraits of the Emperor front and back. He is also set apart by his decorated boots.

The basic regalia garment for most ranks was a *kavadion*, and similarly many ranks carried some kind of baton. The rank of *prôtovestiarios* (right) was one of the higher ones. Hence, he wears a decorated *skiadion* and *aer* (neck flap), and a *tabarion*. His *kavadion* is unusual in being made of counter-changed panels.

PLATE

22

LADIES OF THE UPPER COURT, PALAIOLOGIAN ERA

The period of the Western cultural movement extolled by its proponents as 'Renaissance' may have been a boon for the fine arts, but it was accompanied by negative social trends, especially in relation to the position of women. In Byzantium, in the wake of the vast cultural, social and economic harm done to the realm by the Fourth Crusade and Latin interregnum, the phenomenon was all the more severe. It was manifested in the now limited art of the court with a far greater severity and constraint. High court women still wore the *delmatikion*, made of one or other of the regulation brocades, but in a form that was plainer, looser and more all-enveloping, and more buttoned-up, than ever before. Their headgear consists of one style of flaring pointed coronet, like that of the empress, but lower. There is no sign of the *propolôma*, and the *maforion* had become confined to the use of the *augousta*. No other accessories were in evidence.

JUNIOR COURTIERS, PALAIOLOGIAN ERA

The undress garments of the court retain the motif first borne by the *skaramangion* in previous eras – sleeves very much longer than human arms. The less eminent version, the *lapatza*, was worn with its sleeves folded back and tucked through the belt, with freedom of movement allowed by openings in the armpit in a manner harking back to one form of military coat of the tenth century. Left: this man is a *prôtoallagator*, a military judicial officer who carries a selectively gilded mace as his emblem of office. His outfit is completed by the junior form of *skaranikon*.

The court still needed a throng of folk to keep it running day to day. It is not surprising to find that the *kortinarioi*, staff of the imperial tent, had designated clothing. Right: that the headscarf is called *skoufia*, a word derived from Arabic, suggests it was a re-introduction rather than a recollection of the *maforion* of past Byzantine use. The *kortinarioi* are further unusual in that their leg- and footwear are regulated, which is otherwise only true of the emperor and a couple of ranks below him.

PLATE

24

On the edge of the court, Palaiologian era

As noted elsewhere, women's clothing always tended to change more slowly than that of men, and with the increasingly difficult circumstances of the empire and the deteriorating position of women in the fourteenth and fifteenth centuries, that can only have become worse. This women is of sufficient status and wealth that she could endow a church and have her portrait painted therein, yet the plainness and conservatism of her clothing may not simply be a gesture of humility. Striped women's headgear is a motif that goes back to Late Antiquity, but was much less in evidence in the middle Byzantine period. Its recurrence here probably has more do with the fact that stripes are the simplest, and hence cheapest, decorated fabric to weave.

AGE OF CHANGE

1025 TO 1204

4

Tracing developments in regalia and clothing through the eleventh to thirteenth centuries is problematic. There are no traces of *taktikon* manuscripts from this period.[1] The absence in the Komnênan and Angelid periods does seem curious. Scattered references from the moderately abundant literature of that era indicate significant changes in titles and regalia. Perhaps that in itself is part of the explanation. It may have been that the state of the *taxis* was in such flux that there was no time to compose a record of sufficient literary merit that it was deemed to deserve preservation. Another factor may be the converse of the re-integrative and reaffirming need associated with the tenth-century and fourteenth-century sources. Notwithstanding the encroachments of the Normans from the West, and the Seljuk Turks from the East, which were, in any case, turned back from time to time, the eleventh and twelfth centuries were a time of economic growth for Byzantium.[2] Economic conditions and social confidence are bound up inextricably, so we may well infer that the expansion in the economy was mirrored by some sense of optimism and assurance in the aristocracy and court that reflected less of a need for the reassurance of strongly traditionalist ritualism. Certainly this era sees the greatest internally generated changes in the court and its accoutrements.

Yet the nature of the literature of the eleventh and twelfth century does not unequivocally support this theory. Its relative abundance supports the notion of greater affluence and stability. Its greater secularity could be taken to support the idea that greater assurance required less bolstering from religion. Yet in the actual construction of the texts we see the triumph of another form of traditionalism – Atticism. The imitation of classical authors was by no means a novelty in the eleventh century. It had been in evidence since the first century BCE, and had enjoyed a fluctuating career through the eras.[3] The notable authors of the eleventh and twelfth centuries took to it with renewed enthusiasm, avoiding, as far as they could, any mention of terms, objects and even people that were not known to the ancients, and recycling one antiquated expression after another to describe items of more recent provenance when detail was deemed to be a desirable adornment to the text.[4] It certainly much surpassed the sort of 'soft-core' antiquarianism that can be detected in the Porfurogennêtan literary corpus, which is delightfully rendered into pictorial form in sources such as the *Menologion of Basil II*. Did this reflect some psychological undercurrent, or should it simply be regarded as a contrived literary fashion of no wider significance? No certain conclusions on that can be offered, and it can merely be observed that it makes the task here all the harder in depriving us of much detail for much of the eleventh century and the Komnênan era.

The later eleventh century was a period of some change in the upper echelons of the court, both in its structure and consequently to a lesser degree in the regalia. The twelfth century saw even greater upheavals in both areas. For the lower ranks the conclusion presented in the previous chapters, that almost all the non-imperial regalia tunics named in the *Book of Ceremonies* had *persikomanikia* and were distinguished according to rank and name by colour and decorative scheme, is strikingly borne out in pictorial sources of the eleventh and twelfth centuries. Two of the emperors in the second and third quarters of the eleventh century, Constantine IX and Michael VI, are noted, albeit by commentators already disposed to be critical of them, for having inducted unusual numbers of new courtiers and thereby devalued some ranks.[5] A new rank had appeared in the first half of the eleventh century which was to become very visible in the latter part of the century, that of *prôedros*. The new rank was evidently a somewhat populous one, unlike the singular *prôedros* of the Senate, which had briefly existed in the previous century. Alexios I is also well known to have multiplied the number of higher ranks (Table 1).[6] His Son, John II, then counteracted the effect by eliminating ranks such as *patrikios*, which had been modest enough in the tenth century and had become further devalued. These changes evidently did have an influence on the regalia system, albeit at first only at the higher ranks, while the lower ranks show signs of little change into the twelfth century.

One complex of changes appears to have served to systematise the court in a distinctly different way from tenth-century practice. In the earlier period court functional ranks were dominated by, or confined to, eunuchs, but honorific ranks were open to both eunuchs and entire males, whilst within each specific rank, the eunuch component was deemed to be superior. In the middle portion of the eleventh century it seems that upper ranks were split along this artificial gender line, with the prefix *prôto-* coming to designate the eunuch component. This phenomenon is most clearly visible with the creation of *prôtoprôedros* in the 1060s. This trend was evidently reversed in the reforms initiated by Alexios I Komnênos, under whom the influence of eunuchs in the court diminished, and the prefix simply became a way of multiplying rank distinctions.[7] We have, alas, little or no definite information as to the regalia with which many of the new ranks were vested.

In the second half of the eleventh century we have the benefit of some remarkable and unique documents for our study. Most significant is folio 2r of the Paris manuscript of the *Homilies of John Chrysostom* (Coislin 79) which shows the emperor attended by four courtiers. Each of these men is labelled with his rank and duty and all are dressed in a manner that evidently represents the regalia of the time. Three of the attendants hold the rank of *prôedros* and the fourth that of *prôtoprôedros*. Amongst the texts there are the wills of Kouropalatês Sumbatios Pakourianos and his wife Kalê, both made in the last decade of the century.[8] Neither of these contain garments which can be conclusively identified as regalia, but do include high possibilities. The precise identification of garments in these documents is made somewhat difficult by the prevalent use of the ancient generic term *himation*. In the will of Kouropalatissa Kalê Pakourianê it is at least clear enough that they refer to dresses, mantles being indicated by *manduas* and *sagion*. In the bequest of Sumbatios Pakourianos it does seem likely that the *himatia* are also main garments, in view of the general evidence that cloaks had ceased to be everyday wear for middle Byzantine men, and had become restricted to regalia. A coat (*kavadion*) is also mentioned, yet it would not be safe to conclude that the garments described as *himatia* necessarily could not include coats. One of the *himatia* was given to Sumbatios by Emperor Alexios I. However, even this cannot be taken necessarily to indicate regalia – despite the fact that the *Klêtôrologion* says that a *kouropalatês* receives his regalia garments from the hand of the emperor,[9] and the *Book of Ceremonies* describes how the emperors place the cloak upon the man being promoted[10] – for gifts of clothing were a common sign of favour, which might even be actively sought.[11] All the garments mentioned in Pakourianos' will are given to two of his 'men' – servants, or possibly amongst the slaves freed by the testament – which makes it still less probable that they were regalia. One wonders, therefore, what became of his regalia, which must have consisted at least of a tunic and cloak, each made of one of the regulation brocades. In the normal course of events anything not explicitly disposed of by Sumbatios' will would have passed on to his wife, Kalê, who survived him, a process which would well explain why his will is brief while hers is very extensive and detailed. Indeed, amongst the things Kalê Pakourianê disposes of are some garments which had manifestly come from her husband, and others which might well be his regalia. These will be discussed at a suitable point below.

Moving into the twelfth century, sources are more scattered, yet sufficient to indicate major changes. In the literary field, the pre-eminent sources are John Kinnamos' account of the reigns of John II and Manuel I Komnênos, and Nikêtas Khoniatês' chronicle up to and including the sack of the City by the Fourth Crusade. In art, the most familiar, indeed, sometime over-used, source is the illuminated Madrid manuscript of the chronicle of Skylitzes. It is nowadays recognised that this volume dates to *c.*1150,[12] and it has been convincingly argued that this manuscript is a novel creation produced in the court of Norman Sicily, and, in addition, that the illuminators who painted it seem to have been of mixed nationality according to their styles, and that even those working in a highly Byzantine style may never have been to Constantinople.[13] I would go further and suggest that some of the models that the illustrators must have worked from, for details they were not so well acquainted with, could themselves have been as much as a century old.[14] Approaching this manuscript cautiously with these considerations in mind, it does, none the less, provide us with some useful evidence. The very fact of the painters being taken out of a milieu of Byzantine aristocratic patronage allowed the Byzantine artists to depict items of common use which were not conventionally acceptable in Constantinople. An example of this is the long-sleeved tunic, *skaramangion*, which is rare in strictly Byzantine art, but which has been seen to have been a normal part of court dress for centuries.

A dramatic contrast to the sparsity of evidence is the extensive detail concentrated in the *Eisitêrioi for Agnes of France* composed and illustrated in 1179.[15] It is accepted that this was an official document prepared within the court to record the wedding of a Western princess to the *kaisar*. Spatharakis specifically noted that the clothing shown confirmed the date as much as any other factor, and Jeffreys justly observed that this manuscript has the potential to make a great contribution to the understanding of Komnênian court dress.[16]

Fabrics, Colours and Decoration

The art of the later eleventh century suggests a very significant change in the presentation of the court which probably began with the emperor's *divêtêsion*. We have seen that the venerable picture presented in the *Book of Ceremonies* is of the regalia of the whole court being overwhelmingly in plain-coloured cloths. Notable exceptions to the pattern are the single appearance of brocaded (*trivlattia*) *divêtêsia* worn by the rulers during military triumphs, and the rarely-worn *trivlattion kôlovion* called the 'cluster' (*votrus*).[17] To throw this observation further into relief, it can be contrasted with the frequent occurrence in the *Book of Ceremonies* of variously coloured and figured cloth in the lesser mantles and casual garment of the court, the *skaramangion*.[18] The art of the period

FIG. 45. Mosaic of Constantine Monomakhos and Zôê in Hagia Sofia, 1028–42, one of the earliest representations of figured cloths in middle Byzantine regalia. Constantine bears an *apokomvion*, while Zôê holds the *akakia*.

confirms this image very consistently. The imperial manuscript par excellence which ushers in the eleventh century, the *Menologion of Basil II*, also reflects this established pattern of court dress, even to the single illustration which shows the earliest surviving representation of a *divêtêsion* made of a brocaded fabric.[19] Within quarter of a century garments of figured cloth became standard for royal portraits, from which there is little deviation for as long as pictures show this garment.[20] In contrast, it should be noted that religious figures, angels and saints, largely retained their plain-coloured garments with *persikomanikia* throughout this period. One of the earliest examples of this process is the mosaic of Constantine Monomakhos and Zôê in Hagia Sofia (fig. 45). The rulers are wearing robes made from a brocade of gold on purple in a geometric tessellation descended from examples seen in early medieval period (fig. 5, right). Interestingly, this is the very same fabric shown in a mosaic of Saint George in high court dress in the Monastery of Xenofon on Mount Athos believed to have been set around 1083 (fig. 46). The mosaic showing Irênê Komnênê (with her husband, John II), set in Hagia Sofia after 1118 provides further evidence on the development of the economy of the court. Irênê's regalia *delmatikion* is made of a red brocade figured with palms worked in gold (fig. 47). This cloth is evidently of the same family as the brocades designated for regalia cloaks of the *proedroi* of the Paris *Homilies of John Chrysostom* manuscript (Coislin 79) and similar ranks depicted late in the previous century. This array of evidence strongly suggests that by the late eleventh century the situation refered to in the *Treatise on the Offices* of there being a set repertoire of brocades manufactured for the court from which courtiers might make a choice was already somewhat in place.

The *Eisitêrioi for Agnes of France* is a further rich source for the evolution of brocade patterns. Several of the women's dresses, the tunic of the man who is probably *megas domestikos* and the furnishings of the tent provided for the princess, exhibit the large rondel motif seen on the garb of the Coislin 79 *prôtoprôedros* and slightly later sources. The other dresses and some of the men's cloaks show a newer style of a tessellation with a motif in each panel which are plainly precursors of the standard court brocades shown in the *Lincoln Typikon* (fig. 60). Brocades of this pattern were produced in the eleventh century, but apparently only in monochrome.[21] Evidently there were advances in technique which allowed such silks to be produced in greater quantities.

FIG. 46. Saint George depicted in the regalia of a high courtier of the late eleventh century. His deep purple *khitôn* and red *khlamus* are opulently figured in a manner which had begun with the rulers and then become typical as the century advanced. Mosaic, Monastery of Xenofon, Athos.

Regalia Items Common to Various Ranks and Functions

Headgear

This is an area which saw one of the most visible changes from the custom of the tenth century. In that period, cloth hoods and headscarves, *vêlaria*, *maforia* and *felônia*, were the only non-imperial headgear used by men as regalia, and the wearing of hats was forbidden in the emperor's presence. By the third quarter of the eleventh century this prohibition on hats had been abandoned, as we see primarily illustrated in the Paris *Homilies* manuscript (Coislin 79). The four courtiers attending the emperor on folio 2r all wear hats. The two on the left wear a plain, white dome (chart 8.4a), and those on the right sport a red hat with a long point falling to their left which has a three-lobed fin at the end (chart 8.3). Both these hats are also very commonly illustrated in the Madrid Skylitzes, and can be corroborated from other eleventh-century sources. In considering these images we are confronted with a number of issues. The men in the Coislin 79 picture are manifestly dressed in regalia according to their main garments. Yet the distribution of hats does not follow a similar pattern, which would require the three *proedroi* to be wearing a common type of hat, while the *prôtoprôedros* wore another. Two possible hypotheses may account for this. One is that although hats had become customary court wear, the precise form of them was not regulated at this time, and so the illuminator was at liberty to compose his picture symmetrically. The other possibility is that hats may have come to relate to a different set of parameters, that of function within the court rather than position in the hierarchy. The Coislin 79 courtiers are labelled with their functions as well as their ranks. These range from lowly *dekanos* and *epi tou kanikleiou*, to the highly placed *megas primikêrios* and *prôtovestiarios*. These functions, however, also do not correlate in any obvious way with the distribution of headgear, so this theory must be discounted.

The acceptance of hats in the imperial presence should not be taken to imply a swift or complete disappearance of the *felônion*. In its context as regalia, pictorial sources continue to show it into the twelfth century. The anomalous depiction of a hat on the *eparkhos* shown in the Madrid Skylitzes may be indicative of a change, but equally may illustrate the artist's

FIG. 47. John II Komnênos and Irênê. Once again, in the conventional manner, the Emperor holds an *apokomvion*, while the Empress bears the *akakia*. Note the arched superstructure of John's crown, so much more prominent than earlier versions, and Irênê's *pniktarion*, the oval brooch holding the top of her *lôros* tail and the fact that she wears a *delmatikion* rather than a *divêtêsion*. After 1118. Hagia Sofia.

unfamiliarity with Constantinopolitan practice, as hitherto noted. More evidence is needed to resolve that particular issue. The conspicuous absence of any mention of headgear from the encomium on the eparkhial regalia written by Christopher of Mitylênê can be easily explained by the fact that he was commenting upon regalia unique to that position.[22] Support for the conclusion that twelfth-century representation of the *felônion* is not just a matter of iconographic continuity can be seen in Khoniatês' specific mention of senatorial headgear (*kalumma sunklêtikôs*).[23] His description of this item as 'well-woven' (*exufasmenon*) shows that it is not a type of hat, which are usually made of non-woven materials such as fur or felt. The practice of assembling hats from cloth was known,[24] but it is unlikely that such an item would merit the description 'well-woven'. Hence, this item should be recognised as the continuation of the hood or headscarf that had been part of senatorial regalia since the fourth century, and which continued to be well illustrated through this century in more realistic sources as well as stylised ones. This reference in Khoniatês shows furthermore that the evolution of regalia that is so evident higher up the hierarchy had had a much lesser effect at lowly levels, such as the much-diminished Senate.

In manuscripts of the eleventh century two hats began to be depicted which are plainly the ancestors of the two forms of *skaranikon* of the fourteenth-century *Treatise on the*

FIG. 48. A man in a Bulgarian hat and *zoupa* assaults a Byzantine gentleman wearing the common ensemble of *kausia* and *skaramangion* while a lady wearing a *propolôma* looks on out of window. Eleventh century. St. Mark's Library, Venice, ms 479, *Kunegetika*, f. 33r.

Offices. They are both descended from the Persian *kalansuwa* or *kulâh*.[25] As noted above, the form commonly illustrated in court contexts, or on men of higher status, is a white dome which is usually plain. In addition to the Coislin 79 group portrait, it is worn by Prôedros Iôannês, donor of the *Speer Lectionary*, various males in the Venice *Kunegetika* (fig. 48, right),[26] pictures of Julian the tax collector, addressee of a homily of Gregory of Nazianzos (fig. 54),[27] and various men in the *Eisitêrioi for Agnes of France*. In the majority of cases this hat was worn in company with informal garb rather than regalia. Some examples in the Madrid Skylitzes manuscript have a line of three to six dots running up the front (Chart 8.4b),[28] and a very few of them are red, in place of the standard white.[29] The less-common type exclusively seen on common men is a truncated black cone, derived from the form of *kalansuwa* called *tawîla* – 'tall' (Chart 8.5).[30] Steingass' modern definition of *kulâh* specifies the same form and colour as are seen in Byzantine sources.[31] This hat appears together with both the dome form and the red shaggy fishtailed hat in an eleventh-century manuscript in the Bibliothèque Nationale, Paris.[32] The commonality of the name in Persian use does much to explain the otherwise somewhat perplexing practice in the late sources of giving the same name to hats of such different shape. In the eleventh and twelfth century, they also undoubtedly shared a title, probably *kausia* as an adaptation of *kalansuwa*.[33]

The red, shaggy hat with a trifurcated tail is evidently one of the many foreign borrowings assimilated into Byzantine use in the tenth or early eleventh century. Aside from the Coislin 79 group portrait, the other reliably eleventh-century source in which this hat appears is the Venice *Kunegetika* (fig. 48, left).[34] There, it is part of a style of dress that is used as a signifier of Bulgarian identity, in which context it is corroborated in the Madrid Skylitzes.[35] This hat is also seen in the company of the *kausia* in the Coislin 79 portraits. The herald of the *Eisitêrioi for Agnes of France* is probably also wearing this type of hat, which could well be the latest date of its appearance in Byzantine art.[36]

In terms of pictorial sources of this era, one hat, a simple cylinder, mostly red,[37] seems to be almost unique to the Madrid Skylitzes, yet it may be the survival of an ancient form. Virtually identical headgear appears on reliefs of the earlier Roman

FIG. 49. Coronation of Leo V as co-emperor with Michael I as presented in the Madrid Skylitzes manuscript. Notable aspects are the *lavara* held by the royals, the senior ruler's *kontomanikion*, the hats on the two courtiers at right, and the senior eunuch on the left wearing a *lôros*. Biblioteca Nacional de España, Vitr. 26-2, f. 10v.

Empire, including the porphyry group of emperors now built into the facade of Saint Mark's basilica in Venice.[38] It is likely that this is the 'Pannonian' that Vegetius recommended that Roman soldiers wear in order to accustom themselves to headgear.[39] A hat made as a simple closed cylinder of felt was found at Mons Claudianus in Egypt, dating from the second century, and such a construction may have survived.[40] Later depictions in the round seem to suggest they were made in a manner similar to the *propolôma*: a straight-sided felt 'sleeve' (to use modern millinery parlance) with the domed end turned up into the body, which is left open above.

Some courtiers depicted in the Madrid Skylitzes (fig. 49) and later in the *Eisitêrioi for Agnes of France* wear a large, white asymmetrical hat. This hat is evidently related to the women's *propolôma* (figs 44, 57) and constructed in a very similar manner.[41] A large conical 'sleeve' of felt has the closed end turned partly up into the body. Then the open end is flattened and sewn shut. In a *propolôma* the 'sleeve' is left whole and hence remains symmetrical, while for the male version the open end is cut to a slant or descending curve before being closed (Chart 8.10). The male and female versions were plainly worn differently as well, with the long axis of the *propolôma* following the line of the shoulders side to side (Plate 17), while the man's hat was worn with its spine running front to back with the point forward (Plate 19, left). It may be significant that this arrangement bears some resemblance to the imperial triumphal *toufa,* with which it is clearly conflated in late Byzantine art[42] (Plate 12, centre. fig. 25). As with the *propolôma*, it is evident that this hat was a distinct affectation of the high levels of the court, and more eminent than the Bulgarian hats, which appear to have had more mundane uses, and the white dome *kausia* discussed above. The latter observation indicates that this hat pertained to ranks higher than *prôedros*. There is no term that can be firmly identified as potentially applicable to this hat, but *kapasion* might be employed because, as will be explained later, the hat which should be identified as *kapasion* in the fourteenth-century court can be seen to be a truncated form of this one.

Evstathios of Thessaloniki describes the garb 'foisted' upon Andronikos Komnênos by his partisans when they sought to elevate him to the throne in 1183. The ensemble consisted of the expected red shoes and crown, but also red clothing and a 'smoky covering about his head'.[43] The author attributes the two latter elements to the customs of the Laz (Georgian) mercenaries who were much behind the movement. The hat seems to have become something of a trademark for Andronikos for it is also mentioned by Khoniatês. In his account of the siege of Thessaloniki, Evstathios is the first to use the term *skiadion* ('little shadow') in referring to a hat captured from the attackers.[44] A passage from Nikêforos Gregoras describes a *skiadion*, saying that its 'upper part presented a pyramidal appearance, while its lower portion was also somewhat hollow, but completely smooth'.[45] A white hat with a conical upper and broad brim, a certain contender for the name 'little shadow', can be seen on a country dweller in a nativity in a manuscript in the Great Lavra on Athos (fig. 50). This is another hat which will become very prominent in the regalia of the Palaiologian era.

FIG. 50. Detail of a nativity scene showing a man wearing a *skiadion*. Great Lavra, Athos, codex. 1.1., f. 114v.

Cloaks

Cloaks evidently retained the importance indicated for them in the *Book of Ceremonies*. The range of portraits of the later part of the eleventh century give us a good indication of the ways in which they have changed at the upper end of the court. The most commonly worn regalia mantles in the tenth century were plain colours, and only the minor ones, overwhelmingly of the *sagion/mantion* type, were made of patterned fabrics.

As was previously noted, the ancient form of the *khlamus* was oval, and worn folded along the long axis, which was crossed by the *tavlia*. This probably survived into the tenth century for some ranks, but at some point between the

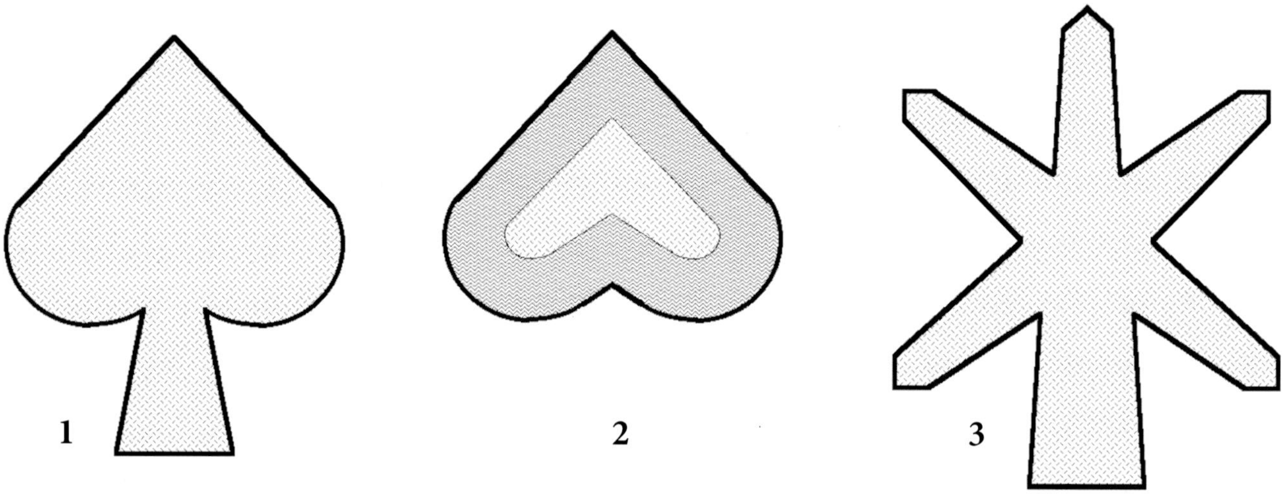

FIG. 51. Motifs worked into court brocades in the late eleventh and twelfth centuries: 1: ivy leaf (*kissofulon*), 2: droplet (*vdellion*), 3: palm tree (*foinix*).

middle of that century and the middle of the eleventh century it underwent a major transformation that had spread across the court. It had been split along that main axis, and was now a semi-oval with a straight edge, a shape much closer to the lesser capes. This change also facilitated the *khlamus* being adorned with a border visible all the way around, which we have seen hitherto on the cloak of St Helena depicted in the last quarter of the ninth century (fig. 14). The increasing use of brocades through the court first manifested itself by application to the *khlamus*. Following these changes, the mantles show a thorough merging of the characteristics of the *khlamus* and the *sagion/mantion* as the century progresses. No longer do they conform to the distinction which had been largely preserved since the time of John Lydos in the sixth century, that the *mantion* 'falls no further than the knee' and 'does not have the decorations we call *tavlia*',[46] and that the *khlamus* is fastened on the shoulder while the *mantion/sagion* is pinned in the centre of the chest. This conflation is most clearly illustrated in the four courtiers of the Coislin 79 manuscript. Most significantly, their fabrics are entirely brocades of a red base with a variety of gold figures. In this colour scheme, and in the fact that ivy leaves are one of the emblems, we may see some visual continuity with the old regalia of the *prôedros* of the Senate, perhaps suggesting some carry-over of regalia from that office to the later *prôedros*. The gold figures used on the capes are ivy leaves (*kissofula*) alone (Coislin 79, f. 2r, left), droplets (*vdellia*[47]) alone (Coislin 79, f. 2r, inner right), palms (*foinikes*) mixed with droplets (Coislin 79, f. 2r, far right) (fig. 51). It is clear from this that at this point, midway through the second half of the eleventh century, the stipulation for some regalia garments had already become something like 'a brocade such as would be chosen from the accustomed ones', in the words of the Palaiologian *Treatise on the Offices*.[48] These emblems were to become standard for court brocades through the eleventh and twelfth centuries and beyond.[49]

The account of a donation to the Monastery of Farfa in Italy made by a *prôedros* named Arguros in 1057 sheds further light upon the late eleventh-century regalia cloak. The chronicler recounts the details of the gift: 'six thousand bezants and a precious cloak [*mantum*] wholly of silk and figured with gold, which was the noble garment of his rank, that had a value greater than a hundred pounds of the purest silver'.[50]

In translating this passage, Guillou loosely rendered *mantum* as 'coat' in accord with modern French, but we can see that the chronicler phrased his account with technical precision in employing the Latin cognate of *mantion*.[51] Even allowing for some exaggeration, it is a remarkable insight into the phenomenal cost entailed by being a high courtier in the eleventh century. The description is very redolent of the mantle of the donor of the Monastery of Dionysiou codex 61, whose tunic as well as cloak suggests that he may well have held this rank or something close to it (fig. 52).

The will of Kouropalatissa Kalê Pakourianê, who distributed her personal effects in 1098 as she entered a monastery, contains a number of garments which can be reasonably inferred to have come from her late husband Sumbatios. The clearest example is the *epilôrikion* which she left to a freedman (*apeleutheros*).[52] Amongst other items which may have come from Sumbatios Pakourianos is a cloak which was undoubtedly part of his regalia. Hence a *kouropalatês* would also have worn a red silk cape figured in gold like those illustrated on the *proedroi* in the various sources previously noted. The cloak left by Kalê Pakourianê is described as 'my red *mandion* of fine silk with gold bands running down it'.[53] This description admittedly does not make it explicit that the 'gold bands' (*khrusonarthêkôn*) are bands of distinct motifs, as on the cloak of a *prôedros*, but such fine precision can hardly have been necessary in the context, while the loose terminology of the time and the context leaves that possibility open, as the editors

FIG. 52. A high courtier, possibly a *prôedros*, of the mid-eleventh century. His lack of beard may indicate he is a eunuch. Observe the finely rendered Persian sleeve, and typical patterning of ivy leaves and palm trees worked in gold on the red field of his *khlamus*. Dionysiou Monastery, Athos, codex 61, f. 1v.

of the document acknowledge.[54] The fact that Pakourianê left this cape to a *prôedrissa* offers further support to the possibility of it being regalia, for the recipient or her husband would have been fully entitled to wear such an item.

Edged cloaks continued through the twelfth century. The donor portrait of Basil the Prôtospatharios from before 1169 shows his as being more in the style of the older *khlamus* – plain red cloth with gold *tavlia* as well as gold edging, worn fastened on the shoulder (fig. 53).[55] In contrast, the anonymous donor of a manuscript in the Lavra on Mount Athos, probably also from the first half of the century, would appear to have a rather higher rank.[56] His cloak is a purple brocade with gold squares and gold edging, but lacks *tavlia*, and is worn fastened more centrally.

Khoniatês tells that in addition to their 'well-woven head coverings', senators of the late twelfth century were still wearing a white linen cape, harking back to the *savanion* of the tenth century.[57] This again shows that at the bottom end of the aristocracy changes in regalia had been far less pronounced that at the top, and old forms tended to persist.

'Persian-sleeved' garments and their successors

The continuity of 'Persian-sleeved' garments through the eleventh century and into the twelfth is unproblematic. In addition to the royal portraits, there are pictures of various other ranks to confirm the spread across the court (figs 22, 30, 32, 33, 34, 40, 46, 52, 53). An invaluable survival is a donor portrait of Theodore Gavras in a dated manuscript executed in 1067.[58] Gavras is recorded in the picture as holding the rank of *patrikios* at the time of its production. This was a junior rank in the tenth century, and was to slip further with the proliferation of higher ranks. The regalia garment of a bearded *patrikios* had been a white tunic in the style of the *divêtêsion* with gold decoration, according to Filotheos, and it was called *kamision* in both the *Klêtôrologion* and the *Book of Ceremonies*; at the time Gavras had the portrait painted this was not yet likely to have been altered by the trend for patterned fabrics trickling down from above. The garment Gavras is depicted wearing in his portrait is definitely fitted with 'Persian-sleeves' with contrasting cuffs and sleeve bands. The range of colours used in this manuscript is very limited, and seem either to have been of poor quality or degraded. The colour of the body of Gavras' *kamision* is now quite a dark blue-grey, with the cuffs and sleeve bands a tan shade. His *esôforion* is a lighter grey. The tincture of the cuffs and *sêmenta* of the *kamision* might well be a poor-quality representation that was meant to be gold. The colour of the body, however, even allowing for some deterioration over time, is not likely to have been a regalia colour by any estimation. The most probable explanation is that Theodore Gavras had himself painted wearing a style of garment he was entitled to, but not his actual formal regalia. This presumes that as a man entitled to wear a tunic with *persikomanikia* he might have more than one – his regalia *kamision* with its expensive gold embroidery and all-too-readily-besmirched

FIG. 53. By the late twelfth century, the ranks of *prôtospatharios* and *prôtospatharissa* had slipped a long way down the hierarchy. Hence the donor, Basil, still wears the old regalia with Persian-sleeves, rather than the newer styles borne by the upper court, and a very plain *khlamus*. 1169. Koutloumousiou Monastery, Athos, codex 60, f. 1v.

white colour, which he would wear only on suitable court occasions, and less precious and delicate ones which he could wear on a day-to-day basis and so still exhibit the fact that he had a place at court. This scenario could further explain the tenor of the passage in Achmet with its implication that wearing such a garment was nothing very remarkable.

The last we see of 'Persian-sleeves' is the donor portrait of Prôtospatharios Basil of *c.*1169 (fig. 53).[59] *Prôtospatharios* was the rank immediately above *patrikios* and by the late twelfth century was so degraded by the inflation of offices that it goes without mention in any textual sources of that century, leading to the suggestion that it had been eliminated.[60] Certainly, while his tunic and cloak both retain the crimson colour of the old prôtospathariate *spekion*, there is none of the opulence to them that would once have been seen, or is now seen in higher ranks. In retaining 'Persian-sleeves', Basil's tunic lags far behind the 'state of the art' in the higher court. From the mosaic in Hagia Sofia, believed to have created very early in his reign, and portraits closely following,[61] John II Komnênos is shown wearing sleeves which fit tightly down the entire length of his forearm (fig. 47). The finely detailed donor portrait of Theodore Lêmniotês in the Church of St Anagyroi at Kastoria demonstrates how this is a simplified form derived from the 'Persian-sleeve'. Rather than an attached cuff with buttons, the new form is a one-piece sleeve with a greater number of buttons securing an opening almost the entire length of the forearm (Chart 3.7). This was a construction destined to prevail to the end of the empire, and exerted a major influence on Western fashion in the late thirteenth and fourteenth centuries. It seems fitting to accept that John was responsible for embracing this innovation. The Komnênoi saw themselves as embodying a new phase for a reinvigorated empire. John sought to continue his father's campaigns of consolidation and recovery of territory, and could well have seen such a 'streamlining' of the regalia as a suitable symbol of that outlook. Certainly Khoniatês records his attention to the style of courtiers' hair and footwear and it is not likely that he would neglect more conspicuous aspects.[62]

Half a century later, the *Eisitêroi for Agnes of France* reveals a further major change in the dress paradigm. While the emperor and *kaisar* are wearing close-fitting sleeves which are a simplified version of 'Persian-sleeves' (Chart 3.7), the courtiers are wearing garments with wide, straight sleeves, the *kôlovion* of the tenth century (Chart 3.2). It is also notable that these tunics also have V necklines which have broad edging, but not the 'lapels' of the eleventh-century fashion (see figs 44, 54; Chart 2.6).

Skaramangion

The frequent appearance of the long-sleeved *skaramangion* in the Madrid manuscript of the Skylitzes Chronicle has been taken as being characteristic somewhat more of the eleventh century than the twelfth, yet there are two sources which indicate that this garment did continue in use in the twelfth century. They are the image of a mourner in an icon of the raising of Lazarus in a private collection in Athens, and the portrait of the donor of a manuscript held in the Bodleian Library, Oxford, dated to the late twelfth century, but showing features present in non-regalia tunics of men from at least the late eleventh century if not before, such as the V neckline with lapels (fig. 54; Chart 2.6a/b).[63] Supporting its credibility and sense of continuity, the latter also bears one of the white dome hats noted coming into use in the later eleventh century.

FIG. 54. Julian the tax collector in later eleventh-century garb of a plain white *kausia* and a *kavadion* or tunic with wide lapels and falling collar. Dionysiou Monastery, Athos, codex 61, f. 28v.

Footwear

Christopher of Mitylênê's poem in honour of the appointment of his friend Iôannês to the position of *eparkhos* of the City gives us invaluable evidence of a significant change in this area. In the first instance, it betokens a decline in the stylisation of the regalia. In the tenth century the regalia of the *eparkhos* incorporated *kaligia/kampagia*, still an antiquated sandal-like form of footwear. By the mid-eleventh century this was evidently no longer the case, and we find the first evidence for the proliferation of colour-coded footwear denoting non-imperial rank. Christopher writes of the 'tawny-orange footwear, stridently bright in colour'.[64] The pictures of *eparkhoi* of the eleventh and twelfth centuries do indeed all show boots which are distinctly different in shade from other footwear in the same sources (fig. 34). The boots of the Eparkhos of Kappadokhian Kaisaria are most clearly and distinctly orange,[65] while the others are certainly within a range of shades that could represent that colour, especially the Skylitzes *eparkhos*. This transition from *kampagia* to boots is unlikely to have been confined to the *eparkhos*, so it may be inferred that the Senate also abandoned the antique sandals in the wake of it. The tendency for changes in junior regalia change to lag behind their betters may have delayed this process, but it probably had happened by the middle of the eleventh century.

Al-Kafartâbî, an Arab visitor to Constantinople in 1071, who saw Emperor Rômanos IV Diogenês during the Easter festivities, asserted, after mentioning the red imperial boots (*tzangia*), that ranks below the emperor wore one boot that was red and one that was black.[66] As noted previously, earlier Arab visitors had commented upon the presence of odd-coloured footwear, and had recorded that that practice was confined to the heir apparent. If that information is correct, then evidently this custom had also been the subject of deflation since the tenth century. We are left speculating precisely which 'ranks below the emperor' the visitor was referring to. The courtiers depicted attending upon Emperor Michael Doukas in MS Coislin 79 are shown wearing boots of the same colour, the prosaic black where the shade is discernible, but there were several ranks between them and the emperor. Immediately below the *kaisar* were the *prôtosevastos* and *sevastos*, relatively new ranks normally associated with people with intimate relationships to the emperor and both perhaps created by Constantine Monomakhos.[67] The ancient rank of *nôvellissimos* was also reserved for members of the imperial family, as presumably was the new rank inserted above it, *prôtonôvellissimos*.[68] The boots of mixed colour can be confidently attributed to those four ranks, while the two classes remaining above *prôtoprôedros*, that is *prôtokouropalatês* and *kouropalatês*, who were drawn from the rank and file of the court, would have worn the common black. The tendency for the regalia of the *kaisar* to quite closely resemble that of the emperor, which was already well established in the prior period, makes it almost certain that with this devaluation in the bicoloured footwear, the *kaisar* would have been elevated to wearing entirely red footwear like those of the emperor in order to preserve the prestige of his position. This change may have taken place in the second quarter of the eleventh century, as part of the reforms which gave the *eparkhos* orange boots in place of his *kaligia*.

Footwear is quite frequently mentioned in sources of the twelfth century. Nikêtas Khoniatês tells us that Emperor John II sought to curb foreign influences, particularly in this area, inspecting the shoes of courtiers for the 'form of their fitting'.[69] This probably means that he disapproved of the fashion for longer toes which was developing in Western footwear at this time.[70] An anonymous encomium of the twelfth century, probably for Emperor Manuel I, mentions royal footwear decorated with eagles worked in pearls.[71] Evidently this is an innovation, for nothing in previous literature or art hints at it. It is a practice which survives the dislocation of 1204 and is seen in the late Byzantine court, probably because it was swiftly imitated by neighbouring kingdoms. The stipulation of colour-coded footwear which had been extended to other high ranks and offices in the eleventh century continued to spread in the following century. Writing of the period leading up to the death of John II in 1143, Kinnamos refers to the blue (*kuanos*) footwear of the *sevastokratôr*.[72] This is confirmed in later sources.[73] Anna Komnênê refers only to the crown granted to the *sevastokratôr* as regalia, and since, in addition to the numerous references to the imperial footwear, she does make reference to coloured footwear granted to other people, the absence of any such reference in this case seems significant.[74] Hence, it appears that Alexios did not institute the use of blue boots for the *sevastokratôr*, and that this must also have been an innovation of John II. This change must have had a knock-on effect. The rank of *sevastokratôr* had been placed above that of *kaisar*, who previously had worn red boots like the emperor. Once the blue footwear had been implemented for the *sevastokratôr*, without any further adjustment there would have been the anomalous situation of a now inferior rank wearing the royal colour. The *sevastokratôr* and *kaisar* wore identical crowns from the outset, and it would have been natural that this potential anomaly should have been resolved by making their footwear identical also. Thus, Brand's suggestion that the *kaisar* wore blue boots may be accepted without hesitation.[75] Khoniatês further gives the information that by 1197 the shoes of the *prôtovestiarios* were 'distinctively hued' in a shade he describes elsewhere as 'frog-coloured' (*vatrakheios*).[76] Unfortunately there appears to be no further evidence which would allow us to fix the date of this change more precisely within the twelfth century. It seems probable that with the proliferation of coloured footwear in the upper ranks, the old practice of some high courtiers wearing red and black parti-coloured footwear fell out of use.

Belt

In his account of the sack of Thessaloniki in 1185, Evstathios makes reference to an Alexios Komnênos who 'wore the belt [*zônê*] of *prôtosevastos*'.[77] This belt may be something akin to the gem-encrusted *valtidion* described in the *Klêtôrologion*, or, in view of the high level at which this rank was inserted into the hierarchy, it is perhaps more likely to refer to a *lôros*, as we have seen this term used thus with the *zôstê patrikia* and in Achmet's *Oneirokritikon*.[78]

Batons

Also from Evstathios of Thessaloniki we have confirmation of the continued use of batons as emblems of rank into the twelfth century.[79] The *doux* of Thessaloniki, David Komnênos, belaboured a critic of his defensive policies with his staff (*ravdos*).[80] The position of *doux* became established in the Byzantine court in the period between the completion of the *Book of Ceremonies* and the drafting of the *Escorial Taktikon* between 971 and 975. It seems plausible to attribute this innovation to Emperor Nikêphoros II – it would befit his interest in, and reforming zeal for, the empire's military organisation, for it was a military rank approximately at the level of *stratêgos*, but which at different times could function in effect above or below that rank.[81] The distribution of batons in the *Klêtôrologion* and *Book of Ceremonies* does not follow any obvious logic, but they are associated with some military ranks of no great elevation,[82] so it seems likely that a *doux* carried a baton of rank from the inauguration of the position, and that this persisted through the eleventh and twelfth centuries.

Regalia According to Male Rank or Function

The emperor

Headgear

Art of the eleventh and twelfth centuries has bequeathed a goodly quantity of formal royal portraits. In the case of imperial headgear they show consistent patterns which indicate significant changes from the tenth century which cannot be attributed to transient personal preferences of different emperors and empresses. These patterns reflect both physical changes in the articles themselves, and changes in conventional representation.

Stemma

In the tenth century, imperial figures of both sexes were customarily depicted wearing the junior coronet, called *stefanos*, *diadêma* and *kaisarikion*. The standard imperial *diadêma* of the tenth century was a metal band with two longitudinal strips of ornament flanking a single panel at the front which sometimes extended in a semicircular peak above the top of the body of the crown, and was then often surmounted by a pearled cross for the emperor and a variety of emblems for the empress (Chart 7). On the ivories of Constantine Porfurogennêtos the diadem band is narrow and the top of the emperor's head is visible above it (fig. 24). As we move into the eleventh century we see the first suggestions of *stemmata* in which cross-shaped superstructures start to appear, alongside continued depiction of the *stefanos*. The triumphal portrait of Basil II shows the first change in the pattern of depiction. He wears a crown which has a wide brow band with no visible superstructure. Yet over his head Christ lowers another crown, holding it by one of the transverse bands of the superstructure, thus showing it to be a *stemma* not merely a *diadêma*. A close inspection of the detail of this second crown shows that it is, in fact, the very same crown as the one Basil wears below. The poem which accompanies this picture reaffirms this, explicitly saying, 'Christ tenders with his life-bearing hand from heaven the crown [*stemma*], symbol of rulership.'[83]

That the brow band on these later tenth- to eleventh-century *stemmata* is significantly wider than that of the *diadêma* accounts for why the cruciform superstructure is largely concealed. The royal portraits of Coislin 79 clearly show the tops of the *stemmata* as being filled in with some sort of material but do not show any evidence of the structure of the upper section of the crowns. A close inspection of the crown being bestowed upon Rômanos IV Diogenês on the Cabinet des Médailles ivory plaque shows the domed superstructure of a *stemma* under Christ's hand, but it remains quite a low arch (fig. 27).

The account of Abû al-Fadl Ibrâhîm ibn 'Alî al-Kafartâbî, who witnessed the Easter rites of 1071, confirms the continuity of the multiplicity of crowns mentioned in the *Book of Ceremonies* into the late eleventh century. He specifically mentions what is evidently the 'great white *stemma*' of the earlier source:

> the Byzantine emperors had crowns for different occasions that were suspended over [their heads]. One was called the 'Largest Crown', which was of gold, adorned with various [colours of] corundum, together with a variety of [other] jewels. The crown was usually suspended over the emperor's head when he sat in his audience chamber to receive the natives of his empire and the envoys of kings.[84]

This account may serve to explain some aspects of the earlier sources, and also hint at reasons for the later evolution in crowns. The *Book of Ceremonies* confirms the practice of suspending the crowns in the Khrusotriklinos.[85] This practice is partly for the purpose of maximising the ostentation of court display, particularly when multiple crowns are hung simultaneously, but in the context mentioned by our Arab visitor another factor is likely to have been the weight of the crown. In the course of a long series of receptions a *stemma* could well become very burdensome.

Portraits of the early twelfth century show a major change in the form of the *stemma*. In the mosaics of Hagia Sofia dating from the late 1110s or 1120s, and manuscripts from similar dates, the upper part of the *stemma* has become conspicuously visible as a full hemisphere bearing the same sort of decor as the brow section. Although it has been shown that Alexios I did not originate the cruciform superstructure of the *stemma*, as Anna Komnênê claimed, reference to it as 'hemispherical' probably indicates that he was responsible for making it somewhat more prominent than it had been.[86] Yet Komnênê's qualification that it 'fitted the head well', and the observation that the portraits of Alexios I preserve the convention of the eleventh century in showing the upper part as not so prominent, undermine this notion.[87] On the weight of the evidence, the advent of the grander and more visibly hemispherical crown should be attributed to the emperor first shown wearing it: Alexios' son and successor, John II, who perhaps inaugurated it as compensation for being in the shadow of so successful a predecessor (fig. 47).

Stefanos/kaisarikion

Michael Psellos confirms the continuation into the later eleventh century of the distinction in crowns between emperor and *kaisar* by describing the indulgence granted to the rebellious Isaak Komnênos by Michael VI.[88] The author uses the technically precise terms *stefanos*, for the *kaisarikion* that ought to have been the best crown that Komnênos was to wear, and *stemma* for the imperial crown that Michael saw fit to concede to him.

While there is good reason to doubt that Alexios Komnênos originated the *stemma* with the cruciform superstructure, what can certainly be accepted from Komnênê's account is that, in creating the rank of *sevastokratôr*, her father endowed its incumbents with the right to wear a *diadêma* or *kaisarikion* along with the *kaisar*.[89] One significant eleventh-century illumination shows a *stefanos* of substantially different form to that shown in earlier pictures (fig. 55). The band is narrower and plainer, while a semicircular panel projects upwards in the centre. This can be accepted as accurate, for it clearly presages the *stemmatoguron* of the *Treastise on the Offices*.

FIG. 55. An early depiction of the very simple coronet that would be called *stemmatoguron* in the fourteenth century. Mid-eleventh century. Dionysiou Monastery, Athos, codex 587, f. 129r.

Two sources indicate the survival of this type of *stefanos* through the twelfth century, although its status is questionable. The earlier example is a marble relief now in the Dumbarton Oaks collection.[90] It has been suggested that this represents John II when he was *kaisar*.[91] The second is the portrait of Alexios V Mourtzouflos from the Vienna manuscript of Khoniatês.[92] Spatharakis noted that this depiction lacked the normal imperial accoutrements, showing the subject in a *kavadion* rather than regalia.[93] In this case it would be reasonable to assume a continuation of the long-established principle of the emperor wearing a coronet with informal dress. The Dumbarton Oaks marble, in contrast, must be passed over as an unreliable source, for there are major problems with the way in which the regalia is depicted, such as the unprecedented combination of a *khlamus* over a *lôros*, and fact that the *lôros* is itself not continuous.

The question that hangs over the use of the *kaisarikion* in the twelfth century results from the observation that in formal portraits (including coinage) the *kaisar* is always shown wearing a crown that is virtually identical to that of the emperor. The inference to be drawn is that in formal contexts, this coronet was only worn by a *sevastokratôr*.

Toufa/tiara

The survival of this item is again confirmed by Abû al-Fadl Ibrâhîm ibn 'Alî al-Kafartâbî who, in addition to referring to the 'great white *stemma*', also describes the triumphal *toufa* of the late eleventh century in minute detail which does much to corroborate the Bamberg Tapestry (fig. 28): 'Another was the Crested Crown, which he set on his head when he returned from a campaign in which he vanquished his enemy. This [crown] was studded with precious stones, and its crest, which protrudes over his face, was of ruby stones.'[94]

The twelfth century is conspicuously devoid of both pictures of, and references to, the *toufa*. It is very possible that it ceased to be used following the major regalia reforms that took place that century.

Main garments

The *divêtêsion* is very well illustrated through the eleventh century. An addition which made its appearance as the century advanced were decorative panels partly or wholly encircling the upper sleeves. As straight strips, these had been a feature of Byzantine dress since Late Antiquity,[95] while court dress had preserved the older pattern of decoration falling off the shoulder from the yoke. After they made their first appearance on formal court dress, the sleeve motifs continue in the rounded form which was common to the shoulder-placed style of Late Antiquity. This change in decoration, with the adoption of figured cloth, illustrates the beginning of a tendency for court dress to shed its artificiality and begin to look more like everyday clothing, albeit much more ornate. This process also doubtless reflects an outcome of the economic revival which took place through this and the following century.[96] Apart from these two changes, the other characteristics of the *divêtêsion* are preserved through the eleventh century: the gold-embroidered and jewelled yoke and hem band and, of course, the full sleeves pleated into long, narrow cuffs which ultimately define the class of *persikomanikia*.

Once more, al-Kafartâbî, after seeing Emperor Rômanos

IV during Easter 1071, described what was undoubtedly his *divêtêsion* thus:

> a garment of the kind their emperors wear with great difficulty, as they are neither able to hold it up properly nor sit in it because of its heavy weight and because they are too weak to carry it ... the garment contained thirty thousand pearls, each of which weighed one *mithqâl*, and ... was priceless, nothing comparable being known on earth.[97]

As discussed above, early in the twelfth century, a simplified descendant of the *persikomanikion* came into use. It retained the mode of being buttoned closely to the forearm, but with a simpler structure, being made in a single piece. Accompanying this, a garment which was quite marginal in the tenth century, the *kontomanikion*, gained a new prominence, being illustrated in royal and quasi-royal portraits[98] (fig. 59) and represented in a surviving example derived from Constantinopolitan practice (fig. 19).

Over-garments

The *lôros* is more evident in art of the eleventh and twelfth centuries than ever before, showing it in use by non-imperial persons for the first time since the consuls of Late Antiquity. The pictures of non-imperial *lôroi* still do not match the broad distribution described in the *Book of Ceremonies*, but are entirely confined to the person of the *eparkhos*. It is possible that this could match an actual change in court practice. It would have been fitting for the *eparkhos* to continue to wear a *lôros* as a symbol of his wielding of delegated coercive imperial power, while the other members of the court, who had worn it for no particularly good reason, may have ceased to have it as regalia. I have previously noted the example of Prôtosevastos Alexios Komnênos of Thessaloniki in 1185, who wore a regalia 'belt' (*zônê*), which probably means a *lôros*.[99] The most probable scenario is that in the context of the modernisation of the regalia and simplification of regalia systems in the eleventh and twelfth centuries, and the tendency for the proliferating upper ranks occupied by members of the extended royal family to gain quasi-imperial attributes, those occasions which saw widespread *lôros*-wearing in the tenth century were dispensed with, while the highest ranks wore them more routinely, perhaps with the degree of ornamentation reflecting a hierarchical structure.

Both imperial and lesser *lôroi* show similar features of evolution, alongside the continuation of the generic form. The yoke of the 'T pattern' *lôros* (Chart 6.4) became wider in the early eleventh century, extending inwards to the neck of the wearer. The decoration on the *lôroi* then produced two distinct appearances overlying this basic shape. One preserved the dominant appearance of the yoke, whilst the other suggested straight edges with 'epaulettes'. The overall shape of these two forms is identical, with the distinction being suggested purely by the distribution of the decoration on them. This century saw another rare form of *lôros* – a single, very wide straight band, the 'tabard style' (Chart 6.5). It is only shown unmistakably on the Rômanos coronation ivory (fig. 27) in the Cabinet des Médailles, Paris.[100] In addition to the Rômanos ivory, the Dionysiou *eparkhos* may be wearing a *lôros* of this type, however his *felônion* precludes certainty, and it may also be a 'epaulette / yoke'-style *lôros* (Chart 6.6). The *eparkhos* of the Madrid Skylitzes wears an older, rare type of *lôros* – the 'Porphyrogennêtan' (Chart 6.3).

Prôedros

Prôedros has the distinction of being one of the most copiously illustrated ranks in the court, other than the emperor. In addition to the three *proedroi* of the Coislin 79 manuscript, there is also Prôedros Iôannês, the donor of the *Speer Lectionary*.[101] As is to be expected, this picture is a much poorer-quality painting, but shows great similarities to the Coislin 79 picture. Iôannês wears a dome hat (*kausia* discussed above) like two of the Coislin 79 courtiers, although only the outline remains, so it is not certain that it was the same white. The Coislin 79 *proedroi* all wear split over-tunics all made of the same brocade of a diaper pattern on a blue base. Unfortunately, due to the fact that their upper bodies are fully enveloped in their cloaks, it not possible to discern the crucial point of detail in their sleeves and cuffs. The tunic of Prôedros Iôannês' is a little different. It does not show a split in the skirt, and although blue, appears to be of a plain cloth with modest contrasting cuffs, hem and *klavoi* in gold. The sleeves may appear to be the simple *roukhon* type, however comparisons with other sources show that to be deceptive. They are, in fact, *persikomanikia*, but in his more pronounced donatorial gesture, the fullness of Prôedros Iôannês' sleeves falls further into the crook of his elbows and is therefore much less readily discernible than in other pictures. The style of Iôannês' tunic is well in keeping with older styles, and artistic, or perhaps personal, traditionalism *may* account for the various contrasts with those of the Coislin gentlemen, although there is another possibility suggested by the further evidence of another donor portrait of a man of unspecified rank.

The portrait from the late eleventh century is that of the donor of Dionysiou codex 61 (fig. 52).[102] There is no written information about this individual, but his clothing offers strong clues.[103] When we compare the Dionysiou donor to the other pictures of *proedroi* we find there are resemblances and differences which are too precise to be insignificant. As noted previously, his cloak is again made of a brocade of a red field bearing gold ivy leaves and palms, edged with gold but with no *tavlion*. It is fastened with a single round brooch in the manner of the *Speer Lectionary* manuscript donor, instead of the two round brooches of the men of Coislin 79. This brocade is not identical to any of the labelled *proedroi*, but, as has been seen, none of those are identical to each other, and this is unquestionably in the same ornamental repertoire. The lack of *tavlion* resembles the *Speer Lectionary* donor. Most interestingly, the Dionysiou donor wears his cloak in the manner of a *khlamus*, fastened on the shoulder rather than on the chest like the others. Thus it is clear that *khlamus* and *sagion* had been thoroughly conflated by this period, not merely in decoration, but in the manner of wearing also. Having diverse ranks of the court wearing identical cloaks was a long-established pattern which probably continued through the eleventh century, so there are only two conclusions that may be drawn from the cloak. One is that this man must be of the rank of *prôedros* or higher. The second is that this picture is likely to be a little earlier than the Coislin 79 portraits. The characteristics of the man's tunic are equally precise. Like all the others it is dark blue, but a plain cloth like that of the *Speer* donor. Again, like the tunic of the *Speer* donor, it has gold cuffs and hem with *klavoi*. The Dionysiou portrait also shows the tunic to have a large gold yoke and sleeve bands matching the hem and cuffs, and, crucially, *persikomanikia*. These *persikomanikia* have only a modest volume, and the pouching is shown falling well away from the cuffs. The cuffs themselves are wider than those of the *Speer Lectionary* donor, but narrower than those of imperial *divêtêsia*. The sum of the similarities and differences between the Dionysiou donor and the other pictures suggests that the Dionysiou donor was probably of a rank somewhat higher than *prôedros*, most probably *kouropalatês* or *nôvellissimos*.

The consistent differences between these two groups suggest a further possibility. The date of the Coislin manuscript is known with considerable precision – the 1070s.[104] The other two are matters of debate, neither being dated more precisely than the second half of the eleventh century on stylistic and prosopographical grounds.[105] It seems likely that the similarities within, and the differences between, the two groups of men are not simply haphazard – they represent a definite change in the regalia. In view of two discernible trends through this period – one being the tendency for regalia tunics to have been simplified in their applied decor, and the other being the trickle-down effect in the use of brocade – the *Speer*/Dionysiou group may be seen to represent an earlier stage. A change in the regalia of the *prôedros*, and perhaps *kouropalatês*, from monochrome blue tunics with gold embroidery to blue diapered brocade, and from simply-edged cloaks to cloaks also with *tavlia*, could reasonably have coincided with the creation of the rank of *prôtoprôedros* in the decade before the Coislin portrait, the 1060s.

Despite the lack of more fully detailed literary sources, the combination of these pictures with the passage from Italy given above which describes the regalia cloak of the *prôedros* makes the regalia of the late eleventh-century *prôedros* one of the most precisely defined non-imperial outfits of the middle period court.

Prôtoprôedros

The fourth courtier of the Coislin 79 party is a eunuch and a *prôtoprôedros*. This was a very new rank at the time this manuscript was made, having only been created in the 1060s.[106] *Prôedros* had originally been a rank restricted to eunuchs, but around the middle of the eleventh century there came to be bearded *proedroi*.[107] In effect this was a devaluation of the position, and so the rank of *prôtoprôedros* was probably created for eunuchs, to restore their pre-eminence. The manuscript is quite worn in the relevant areas, but it does appear that the tunic of the *prôtoprôedros* has 'Persian-sleeves'. This would be in accord with the pattern of distribution established in the *Book of Ceremonies*, wherein eunuchs wore garments more closely resembling those of the emperor than their bearded colleagues. The robe is made of a brocade of large interlaced roundels containing lions rampant, of a type well corroborated in surviving textiles. Its cuffs, collar and breast panel are made of a contrasting dark brocade bearing a finer vine-scroll pattern.[108] The skirt of the tunic is split, although less pronouncedly than those of the *proedroi*. He does not wear a cloak, and with his hands thereby uncovered he adopts the formal posture of respect that the Roman court had inherited from ancient Persian practice.[109]

The Twelfth Century

The twelfth century offers us no recorded upper court ranks or functions associated with artworks. A further complication is that, while to some degree it is possible to trace the changes in the rank structure of the court, there is virtually no information about the evolution of functions. Some conjectures may be made, however, by comparing pictures of the *Eisitêrioi for Agnes of France* with earlier and later practice.

It has been suggested that the man standing behind the throne holding a sword in folio 1v of the *Eisitêrioi* was a *prôtospatharios*.[110] This would indeed have been the place for a man of that rank according to earlier custom, but such precedents cannot be confidently carried over to this era.[111] We have seen that the evidence overwhelmingly suggests that this rank was extremely degraded by this time, if not discontinued. If it did still exist, the regalia shown in the *Eisitêrioi* would indicate a dramatic restoration in the position of *prôtospatharios* in the short space of time from the donation of Koutloumousiou codex 60. This man wears a tunic of scroll-pattern brocade very much like that worn by the *prôtoprôedros* of Coislin 79, and a *kapasion* (the asymmetrical hat) marked with two bars, a motif suggestive of a rank badge only seen on two men immediately flanking the throne on folio 2v. In the *Treatise on the Offices* the grand domestic (*megas domestikos*) is the rank primarily charged with the task of carrying the emperor's sword, with several other ranks designated as a hierarchy of stand-ins.[112] Hence, it seems more likely that it is the *megas domestikos* being represented in this picture of the *Eisitêrioi*, rather than a *prôtospatharios*.

The scenes of the second legation preceding the arrival of Princess Agnes (folio 2v) shows an emissary passing through the care of a number of officers. One meets him at the docks as he disembarks. Unfortunately the image of this man is too damaged to yield any information. Next, a man in a plain *kapasion* and a white dress tunic trimmed with gold passes him onto an evidently inferior functionary wearing a *kausia* (white dome hat) and a red tunic with the usual gold decoration. This occasion would have been quite unique, and even in the *Book of Ceremonies* there is little indication as to who these men might have been even in the tenth century. The man in white could be the *eparkhos*, for it might well still be within the scope of the duties of that official to greet an expected high dignitary on his arrival in the city. The white of his tunic is a plausible element of continuity with the preceding centuries in contrast to the red and brocades of the courtiers. Even in the eleventh century the eparkhial regalia held to older, simpler forms while the court began increasingly to wear brocades.

A man standing to the left side of the emperor in *Eisitêrioi* folio 2v holds a very plain staff of red. A red baton was the mark of the function of a *mandatôr* at the time of the composition of the *Klêtôrologion* and this has prompted the suggestion that he may have been the ambassador who negotiated the marriage that the manuscript commemorates.[113] This is unlikely, for *mandatôr* had been a lowly and populous function,[114] while the placement of this man and his regalia, a double-barred *kapasion*, a red tunic with gold armbands and a cloak of gold-on-red brocade quite reminiscent of those seen in the eleventh-century pictures with a gold edging, all indicate very high status. His placement and apparent function is more like that of the *ostiarios* of the *Book of Ceremonies*, yet the plain colour of his baton is so unprepossessing compared to the gold of the tenth-century officer. In the later *Treatise on the Offices* there are also staves of plain wood, yet again they are confined to men of low rank or function. This man evidently represents a particular development of the twelfth-century court which was a significant departure from earlier practice, and which was not preserved in the restored late Byzantine court. Without further evidence it is impossible to suggest what rank and role he held.

MILITARY AND MILITARY-DERIVED DRESS

As noted in the previous chapter, the basic serviceable forms of military clothing were long established, and there are no discernible developments in this period. In one area some changes can be inferred, that of over-garments. The *epilôrikion* or *epanoklivanon* of the tenth century is described in the manuals as retaining full-length sleeves, which really served little or no practical purpose, and this seems to match actual practice (fig. 42). In the twelfth century those sleeves were truncated to a vestigial elbow-length tube or flat flap. This development is not directly evidenced within the empire, but can be inferred from the clearly military-derived clothing shown in slightly later sources from surrounding kingdoms who looked to Constantinople, such as the royal portraits in the *Queen Keran Gospels* and the pictures of the falconry book of Frederick II, as well as from the dispersal of the fashion for surcoats across Europe.[115]

In her will of 1089, Kalê Pakourianê bequeathed two *epilôrikia*, one described as red and 'Antiokhene' and the other figured with cross motifs (*staurôton*). As Parani noted, the bequest contained no other military equipment.[116] These garments should therefore be recognised as early examples of the civilianised forms which become visible in the later twelfth and early thirteenth centuries, and which are notable as regalia in the fourteenth century.

Khoniatês recounts an episode in which Emperor Manuel I was to have a parlay with the Turkish sultan. The emperor was wearing a purple surcoat figured with gold, and described as *kholobafos*, 'dyed with bile'.[117] He removed it when the man acting as emissary between rulers advised the ruler that it was an inauspicious colour and out of keeping with a season of war (Plate 19, right).[118]

Droungarios of the watch

Foremost of the secondary characters in the account, and hence representations, of the Crucifixion is the mocking centurion, Longinus (fig. 56). The manner is which he is depicted is often quite unusual in the array of soldiers in Byzantine art and surprisingly consistent across the eleventh and twelfth centuries, and this has led to a wide range of speculations as to what models the artists used, or what allusions they might

FIG. 56. Longinus, the centurion at the Crucifixion, depicted in the guise of the *doungarios* of the watch, the head of the Constantinopolitan police. Eleventh century. Mosaic, Church of Nea Moni, Khios.

have been making. In popular literature the notion has long circulated that the Crucifixion centurion was modelled on a Varangian, and this has led on to a persistent misapprehension that there was a definable Varangian 'uniform'. The germ of this idea dates back to a caption in *The Vikings* by Frank R. Donovan published in 1964. The author presented the picture and ventured the opinion that Varangians were 'probably dressed in the style of the hooded guardsman' in the mosaic of the Crucifixion in the Church of Nea Moni on the island of Chios. In the late 1970s a book by Terrence Wise[119] and two volumes by Ian Heath[120] took up the idea and turned Donovan's cautious statement of analogy into a definite hypothesis, which has continued in use to the present.[121] Beyond the vague analogy, there is no basis for connecting these men with Varangians, but the headscarves with the circular decoration bearing such a precise resemblance to those of the various *eparkhoi* point to a more plausible candidate. The *Book of Ceremonies* tells us that all the judicial staff wore such hoods, and this is corroborated by an array of pictures showing mature men as well as military men, and even the odd occasional woman, wearing *felônia*, usually with very similar circular patterning.[122] They were to be present at various ceremonies wearing this distinctive item. Amongst the law-enforcement personnel, the commander of the city watch (*droungarios tês viglas*) had special mention. That was in relation to implements he was to carry, but it does not rule out the possibility that he had a particular customary garb, even in the tenth century. With the indications of extension of regalia in the eleventh century, it is plausible that the *droungarios* of the watch could have gained the distinctive outfit shown on the Crucifixion centurions – a red tunic trimmed with opulent gold cuffs and hem, and a royal blue *khlamus* with gold *tavlia*. As the sort of responsible post that could be held by a man of a populous rank like *prôtospatharios*, he might well already bring to the post a gold-hilted sword such as is shown on the Nea Moni mosaic and other such pictures. Hence, I conclude that the artistic conventions of this era matched the practice of depicting Pontius Pilate as the Eparkhos of Constantinople with another of showing Longinus as the commander of the city watch.

WOMEN

The very scanty information that exists tends to suggest the elite clothing and regalia practices of women in place in the tenth century underwent little change in this period. The text of the will of Kouropalatissa Kalê Pakourianê written in 1081 makes a great deal of recording the status of both Pakourianê's male connections, and the women to whom she bequeathed items. By this date the rank of *kouropalatês* had slipped significantly from its once-exalted position, and it seems likely that if had Pakourianê also held either of the two distinctly female ranks of *zôstê patrikia* or *koubikoularea* (if either still existed) it would have been mentioned.[123] In fact, Pakourianê's will contains nothing which can be even conjectured as being regalia of her own, but many opulent items which would certainly not have looked out of place at court. As noted at the beginning of the chapter, in terms of more literary works, the practice of 'Atticism' denies us contemporary terminology, although at times the lengths the authors have gone to in order to avoid contemporary language can itself be informative.

Common items

Headgear

The large, flaring hat which was previously identified as the *propolôma* becomes quite frequently illustrated in eleventh- and twelfth-century manuscripts.[124] In the tenth century white *propolômata* were worn by three ranks, *zôstai*, *magistrissai* and *patrikiai*, and by the ladies-in-waiting (*koubikoulareai*) – by far the great majority of the female population of the court – and there is no reason to assume this had changed. In the eleventh century on occasion they exhibited considerable ornamentation, which was quite a change from the stark white suggested by the *Book of Ceremonies*, and the simple, white-based style of the late twelfth century (fig. 51).

The *propolômata* shown on the round of Miriam and the Israelite women, dated to around 1059, are purple with gold decoration.[125] These colours are likely to imply that these women were members of the extended royal family, or of the very highest of the non-imperial ranks. Overlying this base colour there were bands of decoration which might run across the hat horizontally, diagonally, or crossing. In the earlier pictures, such as the virgin of the *Smyrna Octateuch* and especially the dancing circle of Miriam, the distribution of the bands of decoration suggest that they were at that time purely ornamental. The only case of a woman wearing a *propolôma* whose rank is known to us is Irênê Gavraina, a donor of a *tetraevangelion*, who was a common *patrikia* in keeping with the rank of her husband and co-donor.[126] The decor on Irênê Gavraina's *propolôma* is a single pale-blue band which slants across almost the entire width of the hat on a low diagonal, just as on some of the Israelite women. However, this picture does date from 1067, within the period in which the decor was probably still ornamental rather than symbolic. A little over a century later, in the *Eisitêrioi for Agnes of France*, the banding is simpler and more consistent. There are two or three gold bands running either near vertical, or parallel to the top. The distribution of these motifs in the pictures strongly suggests a hierarchy in which three bands were superior to two, and vertical more eminent than horizontal. There are two possibilities for when an alteration from ornament to badge may have been implemented. It may have been a consequence of the extensive changes in the structure of the court initiated by Alexios I, to which Guilland has attributed the disappearance of the patriciate.[127] It seems more likely, however, that it was an element of the more sweeping changes of the twelfth century, initiated by John II.

Amongst its many bounties, the *Eisitêrioi for Agnes of France* bring us the first pictures of the *maforion*, the hood or headscarf that the *Book of Ceremonies* said was worn under the *propolôma*.[128] The differences from an everyday *vêlarion* are evident (fig. 57, lower right). It is clearly quite a stiff and carefully shaped affair, which does not meet over the throat. All the *maforia* of the *Eisitêrioi* are a golden colour with two white bands running parallel with the lower edge, as distinct from the white of the earlier version. In the *Book of Ceremonies* there was no suggestion that the empress wore this item, yet we see it on the newly-crowned *augousta* in the *Eisitêrioi*. From there, it goes on to be a conspicuous and unique element of the augustal regalia in the late Byzantine era. This appears to be a case of the empress' regalia being dragged down into conformity with that of lesser women.

A marked contrast to such elite headgear is that of the late twelfth-century *prôtospatharea* who was joint donor of a gospel lectionary now in Koutloumousiou Monastery (fig. 53). According to the *taxis* of the tenth century, a *prôtospatharea* was a rank below that permitted to wear a *propolôma*, and, as has been noted, by the second half of the twelfth century her position had declined, so it is no surprise to find her depicted wearing a common woman's *savanion*, a cylindrical headdress comparable to a turban (fig. 58).[129]

Delmatikion

Pictures of the *delmatikion* become extremely common in the eleventh century, while at the same time there is no trace of the term. Almost every woman who is *not* being represented as a saint or a martyr is shown wearing a dress with very wide sleeves (fig. 58). This is even true of serving women such as Salomê and Imêa, the women who washed the infant Jesus with the sleeves of their presumably hand-me-down *delmatikia* tied behind their backs. Most of the pictures show the drop of these sleeves at

FIG. 57. Princess Agnes meets the *porfurogennêta* from the *Eisitêrioi for Agnes of France*. 1179. Vatican Library, ms Gr. 1851, f. 6r.

the wrist as being a great deal larger than earlier representations, such as the saints of the Church of Saint Maria in Valle (fig. 15). Nevertheless, many of these dresses were very plain, with simple close-fitting round necks and no decoration, and were worn with bare heads, light fillets or simple headscarves, thus implying they were quite common garb. As previously observed, the general use of the *delmatikion* amongst the more affluent classes was probably a situation that had existed in the tenth century. By the middle of the eleventh century one distinct innovation was certainly visible: the *delmatikia* of women of the higher echelons were set apart from others by having a plunging V neckline with broad lapels and a wide falling flap at the back, rather like a latter-day sailor's tunic (Chart 2.6a/b; Plate 17, right).[130] This was undoubtedly the adaptation of a recent Persian fashion, for a modest version of it is found on a late tenth- or early eleventh-century silk coat held in the Textile Museum in Washington.[131] This collar style also made its way into men's dress in the later part of this century (fig. 54).

FIG. 58. A noble lady dressing down, wearing a *savanion* on her head rather than the more formal *propolôma*. British Library, Add. 19352, f. 29v.

Kalê Pakourianê listed far fewer main garments in her bequest than mantles, and then only ever with the generic term, *himation*. However it is clear that, as extensive as her named wardrobe was, it was still not all of it, as implied by the decree that one legatee was to have 'one dress and one cape from the better clothes', and another 'a dress and cape from my fine silks'.[132] In view of the pictorial evidence it must be inferred that many, if not most, of these *himatia* were *delmatikia*. The very ubiquity of this style of garment may be another aspect of the disappearance of a distinct term for it. Certainly Atticising artifice cannot be attributed to the literary style of Pakourianê's will to explain the lack of this expression.

In the late twelfth century, the *Eisitêrioi for Agnes of France* presented a very different picture from the diversity of dresses depicted or implied by the earlier sources. The less formal *delmatikia* could be red or blue brocade (folio 6v; fig. 57, lower right, first and third), while the more formal dresses were all a uniform red brocade (fig. 57 all other women). Whether more or less formal, these dresses are all very much of the same style. Gone is the elegant V neckline of the eleventh century. These gowns are all fastened firmly, high on the throat. Combined with the stiff *maforia* and *propolômata* the effect is one of great severity, perhaps reflecting more straitened circumstances for women in Byzantine society generally.

The Empress and other royal women

Headgear

In the previous chapter it was argued that a similar distinction was made between the senior crown (*stemma*) and the junior coronet (*diadêma*) for royal women as for men. Art and survivals of the eleventh century provide much greater support for this idea. We certainly see a comparable change in the portraits, with empresses' crown becoming larger, showing a more pronounced feature of being somewhat conical (compare the crown of Evdokia in fig. 27 to that of Zôê in fig. 45). These form a considerable contrast to the woman's coronet which forms the basis for the 'Holy Crown of Hungary'. That has the expected projections along the top, but mounted on a very narrow, parallel-sided band much more reminiscent of a tenth-century male *kaisarikion* – indeed, Saint Helena's coronet shown on the Staatliche Museum ivory, and the pictures in BNF Gr. 510 (fig. 14) – than to any of the crowns shown in eleventh-century empress portraits.

The twelfth century continued the trend for the flaring augoustal *stemma* (fig. 47). Near the end of the century, the *Eisitêrioi for Agnes of France* explicitly confirmed the distinction in the crowns, showing the *porfurogennêta* and prospective bride in low coronets, and the newly crowned *augousta* in the grander, semiconical *stemma* (fig. 57, lower left).

Main garment

The very few formal portraits of empresses and saints in imperial regalia from the ninth and tenth centuries showed them wearing the *divêtêsion*. This did still occur through much of the eleventh century (figs 27, 45),[133] while the evidence suggests that this pattern in regalia practice underwent a dramatic change over quite a short period near the end of the century. In the 1060s Evdokia Makrembolitissa was the first empress to have herself depicted in formal portraits wearing a *delmatikion* rather than a *divêtêsion* on a series of seals.[134] A reliquary for Saint Dêmêtrios bearing a labelled portrait of Emperor Constantine X Doukas and Empress Evdokia shows that this was not yet a fixed policy, for the empress' garment has *persikomanikia*.[135] Similarly, *persikomanikia* appear on a *staurothêkê* (reliquary for a portion of the true cross) incorporating a portrait deemed to be of Saint Helena, but which is only dated to 'late eleventh or early twelfth century'.[136] More precisely dated between 1078 and 1087 is the so-called *Egbert Psalter*. Various leaves of this manuscript show Queen Mother Gertrude, Queen Irênê of Kiev and Saint Irênê all garbed in *divêtêsia*. In contrast, such variability ceases with the successor of Evdokia Makrembolitissa, Maria of Alania. In addition to her most famous portrait in the Coislin 79 manuscript, there is also an enamel of Maria with Michael Doukas, dated 1076–81, in which she wears a *delmatikion* rather than a *divêtêsion*.[137] Thereafter, with the possible exception of the nebulously dated *staurothêkê* just mentioned, there are no surviving representations of an empress, a female saint or allegorical figure wearing a garment with 'Persian-sleeves'. The weight of the evidence strongly indicates that with Maria of Alania the practice of empresses wearing the *divêtêsion* as the augustal regalia ceased in favour of the *delmatikion*, and that this practice perhaps diffused more slowly into surrounding nations who looked to Constantinople as a model (fig. 47). The implications of this were probably much greater than might be immediately apparent. It has been shown that in the tenth and eleventh centuries the empress played a very important role in court. Furthermore, the eleventh century had several examples of empresses who ruled in their own right, or who openly determined male imperial rule and succession. The profound symbolic power embodied in the fact that the regalia of the *augousta* was identical to that of the *vasilieus* must have made a significant contribution to the ability of those women to wield such power. After the empress' primary regalia garment fell into conformity with the paradigms of ordinary women, we never again see evidence of such overt female power in the court, and the position of women manifestly steadily declined from then to the end of the empire. This not to suggest a causal link, but rather that the change in dress is the visible face of underlying social trends.

Sceptre

In the eleventh century the practice continued of the *augousta* at times carrying the cruciform *skêpiôn* (fig. 31.1). Yet this century also furnishes evidence, primarily numismatic, for significant innovations in augustal sceptres.[138] Some of these can be associated with particular empresses who were noted, not surprisingly, for their above-average authority. The first two appeared about the same time. One, held by Zôê, has a terminal of three distinct lobes and closely resembles the description of an augustal sceptre in the late Byzantine romance *Belthandros and Chrysantza* (fig. 31.2).[139] The other, held by Zôê and Theodôra on one of their joint coins, is a sceptre of variously sized knobs arranged in line (fig. 31.3). The third, seemingly created for Theodôra, has the precise form of the 'Golden Bough' (*khrusoun vaion*) of the late Byzantine-era *Treatise on the Offices*, as shown in the imperial portrait of Louvre manuscript Ivoires 100 of 1402 (fig. 31.4). In contrast to these, Maria of Alania appears to have reinvented the *skêpiôn*, adding a crescent-shaped cross-piece and knobbing on the shaft (fig. 31.5). As noted by Grierson, this sceptre was illustrated in Maria's hand in the enamel, now part of the Kharkuli Diptych, as well as her portrait in Coislin 79.[140] Very soon thereafter this sceptre migrated across the gender line and was henceforth regularly seen in male hands.[141]

Lôros

It was long believed that the eleventh century saw the advent of a distinct *lôros* for the empress with the reshaping of the long end to create the kite-shaped panel which was in the past mistakenly identified with the term *thôrakion*. It was shown earlier that there is evidence for this practice extending back to the beginning of the tenth century (fig. 43). This modification of the chronology consequently again recasts the eleventh century as a period of continuity rather than innovation in respect of this insignium. Otherwise, the empress' *lôros* shows the same patterns of evolution as that of the emperor, with the development of the 'yoke/epaulette' style (Chart 6.6) from the tabard-pattern *lôros* of earlier in the century (Chart 6.5). The 'yoke/epaulette' style continued throughout the twelfth century. The *Eisitêrioi for Agnes of France* reveals a dramatic change in the practice: the tail of the *lôros* is now draped over the empress' left arm in the same manner as the men, rather than pinned at the waist in the earlier manner.[142] This is bound to be a response to the effect of the *delmatikion*. The vast expanse of the *delmatikion* sleeves would very often have hidden the pinned *lôros*, while draping it once again over the arm would have restored its visibility.

RESPLENDENT TWILIGHT

1204 TO 1453

5

THE FOURTH CRUSADE AND THE LATIN INTERREGNUM

The thirteenth century is a very poor source of evidence for this study due to the devastation of the Fourth Crusade, the Latin interregnum that followed and the grinding struggle to rebuild once the capital was regained and the empire restored. However, it is during these disastrous events that many of the changes in dress and regalia which are visible in the fourteenth century are to be found.

The essential question is to what degree and what types of continuity in court practice fed through into the surviving claimant centres to imperial authority. Treadgold's observation that the ultimate triumph of the Empire of Nikaia was an outcome which was no more likely than any other through much of the interregnum period is well made, for it has been estimated that at least as many refugees from Constantinople went west into Epiros as went east to Nikaia.[1] Yet it is fortunate for researchers that Nikaia should have been the centre to finally take sole possession of the sceptre, for it happened to be the haven for chroniclers of this period, notably Nikêtas Khoniatês. The modes of continuity which may have impinged upon the exiled courts of the Latin interregnum period, and helped to shape the court which was eventually restored to Constantinople, are fourfold: material, personal, literary and artistic.

The harrowing account left by Khoniatês of the flight from the City by his family, friends and others makes it clear that physical continuity was minimal. He and his companions left with no more than they could each carry concealed on their persons.[2] In such straitened circumstances, while clothing was necessarily one of the essentials to be included in the refugees' loads, the often-specialised impedimenta of participation in court ritual cannot have figured highly. Khoniatês records that Alexios III Angelos fled with one thousand pounds of gold 'and other imperial ornaments compounded of precious stones and shining pearls'.[3] These may have been some of the crown jewels, as has often been suggested, but it is clear enough from our prior sources, and surviving examples, that virtually any 'ornament' that was deemed 'imperial' was decorated with gems and pearls, so this loot might have been anything from crowns to swords to Bible covers. In any case, even if these ornaments were regalia, it can be confidently accepted that they would have been consumed: that is, sold for ready cash – in order to fund Alexios' designs for an imperial resurgence in the period following the fall of Constantinople – as he perambulated from his initial refuge in Thrace to an ultimate haven with the Sultan of Konya. It is possible that prior to the first invasion, and between that and the final sack, other highly-placed persons may have been able to send property away to some point of supposed safety. Yet, once again, court vestments and accessories are very much less likely to have featured in such provisions than more densely portable forms of wealth. In all, it seems fairly certain that little in the way of court regalia escaped the ravages of the Crusaders, and so the physical appurtenances of a court must have had to be reconstituted very largely from scratch, according to whatever surplus resources could be found.

That reconstitution necessarily drew upon the three other forms of transmission, firstly the personal. This itself has two facets. On the one hand there were the recollections of those who had had first-hand experience of the functioning of the court, men like Khoniatês and his companions. From them could be pieced together a goodly amount regarding the form of the ritual and regalia. It seems that this was certainly done for the inauguration of the Empire of Nikaia.[4] However, to realise the reconstruction of regalia, another class of personal continuity was required. The diverse coterie of elite artisans who produced court regalia had also naturally been concentrated overwhelmingly in the capital, and had consequently felt the depredations of the sack as much as the aristocrats. Some doubtless survived and fled to the same localities as the courtiers, yet even with the fullest will to resume their previous occupations the circumstances cannot possibly have been conducive to recovering the style and quality of production that the capital had known with any great speed. Specialised workshops were needed. Most items of court dress alone required the participation of numerous distinct skills: weavers, dyers, tailors, embroiderers, jewellers, enamellers.[5] Even if such a diverse industry could have been regrouped, the surplus wealth hardly existed to pay for anything like the opulence of the old Constantinopolitan court. This last circumstance of relative impoverishment continued to the very end of the empire; as it continued through the interregnum period, the potential for personal transmission of both the concepts and skills upon which the old court life was based must have withered away as both courtiers and artisans with first-hand experience died, dispersed further or redirected their activities. Still, a silk industry was fostered in Nikaia to supply the court, and continued to do so after the recovery of the capital.[6]

As the Empire of Nikaia grew and underwent economic recovery, which would generate some surplus wealth that could be employed for the adornment of the court, the last two forms of transmission, literature and art, must have come to have greater effect, providing potential models of court life. This in itself initiated changes. The stylisation of both elite literature and art is well known to us, and cannot have been entirely outside the awareness of the Byzantine aristocracy. Nevertheless, it is clear that elements from those sources were embraced selectively and willfully. Some of the reason for that is plainly that the same need for redressive action and re-integration which influenced the recodification of the life of the court undertaken by Constantine Porfurogennêtos. As with that process, this introduced new archaisms. Later emperors of Nikaia were raised upon a shield as part of the coronation rite, in a ceremony that had not been used in the Roman Empire for many centuries, but which was well illustrated in manuscripts through the period under study (fig. 49).[7] It has been suggested that this archaising innovation should be projected back from the first recorded date of 1254 to the inauguration of the Nikaian Empire,[8] however this seems unlikely. The courtiers present in the newly established court, like Khoniatês, or, indeed, the new emperor himself (Theodore I Laskaris is noted as an antiquarian[9]) must have been aware of its lack of currency, and are more likely to have wanted to enact the most secure form of continuity they could. Furthermore, the raising on the shield necessarily has strong symbolic ties to military triumph, and would surely have seemed incongruous in a court formed of refugees from a devastating defeat. It is rather more likely that this innovation did truly date from the coronation of Theodore II in 1254, when living memory of the old court had largely dissipated and influences from art and literature could exert more of an effect.

The clearest illustrations of how portions of the court culture were reconstructed from a mixture of ill-understood literary and pictorial sources lie in two ceremonial guard units of the Palaiologian court, the Varangians and the 'romfaia-masters' (*romfaiokratôres*). The Varangians are well attested by the chroniclers of the eleventh and twelfth centuries, often labelled 'axebearers' (*pelekunoforoi*).[10] Scattered evidence also records that various corps of Varangians survived the sack of the city and dispersed to successor courts, including Nikaia, and continued the tradition as an axe-bearing guard through to the time of the composition of the *Treatise on the Offices*.[11] Yet in addition to the clear references to the Varangians, Psellos, Attaleiatês, Komnêna and Bryennios all wrote that some of the closest guards of the emperor carried a weapon called *rhomfaia*, without making it at all clear who wielded them or what precisely the weapon was.[12] Modern scholarship recognises the term as an Atticising euphemism for the great two-handed axes carried by the Norsemen and Saxons who served as Varangians in the tenth to twelfth centuries, but it was not so clear at the time. Nor was there a living tradition of guardsmen carrying any sort of weapon called a *rhomfaia*. Nevertheless, with such august literary precedents, it was evidently decided that in the restored court it must be seen to be so as well, despite the difficulty of recognising precisely what this obscure weapon was, or who carried it. Therefore, in restoring it to court ceremonial, other sources had to be brought to bear. The word appears very extensively in Late Antique and middle Byzantine literature as the divinely-ordained weapon of the righteous. In most cases there is no indication (or need for one) as to the specific character of the implement. The more technical texts are often internally contradictory. The Suda lexicon is typical. It reads '*rhomfaia* – the large javelin or short sword'.[13] Another source may have been more influential for its authoritativeness. The frontispiece of the *Psalter of Basil II* shows him being crowned from above and presented with a spear by an angel, while he holds a sword behind him on the left. On the facing page there is a poem on the subject which speaks of an 'incorporeal being' placing in the hand of the emperor a 'weapon which scares enemies away', which is called *rhomfaia* by name.[14] A short sword, as suggested by the lexicon, is hardly an imposing weapon, and in practicehad been long superseded by the adoption of the *spathion*, so in such a context a spear is the only viable interpretation for *rhomfaia*, and those recreating the regalia and ceremonial of the late Byzantine court evidently thought so as well. The existence of an occasional imperial guard called the '*rhomfaia*-masters' who carried spears shows that middle period literature and art were highly influential in the re-establishment of the court, clearly filling a void of directly transmitted familiarity with actual practice, and perhaps even literary convention, from before the arrival of the Fourth Crusade. Yet its very existence in addition to the corps of Varangians also shows that Byzantines of the Palaiologian era did not comprehend the literary stylisation practised by their own ancestors, a profound illustration of the cultural disjunction caused by the Fourth Crusade.

THE COMPOSITION OF THE *TREATISE ON THE OFFICES* AND ITS BASIS

It is well accepted that the *Treatise on the Offices* was written between 1347 and 1368,[15] perhaps after 1360.[16] Verpeaux described the anonymous author as a 'functionary of the service of protocol or a dignitary very conversant with etiquette and precedence.'[17] The striking lacunae in his account, if not its somewhat sketchy nature, must lead one to doubt the first half of Verpeaux's proposal. Manifestly the writer had nothing like the specific expertise of the *atriklinês* Filotheos who wrote the *Klêtôrologion*, or the lofty oversight of Constantine Porfurogennêtos in expanding that work into the *Book of Ceremonies*. The rank of *kouropalatês* was attributed to the author in an early edition, and although that is not well supported by evidence, it might well be an involved but non-specialist point of view such as that which could allow a man to write such a work as the *Treatise on the Offices*.

In addition to the more dispersed evidence discussed previously, the *Treatise* itself contains quite clear evidence for the conclusion that the bulk of the process of restoring the ceremonial and regalia paradigms had been completed in the Lascarid period. The process of the multiplication of offices which had begun in the eleventh century and continued apace in the twelfth century seems to have undergone a further surge in the restoration period. The *Treatise* has many more titles and functions than ever before, but with the regalia being simpler and less diverse than hitherto, this merely means that many ranks differed in name rather than appearance. It probably still remained somewhat fluid up to the accession of Michael VIII, with the reoccupation of Constantinople serving as the catalyst for the solidification of the evidently quite stable structure embodied in the *Treatise on the Offices*.[18] Certainly, the essential reliability of the *Treatise* is assured. A wide range of other sources confirm the stipulations of the work in greater or lesser detail, including Emperor John VI Kantakouzenos' account of the coronation of Andronikos III, and other accounts of coronations given by Pachymerês and Gregoras, as well as sporadic accounts of events and regalia scattered throughout the literature and art of the period.[19]

The regalia

Colours

We have seen that the court from Late Antiquity to the mid-eleventh century was overwhelmingly monochrome, predominantly white or purple with highlights of gold, with rare instances of brocaded cloths used as ground fabrics for distinctive garments, usually mantles; this began to change in the eleventh century, with brocades becoming more common at the imperial level and then trickling down the ranks. This evolution culminates with the Palaiologian scheme in a total inversion of the mid-eleventh-century pattern. The vast bulk of the court wore main garments, usually *kavadia*, made of some brocade chosen from a set range of patterns, densely figured in gold or silver on a ground of red, green or blue (fig. 60). Single-coloured cloths were very rare and apparently reserved for those of the highest ranks: emperor, empress and *despotês*

FIG. 59. Emperor Andronikos II (1282–1328) clad in a *stemma*, tight-sleeved *roukhon* and *diadêma* (previously called *lôros*). This picture well illustrates how black had supplanted purple as the royal colour, and how larger, textile-based *stemmata* had replaced the metal of past eras. Byzantine Museum, Athens.

(fig. 59). With the very scant details given for the emperor in our source, the only colours ascribed to him directly are the black (*melas*) of one of his *sakkoi*,[20] and the gold of his coronation *manduas*.[21] The latter reminds us of the gold *sagion* unique to the emperor and *kaisar* (named *kaisarikion*) in the *Book of Ceremonies*, yielding one of the few straightforward instances of correlation between the two periods. We learn indirectly from the description of the regalia of the *despotês* that the emperor's more common garments are red (*kokkinos*). The information regarding the empress is even more sparse than for the emperor. In fact, we are only given any details at all for the time of her widowhood, when her son is to succeed to the throne. Then, her colours are black (*melas*) for her main garment (called *himation*), and purple (*oxus*) for her *manduas*.[22] It is evident that this combination is specific to her new status, and not typical of her attire when her husband was alive. The portraits of Empress Helena, wife of Manuel II, and Empress Anna, wife of Andronikos III, support the theory that a reigning empress wore main garments in one of the designated court brocades, as did all other women of the court.[23] The regalia of the *despotês* closely follows that of the emperor, being predominantly red (*kokkinos*), but he does have the alternative choice of a purple coat (*oxun kavadion*). This description of the variants of the regalia of the emperor and *despotês* is quite accurately reflected in the illuminated *Alexander Romance* probably executed for Alexios III of Trebizond (1349–90), indicating that vestimentary practice was very much alike in the courts of Constantinople and Trebizond.[24]

The *Treatise on the Offices* does assign specific colours to several ranks below *despotês*. *Sevastokratôr* and *kaisar* also have red (*kokkinos*) for their tunic (*roukhon*), coat (*kavadion*) and cloak (*tabarion*). The *prôtovestiarios* wore green (*prasinos*) garments, doubtless an extension from the green footwear that the rank had been granted in the twelfth century, and that colour was also given to the *prôtosevastos*, an innovation attributed to Michael VIII.[25] Yellow-orange (*kitrinos*) was the prerogative of the *panupersevastos*, and from there of the *eparkhos* by the grace of Andronikos II.[26] The very explicit correlations noted by Spatharakis which can be made between the *Treatise* and the portraits of the very nearly contemporary *Lincoln Typikon*,[27] show that these colour attributes refer to the base tincture of brocades, rather than to monochrome fabrics.

Garments and accessories

In chapter 3 a system of categorisation of male regalia garments was described which initially separated them from common dress and each other by sleeve form, and then by a hierarchy of degree and extent of decoration. It was subsequently observed in chapter 4 that in the twelfth century the details of that system began to change, but that it did continue. The very much simplified regalia of the Palaiologian court still showed that system of division. The most common regalia garments (*roukhon* and *kavadion*) were still distinguished from everyday clothes by being fitted very closely to the forearm and wrist, as we can see most simply by comparing the loose-sleeved *kavadion* of the donor portrait of Theodôros Metôkhitês in everyday dress (fig. 64) with the *kavadia* of the men in the *Lincoln Typikon* with their tight cuffs (fig. 60). The sleeve-derived system of

FIG. 60. The donor portraits of the so-called *Lincoln Typikon* of 1327–42 reflect the stipulations of the *Treatise on the Offices* very precisely.

definition was then further elaborated by the other variants of the *sakkos* and *epilôrikion*, and the extremely long sleeves of the *granatza* and *lapatza*. The next layer of definition was how the garment was opened and put on, distinguishing garments pulled on over the head (*roukhon* and *sakkos*) from those fully opened down the front (*kavadion*, *epilôrikion*, *granatza* and *lapatza*). Finally, *granatza* and *lapatza* were distinguished from each other by the openings in their sleeves (see below). The differentiation between ankle-length aristocratic clothes and knee-length garments harking back to common or military dress (*paganos* or *ta pagana* in the earlier source, fig. 30) had ceased to be used in the late court.

Mantles, already an anachronism in the sixth century, were now very rare. The type open at the centre of the chest (*manduas* and *sagion* in earlier times) had become mostly confined to religious vestments, with occasional use by the rulers. The form fastened on the right shoulder (named *khlamus* hitherto and now called *tabarion*) were only worn by the very highest ranks on the most august of occasions.

A further result of the inflation of offices which had begun in the eleventh century and the simplification of the regalia system is that there was now virtually no garment or accessory which was specific to any single rank.

Headgear

Crowns

The crowns of the Palaiologian male royalty show one of the highest degrees of continuity with the previous periods. The *Treatise on the Offices* mentions the *stemma*, *stefanos*, *stemmatoguron* and the 'triumphal crown' or 'Justinian crown', all of which can be directly related to forms of the prior eras.

Stemma

The *stemma* as shown in late Byzantine art, and described in the *Treatise on the Offices*, is in one respect the culmination of a development which began in the twelfth century, and in another embodies a practice which is first seen in the thirteenth century. We have seen that in the early twelfth century the shape of the *stemma* began to change with the hemispherical superstructure becoming larger than it had been hitherto. By the end of that century the *stemma* was rather more than hemispherical, as we see from the *Eisitêrioi of Agnes of France*. After the Fourth Crusade the pictorial sources show that this trend continued. The crown tended to become taller than previously, although this appears to have varied somewhat from emperor to emperor. This form continued until the end of the empire, while the slightly waisted form, preserved in the Eastern Orthodox patriarchal mitre to the present day, developed after the final fall of Constantinople (fig. 61).[28]

At some point the metal-framed *stemma* gave way to a crown made with a fabric substrate. There is early evidence of this from outside the empire in the crown of Queen Constance of Aragon, which was buried with her in 1220.[29] The earliest explicit Byzantine evidence is found in Pachymerês' account of the coronation of Michael VIII and the young John IV. Pachymerês writes that John followed the senior emperor 'not in a royal crown [*stefei vasilikôs*], but only in a linen bonnet [*kekrufalôs hêmitumviôs*] decorated with gems and pearls'.[30] This obscure expression is a compound of ancient terms for a woman's hair-net and linen cloth respectively.[31] In this can be seen a direct parallel with the description in the *Treatise* of the fourteenth-century *stemma*: 'This was silk with gems and pearls. It is placed on the front of the Emperor and then tied about the head at the back.'[32] (It is worth noting here that this description evokes the ancient meaning of *diadêma*, 'a thing bound around', which had been preserved as a term for coronets long after they had become solid circlets, but which in the late Byzantine court was applied appropriately to the *lôros*.)

The question raised by Pachymerês' account concerns what made John's headgear worthy of note compared to that of Michael. One inference would be that the textile substrate distinguished it from a metallic basis for the 'royal crown', yet, as previously discussed, the globular form of the later twelfth-century *stemma* especially tends to suggest that a transition to lighter materials had already taken place prior to the Latin interregnum. The conclusion that presents itself is that John's crown was distinguished by being made of inferior materials, linen rather than silk, perhaps because Michael was already committed to a plan to eliminate the boy-emperor and rule alone.[33] Pachymerês may have been alluding to this himself with a play on words, for the Suda glosses *hemitumvion* as a 'small grave'.[34]

In his own account of his coronation, John VI Kantakouzenos writes that for his first coronation at Adrianople he commanded 'crowns [*stemmata*] to be made by goldsmiths'. This may suggest metallic crowns, yet this passage could just as well refer to the gem mounts needed to make even a fabric-based crown, as can be seen from the crown of Queen Constance of Aragon. There may be yet another explanation resulting from the pressing circumstances of the moment. When describing the same incidents, Gregoras uses the older term *tainia* for the crown John VI was vested with at the first coronation. This word saw quite extensive use in prior times as a synonym for *diadêma* in the middle Byzantine sense, that is to say the simpler *stefanos* or *modiolos* more usually worn by the *kaisar*.[35] Such a crown is more likely to have been made in metal, and to have been done so quite rapidly, and possibly cheaply from a gilded base metal, rather than pure gold, by the artisans in Adrianople. Kantakouzenos' version of the events would then be accurate as to the creation of the crowns, but showing an understandable measure of hyperbole as to their form and eminence.

In 1343 the crown jewels were pawned to Venice by Anna of Savoy, acting as regent for Emperor John V, for the sum of 30,000 ducats, and lodged in the treasury of the Cathedral of San Marco.[36] They were never redeemed. In this case, the expression 'crown jewels' is quite precisely used, for the inventory consists entirely of gems in isolation. These gems are all stones of red hue. The inventory uses the terms *rubino* and *balasso* in a manner that evidently represented some fine distinction at the time, although that has since been lost, with both words being applied today to ruby.[37] One item is of particular interest, described uniquely amongst the gems as 'a plaque of ruby' (*una tavola di balasso*). The most conspicuous feature of *stemmata* from the middle Byzantine era, if not earlier, to about this date is a large panel on the centre front of the crown, which dwarfs all the other decorative elements, and which is almost always represented as red in coloured depictions. This pattern is preserved up to one of the portraits of Andronikos III,[38] alongside a trend for the decorative elements all being of

FIG. 61. To this day, Eastern Orthodox mitres preserve the form and techniques used in the Palaiologian *stemma*, as well as the antique regalia mode of bearing an image of the person(s) to whom the wearer owed fealty. Museum of Religion in Lvov, Ukraine.

a more consistent, smaller size. From the Dionysiou Khrusobul of Andronikos III (fig. 63) the more homogeneous style of decoration prevails through to the end of the empire, and indeed beyond, as elements of court regalia were incorporated into that of the Eastern Orthodox churches. It is likely that as the wealth of the empire declined further, later *stemmata* may have been made not only with stones of inferior quality and size, but possibly even with glass substitutes, in keeping with the substitution of goblets made of gilded earthenware and lead for metal vessels on the imperial table during the coronation feast of John VI.[39]

Stefanos

In those places where the author of the *Treatise* does not use *stefanos* in the generic sense noted by Verpeaux,[40] it is evident that it has a meaning entirely consistent with the way it was used in the *Book of Ceremonies*, designating the simpler, cylindrical coronets of the ranks immediately below the emperor. It refers to the coronet having four small arches worn by the son of an emperor who has not yet been crowned co-emperor, and the coronet with just one arch called *stemmatoguron*.[41]

FIG. 62. A fine example of a Palaiologian *stemmatoguron* from the Khôra Church, Istanbul.

Stemmatoguron

The *stemmatoguron* is the simpler form of the crown of the *despotês* given to one who is a *gambros*: that is, a close male relative but not the emperor's son. The *Treatise* describes this in detail as having '[a small arch] at the front only' just as is visible in the Khôra Church (fig. 62).[42] This form is seen in earlier pictures (fig. 55) and exists in a pair of surviving base metal votive crowns which may date to the tenth century.[43] Their form mimics in a simplified way the dominant pattern of the brow band of the later eleventh- and twelfth-century *stemmata* which had an ornament with a rounded top on the front, which later projected above the brow band. The *Treatise* asserts that Emperor John VI instituted blue gems for the *stemmatoguron* of the *sevastokratôr*, thus introducing another layer of difference from the imperial *stemma*, and almost certainly from the *stefanos* of an emperor's uncrowned son, which had rubies and other red stones.

Triumphal crown

Verpeaux properly identified the 'triumphal' or 'Justinian crown' with the *toufa* or *tiara* of the previous periods, clinching the argument with Tzetzes' statement that the equestrian statue of Justinian which stood before Hagia Sofia wore this crown.[44] This item, therefore, may have pride of place in terms of continuity, remaining essentially unchanged in both form and role for close to one thousand years, if the lack of pictures and references noted for the twelfth century does not indicate a hiatus in use.

Other headgear

Aêr

Medieval Greek has a quite remarkable array of largely interchangeable terms for textile coverings, which may often denote headgear as well as other uses. *Aêr* is a further addition to the catalogue. In connection with the *skiadion*, Du Cange's suggestion that it refers to the brim of the hat is initially attractive.[45] This notion is dispelled, however, by the description of the headgear of the *megas domestikos*, whose *skiadion* and *aêr* are described in identical terms. This would be understandable if they were separate objects, but is redundant if they are parts of the same object, and implies that the *skiadion* and *aêr* are conceptually separate items, rather than the latter being a component of the former. This conclusion is accepted by other commentators.[46] Liturgically, *aêr* refers to a square cloth used to cover chalice and paten.[47] In the *Treatise on the Offices* it is a flap, again presumably rectilinear, which hangs off the back of some *skiadia*. This practice was probably originally adopted to give the wearer's neck additional protection from the sun. The *despotês*, *sevastokratôr*, *kaisar* and *megas domestikos* have *aêres*. The first three have their names embroidered in gold upon the cloth, while the third has unspecified gold embroidery on a field of red and gold. The field colour of the three senior *aêres* is not stipulated in our source, but it is reasonable to suppose they are red, for that continues the colour scheme of their other garments and would provide a conspicuous ground for the gold embroidery.

Angourôton

This quite mysterious item is worn by the *vardariotai*, the capital's long-established police unit. It is said to be Persian, although in view of the dubious attributions made by the *Treatise* this must be approached with some caution. The form of the word suggests an entirely Greek derivation, and there appears to be nothing resembling it in Persian. All that is said of this hat is that 'in place of a braid, it has yellow-orange cloth [*panion kitrinon*].'[48] If the Persian attribution is valid in this case, this might hint at a resemblance to the bulbous hat seen in ancient Persian art which often had piece of cloth or ribbon tied around the brow.[49]

Kapasion

The Tzakonians have the sole distinction of wearing the *kapasion*.[50] This term is otherwise found in a paraphrase of Khoniatês, substituted once for *pilos* and once for *kaluptra*.[51] Hence, it is some sort of hat, continuing the long tradition of such terms having the generic sense of a covering. The hat shown on three portraits of John VIII and various other fourteenth-century sources, is a plausible candidate for a *kapasion*.[52] That hat appears to be a version of the asymmetrical court hat of the later eleventh and twelfth centuries which has been modified by having the turned-up outer layer cut down, and the inner dome extended upwards. No colour is indicated for the Tzakonians' *kapasia*. We may infer the basic white which had been a common colour for men's hats for many centuries, and which was the uniform colour of the asymmetrical hat and is the tincture of the body of the hat on the painted portrait of John VIII.

Skaranikon

The wealth of court portraiture from the fourteenth century has made the nature of the *skaranikon* a simple matter. Previous authors have effectively dispelled the old view which regarded this item as a body garment.[53] The *skaranikon* was the festival-day alternative to the *skiadion*.[54] It existed in two classes, with the more elite class, at least, in two variant forms. The forms of the superior type are represented as a bulbous dome of a shape quite like the *stemma*, and evidently descended from the white dome hats (previously identified as *kausia*) which came into court use in the eleventh century (figs 48, 54), and alternatively as a cylinder deriving from the Persian *kalansuwa tawîla* or *kulâh*, which, again, begins to be extensively seen in Byzantium in the eleventh century.

No depictions of the lower-class *skaranikon* appear to have survived. It is described in the *Treatise* as 'covered in red silk, having a small tassel at the summit' (Plate 23, left).[55] This type may also have existed in the same two shapes as the elite version, but we can be sure it existed in the cylindrical form, for it clearly survives in the latter-day Turkish fez.[56]

The elite *skaranikon* was extremely ornate. That of the *despotês* was 'red, dusted with gold, gems and pearls'.[57] The author of the *Treatise* admits that he is still trying to find out the nature of the *skaranika* of the *kaisar* and *sevastokratôr*, but in view of the consistent similarity that all the other regalia items belonging to these two ranks bear to those of the *despotês*, it is reasonable to infer that their *skaranika* are also identical.[58] The *skaranika* of the ranks from there down to *prôtohieratikos* also have large amounts of gold decoration upon them. There is a hierarchy of base colour for these ranks. For the *megas domestikos* and the four ranks below, the base colour is red (*kokkinos*). Seven ranks from *megas primikêrios* to the *parakoimomenos* of the chamber have a pink base colour (*verikokkokhroös*) for their hats.[59] The author of the *Treatise* takes some pains to describe this pink shade, saying it is halfway between red and white. He thus makes this group a link between the foregoing and the next group of six, whose *skaranika* are of a white-and-gold brocade (*khrusaspron vlation*).[60] The remainder have hats of an orange-and-gold brocade (*vlation khrusokitrinon*).

The main elements of the decoration on all these elite *skaranika* are portraits of the emperor. According to the *Treatise*, on the front the emperor is shown standing, while on the back he is enthroned. This scheme of decoration is confirmed on all the donor portraits showing *skaranika*, but with one significant quirk. Spatharakis noted that the hats of the males depicted in the *Lincoln Typikon* are back to front, showing the seated emperor rather than the standing one (fig. 60).[61] This characteristic is repeated on all the other regalia-clad portraits as well, Megas Droungarios Alexios Apokaukos,[62] Megas Logothetês Constantine Akropolitês[63] and Megas Primikêrios Iôannês.[64] Whether this is a convention of Palaiologian court portraiture, or whether the author of the *Treatise* was mistaken, is impossible to say.

Skiadion

It has been seen that the account of the sack of Thessaloniki by the Franks in 1185 written by Bishop Evstathios, brought us the first use of the specific term *skiadion*. Supporting the impression given by Evstathios, whilst describing what is evidently the imperial *skiadion*, Akropolitês also states that it is a 'Latin hat' (*kaluptra latinikê*), while Khoniatês leads us to believe it derived from the Georgians.[65] It has been noted that the etymology of *skiadion* denotes a protection from the sun, literally 'little shadow'.[66]

Gregoras describes the *skiadion* of a *megas logothêtês*, saying that 'its upper part presented a pyramidal appearance, while its lower portion was also somewhat hollow, but completely smooth.'[67] Byzantine art presents reasonably common depictions of broad-brimmed hats which could provide the sun protection and fit the various elements of the written sources. What appears to be the earliest such picture is within a nativity scene in a manuscript in the Great Lavra on Athos, presently attributed to the eleventh century (fig. 50). More reliably dated, and more in line with the literary sources, is that of the oarsmen of the boat bringing the emissary to Constantinople to arrange Princess Agnes's wedding in the *Eisitêrioi* of 1179.[68] The pictures which most precisely correlate with both Gregoras' description of the form, and the *Treatise*'s descriptions of their colours and decorations, are found in a late thirteenth-century gospel book held in the Kupferstichkabinet in Berlin. There, the hats are shown with a quite sharply pyramidal crown, and a less steeply conical brim, and painted in the prevalent court colours of red and gold.[69] Therefore, in terms of fourteenth-century sources it is a simple matter to concur with Spatharakis in identifying the pointed, wide-brimmed hats worn by the attendants of Emperor John Kantakouzenos at the Ecumenical Council of 1351 and other sources as *skiadia*.[70]

Akropolitês fills the silence of the *Treatise* by describing the appearance of the imperial *skiadion* as 'the (whole) form worked with pearls and the top also with red stones'.[71] This relates in a satisfactorily hierarchical way with *Treatise on the Offices*'s description of the *skiadion* of the *despotês* as 'wholly pearled'.[72] The *skiadia* of the emperor's close relatives (*gambroi*) who are also *despotai*, are of 'red and gold [brocade] with gold embroidery having crosses and circles worked in pearls'.[73] Verpeaux interpreted this last clause as meaning that there were pearls around the circumference of the hat. Yet the term used is unmistakably plural, so it is much more likely to mean the cross-within-a-circle motif we see on the so-called 'Vatican *sakkos*' and which became such a standard feature of church regalia to this day.[74] The *skiadia* of the *sevastokratôr* and *kaisar* are merely red and gold (brocade) with gold embroidery.[75] The ranks from there down to the *megas konostaulos* wear hats of the red-gold without embroidery. The next group of ranks, from *prôtosevastos* to the *parakoimomenos* of the bedchamber have *skiadia* of green-and-gold brocade.[76] The *logothetês tou genikou* has a hat of white silk with bands.[77] In view of the commonality of other items of regalia from this rank down, it is reasonable to infer that this is also what is meant by the single adjective, *klapôtos*, which is applied to almost all the *skiadia* which follow.[78] This would be quite in accord with the quantity of *skiadia* of this colour and pattern shown in the picture of Emperor John Kantakouzenos at the Ecumenical Council.[79] The one exception to this scheme is the hat of the *prôtasêkrêtis*, which is purple and white silk with wide bands of gold embroidery.[80]

Skoufia

When in attendance at the palace, the staff of the royal tent (the *kortinarioi*) wear upon their heads red *skoufiai* without *kapasia* (Plate 23, right).[81] Sphrantzes also refers to a Thessalonikan *skoufia* with red and gold silk.[82] Du Cange notes the equivalence of *skoufia* with *koufia*, and equates it with the Latin terms *cuphia* and *birretum*.[83] Previous commentators have overlooked the correlation with the Arabic *skuffiya*/*kufiyya*, well known as a male headscarf back into the early Middle Ages.[84] This accessory puts one in mind of the ceremonial hoods and headscarves of the middle Byzantine period, yet one cannot say whether its use was inspired by an awareness of the earlier practice, albeit renamed, or whether like the name it was a new import from the Arab world. Comparable instances in this era could prompt a conclusion either way.

Seia

The *seia* are items associated with the *skiadion* and *aêr* of the ranks of emperor to *megas domestikos*. The derivation of the term is the same as one for the pendants of the crowns of the Porfurogennêtan era, the *kataseista*, and in context we may viably accept that the *seia* are something analogous.[85] The earlier *kataseista*, or *praipendoulia*, are depicted as a string of pearls with a cluster of two or three at the bottom. This continues to be the case with the pendants shown attached to Palaiologian crowns, although the descriptions of the *seia* indicate a different construction. The *seia* of the *megas domestikos* are simply described with a term employed for many of the elite garments and accessories, 'gold-red' (*khrusokokkinos*), and those of the *despotês*, *sevastokratôr* and *kaisar* are 'like those of the emperor except for the knot and the palms'.[86] None of these descriptors can be readily equated with a string of pearls. A more likely interpretation is that *seia* are tapes or strips of silk, probably a gold-and-red brocade, worked with various figures for the four highest ranks.

Turban

The appearance of the turban amongst the regalia in the *Treatise on the Offices* is a further instance of the mundane making its way into court ritual more than in prior eras. There is ample evidence that such headgear had been in common East Roman use for many centuries by the fourteenth century, although its use may have had a recession in the late thirteenth and fourteenth centuries in favour of European styles of hat that begin to be seen in Western-influenced manuscripts of the time.[87]

Only a relatively few ranks have turbans amongst their regalia: the *logothetês tou dromou*; *logothetês tou Ssratiôtikou*; *logothetês tou oikeiakou*; and the *ageloi*, the *megas logariastês*, the *prôtasêkrêtis*, the *epi tôn deêseôn* and the *mystikos*. In contrast, none of these ranks have a *skaranikon*. A turban is almost always accompanied by an *epilôrikion* across these ranks. On occasion, the emperor wears a turban, which is specifically defined as the sole fitting accompaniment of an *epilôrikion*.[88] The one ceremony explicitly described for this imperial outfit culminates with the veneration of Mary as 'mother of victories'.[89] This indicates that this ensemble of a turban and *epilôrikion*, which we first saw as imperial triumphal regalia by the early tenth century, had retained its military associations. This is one of the simplest examples of detectable ceremonial vestimentary continuity between the tenth and fourteenth centuries. It is notable that no colour of these ceremonial turbans is specified. It seems probable that they were white, since that is the colour shown consistently across Byzantine pictorial sources throughout the middle and late Byzantine eras, a marked contrast to the variety of shades illustrated in Islamic sources. These regalia turbans have an ornament hanging over the left ear. The name given to this ornament is somewhat obscure: *margelion surmateïnon*.[90] It may mean a 'train of pearls', 'pearls strung on gold' or a 'gold braid' (Plate 20, right).[91]

In contrast to other well illustrated-items, there appear to be no depictions of Palaiologian regalia turbans amongst surviving art.[92] Even without any pictures it is possible to make a strong hypothesis as to the form of the Palaiologian regalia turban. While a recent suggestion that turbans were 'a concession to Turkish fashion'[93] is as false as the claim in the *Treatise* that they were derived from Persia (see the discussion in chapter 3), there is still a Turkish connection, but in the other direction. We have seen that turbans wrapped over heavy caps were already in Byzantine use in the tenth century.[94] Over the following centuries this practice became quite ubiquitous across the eastern Mediterranean cultures, with the caps themselves increasing in opulence and size.[95] Tall, pointed turban-caps may be seen in Byzantine and Byzantine-derived sources, including the Madrid Skylitzes and others from the eleventh to the thirteenth centuries.[96] The same style appears in the earliest Ottoman portraits, such as the contemporary painting of Mehmet II, and thereafter are a characteristic feature of elite Ottoman dress.[97] It is therefore reasonable to conclude that Palaiologian regalia turbans consisted of a fine, white cloth wrapped over a tall cap which protruded from the top, and almost certainly sewn to shape that they might be put on like a hat.

Pull-over garments

Sakkos

The *sakkos* has been the subject of significant scholarly attention, although without resolving several crucial issues, and sometimes confusing the issue more than elucidating it.[98] The observation upon which scholars agree, and which is beyond question, is that the *sakkos* was originally a coarse, shapeless bag worn as a garment of penitence.[99] Apparently unrecognised to date is the fact that as a long sack with holes cut for head and arms, the penitential *sakkos* is, in effect, a rustic form of the original *colobium/kôlovion*. We have seen previously that from the fourth century the *kôlovion* began to be gentrified, gaining long, loose sleeves and becoming conflated with the *dalmatica/delmatikê*. In doing this, it carried its name with it in male use, thereby creating a terminological confusion, or perhaps even a void, for the old, sleeveless, sack-like form. That the potent significance of the ancient type was by no means lost can be seen in the iconography of the sixth to eleventh centuries, when the crucified Christ was commonly depicted wearing this garment rather than the loincloth of Western and later Orthodox iconography.[100] Thus, the already-established term *sakkos* may have increasingly been employed to ease the confusion of nomenclature, or fill the void, from the sixth century onwards. It should be noted that late Byzantine theology was well aware of the antecedence of the *sakkos* and its connection with the Crucifixion *kôlovion*. While discussing the significance of vestments in the fifteenth century, Symeon of Thessaloniki wrote that patriarchs and archbishops 'wear *sakkoi* conspicuously recalling that He above us wore a *sakkos* in his suffering and death upon the cross'.[101] Similarly, he equates the *sakkos* with the purple that Christ was dressed in during the passion, thereby once again recalling early iconography which invariably paints the Crucifixion *kôlovion/sakkos* as purple, or a dark blue shading towards purple.[102]

One natural assumption underlying the discussion is that the imperial *sakkos* must be of the same form as the religious vestment. This assumption is, however, questionable. Although the emperor had so great a religious role that it led Runciman to characterise the entire system as a theocracy, the evidence from earlier periods is that religious symbolism was projected onto secular regalia rather than religious items being co-opted into the lay sphere, and that lay and religious garments bearing the same name could have significant differences. A close inspection of the chrysobull of Alexios III of Trebizond in the Dionysiou Monastery suggests that this is true of the *sakkos* (fig. 63). At the cuffs one can see that the inner layer shows the cuffs fastened tightly to the wrist of a regalia *roukhon* or *kavadion*. The outer garment, however, has the straight, loose sleeves of the middle Byzantine-era *kôlovion*. Its fabric is the very black that *Treatise on the Offices* attributes to the imperial *sakkos*, a colour that we have seen is rare in lay use. Thus it seems that while the ecclesiastical *sakkos* preserved the ancient sleeveless form of the *kôlovion*, and may have done so throughout the medieval period, the lay regalia form of late Byzantium once again derived from the gentrified style with wide sleeves, which became so prominent in the regalia in the later twelfth century. Whether the term *sakkos* was used for the sleeved lay garment throughout, or re-attributed to it is a question upon which the sources seem to be silent.

It has been said that in Palaiologian court practice the *sakkos* had supplanted the *divêtêsion*.[103] The parallel is not quite as simple as that. Certainly it is the main focus of the coronation ceremony, as the *divêtêsion* had been, but the resemblance ends there. The *sakkos* is the sole prerogative of the emperor amongst laymen, whereas the *divêtêsion* was worn by various ranks at different times. The *divêtêsion* was a wholly secular garment, with its iconographic use upon the figures of Christ and angels being a projection from the secular realm into the spiritual,[104] while the *sakkos* necessarily retains some religious ramifications despite its difference from the pure ecclesiastical form. Hence, the *sakkos* distinguished the emperor from the

FIG. 63. Emperor Alexios III Komnênos (1328–41) of Trebizond and Theodôra. The loose sleeves of the emperor's *sakkos* are a distinct contrast to the close sleeves of the *roukhon*. It is notable that the empress is wearing a crossover coat derived from the Turkish *yalma*, and that she is dressed somewhat informally, without *diadêma* or *maforion*. Khrusobul, Dionysiou Monastery, Athos.

rest of the court in a way that the *divêtêsion* did not. A further difference is likely to be when, and how often, the *sakkos* was worn. A full assessment of this is hampered by the fact that the *Treatise on the Offices* says surprisingly little about the regalia of the emperor. The impression to be gleaned from scattered hints is that the *sakkos* was not worn so very often, and that the emperor might just as often be wearing a *roukhon*, a *kavadion* or even an *epilôrikion*. Supporting this observation is a major symbolic difference. The *divêtêsion* was central to the iconography of emperorship in the tenth to twelfth century, yet the *sakkos* is less visible in late Byzantine royal portraits, in which the emperors are more often depicted wearing either a *roukhon* or *kavadion*.

Roukhon

Roukhon was a long-used term for a main garment, principally a tunic.[105] The *Composition on Warfare* of Nikêforos Fôkas shows that the term *roukhon* had been in vernacular use since the the early tenth century if not earlier, evidently bearing a quite general meaning of 'garment', and deriving from Slavic, according to Mihaescu.[106] As we may see from the employment of terms like *himation*, there had been a common tendency over a long span of time for such basic terms to refer to a main garment, a man's tunic or or woman's dress, when there is no other information given in the context. This phenomenon must surely have been the foundation for the more specific use of *roukhon* in the late Byzantine era, at least in the court milieu. Du Cange gives a number of citations of the term, many of which appear to be late redactions of earlier sources. Of particular note is a metaphrase of Khoniatês' *Historia* now in the Vatican Library which shows extensive revisions from the earlier versions. Due to the nature of the alterations in this version, and the brevity of Du Cange's quotations, three of the four occurrences are impossible to relate to earlier editions. In one which can be correlated, *roukhon* has evidently been interpolated in order to ameliorate Khoniatês' Atticising circumlocutions, and it seems likely that the others were inserted for the same reason.[107] The context of that passage, a description of a statue of Andronikos I, makes it sufficiently clear that a tunic is indeed what is being described. In another place, *roukhon* is also manifestly equivalent to tunic, 'a split *roukhon* of two colours'.[108] This plainly refers to the adoption of the parti-coloured tunics which were a prevalent fashion in Western dress from the thirteenth century,[109] and which begin to be illustrated in Byzantine art in the fourteenth century.[110] *Roukhon* is also found used for women's dresses in Iôannês Kananos' account of the siege of Constantinople that took place in 1422, directly paralleling the employment of *himation* throughout the period and even in the present source.[111]

The *roukha* of the *Treatise on the Offices* are distinguished from other tunics called *kamisia*, *stikharia* and *himatia*, which are worn by ecclesiastics. Spatharakis attributes this tunic to the *sevastokratôr* shown on the first page of the *Lincoln Typikon*.[112] This may be so, but identifying this garment with any confidence in artworks of this period is rarely possible, for the crucial area for distinguishing a *roukhon* from a *kavadion*, the centre front where a *kavadion* opens, is almost invariably covered by another item of regalia, either the *tabarion* or *diadêma*. One pictorial source made under imperial or quasi-imperial patronage in the fourteenth century, the illuminated *Alexander Romance*, does show tunics with very close-fitting cuffs employed as royal regalia. They are predominantly red for the senior emperor, just as the *Treatise* says, or occasionally purple or blue, and a purple-based brocade for the emperor designate.[113] Unfortunately, this manuscript was produced in the rival empire of Trebizond, and, while there are discernible parallels, it is difficult to assess just how close its court practices were to those of Constantinople. In addition, due to the paucity of terminology in sources of the eleventh to fourteenth centuries, it is impossible to make any guess as to when the transition of terms to *roukhon* might have taken place.

The regalia *roukha* in the *Treatise* are worn by the highest four ranks: the emperor, *despotês*, *sevastokratôr* and *kaisar*. That of the emperor is only described as 'pearled' (*margaritareinos*),[114] but from the description of the *roukhon* of the *despotês* we learn that its colour was red (*kokkinos*) and that it had borders (*rizai*) bearing military symbols. These borders were presumably embroidered in gold or braid woven in gold. The *roukha* of the *despotês*, the *sevastokratôr* and the *kaisar* are all the same red as the emperor's tunic but varied in their trimming. The *roukhon* of the *despotês* had borders without military emblems, while those of the *sevastokratôr* and the *kaisar* lacked such borders. If the red fabric was not figured in some way, this description makes them remarkably plain for regalia garments of such high rank, yet that fact probably made them all the more distinctive in an assemblage of the court mostly dressed in multicoloured brocade *kavadia*.

Divided garments

Hitherto in this volume it was concluded that by tenth century the form of sleeve that a garment possessed, or lacked, was often what determined its identity and place in the scheme of regalia, and, indeed dress practice more generally. The reduction in stylisation of the late Byzantine court had reduced this feature of vestiary practice, but there were still traces of it. The identities of garments in this category are founded upon that fact.

Kavadion

We have seen that the essential nature of the *kavadion* is not a problematical issue – a coat opening vertically down the front. Already common in everyday men's dress in the sixth century, it had become ubiquitous by the fourteenth century. This is amply attested by pictorial sources from the twelfth to fifteenth centuries.[115] A surviving coat of the fifteenth century, undoubtedly modelled on Byzantine style is held in the Museum of Art, Bucharest (Chart 5.4).[116] The prevalence of this garment is reflected in the regalia rules of the *Treatise on the Offices* by the fact that virtually every listed rank has a *kavadion*. This phenomenon illustrates one conspicuous way in which the Palaiologian court was dramatically less stylised than the court of Constantine Porfurogennêtos and his immediate predecessors and successors. Only the *kavadion* of the *despotês* is specified with any precision. It is purple (*oxus*) or red (*kokkinos*) according to the wearer's preference, with pearlwork (*margariteinos*).[117] All the other ranks were to have *kavadia* made of 'a brocade such as will be chosen from the accustomed ones'.[118] In this we see the continuation of the practice initiated in the later eleventh century, and particularly illustrated in the garb of the *proedros*.

The Palaiologian court *kavadion* has the distinction of being very nearly the most often and accurately represented item of clothing in the Byzantine repertoire, surpassed only by the *khlamus*. Its appearance in art has been often noted by previous scholars.[119] It is most copiously depicted in the *Lincoln Typikon* (fig. 60), most familiarly seen in the oft-reproduced portrait of Megas Droungarios Alexios Apokaukos,[120] and visible in other donor portraits bearing recorded ranks.[121] A significant characteristic of the majority of these regalia *kavadia* is that they are entirely devoid of any trimming. The unvarying characteristic of these coats which defines their nature as regalia is the form of their sleeves. They are all very tight to the wrist, in a manner which harks back to the *persikomanikion* of much earlier times. A source which throws this fact into sharp relief is the donor portrait of Theodôros Metokhitês in the Church of the Holy Saviour in Khôra (fig. 64). Some have assumed that Metokhitês is depicted in regalia as is normally the case.[122] However, according to the *Treatise on the Offices*, the regalia proper to his rank of *megas logothetês* should show a *skaranikon*, as do the other donor portraits of this era, rather than the turban-like affair he wears. His *kavadion* has rather loose sleeves, rather than the close-fitting cuffs which, again, can be precisely corroborated by the other donor portraits. Furthermore, Metôkhitês' *kavadion* has contrasting edging, again quite unlike regalia coats. Hence, Metokhitês has chosen to be shown in everyday clothing, presumably as a gesture of humility.

Spatharakis is particularly acute in identifying a rare variant of the *kavadion* in the garment worn by Alexios V Mourtzouflos.[123] This particular *kavadion* is a development of the Persian style dating back to the *kandus* of the Sassanian era and *fiblatôrion/zôstarion* of Roman Late Antiquity which has the edge of the front panel opening offset to the left (fig. 8; Chart 2.4).[124] In addition to having sleeves loose at the wrist and the unusual patterning, this once again suggests that Mourtzouflos' coat is not a regalia *kavadion*, for all the other identifiable examples have the opening down the centre front. We may also compare the non-regalia coats of the illuminated *Alexander Romance* and other sources, which are cross-over coats with slanting front-panel edges from the Armenian tradition, or of the type called *yalma* in early Turkish.[125] The fact that Mourtzouflos wears a very plain *stemmatoguron* rather than anything more eminent also indicates that he was dressing down for this portrait.

FIG. 64. In contrast to most donor portraits of the Palaiologian era, Theodôros Metokhitês had himself depicted in everyday dress, rather than his regalia as *megas logothetês*. Khôra Church, Istanbul.

Epanoklivanon

This term is commonly synonymous with *epilôrikion* throughout our period, and should be taken so here.[126] The precise form will be explained in the next entry. The garment worn by the Tzakonians is blue with white lions 'confronted statant' (in European heraldic terminology) worked onto the chest. This design is reminiscent of the *leukoleôn* capes of the *Book of Ceremonies*, and the surviving fabrics that bear such designs (fig. 21).[127] In view of the virtual disappearance of regalia capes in the Palaiologian scheme, it is not remarkable to find this popular and persistent motif applied to such coats.

Epilôrikion

In chapter 3 it was observed that the military manuals of the tenth century were quite precise about the forms of the arming coats which they variously called *kavadion*, *epanoklivanon* and *epilôrikion*, and that those descriptions dwelt upon the nature of the sleeves. The most relevant type for the continuance of the terms *epanoklivanon* and *epilôrikion* is that described by the *Composition on Warfare* which had openings in the armpits through which the arms could pass, leaving the sleeves to hang free. From the eleventh century some form of these military garments made their way into civilian use, preserving the name *epilôrikion*, evidently to distinguish them from the standard civilian *kavadion*. *Epilôrikia* are mentioned several times in *Digenês Akritas*, where they are luxurious and colourful garments, while still retaining their military purpose.[128]

Thereafter, in chapter 4 I outlined the trend for the sleeves in these garments to be attenuated, initially to elbow length around the turn of the thirteenth century. This process continued and by the time of the creation of the *Treatise on the Offices* the *epilôrikion/epanoklivanon* was entirely devoid of sleeves. It is illustrated in this form on the junior figures of the donor portraits of the *Gospels of Ivan Alexander*.[129]

The author of the *Treatise* assigns the origin of the *epilôrikion* to the Medes in the time of King Cyrus, along with the turban.[130] As Grabar has observed, this is a fiction designed to give an ancient and admirable cachet to these garments.[131]

Granatza and *Lapatza*

These garments are treated together because the author of the *Treatise on the Offices* regards them as being the same garment, and confesses confusion as to why they have different names.[132] A careful consideration of how they are worn from a practical standpoint will reveal a physical distinction.

The earlier term used for the surcoats of the *Stratêgikon*, *gounion*, is traceable back to the Aramaic *gônakka*, which also entered antique Greek as *gaunakê*.[133] For several centuries there is a hiatus in the sources. *Gaunakas* appears in the Suda glossed with a single word – 'garment' (*ampekhomenon*), suggesting that in the tenth century there was little recollection of what sort of garment it had been at an earlier time.[134] It seems otherwise unknown in medieval Greek. In the West it reappears quite extensively from the early thirteenth century in late continental Latin as *garnachia/garnacia/guarnachia*, in Anglo-Latin as *warnache* and in French as *garnache*, all these referring by explicit description to the sleeveless surcoat that had become a feature of European dress, both civil and military, from the late twelfth century.[135] The phonology of *granatza* as given in the *Treatise on the Offices*, that is the interpolated 'r' and the equivalence of 'ch' to 'tz' commonly observed in medieval Greek, suggests that this term had re-entered Byzantine usage from the West. Yet we are confronted with an apparent contradiction in that the recorded European *guarnachia* was a sleeveless pull-over garment, whereas the late Byzantine *granatza* had sleeves and was a divided garment. This is not remarkable – it is a very common phenomenon for a clothing term borrowed from one culture to another to be applied to a different garment. A recent example is the use in the third quarter of the twentieth century of 'caftan' for a pull-over tunic, when its ancient and proper use was for a coat.[136] It may be that the initial mis-application was in the Western adoption, while the re-assimilation into Greek restored it to its antecedent use, probably because while *gaunakê* was still in use, it seemed old-fashioned, whereas *granatza* seemed new and trendy. Whatever the precise route of transmission, it seems clear that *granatza* was reapplied to a form of *gounion* related to that of the *Stratêgikon*, a loose, heavy coat with ample sleeves particularly for outdoor wear in inclement weather.

The evolution of the *lapatza* and the derivation of its name are issues for which there is even less evidence than for the *granatza*. Phonology again suggests it was a foreign import, which Hemmerdinger derives from the Persian *lapacha* – 'an outer garment'.[137] Other than that, there appears to be no other precedent for it in Greek, and only tenuous hints in Latin.[138] According to early thirteenth-century Latin sources, the *lapatia*, or more commonly simply *lapa* in Western ecclesiastical use, was worn unbelted, illustrating yet again the alterations in custom and style which occur as garments and terms cross cultural boundaries.

Thus a consideration of etymologies does not shed any light on why two names are used, but the description of how they are worn is more forthcoming. The *Treatise* tells us that the sleeves of the *granatza* and *lapatza* were very long, to the ankle in fact, and we see a garment showing this characteristic in a damaged fresco from the crypt of the Church of the Holy Saviour in Khôra (fig. 65).[139] We have seen that coats with very long sleeves had a very ancient history in the Near East, and were known to Rômaioi in the tenth century, as with Achmet's *kavadion skaramangion*. The extending of the ample *gaunakê* sleeve, which doubtless began as protection for the hand and then was taken further as a token of opulence as the garment was gentrified, introduced a new permutation. Whereas the long *skaramangion* sleeve had to be pulled back onto the forearm to free the hand, the fullness and weight of the *gaunakê* sleeve made that impractical. To evade this problem two expedients were applied, which in one case had been first seen in ancient garments, and in the other were applied to military garments of the tenth century. The first is to have an opening in the armpit to pass the arm and allow the entirety of the sleeve to hang empty. Pictures from the early imperial era show this practice in tunics, while it is later found in some of the so-called 'Persian riding coats' excavated in Egypt.[140] As has been noted, it is explicitly described as being a feature of the padded military *kavadion* and *epilôrikion* in the tenth-century *Composition on Warfare*,[141] and once more appears in short-sleeved civilian tunics in the donor portraits of the *Queen Keran Gospels* manuscript of 1272.[142] A manuscript in Berlin from the turn of the fourteenth century or slightly later shows a coat precisely of this form, but of the more mundane type, merely knee-length in the body and with sleeves not unduly long.[143]

The other method of allowing free use of the hands is to place an opening for the arms at the elbow. Once again, this is presaged in a tenth-century military manual, the *Sullogê Taktikôn*.[144] It takes a long while for it to become illustrated however. The earliest representation dates from *c*.1225, when it is shown as the travelling garment of Richard I of England

FIG. 65. The coat on the left of this fresco is evidently a *lapatza* as the ends of the very long sleeves are visible on either side. Note the seam lines on the boots. Khôra Church, Istanbul.

in the *Liber ad Honorem Augusti* of Peter of Eboli (fig. 37).[145] It is significant that it appears that, as far as the illustrator of this manuscript was concerned, this was a distinctively English fashion in the European context, for no other person in the manuscript is shown wearing such a garment. This strongly suggests that this sleeve style could have already been taken back to Britain by men leaving service with the Varangians or other Roman units from the eleventh century onwards, who must have had far more long-term day-to-day exposure to Byzantine customs than anyone else from the far West. In fact, the pictures of Richard show both sleeve openings on the same garment. Thereafter, there is a gap in the pictorial sources in both East and West until the fourteenth century, at which time they suddenly become common, being particularly well illustrated in the *Alexander Romance*.

How these two forms relate to the description in the *Treatise* hinges upon the use of the belt. The author says that the *lapatza* was worn with a belt through which the sleeves were threaded (Plate 23, left), while the *granatza* was worn unbelted. This can only mean that the *lapatza* had openings in the armpits, for if had the openings in the elbow, the construction of the sleeves through the belt would have made any use of the arms nearly impossible. It can be inferred from this that the *granatza* had the elbow openings, with freedom of movement permitted by the absence of the belt.

Diadêma

The ornamental drape descended from the ancient *toga* remains an essential component of imperial regalia in the Palaiologan period, just as it had been earlier. The term *lôros* is no longer used, for the garment has taken over the name *diadêma* from the old coronet, as the author of the *Treatise* takes some trouble to explain.[146] The word *zônê* (belt) is also used, just as it was in the middle Byzantine period.[147] The only significant observation to be made in comparing the custom described in the *Treatise* to prior times is that by this period the use of the *diadêma* has become confined to the emperor, whereas in the *Book of Ceremonies* various ranks also wore it on occasion. The reason for this is simple. When looking at older works of art for examples upon which to base their reconstitution of a court, the rulers and courtiers of the post-1204 realm are quite likely to have seen nothing but royal portraits showing the *lôros*. Even had they seen the very few pictures illustrating non-royals wearing this accessory, they would have seen them as what they purported to be, pictures of Pontius Pilate, having no framework for contextualising him in the judicial role of an *Eparkhos tês Poleôs*. The *Treatise* stresses that the *diadêma* was always worn with the *sakkos* (fig. 63),[148] while giving no indication that it could be worn with another garment, as art shows (fig. 59). The form of the *diadêma* shown in the art of this era is very consistent. It bears most resemblance to the 'yoke-style' *lôros* of the later eleventh century (Chart 6.6).[149]

Mantles and cloaks

The abandonment of the cloak or mantle in men's dress in favour of the coat, noted in earlier sections, is now so complete that no one but the highest royalty wears them as regalia. The distinction in form that was present in the tenth century but disappeared in the late eleventh century has been restored, however.

Manduas

The *manduas* figures rarely in the *Treatise on the Offices*, but in some significant ways. In one case its presence reflects the survival of this cape as a basic part of women's everyday attire. The mother of an incoming emperor wears a purple (*oxus*) *manduas* to the coronation.[150] (See below for further discussion of this.) Also unremarkable is the fact that the higher ranks of the priesthood wear *manduai* with stripes (*potamoi*) at the elevation of a patriarch. Such capes are a standard part of their vestments, as our source makes evident.[151] More significant is the appearance of a gold (*khrusoun*) *manduas* amongst the emperor's garb during phases of the ceremonies at his coronation. Recalling the information given by Constantine Porfurogennêtos defining the equivalence of *manduas* and *sagion*, these references hark back to the gold and gold-edged *sagia* of the emperor in tenth-century ceremonies. Yet the difference in the employment of these otherwise-identical capes is very important. The tenth-century *sagia* were worn very often in all manner of ceremonies. The golden *manduas* of the fourteenth century was only worn in those portions of the coronation rituals which were most specifically religious in nature.[152] In one, the *manduas* was worn with a *sakkos*, another item with religious associations.[153] This transformation illustrates another aspect of the disappearance of capes in Byzantine dress that has been discussed elsewhere in this work in relation to the *khlamus*/*tabarion*. Whereas the latter disappeared from all common use, the *manduas* simply shed its secular aspect and was preserved in the much more conservative milieu of the Church as a religious vestment. It is in that capacity that it returns briefly to imperial use in these ceremonies. This observation serves also to confirm that the form of the *manduas* remained essentially unchanged as a semicircular cape worn fastened at the centre of the chest.

Tabarion

Du Cange established the equivalence of *tabarion* (ταμπάριον) with *khlamus* in noting the substitution of terms in a fourteenth-century redaction of the chronicle of Khoniatês.[154] Following that, Spatharakis identified an example appropriately worn by Sevastokratôr Constantine Palaiologos in the *Lincoln Typikon*: a semicircular cloak fastened with a brooch on the right shoulder in time-honoured fashion.[155]

The basic survival of this garment is quite unremarkable, but the dynamics of its transmission and evolution in form and terminology demand elaboration. Previously, the conclusion was presented that even in the tenth century the *khlamus* was an anachronistic garment not present in everyday Byzantine male fashion, and therefore that its usage in court was even then an expression of stylisation. The prevalence of cloaks worn in identical or similar manners by Western men would have struck Byzantines as indicative of the backwardness of such visitors in that period. The later eleventh and twelfth centuries saw a further recession in the *khlamus*, as its distinctive features became diffused, with the *tavlia* placed on capes fastened on the chest, and unadorned mantles being fastened on the right shoulder. This left the true *khlamus* further confined in use to imperial and near-imperial ranks, and hence all the more central to imperial iconography, especially in durable, widely-seen media such as coinage. In the reconstitution of court practice and regalia following the Fourth Crusade, the resumption of *khlamus*-wearing would have been a rapidly embraced visible claim to power, one which would be relatively easy and inexpensive to implement and which would serve to conceal deficiencies in regalia which was more costly or less easily replaced, such as the *lôros* or crowns. The prior contraction in its use also lays the foundation for the restricted use of the *tabarion* reflected in the *Treatise on the Offices* – it is confined to the emperor, *despotês*, *sevastokratôr*, *kaisar*, *panupersevastos* and *prôtovestiarios*.

The term *tabarion* has been connected with the Italian *tabarro* attested in use in the thirteenth century.[156] The spelling of *tabarion* is an early example of the use of *mu-pi* to represent the Latin phoneme 'b', as persists in Greek to this day.

The *tamparia* of the *despotês* and *sevastokratôr* are both red (*kokkinos*), like their *roukha*, and adorned with pearlwork.[157] The same is presumably true of the cloak of the *kaisar*, since his other regalia is identical to that of the *sevastokratôr*. The *tamparia* of the other two offices are also decorated with pearlwork, on a yellow-orange (*kitrinos*) field for the *panupersevastos* and a green (*prasinos*) field for the *prôtovestiarios*.[158]

Leg- and footwear

Stockings

Stockings (*kaltzai*) are an unusual addition to the regalia.[159] The *Book of Ceremonies* makes no mention of the hose that anyone was to wear on a day-to-day basis, merely specifying those occasions upon which the rulers were to wear military leggings (*kampotouva*). Leg-wear was hardly ever to be seen between the normal ankle-length robes of aristocrats and the boots that were commonly worn across our period. The only time they would have been visible was while the wearer was mounted, as the skirts of the clothing rode up or blew aside. The reason for the addition may have been to assure the chromatic unity of the most eminent outfits, and to distingish them from the next category down. Thus, the hose of the *despotês* are the same red (*kokkinos*) as his *skiadion*, *skaranikon*, *roukhon* and *tabarion*.[160] In contrast, the stockings of the *sevastokratôr* and *kaisar* are blue (*êeraneos*) matching their boots, but clashing with the red of their other garments.[161] Curiously, the only other courtiers to have regalia *kaltzai* are the staff of the imperial tent (the *Kortinarioi*), who also have the distinction of red hose.[162]

Boots

Footwear is specified for the six highest ranks. The persistence of long-established practices can be seen in the sole reference to the emperor's boots. Two types are mentioned by venerable terminology, *hupodêmata* and *tzangia*. The *hupodêmata* are evidently his everyday wear, and are not described. The *tzangia* are his true regalia footwear, worn in parades and festivals, and this expression is not applied to the footwear of any other man.[163] That the terminology should be used this way shows a distinct antiquarianism that is very much at odds with the general tone of the work, for as early as the eleventh century *tzangia* had started to become a general term for men's boots, rather than those of the ruler. The imperial ceremonial *tzangia* are described in some detail, which makes it clear that these are high boots extending to the knee in time-honoured fashion. The shaft of these boots is decorated with eagles worked in gems and pearls, as the toe area is also. Our source does not say as much, but there is ample evidence in other sources that the *tzangia* were still dyed red/purple as imperial footwear had been since Late Antiquity.[164] The difference of his less eminent *hupodêmata* may be that, while they would also have been of the imperial colour, they were not decorated to the degree of his ceremonial boots. There may also have been a distinction of form, with the *hupodêmata* perhaps being shorter than the *tzangia*. Byzantine art across the period commonly shows common boots as being quite low on the calf. Anything much longer would have been redundant under the long skirts of noble tunics and coats, and could have been an encumbrance under such full skirts.[165]

The *hupodêmata* of the *despotês* were coloured purple (*oxeos*) and white (*leukos*), and had eagles worked in pearls on the sides of the shaft of the boots, and upon the toe,[166] in the manner seen on the fragmentary royal statue from Tirnovo.[167] The boots (*hupodêmata*) of the *sevastokratôr* were blue (*êeraneos*) with eagles embroidered in gold on a red (*kokkinos*) field in the same layout as those on the footwear of the *despotês*.[168] The overall colour, at least, had been in place since at least the early twelfth century, instituted by John II.[169] Ranks below this had plain-coloured *hupodêmata*. The *kaisar* also had blue (*êeraneos*), the *panupersevastos*, yellow-orange (*kitrinos*), and the *prôtovestiarios* green (*prasinos*). The first and last of these were, again, already in place in the twelfth century.[170] All below that wore the mundane brown and black. Despite the proliferation down the ranks, footwear retained its importance in establishing a major division in the court. An aspect of this is illustrated by the fact that the highest four ranks with decorated boots retained them even when they and the entire court were garbed in black in mourning for an empress or royal heir.[171]

Shoes

As a counterpoint to the regal *hupodêmata* and *tzangia*, common footwear is mentioned twice in the *Treatise* by the name that has survived with a minor change in spelling to the present day, *papoutzia*.[172] The *Kortinarioi* were to wear dark-coloured *papoutzia* with their red stockings, while shoes were part of the minimum presentable dress of the dozen paupers who were invited to an imperial dinner on the Thursday of the Easter festival.[173]

Accessories

Akakia

The *akakia* is almost unique in having endured across the whole of our period unchanged in name, nature and symbolism. It was a cylindrical sachet of silk containing earth representing the humility maintained by the Emperor despite his exalted position.[174] There is one significant difference in the employment recommended by the *Treatise* compared to the *Book of Ceremonies*: it had exchanged hands with the cross, and in the Palaiologian era it was to be held in the left hand.[175]

Cross

The cross was the ceremonial staff of the emperor, counterpart to the golden bough of the empress.[176] It was called *skêpiôn* at the beginning of our period and, according to ample pictorial evidence, remained largely unchanged in form across the centuries. Palaiologian practice did preserve one change from the custom preferred by Constantine Porfurogennêtos. In the later period the cross was held in the emperor's right hand, whereas the *Book of Ceremonies* states that the *skêpiôn* was held in the left hand.[177] Constantine was probably trying to fix a practice which pictorial sources show was in fact highly variable. Fourteenth-century art indicates that the post-Fourth-Crusade restorers succeeded where Constantine Porfurogennêtos evidently failed, for the surviving late Byzantine portraits conform strictly to the right-handed stipulations of the *Treatise on the Offices*.

Baton

The place of the baton (*dikanikon*) in the Palaiologian court is one of the most dramatic contrasts with the practice of the tenth century. In the earlier period batons certainly had a significant part in the ceremonies, yet few ranks had any unique form of baton as a part of their regalia. The few who did were *ostiarios*, *silentiarios*, *mandatôr*, *kouropalatês*, *dekourion* and *ekdikos*. At the end of the empire the great majority of named ranks had a distinctive baton. One substantial group had a form of baton in common – plain wood – but other ranks who had them each had a distinct form, set apart by some combination of metal, colour and decorative details. Compared with how much clothing regalia was common across the ranks, it can be said that baton form was one of the most important signs of rank. These men were even called to functions as a category, 'those who carry a baton', very much paralleling the largely synonymous categories of 'the white-wearers' (*leukoforoi*) and 'the cloak-wearers' (*khlanidoforoi*) in the *Book of Ceremonies*.[178]

Underneath the variations of metal, colour and decor, the *dikanika* occurred in a very limited number of gross forms. The majority of the most eminent were divided into four sections, either by knobs or changes in finish.[179] The next class were divided into two sections by changes of finish.[180] A few had a knob at their top and then a unitary scheme of patterning.[181] A couple had an emblem on top – a *gamma* in one case, and a dove in another – which may have been inspired by the eagle-headed sceptre (*skipiô*) of Late Antiquity.[182] There is a clear implication that most of the plain wooden batons were knobbed, for a few are said to lack them.[183] They must also usually have been in a darker-coloured wood, for one was said to be of a white wood.[184]

Gauntlet

In one of the rare occasions of truly distinctive and representative regalia items within the throng of the junior court, the Prôtoierakarios carried a left-hand gauntlet (*kheirôrtion*) tucked into his belt.[185] This custom represented his position as the head of the imperial falconers.[186] This glove was rather ornate, being worked with purple eagles and having a band woven with pearls around the edge of the cuff.

Gauge

The *megaloi tzaousioi* carried a *saliba* at the left side of their belt.[187] This has previously been taken to be a short javelin or dart,[188] but there is an interpretation which better explains who carried this item. The *Treatise* states that this object is a '*seiromastês* which is commonly called *saliba*'.[189] Both terms were indeed applied to javelins, yet the former gained its name from an older implement, a prod used for testing the depth of grain containers, or ascertaining whether there were pitfalls in advance of a military force.[190] The task of the *megaloi tzaousioi* was to 'procure the good management of the emperor's troupe' under instruction from the *megas primikêrios*.[191] There was no logic to such men carrying darts, whereas for the item to be a grain gauge or pit tester would be fully in keeping with assuring the good order of the imperial company.

In addition to these considerations, the placement of the *saliba* on the left side and the singularity of the noun argue against it being a dart. The practice of carrying darts on the belt goes back to Late Antiquity in Persia, and was continued in later Turkish practice beyond our period, though it was restricted to cavalry. All the evidence across these societies, over a long period of time, indicates that they were carried in a holder suspended from the right side of the belt, much like an arrow quiver, which contained a minimum of three darts. Roman practice was to carry a number of darts either on the back of the shield, or otherwise in the left hand.[192] To attach such a weapon to the left side of the belt would impose a major impediment to it being swiftly and readily brought into play by the predominantly right-handed users. Such a consideration of speed and ease of deployment would not have been relevant to a gauge.

Kerchief

The references to kerchief (*mandulion*) in the *Treatise* are curious and somewhat contradictory. In most cases it is an item attached to the *akakia* which is said to symbolise the instability of human existence and rulership.[193] Once, the emperor was to make a slight gesture with it in order to initiate a new phase of one of the Easter ceremonies – that was one of the very few occasions upon which there was any pretence of the emperor being in charge of the rituals of the court, an indication of how much more ossified the ceremonial of late Byzantium had become compared to the tenth century. In complete contrast to these lofty and symbolically charged applications of *mandulion*, it also saw use in its entirely prosaic incarnation as a table napkin when the *pinkernês* brings the emperor a cup.[194] Later art quite often shows people with a kerchief in hand (hence it was also called *enkheiridion*) or tucked through the belt as an emblem of their refinement (fig. 60).

Fualin

The *fualin* is a minor part of the emperor's regalia. It is evidently not a main garment, for it is worn with a *kavadion*.[195] It is also manifestly not a form of headgear since it is worn with the crown, and possibly other headgear.[196] It does have the usual array of pearls and gems that we expect of imperial regalia. *Fualin* is a form of *fialin*/*fialê* discussed at length above. I concluded in that case that it was a form of decoration which formed a broad yoke with spurs extending down the shoulders. It seems likely that the Palaiologian *fualin* is essentially the same, but detached from any garment. It might be said, therefore, that it is related to the *stêthokarakallon* found among the augustal regalia of the tenth century. Several Palaiologian imperial portraits depict what is probably the *fualin*. In contrast to the stipulations of the *Treatise on the Offices*, these pictures show it in conjunction with the *diadêma* (*lôros*). In this context the motif may be taken as a form of the yoke of the *diadêma*, although there are some subtle points of detail which set it apart. The collar portion of the *fualin* is very much wider than the yoke associated with other late Byzantine *diadêmata* and has a more strongly defined line dividing it from the vertical part of the *diadêma*, while the wings or spurs appear contiguous, whereas the sleeve bands with which they might otherwise be confused are shown as separate on other portraits.[197]

Torque

From the beginning of our period numerous men had the privilege of wearing a torque. At the end there was just one such rank, that of the *stratêgoi*.[198] The *Treatise* says that a man serving as *stratêgos* wore a *strepton* of old as an emblem of their dignity. This again illustrates how a novel validating mythology had been created to underpin the renewed practices of the restored court, for military functions like *stratêgos* had no insignia in the middle Byzantine era, although they were commonly filled by men holding the rank of *prôtospatharios*, who did have a torque amongst their regalia. The *strepton* of the late Byzantine court was made of the three twisted strands of gold, evidently resembling the style well known amongst the Celts more than the solid forms illustrated in earlier Byzantine art.[199]

Military equipment employed in ceremonies

Archery equipment

A unit of the army called *Mourtatoi* routinely carried archery equipment (*toxa*) in major parades.[200] We can confidently envisage this as being somewhat ornate matching sets of bow-case and quiver such as those that survive from the early Ottoman period.

Mace

The *prôtoallagatôr* had the unique distinction of carrying a mace (*matzouka*).[201] This term appears as early as the *Taktika* of Leo the Wise.[202] The Palaiologian regalia mace is described as *argyros kekhrusômenos*.[203] Verpeaux regards this as tautological, citing the variable use of *kekhrusômenos*,[204] however there is good reason to doubt this on the basis of the many ornate ceremonial maces which have survived from this period from cultures which had relations with Byzantium. We can be sure that this *matzouka* is the direct descendant of the all-metal *spathovaklion* of the Porfurogennêtan era, with a head of the globular form which was quite ubiquitous in Eastern Europe and the Middle East at this time. Ceremonial maces of this type were commonly silvered, with the head divided into segments alternating the silver colour with gilded bands. It seems more plausible that this is what *argyros kekhrusômenos* means in this case.

Romfaia

When the emperor attended the elevation of a new patriarch or *despotês* he was accompanied by four courtiers in stylised military dress, who were called *romfaiokratôres*, 'masters of the *romfaia*'. They each wore a gold *epilôrikion* and red *skaranikon*, and held in one hand a shield showing an equestrian picture of the emperor, and in the other a spear with a gilded shaft (Plate 20, left). This spear is called *romfaia* in accord with time-honoured usage.[205] The fact that the late Byzantine court had both *romfaiokratôres* and another unit of guards called 'Varangians' shows that middle Byzantine literature was a significant influence on those working towards the reconstitution of the court, although they read that literature in a somewhat simplistic manner, as was discussed in the introduction to this chapter.

Sword

With one exception, the only sword (*spathê*) mentioned in the *Treatise on the Offices* is that of the emperor himself. This is unremarkable, when a group of the palace garrison are to attend with sword in hand on occasion.[206] Almost all of the references to the imperial sword also deal solely with who should be holding it at a given moment.[207] In keeping with the lack of detail of imperial regalia in the *Treatise* there is no description of the imperial sword, but this is one case when such information would be quite redundant, for it is inconceivable that it should be anything other than gilded and bedecked with gems and pearls, as was the imperial sword of the *Book of Ceremonies*.[208]

One passage dealing with the imperial sword is highly significant. It states that the passing of the sword embodied the transfer of power and authority. This is a noteworthy change from the beginning of our period, when it was the *skêpiôn* that occupied that symbolic role. This major change in symbolism can be seen well reflected in the regalia patterns of the court. One facet of it is the fact that no courtiers now carried regalia swords as they did in the Porfurogennêtan era, and the other facet is the proliferation and devaluation of the baton.

Shield

The few regalia shields in the *Treatise* are referred to interchangeably with the ancient term *aspis* and the medieval term found in the *Book of Ceremonies*, *skoutarion*. There are only four shields in total, divided amongst three categories. The one most often mentioned is the imperial parade shield. It is never described, but we can be certain it was identical to the equivalent object described in the *Book of Ceremonies*: a round buckler, gilded and bedecked with pearls and precious stones.[209] There is also the shield upon which the emperor was raised during his coronation (fig. 49).[210] It is remotely possible this was the same as the imperial parade shield, but it is more likely that it was a rather larger and more robust item, perhaps with some opulent decoration around its edge and plainer in the centre where the emperor would stand. The last group of four shields are those carried by the *romfaiokratôres*. These are round and convex (*strongulos*) and painted with a portrait of the emperor on horseback.[211]

Whip

Each one of the *vardariotai*, an ethnic guard unit which had acted in a policing role since the tenth century, carries a whip (*manglavion*) on his belt.[212] This may not truly be a matter of regalia, but rather a pragmatic response to the possibility of an over-enthusiastic populace, for the author says that their purpose was 'to whip those who deserve to be whipped'. We can see a direct parallel in this with the carriage of a *manglavion* by the *droungarios tês viglas* in the *Book of Ceremonies*, although there it was more clearly ceremonial, since the commander of the city police would hardly ever have had occasion to chastise a miscreant himself.[213]

Women's regalia

Women are rather less well in evidence in the Palaiologian court than they had been in prior centuries. The crowning of an empress was a perfunctory affair, and when a foreign princess arrived to be married she was simply dressed in 'the imperial garments prepared in advance',[214] reminding one of the miniatures of *Eisitêrioi for Agnes of France*. There is no trace of the eminence of the Porfurogennêtan *zôstê patrikia* or *koubikoularea*. The nearest approximation is the mother of the emperor who had minor roles in a few ceremonies. In keeping with this marginalisation, there is very little detail forthcoming of any regalia of any of the women of the court in the literary material. Again, the ample supply of Palaiologian donor portraits comes to our aid, and confirms an inference that can be drawn from the silence of the written sources. If the range of variation in Palaiologian regalia for men is notably less that at the beginning of our period, the range for women has quite vanished. The *Lincoln Typikon* illustrates women explicitly recorded as holding the ranks of *sevastokratorissa*, *prôtostatorissa*, *megalê konstaulissa*, *megalê primikêrissa*, *prôtosevastê*, another (with no remaining rank due to damage) accompanying her husband who was a *megas stratopedarkhos*, and two other young women of unrecorded rank (fig. 60).[215] In addition, we have the portrait of Maria Akropolitissa, wife of Megas Logothetês Constantine Akropolitês.[216] All these women wear identical outfits. Their main garment is a vast brocade sack of no definite shape with a high collar. It is evidently enormously long and caught up in such a way that the upper part falls almost to the knee over a concealed belt. This dress has the falling *delmatikion* sleeves which had been in evidence from the early Middle Ages, and had evolved to a great span by the twelfth century. The upper part of these sleeves continues to be adorned with the decorative panels that had begun as modest bands in the eleventh century, and had then grown to wide rectangles by the late twelfth century, but otherwise the garment is completely undecorated, like the *kavadia* of the women's partners. The dress is worn over a fine white *esôforion* with matching *delmatikion* sleeves. A further aspect of the standardisation of women's court dress in this era is the headgear. The women illustrated are also all wearing identical narrow, jewelled and pearled coronets surmounted by low points (Chart 7).

Clothing

The 'garment called *himation*'

The only time the author of the *Treatise on the Offices* tells us of a woman's clothing is to specify the attire of a widowed empress during the coronation of her son.[217] She is to wear a 'black garment called *himation*'.[218] The employment of *himation* in this way is curious in view of the long use of it as a common term for a woman's dress.[219] Elsewhere in the *Treatise* where it does not simply mean 'clothing' in the general sense, *himation* refers to a particular type of ecclesiastical tunic.[220] Its appearance in this context may support the idea that this expression had been fully supplanted by *roukhon* for women's dresses as well as men's tunics, as is suggested by its use by Kananos. It is impossible to be certain that the use of an apparently uncommon term indicates that the garment has unique characteristics other than its colour and context of use, but, in keeping with the decorum of grief, it seems probable that this dress had simple, close-fitting sleeves, rather than the extravagantly voluminous ones seen on court dresses as commonly worn, nor would it have had their great length.

Manduas

In addition to the black *himation*, a widowed empress wore a purple (*oxus*) *manduas* to her son's coronation. While it is very likely that the *manduas* survived as everyday wear in the lower social classes, it is extremely unlikely to have had any frequent regalia use in this period. The heavy brocades of which Palaiologian court dress was normally made would render capes superfluous and uncomfortable, and we should compare how rare cloaks had become in men's regalia in this period. Certainly the *manduas* is entirely absent from the numerous pictures of women of the Palaiologian court that have survived. Therefore, this combination of *himation* and *manduas* should be viewed as the embodiment of a very traditionalist image of feminine modesty, possibly the most archaising feature of Palaiologian court vestiary practice.

Maforion

Art of the Palaiologian era shows us that one of the most important and persistent pieces of women's regalia, the *maforion*, has all but disappeared. It was evidently not a part of the attire of women of the higher levels of the court. It does survive, however, amongst the regalia of the empress. A *maforion* of the form illustrated in the *Eisitêrioi for Agnes of France* is depicted upon Empress Anna, wife of Andronikos III.[221] Du Cange also reproduces a line drawing of a portrait of Michael VIII with his wife and son, in which Theodôra is also wearing such a *maforion*.[222] Du Cange does not give a clear indication of the source of the picture, and it is not included in Spatharakis' collection. It may be from the typikon of the Monastery of Saint Michael, or some other work now lost.

Accessories

The golden bough

The *khrusoun vaion* is one of the very few pieces of augoustal regalia mentioned in the *Treatise on the Offices* and associated documents. It is described as 'a span [*spithamê*] from top to bottom and encrusted with pearls and jewels'.[223] Spatharakis noted fine representation of the golden bough in the imperial family portrait of Louvre Ivoires 100.[224] That picture shows it as having three pairs of lobes with another at the summit, and that the description in the *Treatise* refers only to the head of the item, which was mounted upon a staff approximately a metre long. As noted hitherto, there had been distinct augustal sceptres from the beginning of our period. Some of the early forms appearing in art and in coinage do bear a considerable resemblance to the golden bough of Palaiologian portraits (fig. 31.4).[225] In counterpoint, the description of the augustal sceptre in the late Byzantine romance *Belthandros and Chrysantza* as 'tri-branched' (*triklônon*) more resembles earlier styles, particularly of the eleventh century (fig. 31.2) and suggests that the earlier form had continued in use, perhaps on less formal occasions than those discussed in the *Treatise*.[226] Prior to the *Treatise* there is no indication of what the sceptre of the *augousta* was called, if it had a unique name at all.

During the coronation ritual an empress received the golden bough from the hand of the emperor immediately after he placed a crown on her head.[227] It then becomes a permanent part of her regalia, as indicated by the fact that she still carried it into the coronation ceremony of her son.[228]

Crowns

Reproducing a pattern visible since the beginning of our period, there is a hierarchy of crowns for Palaiologian women. The mother of an emperor who had been empress herself was entitled to wear a *stemma*, the more eminent type, into the coronation of her son, while his wife wore a *stefanos*. At this point the incoming emperor had himself not yet been crowned, and so, of course, had not yet crowned his wife. Therefore we must conclude that the *stefanos* of the soon-to-be-empress must in fact have been one of the coronets that were noted earlier as being worn by a great number of the women of the court. During the coronation ceremony this coronet was replaced by the *stemma*. The *stemma* of the empress of Louvre Ivoires 100 manuscript, Helena, is in the form of a large inverted cone that was already in use in the eleventh century, surmounted with points in the manner going back to Late Antiquity. The same form is corroborated by the Dionysou Monastery *Khrusobul of Alexios III* of Trebizond (fig. 63),[229] and the *Gospels of Ivan Alexander*, where, again, there is a clearly depicted distinction between the *stemma* of the crowned empress and the more modestly pointed *stefanoi* of other women.[230]

Diadêma

Unsurprisingly, the *diadêma* (the *lôros* of the earlier era) retains its pre-eminence. In fact it may have a somewhat greater status than it held in the tenth century, for while in the *Book of Ceremonies* a number of ranks had the right to wear *lôroi* at various times, in the Palaiologian period the *diadêma* was entirely confined to the emperor and empress. Its form for the empress as well as the emperor was the simpler 'yoke' style which had come into use in the eleventh century (Chart 6.6). As we have seen, the distinct female form with the rounded tail did not survive to the end of the twelfth century.

Conclusion

The nature of the late Byzantine court was characterised by contraction and simplification compared to any earlier era. There can be no question that the much-reduced late empire was considerably poorer than in prior times and that it expressed itself in a smaller court with less diversity and opulence in its regalia.

The ubiquitous garment that all men of the court had in common with each other was the *kavadion*. In form this was a perfectly ordinary coat opening down the centre front, distinguished from those worn on the street by being made of one of the regulation court brocades, and by having close-fitting cuffs. Closely related to the *kavadion* was the *epilôrikion*, sometimes called *epanoklivanon*, by this time a coat entirely without sleeves. Only a few ranks wore this garment, either as an alternative to a *kavadion*, or in place of it. Colour is attributed to the *epilôrikion* just twice, white for the emperor's garment and gold for the *romfaiokratôres*; the others were made of a regulation brocade like the *kavadia*. The pull-over tunic, or *roukhon*, still appeared as regalia, but solely for the emperor, *despotês* and *sevastokratôr*. Similarly restricted was the ancient *khlamus*, now called *tabarion*. The rarity of the cloak was another sign of the long-established dominance of forms of coat in Byzantine dress. The sacral nature of the emperor's position was made more visible than ever in this period by his wearing of the supreme ecclesiastical robe, the *sakkos*.

The informal garments of the court were the almost identical *granatza* and *lapatza*. These were somewhat similar in form as well as employment to the old *skaramangion*, having sleeves very much longer than the wearer's arms, but whereas a *skaramangion* might be a tunic or a coat, these were always of coat form. They were made less encumbering by having openings for the arms in the middle of the sleeves for the *granatza*, and in the armpits for the *lapatza*. The latter was thus the same as forms of the *epilôrikion*, *gounion* or *kaunakês* of the eleventh and twelfth centuries.

Hats adopted from Persia, and in vernacular use since the eleventh century, if not earlier, were now established in the court as the two forms of *skaranikon* dome-shaped and conical. These showed rank by their decoration, imperial portraits on various base colours for those of the upper court, and plain red with tassel, the later Turkish fez, for the rest. The male court hat of the twelfth century, derived from the women's *propolôma*, survived in a truncated form as the *kapasion*. Two other types of foreign headgear, the turban and broad-brimmed Georgian *skiadion*, found similar eminence, the latter attaining the head of the rulers themselves, fitted with a curtain at the back in a practice which probably went back to the twelfth century as a prosaic expedient. Again, these were distinguished from everyday wear only by their decoration. Another, more obscure hat derived from Persia, the *angourôton*, was also in use, and one example of the ancient headscarf persisted, renamed with a term derived from Arabic in the *skoufia*. The emperor's crown, the *stemma*, retained the bulbous form it had evolved in the twelfth century, while the next few ranks wore simpler coronets still somewhat resembling the earlier *kaisarikion*.

Footwear is one item that retained its ancient pre-eminence. The emperor's boots were purple, albeit by this time further adorned with eagles worked in pearls. Those of the *despotês* were purple and white, again with pearled eagles, and eagles appeared on the boots of the *sevastokratôr* as well, this time in red and gold on a blue field. The next three ranks had plain boots in specified colours.

One item had all but disappeared from the Palaiologian regalia, the sword. So much a feature of tenth-century ceremony, the only one that remained was that belonging to the emperor, still replete with gold and gems, just as it was at the beginning of this study. Some military equipment still appeared: mace (*matzouka*), spear (*romfaia*), shield (*aspis*) and archery sets (bow and arrows: *ta toxa*). In contrast to the disappearance of the sword was the spectacular proliferation of the baton. Virtually every rank had one, and they ranged from the expected precious metals at the top to plain wood at the bottom of the hierarchy. A greater number of ranks now carried some accessory that indicated their nominal function in the court, ranging from the glove of the imperial falconer to the grain measure (*saliba*) of the provisioning officers.

The presence and role of women in the Palaiologian court was much less well defined than in previous times. Art shows that they did have a regalia of sorts, despite the complete omission of any reference to it in the *Treatise on the Offices*. It consisted of the type of dress with very wide sleeves that had been called *delmatikion* from Late Antiquity, made out of one of the regulation brocades. It was very much the equivalent of the *kavadion* of the male courtiers. In addition, highly placed women wore a low coronet of many points, evidently related to the *augousta*'s crown of earlier times. The *stemma* of the empress by this time had continued the evolution of the inverted cone form first seen in the eleventh century, becoming higher, and restoring the points seen on early augustal *stemmata*. Below her crown the empress was now the last woman to wear the stiff, stylised *maforion*. This was a major change from the Porfurogennêtan period when the *maforion* was confined to lower-ranking women, but continued the practice first visible in the second half of the twelfth century.

Many of the upper ranks in the Porfurogennêtan court had several quite different sets of regalia, a primary one, and then another or others for special occasions. In addition to the formal wear, such men also had the informal court dress of the *skaramangion*. In stark contrast to that, in the Palaiologian court very few ranks below the top four had any variation in their regalia other than their hat. Not only was there a very much smaller range of regalia, but the regalia in use was significantly less opulent. Certainly, the late court was almost entirely clad in brocaded cloth, which had been rarer in the tenth and early eleventh centuries, yet even the plain cloth of the Porfurogennêtan courtier's garb was liberally worked with panels and trimmings of gold and silver, while such added decoration was much less evident in the final period of the empire. Furthermore, whole classes of regalia had receded from the use of the wider court, notably the *lôros*, for reasons as much to do with wealth as with the simplification of vestimentary patterns. In every way the Byzantine court of the Palaiologian era was a much less resplendent place than it had been prior to the Fourth Crusade.

CONCLUSION

The survival of the Roman Empire in the East for more than a thousand years beyond the fall of the western provinces could be said to be the most remarkable cultural achievement in recorded human history. Century after century saw a remorseless succession of external threats: Persians, Avars, Muslims, Slavs, Rus, Normans, Turks and Crusaders. If those were not enough, internal divisions, both civil and religious, tore at the fabric of the society. Yet not only did the empire not succumb, but from time to time it rallied enough to counter-attack and regain lost ground. The most remarkable example was the recovery from the crushing blow of the Fourth Crusade, which would have more than enough to destroy any less-robust society. One of the foundations of this durability was ideological, the very sense of its earlier history as ruler of the West as much as of the East. Another foundation was its multiculturalism, the ability to welcome people from other nations and assimilate cultural influences from them, employing such things routinely whilst not forgetting their origins. Yet another must have been the effective functioning of government. The historical narratives with their grievous accounts of marital contrivances, political manoeuvring, incompetent rulers, murders and usurpations often give such an impression of mayhem at the top that it seems a wonder that the state did not collapse from that alone. The very inertia of that enormous court and the imperial bureaucracy which administered the realm must have been a marmoreal plinth whose solidity did much to mitigate the effect of tribulations immediately around the throne. The fact that the Ottomans co-opted that bureaucracy, even as diminished as it must have been in the fifteenth century, and relied upon it for centuries after 1453 is a clear testament to its effectiveness.

The ceremonial of the court (and bureaucracy) and the regalia which was integral to it played its own part in the durability of the edifice. The essence of ceremonial and regalia is that it should for a time transform the consciousness of participants and onlookers, linking them into a wider cultural and ideological entity. Decade after decade, century upon century, through the oft-repeated rituals, the regalia presented a visual expression of structure and continuity, linking, for both citizen and foreigner, the present with a past that was recorded, not merely in texts and manuscript illuminations accessible to an elite few, but in architecture, statuary, paintings and mosaics that many people saw every day. A crucial quality of the ceremonial, at least in the middle period, was the way it reached beyond the court, drawing in Romans from common walks of life, visitors, and even prisoners from other nations and religions. For a few hours a humble plasterer or wood-turner might find himself walking in the footsteps of the emperor, clad in a gold-shot garment from the imperial store that was worth more than his entire life's wages. The profound psychological effect in binding that man, and his kin and peers, into the fabric of the state should be be underestimated.

Central to the contribution the regalia makes to the consciousness-transforming effect of ceremony is artificiality, that it should be distinctly different from everyday dress. The evolutionary trajectory of the regalia over the millennium of the Enduring Empire could well be seen to parallel the fortunes of the state in a way that might be as much causal as consequential. The first phase, from the sixth century to the ninth century saw a process of elaboration, with the dress and accessories of the court becoming ever more diverse, artificial and distinct from everyday clothing. By the end of that process, the formal attire of the average junior courtier in his pristine white *kamision* with its tightly buttoned 'Persian-sleeves', swathed in the ultimate anachronism of a white, purple-panel *khlamus,* unchanged in form for centuries, his head perhaps draped in a ceremonial hood, could hardly be different from the practical and colourful garb of a well-to-do man about town, dressed in a brocade *kavadion*, topped by an Armenian turban or Persian hat. This period would have seen a great recovery from the shock of the fall of the West, but for the debilitating internal effects of the Iconoclast Controversy. With the healing of that division, the period from the beginning of the tenth century into the eleventh did see just such a growth, climaxing with the illustrious reign of Basil II, half a century of stability and extensive strengthening and extension of the empire's borders.

Basil had been a conservative. Under his successors things began to change, and the changes accelerated as the century progressed. The artifice of the regalia was an increasing casualty of the wind of change. Amongst the first ancient item to vanish was the *kampagia*, the descendant of the Republican soldier's sandal, replaced by the sophisticated footwear long in common use. After that, the ritual hood (*maforion*) was abandoned, opening the way for the hat to infiltrate the court. Increasingly, the narrow range of monochrome fabrics of regalia garments gave way to patterns and a rainbow of colours like those that had characterised lay fashion for centuries, although this change took a very long time to trickle down the full length of the hierarchy. Near the end of the eleventh century, the most distinguishing characteristic of the regalia of the empress fell by the wayside. No longer would she be seen to partake equally in imperial authority by wearing the same garment as the emperor, the *divêtêsion*. Henceforth she would be just another woman, garbed in the wide-sleeved *delmatikion* that any but the poorest might enjoy. This evolution continued through the twelfth century. At the top, the 'Persian-sleeve' was simplified. It was still buttoned tightly to the wrist below a loose shaft, but was of a less complex construction. Crowns became inflated. The enclosed top of the male *stemma* became taller and more rounded, presaging the Palaiologian crown and the mitre of the post-Byzantine Orthodox Church. The empress' crown became taller. Towards the end of that century, the more populous ranks found themselves wearing something even simpler, tunics with the straight, loose, open sleeves going back to the *dalmatica* of antiquity, and still in plain fabrics, albeit with more extensive applied gold decoration.

The destruction wrought by the Fourth Crusade caused a radical interruption in court culture. The successor states immediately made some attempts at regalia, if only to bolster each new ruler's claim to the legacy of the Golden Throne. Once the rulers of Nikaia had regained Constantinople, a full campaign of reconstitution was undertaken. With no direct continuity, court culture had to be reconstructed in other ways. There was literature and art to provide an indication of past court practice, and it was exploited enthusiastically, although not always understood. The regalia that resulted was very low on the scale of artificiality. Garments and accessories were much like those worn everyday, distinguished only by subtle points of constructional detail or decoration. Main garments, the *roukhon* of the highest ranks, and the *kavadion* of most of the rest of the court, retained the feature of cuffs tightly fastened to the wrist. The *kavadion* and other common regalia garments were made of patterned fabric, but selected from a narrow range of patterns and colours made specifically for court use. Many ranks were only distinguished by details of their headgear or baton. Once again, the very highest male ranks were set apart by garments in plain colours, and by being some of the very few still to wear a cloak, the ancient *khlamus* fastened on the right shoulder, but now called a *tabarion*, a name borrowed from an Italian word. The position of women in this era was more marginal than it had ever been, a development which paralleled those in Europe at the same time. In so much as they had any court dress, it was all alike, a low coronet with points and a *delmatikion* dress, of a regulation court brocade, certainly, but beyond that, plainer and more sack-like than it had ever been before. The story of regalia in Constantinople does not end with the Ottoman conquest, however. The new rulers embraced more than the efficient imperial bureaucracy they found there, but material things besides. The most obvious was a hat. The red, betasselled *skaranikon* worn by the mass of junior courtiers was embraced as the fez, exported to the fringes of the successor empire, then forgotten in the capital, to be re-introduced in the nineteenth century.

One of the most curious observations to be made of this saga, is that, attempts at imperial usurpation aside, there seems to be no surviving record in this span of nearly one thousand years of any transgressions or enforcement regarding the *taxis* or regalia in the court. This is quite remarkable. With the enthusiasm of so many chroniclers in recording the machinations, offences and failings of famous men, surely something ought to have come to light. I suspect that the answer is that within the court, scrutiny was so intense and continual that no presumption to a higher status was viable or beneficial, and, outside the court, rank and its display counted for less than factors like personal authority and money. Similarly, it seems that the regalia scheme had such a degree of variability, and flexibility, that procedural errors, such as wearing the wrong cloak or hat for a given ceremony or festivity, were a matter for embarrassment rather than punishment.

The Roman Empire was not a remote island through the course of this millennial trajectory. Not only did it absorb influences from the East in the earlier phase, and from the West towards the end, but in between it had a profound effect on the culture of both Christian Europe and parts of al-Islamiyya. Most notably early on, Charlemagne looked to Constantinople for paradigms of royalty and Romanity, as did his tenth- and eleventh-century Ottonian successors in Germany with even more enthusiasm and persistence. In the early twelfth century, the rulers of Sicily, as part of their own project of cultural synthesis, embraced Constantinople's imperial precedent with even more enthusiasm, borrowing much more than the iconography for which they are famous, but constructing their own regalia in imitation of the practices at the heart of the Queen of Cities.

In the globalised confusion of the twenty-first century it is very hard for us to appreciate how important clothing and accessories have been in both formal and informal ways for structuring the nature, identity and, indeed, the very consciousness of past societies and their people. I hope I have provided some small insight into the formalities of this narrow slice.

NOTES

INTRODUCTION

1 I vehemently reject the expression 'Byzantine Empire', coined in 1556 by the German Hieronymus Wolff, as a term created for the prejudicial purpose of detaching the entity which endured in the East from the 'true', that is, Western-ruled, Roman Empire. The expression 'Enduring Roman Empire' is my own creation, but 'Rômania' (Ρωμάνια) is found in the literature from the first century of the Common Era. The very word 'empire' is problematical, with all its mostly more recent connotations. *Vasileia Rômaiôn* (Βασιλεία Ῥωμαιῶν), 'Kingdom of the Romans' is the closest phrase to Roman Empire, and was in use throughout the time period covered by this volume, although in the later centuries the Greekness of the realm came to be more acknowledged.

2 Cyril Mango stated the position most extremely thus: 'Nearly all Byzantine painting that has come down to us is religious in content and is based on the faithful reproduction of iconographic formulas that can be traced back to the early Christian period. It is worthy of note that in depicting such stereotyped compositions Byzantine artists carefully avoided any intrusion of contemporary costumes or settings: Christ, the Apostles, the prophets appear in antique garb...': 'Discontinuity in Byzantium', in M. Mullett and R. Scott (eds), *Byzantium and the Classical Tradition*, Centre for Byzantine Studies, Birmingham, 1981, p. 51.

3 In addition to various publications by the present author commenting upon specific practical aspects, see also Lyn Rodley, *Byzantine Art and Architecture: An Introduction*, Cambridge University Press, Cambridge, 1994, pp. 345–6; and in much greater detail see the doctoral dissertation of Maria Parani, published as *Reconstructing the Reality of Images: Byzantine Material Culture and Religious Iconography*, E. J. Brill, Leiden, 2003.

4 I recommend Karel Innemée, *Ecclesiastical Dress in the Medieval Near East*, E. J. Brill, Leiden, 1992. A compendious historical study of the vestments of the metropolitan Eastern Orthodox Church remains very much needed, however.

5 Nicholas Oikonomidès, *Les Listes de Préséance Byzantines des IXe et Xe siècles*, Éditions du Centre National de la Recherche Scientifique, Paris, 1972, p. 24.

6 *Peri Stratêgias*, in G. T. Dennis (ed. and tr.), *Three Byzantine Military Treatises*, Dumbarton Oaks, Washington, DC, 1985.

7 *The Taktika of Leo VI*, ed. and tr. George T. Dennis, Dumbarton Oaks, Washington, DC, 2010.

8 Portions of both the *Composition on Warfare* and *Taktika* are incorporated into Eric McGeer (ed. and tr.) *Sowing, the Dragon's Teeth*, Dumbarton Oaks, Washington, DC, 1995.

9 For an example of this adaptation see T. Dawson, '"Fit for the Task": Equipment Sizes and the Transmission of Military Lore', *Byzantine and Modern Greek Studies*, 31:1, 2007, p. 12.

10 It must be acknowledged here, that there is still considerable disagreement amongst art historians on matters of dating, and it does seem likely that a significant number of surviving works which are presently dated to the eleventh century could well be earlier.

11 A great caution is just how much of the Cleveland Museum of Art's early dress and textile collection turned out to be fake when analysed by exacting modern standards. See Sheila S. Blair, Jonathan Bloom, and Anne Wardwell, 'Re-evaluating the Date of the "Buyid" Silks by Epigraphic and Radiocarbon Analysis', *Ars Orientalis*, 22, 1992, pp. 1–41. The CMA project was the culmination of a long and unusually vitriolic debate amongst various scholars and collections. See also Dorothy Shepherd, 'Medieval Persian Silks in Fact and Fancy', *Bulletin de Liaison de la Centre Internationale d'Études des Textiles Anciennes*, 39/40, Lyon, 1974, pp. 1–240.

12 Examples are the Skjoderhamn outfit, which turned out to be centuries earlier than had been believed (Margareta Nockert and Göran Possnet, *Att Datera Textilier*, Gidlands Förlag, Oslo 2002, pp. 59–61) and the Manazan Caves shirt, which was found to be centuries later than estimated. See Dominique Cardon, 'A Mysterious Group of Textiles, Probably Medieval, Found in the Caves of Manazan, near Tazkale, Karaman Province, Turkey', *Bulletin du CIETA*, 7, 1993, pp. 183–4, and Timothy Dawson, 'Concerning an Unrecognised Tunic from Eastern Anatolia', *Byzantion*, 73:1, 2003, pp. 201–10 for two divergent estimates. Personal communication with Dominique Cardon yielded the carbon-14 date of thirteenth century for the Manazan Caves tunic.

13 For examples of reconstructions done by the author, or under his supervision, see 'Propriety, Practicality and Pleasure: The Parameters of Women's Dress', in Lynda Garland (ed.), *Byzantine Women: Varieties of Experience 800–1200*, Ashgate, Aldershot, 2006, pp. 41–75, 'Suntagma Hoplôn: The Equipment of Regular Byzantine troops, *c*.950–*c*.1204', in David Nicolle (ed), *Companion*

to *Medieval Arms and Armour*, Boydell & Brewer, London, 2002, pp. 81–90, and www.levantia.com.au.

CHAPTER 1

1 John Bagnell Bury, *A History of the Later Roman Empire*, Dover Books, New York, 1958, p. 429 n. 1 and p. 316 n. 2.

2 Rafaele D'Amato, *Roman Military Clothing (3) 400–640*, Osprey Publishing, Oxford, 2005.

3 Rodolphe Guilland, *Titres et Fonctions de l'Empire Byzantine*, Variorum Reprints, London, 1976, p. 210.

4 *Corpus Juris Civilis*, Book XI, §VIII.3 and 4. Justinian I, *The Civil Law*, tr. Samuel Parsons Scott, Central Trust Company, Cincinatti, 1932, vol. 15, p. 175 (hereafter *The Civil Law*).

5 *The Civil Law*, vol. 17, p. 272.

6 John Lydos, *On Powers or The Magistracies of the Roman State*, ed. and tr. Anastasius C. Bandy, American Philosophical Society, Philadelphia, 1983.

7 The eagle sceptre is well illustrated in consular diptychs of the fifth century: diptych of Boethius, 487, Brescia Museum, no. 7; right, anonymous diptych, *c.*490, Bearn Collection, Paris.

8 Lydos, *On Powers*, pp. 4, 18; LSJ, pp. 944, 1014.

9 *Achmetis Oneirocriticon*, ed. Francis Drexl, B. G. Teubner, Leipzig, 1925, p. 179.

10 The lady in the grotto of Khusrau II wears the diagonal shawl that is present in all the *persikomanikion* outfits under her *kandus* and there are a scattering of other such pictures.

11 Johannes Jacob Reiske, *Commentarii ad Constantine Porphyrogennetus De Cerimoniis Aulae Byzantinae*, E. Weber, Bonn, 1839, p. 425. Personal communication from Dr Alan Treloar of the School of Classics, History and Religion, University of New England, New South Wales, Australia, citing Edward William Lane, *An Arabic–English Lexicon*, Frederick Ungar, New York, 1955–6 (London, 1885), part 3, p. 941; Francis Joseph Steingass, *Persian–English Dictionary*, Routledge, London, 1977 (1892), p. 551 gives *dibaj* as 'A vest of brocade'.

12 Shown on a courtier on the right side of the apse arch in the Chapel of St Venanzio, Lateran Baptistry, Rome; on the right-hand saint on an icon of Mary between Saints George and Theodore, St Catherine's Monastery, Mount Sinai; and on Prefect Leontios, Church of St Demetrios, Salonika.

13 Metropolitan Museum, New York, inv. no. 90.5.901.

14 Pergamon Museum, Berlin. Ernst Kuhnel, and Wolfgang Fritz Volbach, *Late Antique Coptic and Islamic Textiles of Egypt*, E. Weyhe, New York, 1926, plates 43, 46, 47.

15 Several in the Victoria and Albert Museum, London.

16 Isidore of Seville, *Etymologies*, tr. Stephen A. Barney et al., Cambridge University Press, Cambridge, 2006, bk XIX, § 22.27: ... *in armos tantum clausa, quasi armiclausa, C litteri ablata* ... His terminology has often confused modern scholars unaware that 'closing' a seam, or a entire garment, remains a current expression in traditional dressmaking parlance. The term also occurs as ἀρμελαύσιον in the *Stratêgikon* at XII B.1.1. The expression survives into the tenth century applied to regalia garment of deme functionaries called *kombinografoi*: *De. Cer.* 71.10.

17 *Menologion of Basil II* (Vat. Gr. 1613), pp. 69, 112, 255 (female), 257 (male). Vat. Gr. 699, passim.

18 Slits on both shoulders: Louvre inv. nos. 21, 74, 191. Pierre du Bourget and Pascale Gremont, *Tissus Coptes*, Musée d'Angers, Angers, 1977, pp. 69, 71. Left-shoulder slit: Metropolitan Museum inv. nos. 90.5.901, 90.5.19a and 89.18.317.

19 Dorothy Burnham, *Cut my Cote*, McKinnon-Moncur, Ontario, 1973, p. 11.

20 The diagram given in Cäcilia Fluck and Gillian Vogelsang-Eastwood (eds), *Riding Costume in Egypt: Origin and Appearance*, E. J. Brill, Leiden, 2004, fig. 68, and copied by D'Amato (p. 45) is incorrect in showing the front overlapping right over left. In that position the body's natural flexing pulls the square panel on the right out of the belt and allows it to flap free, while a left-over-right overlap secures it.

21 Lydos, *On Powers*, p. 30.

22 Lydos, *On Powers*, p. 88.

23 Isidore of Seville, *Etymologies*, bk XIX, § 22.6

24 Xenofon, *Cyropaedia*, bk 8, ch. 3, s. 10: ed. T. E. Page and W. H. D. Rouse, Loeb Classical Library, London, 1914, vol. II, pp. 353–4.

25 The volume edited by Fluck and Vogelsang-Eastwood (note 20 above) discusses the coats extensively.

26 Such as an ivory plaque given in Peter Wilcox, *Rome's Enemies 3: Parthians and Sassanid Persians*, Osprey Publishing, Oxford, 1999 (1986), p. 13.

27 Timothy Dawson, 'Oriental Costumes at the Byzantine Court: A Reappraisal', *Byzantion*, 75, 2005.

28 Isidore of Seville, *Etymologies*, bk XIX, § 22.24.

29 For archaeological survivals see Pierre Du Bourget, *Musée National du Louvre: Catalogue des Etoffes Coptes*, Éditions des Musées Nationaux, Paris, 1964, passim. In art see Kurt Weitzman, Manolis Chatzidakis, Miatev Krsto and Svetoar Radojic, *Icons from South Eastern Europe and Sinai*, Alpine Fine Art Collection, New York, 1974 (London, 1968), p. 6, and Christine Schug-Willie, *Art of the Byzantine World*, Harry N. Abrams, New York, 1969, p. 144.

30 Du Cange, *Glossarium Mediae et Infimiae Latinitatis*, Akademische Druck-U. Verlagsanstalt, Graz, 1954, vol. II, pp.

412f. John Cassian's *Monastic Institutions*, book I, chapter IV gives a very clear description of the characteristics of the garment: Nancy Shevçenko, 'colobium': *Oxford Dictionary of Byzantium*, vol. I, p. 480.

31 Du Cange, *Gloss. Lat.*, vol. II, pp. 412f; Reiske, *Comm.*, p. 186; Albert Vogt, *Constantine Porphyrogénète: Le Livre des Cérémonies, Commentaire*, Paris, 1967, vol. I, p. 113.

32 *Patrologia Graeca*. 88.

33 τῶν δελματικῶν ἤγουν κολοβιῶν: Du Cange, *Glossarium ad Scriptores Mediae et Infimiae Graecitatis*, Akademische Druck-U. Verlagsanstalt, Graz, 1958, col. 272 (title given as *De Initiis Haeresion*).

34 Tenney Frank, *An Economic Survey of Ancient Rome*, vol. V, Pageant Books, Paterson, NJ, 1959, p. 391.

35 Museo Nazionale de Bargello, Brunelt-Denon Collection 19c.

36 Lydos, *On Powers*, pp. 134, 136, 144, 178, 220, 238.

37 George P. Galavaris, 'The Symbolism of the Imperial Costume as Displayed on Byzantine Coins', *Museum Notes*, 8, 1958 (American Numismatic Society), pp. 103–6.

38 Lydos, *On Powers*, p. 88.

39 Lydos, *On Powers*, p. 30.

40 Grotowski's conclusion that the *tavlia* are diamond-shaped is understandable from the impression given by artworks, but contradicted by archaeology as well as Lydos' description. His suggestion that they are separate and applied from the cloak, however, is rather less explicable, even in terms of the art. Piotr Ł. Grotowski, *Arms and Armour of the Warrior Saints*, E. J. Brill, Leiden, 2010, p. 281.

41 Epistle 245: Reiske, *Comm.*, p. 65.

42 Isidore of Seville, *Etymologies*, bk XIX, § 24.2.

43 Du Cange, *Gloss. Graec.*, col. 866, citing Hesychius, Eustathius and the lexicon of Cyril.

44 Isidore of Seville, *Etymologies*, bk XIX, § 23.6.

45 Hesychios 2:230 M 229 [3:70] εἶδος ἱματίου περσῶν πολεμικοῦ ...: There is no reason to take this passage, as Piotr Grotowski has, to mean that *manduas* could refer to a shirt of mail. Soldiers need clothes just as much as armour! Grotowski, p. 140.

46 Andreas Alföldi, *Die Monarchische Repräesentation im Römischen Kaiserreiche*, Wissenschaftliche Buchgesellschaft, Darmstadt, 1980, p. 184.

47 Meyer Reinhold, *The History of Purple as a Status Symbol in Antiquity*, Latomus, Brussels, 1970, p. 64, for an incident involving Emperor Julian.

48 Romilly James Heald Jenkins, 'The Emperor Alexander and the Saracen Prisoners', *Studi Bizantini e Neoelleniki*, 7, 1953, p. 393.

49 Fluck and Vogelsang-Eastwood, passim, particularly Petra Lindscheid. 'Gaiters from Antinoöpolis in the Museum für Byzantinische Kunst, Berlin', for leggings. Footed trousers were found at Halabiye, see J. Lauffray, *Textiles de Halabiye*, Paris, 1951, and the trousers from Thorsberg are a famous example.

50 Lydos, *On Powers*, pp. 30–1. Grotowski's suggestion that the straps of the *kampagia* extend to the knee is not borne out by this passage, which he cites. Grotowski, p. 201.

51 Lydos, *On Powers*, p. 32.

52 Lydos, *On Powers*, p. 86 for the torque, and p. 104 for the belt.

53 *Das Strategikon des Maurikios*, ed. George T. Dennis, tr. Ernst Gamillscheg, Verlag der Österreichischen Akademie der Wissenschaften, Wien, 1981. George Dennis's English translation has some defects, but his volume provides good background information. George T. Dennis, (tr), *Maurice's Strategicon*, University of Pennsylvania Press, Philadelphia, 1984.

54 ἀρμελαύσιον: *Stratêgikon* XII B.1.1.

55 Isidore of Seville, *Etymologies*, bk XIX, § 22.27.

56 *Stratêgikon* I.2, XII B.1.1.

57 The Persepolis reliefs are amongst the earliest and best examples, while the latest are found on Sassanian metalwork such as pieces in the Sackler Gallery in Washington. Veronika Gervers-Molnár, *The Hungarian Szur: An Archaic Mantle of Eurasian Origin*, Royal Ontario Museum, Toronto, 1973, collects numerous examples.

58 See note 7 above.

59 Bargello Museum inv. Brunelt-Denon 19c, an Alexandrine pyxis in the British Museum, inv. M&LA 79,12-20,1.

60 Dominique Bénazeth and Patricia Dal-pra, 'Quelques Remarques à Propos d'un Ensemble de Vêtements de Cavaliers Découverts dans Tombes Égyptiennes', in *L'Armée Romaine et Barbares du Troisième au Quatrième Siècle*, L'Association Française d'Archéologie Mérovingienne, Saint-Germain-en-Laye, 1993, pp. 367–2; Also Fluck and Vogelsang-Eastwood (n. 20 above) extensively.

61 Frank, p. 373, 377. The assumption that a *fiblatôrion* would be some sort of mantle or cape is improbable given that virtually every such garment in use at the time was fastened with a brooch, so none would be distinguished by this characteristic. Nor does the term support Frank's version of a 'cape with a brooch'.

62 *Stratêgikon* I.2, l. 50f. The use of *gounnoepilôrikion* in one version of the manuscript is almost certainly an example of the language having been updated in the copying process. The original text does not mention this garment having a hood, as Dennis suggests in his translation.

63 *Stratêgikon* XII B.1.

64 Unpublished examples in the State Museum, Berlin.

65 See Thor Ewing, *Viking Clothing*, Tempus Books, Stroud,

2006, pp. 72–5 for pictures and patterns.

66 Mosaics showing such detail are on display in the British Museum.

67 Flavius Vegetius Renatus, *Epitome de Re Militari*, ed. and tr. Leo F. Stelton, Peter Lang, New York, 1990, p. 43.

68 Rafaele D'Amato and Graham Sumner, *Arms and Armour of the Imperial Roman Soldier*, Frontline Books, London, 2009, p. 220.

69 Often well illustrated on Sassanian metalwork, such as a plate in the Hermitage (acc. no. S250). See Prudence Oliver Harper, *Silver Vessels of the Sassanian Period*, vol. 1, Metropolitan Museum, New York, 1981, pl. 19.

70 Staatliche Museum, Berlin, Antikensammlung, inv. 30219,505. Robin Cormack and Maria Vassilaki (eds), *Byzantium: 330–1453*, Royal Academy of Arts, London, 2008, p. 168, no. 121. A diptych shows two noblewomen wearing collars that are virtually identical, p. 72, no. 13.

CHAPTER 2

1 Constantine Porfurogennêtos, *De Cerimoniis Aulae Byzantinae*, ed. Johannes Jacob Reiske, E. Weber, Bonn, 1839, p. 502, lines 1–20 (hereafter citations will be abbreviated in the form: *De Cer.* 502.1–20); Oikonomidès, pp. 81–3.

2 *De Cer.* 702.17–20; Oikonomidès, p. 83.

3 Theophanês, *Continuatus*, ed. I. Bekker, E. Weber, Bonn, 1838, bk V, ch. 30, p. 258, ch. 97, p. 348; Arnold Toynbee, *Constantine Porphyrogenitos and His World*, Oxford University Press, London, 1973, p. 592.

4 *De Cer.* 704.3–4; Oikonomidès, p. 83.

5 The *Klêtôrologion* is preceded by the so-called *Taktikon Uspenski*, and followed by the *Escorial Taktikon* and the *Taktikon Beneseviç*. The essential work is Nicholas Oikonomidès, *Les Listes de Préséance Byzantines des IXe et Xe Siècles*.

6 *De Cer.* 703.12–17; Oikonomidès, p. 83.

7 *De Cer.* 705.15–17; Oikonomidès, p. 85.

8 *De Cer.* 605.3.

9 Vogt, *Comm.*, vol. 1, pp. xxvi–xxviii.

10 David Talbot Rice, *Art of Byzantium*, Harry N. Abrams, New York, 1959, p. 74; Ernst Kitzinger, *Byzantine Art in the Making*, Faber and Faber, London, 1977, pp. 2, 104–5.

11 Nicholas I, Patriarch of Constantinople, *Letters*, ed. L. G. Westerink, tr. R. J. H. Jenkins, Dumbarton Oaks, Washington, DC, 1973, letter 32, pp. 218–20; pseudo-Symeon, Reign, Leo VI, ch. 12, p. 705; Toynbee, pp. 7–9.

12 'Powwows, Parades and Social Drama among the Waccamaw Indians', in Pamela R. Frese, *Celebrations of Identity: Multiple Voices in American Ritual Performances*, Bergin and Garvey, Westport, 1993, p. 76. Similar reflections on the use of ritual as a social therapy in Britain can be found in Gerd Baumann, 'Ritual Implicates "Others": Rereading Durkheim in a Plural Society', in Daniel De Coppet (ed.), *Understanding Rituals*, Routledge, Allen and Unwin, London, 1992, p. 100, and Robert Bocock, *Ritual in Industrial Society*, London, 1974, p. 174. A fascinating exploration of an analogous 'state religion' is contained in Christel Lane, *The Rites of Rulers: Ritual in Industrial Society – The Soviet Case*, Cambridge University Press, Cambridge, 1981, especially ch. 2, pp. 24ff.

13 A short chapter is devoted to it in the *Klêtôrologion*: Τῆς Ὀρθοδοξίας, *De Cer.* 761f; Oikonomidès, p. 195.

14 Theophanês *Cont.*, p. 357; R. J. H. Jenkins, 'The Chronological Accuracy of the "Logothete" for the Years A.D. 867–913', *Dumbarton Oaks Papers*, 19, 1965, p. 106.

15 The description in the *Book of Ceremonies*, pp. 5–38, is much more extensive and detailed than that of the *Klêtôrologion*, pp. 741–59; Oikonomidès, pp. 165–91.

16 *De Cer.* pp 708–12; Oikonomidès, pp. 95–9.

17 For more, see Shaun F. Tougher, 'Byzantine Eunuchs: An Overview, with Special Reference to their Creation and Origin', in Liz James (ed.), *Women, Men and Eunuchs: Gender in Byzantium*, Routledge, London, 1997, pp. 168–84.

18 *Klêtôrologion*, ch. 1; *De Cer.* 708–12.

19 χῶρις σταυρικοῦ τῦπου: *De Cer.* 712.1; Oikonomidès, p. 99.

20 Confirmed in *De Cer.* at 258.18 and 259.9.

21 *De Cer.* 745.3 and 770.2; Oikonomidès, pp. 171, 207.

22 The manuscript has σὺν ἐπομίοις καὶ πώλοις. The antique meaning of *pôlos*, foals, is not very plausible, especially given that elsewhere we find the compounds six- and eight- (ἑξάπωλον, ὀκτάπωλον). Hence, it seems more likely that it is a case of orthographic drift deriving from the phonetic merging of omicron and omega, and what is meant is a derivative of πόλος, which can mean a bowl-shape, orbit or even star. LSJ, p. 1436. Star is the most likely, for that would make *kexapôlon* and *oktapôlon* six and eight-pointed stars, which are motifs we do find woven into Coptic textiles. This description, therefore, very likely means with *gonateia* in the form of octograms.

23 μετὰ σπεκίων καὶ ῥωέων σαγίων: *De. Cer.* 745.3 and 770.2; Oikonomidès, pp. 171, 207.

24 *De. Cer.* 777.14, 20, 779.13, 20; Oikonomidès, pp. 217, 219.

25 See Isidore of Seville, *Etymologies*, bk XIX, § 22.29 for an explanation of the derivation of the term.

26 *Composition on Warfare* (traditionally *Praecepta Militaria*) II. 74: Eric McGeer, *Sowing the Dragon's Teeth*, Dumbarton Oaks, Washington, 1995, p. 26.

27 *Achmetis Oneirocriticon*, ed. Francis Drexl, B. G. Teubner, Leipzig, 1925, p. 179.

28 Pamela G. Sayre, 'The Mistress of Robes – Who was She?', *Byzantine Studies*, vol. 13, no. 2, 1986, p. 235.

29 As witness the complaints against Emperors Constantine IX and Michael VI that they upset the order of the court by promoting courtiers by multiple grades: Michael Psellos, *Chronographie*, ed. and tr. Emile Renauld, Société d'Édition Les Belles Lettres, Paris, 1967, bk 6, ch. 29, vol. I, p. 132, and bk 7, ch. 1, vol. II, pp. 83–4; Jean-Claude Cheynet, 'Dévaluation des Dignités et Dévaluation Monétaire dans le Second Moitié du XIe Siecle', *Byzantion*, 53, 1983, pp. 453–77.

30 Helen Evans and William D. Wixom, *The Glory of Byzantium: Art and Culture of the Byzantine Era A.D. 843-1261*, Metropolitan Museum of Art, New York, 1997, p. 249, n. 175.

31 Long after the toga had become an anachronism, at the end of the fourth century edicts could still be made forbidding the wearing of those notable symbols of Barbarism, trousers: Theodosian Law Code, 14, 10, 2-3; Alföldi, p. 180.

32 Reinhold, *History of Purple as a Status Symbol in Antiquity*, discusses the fluctuations of this into the Middle Ages; Rodolphe Guilland, 'Sur Quelque Terms du Livre des Ceremonies de Constantin Porfyrogénète', *Revue des Etudes Grecques*, 62, 1949, p. 334, n. 1.

33 *The Civil Law*, vol. 15, p. 175. As a notable exception to his generally highly restrictive approach, Justinian allowed women to wear wholly silk garments dyed purple: Reinhold, p. 68.

34 *The Civil Law*, vol. 17, p. 272.

35 *De Cer.* 187.13–4 (*stemma*), 189.11 (*skaramangion*), 190.5 (*stemma*), 190.20–21 (*stemma*), and 191.19 (*stemma*).

36 *Leukos: De Cer.* 187.14, 187.22, 188.1, 188.6, 188.9, 189.9, 190.24, 583.18. *Aspros: De Cer.* 8.4, 587.21, 593.19.

37 Rodolphe Guilland, *Titres et Fonctions*, p. 210. The rank of *Kandidatos* seems to have disappeared by the twelfth century: p. 218.

38 *De Cer.* 105.6, 500.15, 505.12; *Imp. Exp.*, pp. 142, 148.

39 Nikêforos Bryennios, *Commentarii*, ed. and tr. Paul Gautier, Byzantion, Brussels, 1975, bk IV.2, p. 131.

40 In medieval Europe, linen was laid out in the sun on meadows of grass specifically maintained for the purpose. The oxygen emanating from the photosynthesis of the vegetation served to bleach the cloth. The same process may have been used in Byzantine territory.

41 Ross E. Griffith, M. David Potter, and Bernard P. Corbman, *Textiles: Fibre to Fabric*, McGraw-Hill Book Company, Sydney, 1967, p. 17.

42 The literature on Tyrian purple is extensive. Some good technical works are: Lloyd B. Jensen, 'Royal Purple of Tyre', *Journal of Near Eastern Studies*, 22, 1969, pp. 104–18; Joseph Thomas Baker, *Studies on Tyrian Purple and its Precursors in Australian Molluscs*, unpublished dissertation, University of Queensland, 1967.

43 *De Cer.* 128.11–14.

44 *De Cer.* 271.20–1.

45 LSJ, p. 1315, for the uses of *porfureos* to mean a red.

46 Vogt, *Comm.*, vol. 1, p. 175.5.

47 *Pourpre foncée*: Vogt, *Comm.*, vol. 1 p. 177.14, pp. 178.17 and 22.

48 Sophocles, p. 916.

49 Du Cange, *Gloss. Graec.*, p. 1048.

50 *De Cer.* 641.16.

51 πορφυρὰν ἐσθῆτα ... μελαὶναν / τνὴ κατακὸρως ὀξεὶαν: Psellos, *Chronographie*, bk. 1, ch. XXXI, p. 20.

52 *De Cer.* 470.10, 11; *Imp. Exp.*, p. 110.

53 Anna Muthesius, *Studies in Byzantine and Islamic Silk Weaving*, Pindar Press, London, 1995, p. 160; *Byzantine Silk Weaving, AD 400 to AD 1200*, Verlag Fassbaender, Vienna, 1997, p. 29.

54 Also on this *De Cer.* 473.7, 11; *Imp. Exp.*, p. 112, for garments *De Cer.* 469–73; *Imp. Exp.*, pp. 108–10 for the leather covering the chests in which the garments are carried.

55 *De Cer.* 227.7.

56 τὸ νικητικὸν σάγιον: *De Cer.* 495.10; *Imp. Exp.*, p. 136, l. 673.

57 *De Cer.* 187.14, 187.22, 188.1, 189.8.

58 *De Cer.* 434.15.

59 *De Cer.* 105.16–17, 105.22, 135.20.

60 τὸ δημοτῶν καμίσιον ... τὸ νικητικὸν σάγιον: *De Cer.* 500.18; *Imp. Exp.*, p. 142.

61 Green: *De Cer.* 188.15, 189.17, 190.15, 581.17, 586.22. Blue: *De Cer.* 190.23, 581.19. 581.21, 586.23.

62 For example, in terms of fabrics, *sendes*: *De Cer.* 468.18; *Imp. Exp.*, 112; Reiske, *Comm.* p. 529.

63 Herbert Weir Smyth, *Greek Grammar*, Harvard University Press, Cambridge, MA, 1959, p. 30.

64 Robert Browning, *Medieval and Modern Greek*, Hutchinson, London, 1969, pp. 32–3, 62–3; Likewise Geoffrey Horrocks, *Greek: A History of the Language and its Speakers*, Longman, London, 1997, p. 259.

65 Edward Lane, p. 1074, and Steingass, p. 574.

66 Reiske, *Comm.*, p. 474.

67 *De Cer.* 181.1, 190.18, 241.21, 242.2, 360.12, 388.11, 389.5, 390.20.

68 *De Cer.* 242.4, 394.15, 405.5.

69 Lydos, *On Powers or The Magistracies of the Roman State*, section 17, p. 31; Suda, vol. 1, p. 406.

70 Charleton T. Lewis and Charles Short, *A Latin Dictionary*, Clarendon Press, Oxford, 1980, p. 188; OLD, vol. I, p. 195.

71 Sophocles, p. 273; Vogt, *Comm.*, vol. I, pp. 170–1.

72 Saints Prokopios, Dêmêtrios and Nestôr, Monastery of Saint Catherine, Mount Sinai: in colour, David Talbot Rice, *Art of the Byzantine Era*, Thames and Hudson, London, 1963, p. 131.

73 See, for example, Psellos, *Chronographie*, book II.10.21 (vol. I, p. 31), book VI. 101.13 (vol. II, p. 16), bk. 7.41.12 (vol. II, p. 171).

74 Anna Komnênê, *Alexiade*, Société d'édition 'Les Belles lettres', Paris, 1967, bk 15, ch. xi.

75 Vogt, *Comm.*, vol. I, p. 30.

76 Constantine Porfurogennêtos, *The Book of Ceremonies*, tr. Ann Moffat and Maxine Tall, Australian Association for Byzantine Studies, Canberra, 2012, p. xxxvii.

77 Examples may be found in Wolfgang Fritz Volbach, *Early Decorative Textiles*, Paul Hamlyn, London, 1969.

78 Du Cange, *Gloss. Lat.*, p. 678; *Gloss. Graec.*, col. 206; Guilland, 'Sur Quelque Terms du Livre des Cérémonies du Constantine VII Porphyrogénète', *Revue des Études Grecques*, 62, 1949 (hereafter abbreviated as: 'Terms', II), p. 334, John F. Haldon, 'Some Aspects of Byzantine Military Technology from the Sixth to the Tenth Centuries', *Byzantine and Modern Greek Studies*, 1, 1975, pp. 205–6.

79 *De Mensibus*, Book 1, section 21, lines 1-6.

80 Guilland, 'Terms', II, p. 335.

81 Robert S. Lopez, 'The Silk Industry in the Byzantine Empire', *Speculum*, 20, 1945, pp. 1–42; Muthesius, *Studies* and Muthesius, *Byzantine Silk Weaving*; Jonathan Shepard, 'Silks, Skill and Opportunities in Byzantium: Some Reflections', *Byzantine and Modern Greek Studies*, 21, 1997, pp. 246–57.

82 Guilland, 'Terms', II, p. 338, n. 8.

83 '... unde triblattion pallium vocatur quod trium cernitur esse colorum.': Guilland, 'Terms', II, p. 340.

84 Before laying this theory to rest, it must be noted that it has most recently been espoused by Anna Muthesius. It behoves us to consider why so eminent a textile historian should embrace it, if it were indeed so weak. Muthesius mentions the theory briefly in an article published in 1993, within a section dealing with terminology from the Book of the Prefect and other sources. ('The Byzantine Silk Industry: Lopez and Beyond', *Journal of Medieval History*, 19, 1993, pp. 1–67, republished in Muthesius, *Studies*, pp. 255–314.) In a later publication, Muthesius goes on to cite her own previous article as though it was a fact that she had established herself, saying 'I have explained elsewhere the terms διβλάττιον and τριβλάττιον as twice- and thrice-dipped purples.' (Muthesius, *Byzantine Silk Weaving*, p. 25.) Closer examination reveals that, in fact, Muthesius draws all of her information from the terse summary of the subject given by John Haldon in the notes to his translation of the *Treatise on Imperial Military Expeditions* (*Imp. Exp.*, pp. 205–7) and that she did not consider the arguments presented by Guilland and other authors directly herself. Muthesius's limited approach to the subject is readily explained in the light of the body of her work. Her overwhelming area of interest lies in the process of production of silk: the breeding of the worms; gathering and processing of the floss; spinning of the yarn and weaving of the fabric. And, indeed, her expertise and authority in these areas merits the greatest respect. However, it is manifest that Muthesius regards the technology of dyeing, although unavoidable, as being peripheral to her work and therefore fit to be treated in such a cursory manner. To further illustrate this we may compare her passing treatment of the *vlattion* compounds with the detailed attention she gives to the numerical compounds of -pôlon (ἑξάπωλον, ὀκτάπωλον and others), which she regards as describing different densities of thread in the weave. (Muthesius, *Studies*, p. 292.) Hence, while deferring to Muthesius's knowledge in the field central to her research, her views on the matter of the *vlattion* compounds are less convincing in the light of the potent reasons for disregarding the multiple-dye bath theory.

85 Guilland, 'Terms', II, p. 345.

86 Pieces examined *in situ*: Metropolitan Museum, inv. 90.5.901, fifth–sixth centuries; inv. 90.5.20, ninth century?; British Museum, inv. 820-1903, sixth–seventh centuries; Victoria and Albert Museum, inv. 409-1890, fifth century; inv. 820-1903, eighth–ninth centuries. Also several of the eighth–nineth-century garments found at Moshchevaya Balka: Anna Ierusalimskaja and Birgit Borkopp, *Von China nach Byzanz*, Baterischen Nationalmuseum, Munich, 1996, figs 1, 2, 3.

87 *De Cer.* 80.11, 188.21, 442.1, 499.4, 502.7; *Imp. Exp.*, pp. 140, 144.

88 *De Cer.* 31. 16; from κεντέω, to stab or prick: LSJ, p. 832.

89 Byzantine and other early surviving pieces which are likely to have been modelled upon Byzantine examples are collected in Marie Schuette and Sigrid Müller-Christiansen, *The Art of Embroidery*, Thames and Hudson, London, 1964, pls 11 to 75.

90 *De Cer.* 80.11.

91 σωλήν: LSJ, p. 1594.

92 Lampe, p.1362; Sophocles, 1065.

93 Reiske spends considerable space on this adjective, but his conclusion is gold tubes hanging from the edges of garments, which does not make adequate sense of the embroidery component of the word (Reiske, *Comm.*, p. 186). In his translation, Vogt does not attempt to render it with any specific sense (Vogt, *Comm.*, vol. I, p. 72), nor

does he even mention it in his commentary (Vogt, *Comm.*, vol. I, p. 113).

94 Schuette and Müller-Christiansen, p. 301, and pl. 65; Kay Staniland, *Medieval Craftsmen: Embroiderers*, British Museum Press, London, 1991, plate 51, p. 46.

95 Vogt decided they meant 'woven with gold threads' (Vogt, *Comm.*, vol. I, p. 30.), while Haldon opted for 'gold-embroidered' (*Imp. Exp.*, p. 143). Haldon's version is untenable, both because there is a specific term for 'gold-embroidered', *khrusokentêtos* as previously discussed, and because the words qualified by gold here are of pure classical provenance, the first a noun meaning 'web', and then second a technical adjective for 'woven' (ὑφή and ὑφαντός, LSJ, p. 1732), as Vogt presumably recognised.

96 An exception is Anna Muthesius. See 'Crossing Traditional Boundaries: Grub to Glamour in Byzantine Silk Weaving', *BMGS*, 15, 1991, pp. 326–65; 'From Seed to Samite: Aspects of Byzantine Silk Production', *Textile History*, 20:2, 1989, pp. 135–49; also Shepard, pp. 246–57.

97 W. Fritz Volbach, *Early Decorative Textiles*, Paul Hamlyn, New York, 1969, pp. 113f and plates 55 onwards; Talbot Rice, *Art of the Byzantine Era*, Thames and Hudson, London, 1963, pp. 70–75 and 104–109.

98 Extensive and detailed regulation of the silk industry is set out in the *Book of the Eparch*, especially sections 6 and 8: Johannes Koder (ed.), *Das Eparchenbuch Leons des Weisen*, Verlag der Österreichischen Akademie der Wissenschaften, Wien, 1991, pp. 90–1 and 102–3. Liutprand of Cremona describes how he fell foul of these regulations: *Embassy to Constantinople*, chs 53–5; Becker (ed.), pp. 204–5; Wright (tr.), pp. 202–3.

99 χρυσοσήμεντος: *De Cer.* 294.15, 296.2.

100 χρυσὰ ὁλοσήμεντα: *De Cer.* 590.2.

101 *De Cer.* 641.8.

102 *De Cer.* 99.9, 110.7, 167.9, 184.4.

103 *De Cer.* 82.3. But never to any *khlamus*, contrary to Vogt, *Comm.*, vol. I, p. 30.

104 Vogt (*Comm.*, vol. I, p. 30) translates this as 'with bands of gold' (à bandes d'or) and refers to the presence of a workshop on the palace complex producing braids, citing Jean Ebersolt, *Les Arts Somptuaires de Byzance*, E. Leroux, Paris, 1923, p. 5.

105 *De Cer.* 72.14.

106 φέγγος/φέγγω: LSJ, pp. 1744–5.

107 These documents were records kept by the Jewish community of Cairo: Stillman, p. 55 and numerous other pages.

108 Accession number 31.106.64.

109 ἔχον φιάλιον: *De Cer.* 528.16.

110 ὑπὸ φιάλιον: *De Cer.* 577.14.

111 ὑποβλττωμένον σχήμτι φιαλίου: *De Cer.* 722. 7; Oikonomidès, p. 125.

112 φιάλη: Du Cange, *Gloss. Graec.*, col. 1675; LSJ, p. 1930.

113 *De Cer.* 180.14, 297.23, 600.4 to cite just a few of the thirty-six occurrences with this meaning.

114 *De Cer.* 125.25, 126.2, 157.22.

115 *De Cer.* 528, 721 tr.

116 *BoC*, pp. 528, 577, 589, 721.

117 Agnes Newhall Stillwell, *Corinth: Results of Excavations Conducted by the American School of Classical Studies at Athens: Vol. XV, part III: The Potters' Quarter, The Pottery*, American School of Classical Studies, Princeton, 1984, pl. 67 especially shows many vessels of this pattern; G. Roger Evans, *Corinth: Results of Excavations Conducted by the American School of Classical Studies at Athens: Vol VII, Part III: Hellenistic Pottery*, American School of Classical Studies, Princeton, 1975, pl. 29 and others of similar form.

118 *De Cer.* 86.1, 188.21, 442.1, 576.11, 576.12, 576.15, 576.17.

CHAPTER 3

1 Toynbee, p. 578, describing the classicising digressions in Constantine Porfurogennêtos, *De Administrando Imperio*, ed. Gyula Moravcsik, tr. Romilly James Heald Jenkins, Dumbarton Oaks, Washington, DC, 1967, pp. 581, 604, with his conclusions regarding *De Cerimoniis.*

2 Averil Cameron, 'The Construction of Court Ritual: The Byzantine Book of Ceremonies', in David Cannadine and Simon Price (eds), *Rituals of Royalty: Power and Ceremonial in Traditional Societies*, Cambridge University Press, Cambridge, 1987, p. 118.

3 Michael McCormick, 'Analysing Imperial Ceremonies', *Jahrbuch der Österreichichen Byzantinistik*, 35, 1985, pp. 1–20; Michael McCormick, *Eternal Victory*, Cambridge University Press, Cambridge, 1986, pp. 175–6.

4 McCormick, *Eternal Victory*, pp. 160–1.

5 Stephen G. Nichols, 'The New Medievalism: Tradition and Discontinuity in Medieval Culture' in Marina S. Brownlee, Kevin Brownlee, and Stephen G. Nichols (eds), *The New Medievalism*, Johns Hopkins University Press, Baltimore, 1991, p. 10.

6 See Michael Featherstone, 'Preliminary Remarks on the Leipzig Manuscript of *De Cerimoniis*', *Byzantinische Zeitschrift*, 95, 2002, pp. 457–79, and 'Further remarks on the *De Cerimoniis*', *Byzantinische Zeitschrift*, 95, 2002, pp. 113–21 for detailed analyses of the source.

7 Liutprand, *Embassy to Constantinople*, ch. 37.

8 Liutprand, *Antapodosis*, bk. 3 ch. 23.

9 Du Cange, *Gloss. Lat.*, vol. 8, p. 98.

10 Du Cange, *Gloss. Lat.*, vol. 8, p. 104.

11 χάσδιον: this term was imported from the Arabic, *ḳazz* or *k͟hazz*. See R. B. Serjeant, *Islamic Textiles: Material for*

a History up to the Mongol Conquest, Librairie du Liban, Beirut, 1972, p. 45 and numerous other places. It is surprising to find Moffat implausibly rendering χασδίου βηλαρίου ἑνός as 'one length of beaver fur', *BoC*, p. 606.

12 μολχάμιον, also sometimes unHellenised, *μόλχαμ*: another import from Arabic, *mulḥam*. Serjeant, pp. 18–19 and elsewhere.

13 Lewis and Short, p. 1964.

14 Achmet, *Oneirocriticon*, ch. 260, περὶ βηλῶν καὶ καλυμματῶν ἤτοι ταπητῶν, p. 214. *The Oneirocriticon of Achmet*, tr. Steven Michael Oberhelman, Texas Tech University Press, Lubbock, 1991, p. 227, although he is mistaken in declaring that this is the only occurrence of the word in Greek.

15 *De Cer.*, 310.11, 339.16, 339.18, 617.7.

16 *Actes d'Iviron II*, ed. Jacques Lefort, Nicholas Oikonomidès and Denise Papachryssanthou, P. Lethielleux Paris, 1990, pp. 180–1.

17 *Actes d'Iviron*, p. 176.

18 De Cange, *Gloss Lat.*, vol. v, p. 166; Migne, col. 1332.

19 Frank, pp. 371–81, passim. The spelling is highly variable.

20 *De Cer.* 623.12.

21 *De Cer.* 374.5, 755.11, 755.19, 756.16, 771.9, 771.10; Christopher Walter, *Art and Ritual of the Byzantine Church*, Variorum Publications, London, 1982, pp. 13–14.

22 *De Cer.* 264.16, 268.5, 268.9, 748.2; Oikonomidès, p. 175.

23 Du Cange, *Gloss. Graec.*, cols. 1670, 1656; LSJ, p. 1912; Lampe, p. 1473; Sophocles, p. 1632, Reiske, *Comm.*, p. 284, Vogt, *Comm.*, p. 80; Oikonomidès, p. 174, n. 163; OLD, p. 1282; Lewis and Short, p. 1289.

24 Walter, p. 9; Oikonomidès, p. 295.

25 Talbot Rice, *Art of Byzantium*, figs 22, 23, 26, 27.

26 Moffat translates it as 'cape' on p. 264, *BoC*.

27 *De Cer.* 522.15.

28 *De Cer.* 80.25, 99.15, 105.7.

29 *De Cer.* 352.12.

30 Sophocles, p. 526.

31 BNP, Gr. 510, f. 149r and 215v; Vat. Gr. 1613, men: pp. 2, 4, 58 (yellow *esôforion*), 78, 159, 206, 280 (red *esôforion*) (other occurrences of white *esôforia* on men in this manuscript are too frequent to be enumerated comprehensively), women: pp. 16, 39, 98, 150, 164.

32 εἰκασταὶ and ἐργάται: *De Cer.* 590.1.

33 *De Cer.* 641, passim.

34 Piotr Grotowski's suggestion, stemming from a confusion between clothing and armour, that the term denotes detached sleeves is not plausible in the absence of any other evidence for such a practice in Byzantine dress. It is particularly curious when he seems to imply that such hypothetical sleeves are to be fastened to *lôroi*. Grotowski, pp. 171–2.

35 Vat. Gr. 1613, p. 75 and elsewhere. In antiquarian art of the eleventh century: Vat. Reg. Gr. 1B, f. 263r, and its sibling in the BNP Gr. 139, F. 1v and 5v.

36 BNP, Gr. 510, f. 149r; Donor of the *Adrianople Gospels* manuscript, to cite just two examples bracketing the tenth century.

37 Moffat recognises the basic derivation, and in the context of the empress' *diakoptês* acknowledges it as a split garment (*BoC*, p. 582), yet curiously decides that the adjectival form means 'with cut segments, i.e. with appliqués' (p. 294).

38 M. Chatzidakis and S. Pelekanides, *Kastoria*, Melissa, Athens, 1985, figs. 20, 23.

39 *De Cer.* 710.13; Oikonomidès, p. 95. The precise meaning of this passage is not completely clear. The figure is given amongst the enumeration of customary gifts that a newly elevated courtier is expected to distribute, mostly to other courtiers and officers. See Grotowski, p. 282 for another theory.

40 Saints Prokopios, Dêmêtrios and Nestôr, Monastery of Saint Catherine, Mount Sinai: Talbot Rice, *Art of the Byzantine Era*, p. 131.

41 *De Cer.* 575.3, 7, 14; 641.3, 14, 16.

42 Ebersolt, *Melanges d'Histoire et d'Archéologie Byzantines*, E. Leroux, Paris, 1951, p. 55; Sophocles, p. 1150; *Imp. Exp.*, p. 204. Accepted by Moffat, *BoC*, p. 575.

43 For example, *Menologion of Basil II*, pp. 100, 130, 408 and others. The style is preserved for a much longer period in the conventional iconography of portraits of the Theotokos.

44 Du Cange, *Gloss. Lat.*, vol. III, p. 629; J. F. Niermeyer, *Mediae Latinitatis Lexicon Minus,* E. J. Brill, Leiden, 1976, p. 457.

45 *De Cer.* 742.8, 756.7.

46 Vogt, *Comm.*, vol. I, p. 30. Commentary *Imp. Exp.*, p. 260.

47 *De Cer.* 495.8; *Imp. Exp.*, p. 136. Reiske was purely speculative in his comments about this garment, both here (Reiske, *Comm.*, p. 574) and in his earlier entry on *sagia* in general (Reiske, *Comm.*, p. 53), and contributes nothing to our knowledge.

48 *Kamision*: *De Cer.* 127.3, 523.18, 574.17–18.

49 Reiske, *Comm.*, p. 244 and at greater length on p. 676.

50 Museo Nazional, Ravenna: see Volbach, pl. 66 (p. 138) and p. 133 for other dated fabrics with the same design.

51 Paul Hetherington and Werner Forman, *Byzantium: City of Gold, City of Faith*, Orbis Publishing, London, 1983, p. 82.

52 *De Cer.* 576.17.

53 *De Cer.* 578.4.

54 Volbach, pls 63 (p. 132) and 64 (p. 137).

55 Sophocles, p. 85.

56 *Imp. Exp.*, p. 222; sea-wool, made from the fibrous material

extruded by various bivalve molluscs, is mentioned in Diocletian's *Edict on Prices*, in Tenney Frank, *An Economic Survey of Ancient Rome*, Pageant Books, Princeton, 1959, vol. V, pp. 379, 385.

57 Serjeant 1972, p. 123, n. 8; Ernst Kuhnel and Louisa Bellinger, *The Textile Museum Catalogue of Dated Tiraz Fabrics*, Textile Museum, Washington, 1952, pp. 88, 89, 91; Lisa Golombek, and Veronika Gervers, 'Tiraz Fabrics in the Royal Ontario Museum', in Veronika Gervers (ed.), *Studies in Textile History*, Ontario Museum, Toronto, 1977, pp. 96–9.

58 Galavaris, pp. 103–6.

59 *De Cer.* 637.18–19; Galavaris, p. 107; Michael F. Hendy, *Coinage and Money in the Byzantine Empire: Dumbarton Oaks Studies*, 12, Dumbarton Oaks, Washington, DC, 1969, p. 66.

60 *De Cer.* 24.6, 20; 26.10.

61 *De Cer.* 641.8.

62 These figures are based upon practical reconstruction.

63 *De Cer.* 227.5; 275.18; 417.4, 7, 8; 432.3; 439.7; 442.22; 639. 15; 742.9; 743.14; 751.21; 752.11.

64 Piltz' suggestion that *kampagia* were the imperial red boots or *tzangia* is completely untenable, given how much of the court wore them: Piltz, 'Costume in Life and Death in Byzantium', *Byzantium and the North: Transactions of the Nordic Research Course in Byzantine Art History*, Almqvist and Wiskell, Uppsala, 1989, p. 157. More recent scholarship accepts that tenth-century *kampagia* were still something resembling antique sandals: Alexander P. Kazhdan and Michael McCormick, 'The Social World of the Byzantine Court', in Henry Maguire (ed.), *Byzantine Court Culture*, Dumbarton Oaks, Washington, DC, 1997, p. 180 and note 67, and similarly at p. 195, citing an article by Cyril Mango.

65 *De Cer.* 742.18; 752.1; 757.19; 759.10; 769.23; 773.14; 774.15; 777.23; 779.10; 780.2; 781.5.

66 *De Cer.* 641.9, 766.21 (Oikonomidès, p. 201), with the *lôros*, 187.10, emperor in *skaramangion*; 766.22–3 (Oikonomidès, p. 201), *patrikioi* in *kamisia*; 778.3 (Oikonomidès, p. 217), many ranks in *kontomanikia*; 781.9 (Oikonomidès, p. 221), much of the court.

67 Ebersolt, *Melanges*, p. 65.

68 Guillaume De Jerphanion, 'Le "Thorakion" caracteristique iconographie du XIe siècle', *Melanges Charles Diehl*, II, 1930, pp. 71–9.

69 LSJ, p. 689, citing Galen 12.493.

70 To cite a representative, rather than comprehensive, spread: an ivory icon of St Dêmêtrios in the Metropolitan Museum (inv. 1970.324.3) late tenth century; the Vatican Triptych (inv. 2441) tenth to eleventh century; very extensively in Vat. Gr. 1613 (*Menologion of Basil II*); the Harbaville Triptych, mid-eleventh century; Kastoria, Mavriotissa Monastery on the centurion at the Crucifixion, late eleventh century; Church of St John the Baptist, Potamos, Kythera, Fresco showing St George with two other saints, late twelfth to early thirteenth century. By the fourteenth century representations have become a highly stylised vestige, as in the census scene from the Church of the Holy Saviour in Khôra, Constantinople.

71 David and companions in Bib. Marc. Gr. Z 17 (Psalter of Basil II), f. 4v, 976–1025; an official at the Crucifixion on an icon held by the Bishopric of Limassol, Cyprus (Evans and Wixom, p. 126).

72 Vat. Urb. Gr. 2, f. 167v.

73 Guido Gregorietti, *Jewellery through the Ages*, American Heritage Press, New York, 1969, pp. 134–5. A fragment which may well be from a similar object is in Gladys R. Davidson, *Corinth: Results of Excavations conducted by the American School of Classical Studies at Athens, Vol XIII: The Minor Objects*, American School of Classical Studies at Athens, Princeton, 1952, p. 306 and pl. 125.

74 *De Cer.* 766.20, 781.9; Oikonomidès, pp. 201, 221.

75 For example on bowls in the Hermitage Museum, acc. S297 and acc. S272: Harper, pls. 18 ad 28.

76 Jennifer L. Ball, *Byzantine Dress: Representations of Secular Dress in Eighth to Twelfth Century Painting*, Palgrave-Macmillan, New York, 2005, p. 50, n. 77.

77 *De Cer.* 441.3, 442.2.

78 *De Cer.* 576.3.

79 *De Cer.* 607.8.

80 Haldon preferred this version for his translation: *Imp. Exp.*, p. 109.

81 *De Cer.* 469.6, 8; *Imp.Exp.*, p. 108.

82 *De Cer.* 661.13, 15.

83 *De Cer.* 677.20–1.

84 Antonietta Amanti Canta, 'Bridal Gifts in Bari', *Medieval Clothing and Textiles*, 9, 2013, p. 10.

85 A man: BNP, Gr. 510 f. 215v.

86 Various males: Vat. Gr. 1613, pp. 159, 206 and elsewhere.

87 Biblioteca Nacional, Madrid, Vitr. 26-2, f. 42v and 47r.

88 Bodleian Rowe MS 6 frontispiece.

89 Helen of Troy: Bib. Marc. Z 454 (=822)(tenth century) f. 1v; Various women: Bib. Marc. Z 478 (=881)(eleventh century) f. 62 r; Two noble women: Vat. Urb. Gr. 2 (1122) f. 19v; The woman at the well: Vat. Gr. 746 (twelfth century) f. 86v.

90 See Dawson, 'Tunic', for a full discussion of the garment and argument for its dating based in part on its construction. As yet unpublished information on the subsequent carbon-14 dating to the thirteenth century courtesy of Dominique Cardon.

91 *De Cer.* 469.9; *Imp. Exp.*, p. 108, and notes p. 219.

92 One of those attending upon the emperor of BNP, Coislin 79, f. 2r (Evans and Wixom, p. 208) has a striped under-tunic; striped garments recur in the Madrid Skylitzes both as underwear: f. 42v, and as outerwear: f. 49v; the chief tax collector in the miniature of Sinai Gr. 339, f. 73v (*c.*1150), and elsewhere.

93 Madrid Skylitzes, f. 47r, showing the Caliph al-Ma'mun, the frontispiece of a copy of Dioscorides, Topkapi Saray Library, Ahmet III, 2127, f 1v (Evans and Wixom, p. 430), and numerous pieces of minai-ware pottery. See also Serjeant, pp. 101, 160, 161, 169, 212, 216, and Stillman p. 44 for references to striped fabrics in Islamic use.

94 Serjeant, *Islamic Textiles*, p. 168, n. 9, mentions cloth patterned with octagons.

95 *De Cer.* 678.2–3.

96 Dawson, 'Oriental Costumes'. For *paragôdês*, see chapter 1.

97 Parani, *Reality*, p. 34.

98 Komnênê, *Alexiade*, bk 3, ch. iii, §5; Komnênê, *The Alexiad of Anna Comnena*, p. 112; Piltz, *Kamelaukion*, p. 31.

99 *De Cer.* 500.9; *Imp. Exp.*, p. 142.

100 *De Cer.* 522.5–8.

101 *De Cer.* 411.15 *diadêma*; 413.10–20 *stefanos* 4 times; 414.17 golden *modiolos*.

102 *De Cer.* 80.14, 84.21, 104.22, 188.10 and 505.12.

103 *De Cer.* 188.10.

104 Iôannês Zonaras, *Epitomê Historiarum*, ed. L. Dindorf, B. G. Teubner, Leipzig, 1868–75, p. 566, l. 17.

105 G. Morgan, 'A Byzantine satirical song?', *Byzantinische Zeitschrift*, 47, 1954, pp. 292–7; Horrocks, p. 259; Pseudo-Kodinos, *Suidae Lexicon*, ed. Ada Adler, B. G. Teubner, Stuttgart, 1971, vol II, p. 79.

106 See following note.

107 Giorgios Monachos, *Chronikon*, ed. John Classen, B. G. Teubner, Stuttgart, 1978 (1834), pp. 832–3.

108 *De Cer.* Vol II. ch. 17, p. 599.

109 *De Cer.* 502.7; *Imp. Exp.*, p. 144.

110 Antonio Santangelo, *A Treasury of Great Italian Textiles*, Harry N. Abrams, New York, 1964, fig. 2 and p. 12.

111 *Persikomanikion*: *Achmetis Oneirocriticon*, p. 179. Oberhelman's explanation that the 'Persian sleeve' was 'a long sleeve which reached the hand and supplied the place of a glove' is negated by Achmet's description of it having a division, although it is characteristic of another Persian garment adopted by the Romans, the *skaramangion*. Steven M. Oberhelman, 'Oneirocritic Literature of the Late Roman and Byzantine Periods', unpublished PhD thesis, University of Minnesota, 1981, p. 537, n. 405. On the identification of the *skaramangion* see Timothy Dawson, 'Oriental Costumes', pp. 97–114.

112 *De Cer.* 502.6; *Imp.Exp.*, p. 144, where Haldon corrects the spelling to *triblattia*.

113 *De Cer.* 33.14–15, 181.4–5. This class division is well illustrated in Byzantine art in scenes like the tax collection of Sinai manuscript 339, f. 73v where the long, ornate robes of the officials are starkly juxtaposed to the short, plain tunics of the farmers. The suggestion that the imperial 'rustic' garments were undecorated has no merit: Reiske, *Comm.*, pp. 138, 244.

114 *De Cer.* 80.11, 86.4, 188.8, 374.4, 561.20.

115 κολόβιον τριβλάτιον χρυσοσωληνοκέντητον, διὰ λίθων καὶ μαργάρων ἠμφιεσμένον, ὃ καὶ βότρυς καλεῖται: *De Cer.* 80.11. κολόβιον τὸν λεγόμενον βότρυν: 86.4.

116 κολώβια, ἤγουν τοὺς κριοὺς: *De Cer.* 188.8.

117 *De Cer.* 575.3, 7, 14, 641.3, 14, 16, and in places where *allaxima* also seems to refer to cloaks: *De Cer.* 575.22, 577.13.

118 *De Cer.* 229.1, 414.9.

119 *De Cer.* 9.10.

120 *De Cer.* 279.19.

121 *De Cer.* 181. 5.

122 Vogt, *Comm.*, vol. I, p. 171.

123 *Paschal Chronicle*, p. 614.1-3.

124 Bargello Museum (illustrated): Talbot Rice, *Art of Byzantium*, fig. 21; Vienna Kunsthistorisches Museum: Haussig, fig. 126. Both are dated to *c.*500 and said to represent Ariadnê and various other empresses.

125 The possible derivation is from *maraon* (τὸ μαράον)/ *maraos* (ὁ μαράος), which in antiquity equated to *pittaxis* (ἡ πίτταξις). (LSJ, pp. 1080, 1409.) Although *pittaxis* was the name of a fruit, and so has no conceivable application to the cloak, the strong koinê tendency to make nouns of this sort into standard neuter could have turned it into *pittakion* (τὸ πιττάκιον), thereby conflating it with an established term for a writing tablet, label or document (LSJ, p. 1409). By such a process, *opsimaraos* could mean 'with a face on a tablet'. It would then be easily contracted through the ancient practice of merging vowels, or simply lazy orthography, to *opsimaros*.

126 *De. Cer.* 583.17, 593.19.

127 *Kaisarikion*: *De Cer.* 522.8–9.

128 For the ancient background see Alföldi, p. 184, and Reinhold, p. 64, for an incident involving the Emperor Julian; *De Cer.* 434.14–15, 558.10.

129 Jenkins, 'Emperor Alexander', p. 393.

130 'Harun ibn Yahya and His Description of Constantinople', tr. Alexei Vasiliev, *Seminarum Kondakovum*, 5, 1932, p. 159.

131 Jenkins, 'Emperor Alexander', p. 393.

132 *De Cer.* 558.10. The Suda suggests this by saying that

strikton is called 'the estenômenon' (τὸ ἐστενωμένον), which may mean 'confined' or 'made scanty' and that they are 'lordly amongst footwear' (κυρίως ἐπὶ ὑποδήμτος).

133 *De Cer.* 638.15. The Book of Ceremonies' use of this term is evidently much more specific than that of the atticisers of the eleventh and twelfth centuries – Psellos, Komnênê and Khoniatês all use the term extensively as a term for any imperial footwear. See also LSJ, p. 1352.

134 Frauberger, Heinrich, *Antike und fruhmittelalterlich Fussbekleidungen aus Achmim-Panopolis* (publisher unknown), Dusseldorf, 1895, pl. IV.17 (sandals), 20 and others (shoes).

135 *De Cer.* 423.3.

136 Du Cange, *Gloss. Graec.*, col. 176,

137 Numerous Late Antique examples survive from Egypt made by 'knotless netting', while the earliest surviving socks made by two-needle knitting are regarded as being of the early twelfth century: Irena Turnau, 'The Diffusion of Knitting in Medieval Europe', in Negley B. Harte, and Kenneth G. Ponting (eds), *Cloth and Clothing in Medieval Europe*, Heinemann, London, 1983, pp. 368–9; François Boucher, *A History of Costume in the West*, Thames and Hudson, London, 1987, p. 159 shows a knitted sock of debated medieval date which is preserved in Switzerland, and points out how unusual it is compared to tailored cloth construction; Louisa Bellinger, 'Patterned Stockings: Possibly Indian, found in Egypt', *Textile Museum Workshop Notes*, Paper 10 (December 1954). It is worth noting that these socks are made of cotton, just as Achmet mentions for *housia*, the term which seems to have supplanted *touvia* for knitted hose, p. 176.

138 *De Cer.* 219.10, 227.8, 439.7, 443.1. Descended from the Latin *campus + tubia*. Achmet, *Oneirocriticon*, pp. 198, 218. Achmet uses *touvia* for these, but makes his meaning clear by listing the varieties of padding. A good illustration is in the *Menologion of Basil II*, Vat. Gr. 1613, p. 257. Grotowski's suggestion that *kampotouva* is contracted from *kampagia + touva* is not viable, as such a collative would naturally be *kampagotouva*, Grotowski, p. 202. Furthermore, the *Book of Ceremonies* contains a number of passages where it is written explicitly that various men are to wear both *kampotouva* and *kampagia*, which would be redundant if the former had the meaning proposed by Grotowski.

139 The earliest explicit mention of stirrups is in the *Stratêgikon* attributed to Emperor Maurikios, and so they had been around in the Roman world some time before 603 CE. It is worth noting here that all the Sassanian art which shows horsemen riding without stirrups also shows them wearing very light loose trousers.

140 See Bénazeth and Dal-pra, pp. 367–82, and several articles in Fluck and Vogelsang-Eastwood.

141 Such as on the four saints on the right wing of the Forty Martyrs Triptych in the Hermitage. See, for example, Grotowski, fig. 19.

142 *De Cer.* 638.15–6.

143 Hilâl al-Sâbi', *The Rules and Regulations of the Abbâsid Court*, tr. Elie Salem, American University Press, Beirut, 1977, pp. 65, 73.

144 Diptych of Boethius, 487, Brescia Museum, no. 7; anonymous diptych, *c.*490, Bearn Collection, Paris, no. 41: Elizabeth Piltz, *Le Costume Officiel des Dignitaires Byzantins à l'Époque Paléologue*, Acta Universitatis Upsaliensis, Uppsala, 1994, pls. 32 and 3.

145 *De Cer.* 639.9–11.

146 *De Cer.* 62.16, 187.15, 591.6.

147 *De Cer.* 25.21, 591.4.

148 *De Cer.* 591.4–6.

149 *De Cer.* 25.21, 187.15.

150 Dumbarton Oaks Collection, no. 47.11: Evans and Wixom, p. 202.

151 ἡ τοῦ Μωσέως ῥαβδος: *De Cer.* 6.24, 10.21, 640.6.

152 Kurt Weitzmann, *The Age of Spirituality*, Metropolitan Museum, New York, 1979, pp. 405, 421, 424, 430; Pierre Du Bourget, *Early Christian Art*, Weidenfeld and Nicolson, London, 1972, pp. 93–3, 97.

153 Weitzmann, *Spirituality*, pp. 412, 445, 501.

154 The *lavaron* is well discussed in the scholarly literature. See variously Hendy, and Parani, *Reality*, pp. 32–3.

155 *De Cer.* 294.17, 589. 18. *BoC*, pp. 294, 589, citing Reiske's *Commentary*, and Sophocles' *Lexicon*.

156 *De Cer.* 439.6, 440.3, 440.7, 474.8, 474.10, 481.7, 490.2, 554.9, 602.22, 752.16, 764.16, 765.15.

157 *De Cer.* ch. 46, pp. 225–6 contains the account of his elevation.

158 Πράσινος, ἔχουσα ῥοδα χρυσᾶ καὶ ταβλία χρυσᾶ: *De Cer.* 227.4.

159 There are no less than three versions of this ceremony: *De Cer.* 143.19–20, ch. 46, pp. 231–2 and ch.47, pp. 236–7.

160 *De Cer.* 528.19–20.

161 *De Cer.* 528.16–529.2.

162 *De Cer.* 495.8; *Imp. Exp.*, p. 136.

163 Grotowski, p. 302.

164 *De Cer.* 81.10.

165 *De Cer.* 148 15, 286 21.

166 *De Cer.* 708.19; Oikonomidès, p. 91; Alice Bank, *Byzantine Art in the Collections of Soviet Museums*, Aurora Art Publishers, Leningrad, 1985, pls. 112–13 for the icon; Talbot Rice, *Art of the Byzantine Era*, p. 131 for the later icon.

167 *De Cer.* 391.14. Grotowski fails to recognise this term in

his discussion of military sashes, which he mistakenly conflates with textile belts and the Palaiologian *lôros*, pp. 277–81.

168 To cite a representative, rather than comprehensive, spread: An ivory icon of St. Dêmêtrios in the Metropolitan Museum (inv. 1970.324.3) late tenth century; the Vatican Triptych (inv. 2441) tenth to eleventh century; very extensively in Vat. Gr. 1613 (Menologion of Basil II); the Harbaville Triptych, mid-eleventh century; Kastoria, Mavriotissa Monastery on the Centurion at the Crucifixion, late eleventh century; Church of St. John the Baptist, Potamos, Kythera, Fresco showing St. George with two other saints, late twelfth- to early thirteenth century. By the fourteenth century representations have become a highly stylised vestige, as in the census scene from the Church of the Holy Saviour in Khôra, Constantinople.

169 *De Cer.* 52.263.

170 Christopher of Mitylênê, *Die Gedichte des Christophoros Mitylenaios*, ed. Eduard Kurtz, August Neumans Verlag, Leipzig, 1903, p. 17.

171 *De Cer.* 524.9–10.

172 Vat. Gr. 1156, f.283v (five elderly men seated at a table with Christ); Vat.Gr. 1162, ff. 76v, 95v, 133v, 142r, 178v, 186r (scenes showing elderly men); Vat. Gr. 1162, f.109r (a woman amongst a group of women); BNP Gr. 74, f.120v (a man in civilian dress).

173 *De Cer.* 524.3.

174 Achmet, *Oneirocriticon*, pp. 171, 205.

175 Sophocles, p. 1161.

176 Lewis and Short, p. 950; *OLD*, p. 1722, both referring to the magisterial *fasces*.

177 Vat. Gr. 1156 f. 195v.

178 *Taktika*, ch. v §3: *PG* 107, col 717; Dennis (tr.), p. 74.

179 See note 73 in chapter 2 above.

180 *De Cer.* ch. 55, p. 269.

181 Alan Cameron, *Circus Factions: Blues and Greens at Rome and Byzantium*, Clarendon Press, Oxford, 1976. p. 259.

182 *De Cer.* 500.18; *Imp. Exp.*, p. 142.

183 *De Cer.* 106.3, 5, 135.20.

184 *De Cer.* 271.20–21.

185 *De Cer.* 255.8.

186 *De Cer.* 607.10, 12, and 470.7 respectively.

187 Reiske, *Comm.*, p. 553; *Imp. Exp.*, p. 223.

188 Examined *in situ*.

189 Especially acc. no. 32.96. Examined *in situ*.

190 *De Cer.* ch. 69 for the protocols of chariot racing; 330.18ff for the award ceremony.

191 *De Cer.* 584.4.

192 *De Cer.* 640.11–12.

193 *De Cer.* 391.14 for *pektorarion* in the promotion of a *kandidatos*. Grotowski, p. 277, n. 579 for earlier scholarship.

194 Rather curiously, Grotowski suggests that these diagonal sashes are a supernumerary cape (*sagion*) which might be tied around even under a *khlamus*, although he presents no reasons why such an awkward practice might be adopted, p. 269.

195 *De Obsidione Toleranda*, ed. Hilda van den Berg, E. J. Brill, Leiden, 1947, §19 (ed. van den Berg, p. 49; tr. Sullivan, p. 159); *Sullogê Taktikôn*, ch. 28 §4, ch. 39 §1; *Composition on Warfare*, III. 29, 36 (tr. McGeer, pp. 34, 46)

196 Leo preserves the *Stratêgikon* usage, ch. 6 §2, while the changed use is recorded in Fôkas' *Composition on Warfare*, III. 29, 36 (tr. McGeer, pp. 34, 46).

197 Taxiarchis Kolias, *Byzantinische Waffen*, Österreichischen Akademie der Wissenchaften, Wien, 1988 only refers to *vamvakion* as a raw material, p. 56, n. 150. The idea that the word could apply to a garment seems to originate with Ian Heath writing for the popular market in *Byzantine Armies: 886–1118*, Osprey Publishing, London, 1981, p. 7. It is clear that Heath had no access to primary sources in the original language.

198 *Sullogê Taktikôn*, ch. 28 §4, ch. 39 §1; *Composition on Warfare*, III. 29, 36 (tr. McGeer, pp. 34, 46).

199 *Composition on Warfare*, I. 20 (tr. McGeer, p. 12).

200 The attribution is made in the *Treatise on the Offices*, 205.8–13, and taken at face value by Ebersolt, *Arts Somptuaires*, p. 143.

201 Piltz, 'Life and Death', p. 158. She repeats this proposition in *Le Costume Officiel*, 1994, p. 53.

202 *Encyclopedia of Islam*, vol. v, p. 734.

203 *Composition on Warfare*, I. 24 (tr. McGeer, *Sowing the Dragon's Teeth*, p. 14).

204 *De Obsidione Toleranda* §15 (ed. van den Berg, p. 48; tr. Sullivan, p. 157)

205 Reiske, *Comm.*, followed by Moffat, *BoC*, p. 381.

206 Described in some detail in the *Composition on Warfare* of Nikêforos Fôkas under the terms *kavadion*, I. 3 and *epilôrikion*, III. 4 (tr. McGeer, pp. 13 and 35 respectively).

207 *De Cer.* 381.11, 18.

208 *De Cer.* 576.3.

209 *De Cer.* 7.5.

210 *De Cer.* 640.15.

211 Justin's coronation: *De Cer.* 429.9; the imperial store: *De Cer.* 640.12–15.

212 For more on such equipment see Timothy Dawson: '"Fit for the Task"', *Byzantine Infantryman: Eastern Roman Empire, c.900–1204*, Warrior Series, Osprey Publishing, Oxford, 2007, and *Byzantine Cavalryman: Eastern Roman Empire, c.900–1204*, Warrior Series, Osprey Publishing, Oxford, 2009.

213 *De Cer.* 506; *Imp. Exp.*, pp. 148–9.
214 Timothy Dawson, 'The Monomakhos Crown – A Toward Resolution', ΒΥΖΑΝΤΙΝΑ ΣΥΜΜΕΙΚΤΑ, 19, 2009, pp. 183–93.
215 *De Cer.* 500.6–8, 505.10–11; *Imp.Exp.*, pp. 142, 148–9.
216 Liz James concludes that Byzantines were much more concerned with intensity of colour and of light than with the shade of them: *Light and Colour in Byzantine Art*, Clarendon Press, Oxford, 1996, pp. 51, 127.
217 David Nicolle, *Arms and Armour of the Crusading Era*, Kraus International Publications, White Plains, NY, 1988, p. 651, fig. 88, p. 652, fig. 95b, p. 654, fig 108.
218 For a survey of the construction methods used in middle Byzantine battlefield *klivanion* and how they evolved from earlier forms see Timothy Dawson, *Armour Never Wearies: A History of Scale and Lamellar Armour in the West from the Bronze Age to the Nineteenth Century*, The History Press, Stroud, 2013, pp. 79–90.
219 *Imp. Exp.*, p. 279.
220 Serjeant, p. 186.
221 Michael C. Bishop and John C. N. Coulston, *Roman Military Equipment from the Punic Wars to the Fall of Rome*, Batsford Books, London, 1993, p. 163.
222 Surviving examples are held in the Sackler Gallery, Washington and other collections. For an illustration: Georgian State Art Museum, v-939/G-76-A, Evans and Wixom, p. 348.
223 Taxiarchis Kolias' attempt to identify this with the curved *paramêrion* is mistaken. (Kolias, *Byzantinische Waffen*, pp. 137–8, 150; McGeer, p. 63). The *Treatise on Imperial Military Expeditions* carefully distinguishes between the emperor's battlefield and parade *spathia* and his *paramêrion* (*De Cer.* 468.14–15; *Imp. Exp.*, p. 108). A thirteenth- or fourteenth-century portrait of the tenth-century Emperor Nikêforos Fôkas made in Trebizond shows him holding before him the scabbard of the *paramêrion* which he brandishes on his shoulder, with the chape resting upon the ground. This scabbard is unmistakably fitted with a baldric.
224 *De Cer.* 80.12, 167.9, 188.24, 190.5, 191.18, 557.14, 640.11.
225 *De Cer.* 81.8, 309.7, 578.19.
226 *De Cer.* 576.3, 576.9, 577.20, 579, various lines and 599, various lines.
227 βάλλω: *De Cer.* 188.24.
228 περιβάλλω: *De Cer.* 80.12, 81.8, 82.4, 188.4, 188.9, 190.5, 191.18.
229 ὑπαλάσσω: *De Cer.* 167.9.
230 φέρω: *De Cer.* 575.1, 576.1, 11, 13, 15, 577.20, 578.19, 599.3, 5, 16.
231 κατέχω: *De Cer.* 81.13, 82.4,10.
232 κρατέω: *De Cer.* 81.9.
233 βαστάζω: *De Cer.* 72.18, 99.5,25, 100.23, 148.6,8,14, 255.17, 286.2,22, 290.20,22, 302.3,19, 309.7, 347.9, 361.24, 542.1, 574.12, 576.16.
234 Parani, *Reality*, pp. 146–7 makes rather too much of the apparent height at which the swords are held in different sources, while Hennessy weakens her already poor case by misreading Parani – 'A child bride and her representation' in the Vatican *Epithalamion. Byzantine and Modern Greek Studies*, vol. 30, no. 2, p. 137.
235 As noted by Mavrogordato: *Digenês Akritas*, Clarendon Books, Oxford, 1963, GRO IV, l. 378: Mavrogordato (ed.) p. 96 and note 1457, GRO l. 645: p. 112. Mavrogordato translates the term as a collative compound, 'sword and mace'.
236 Reiske, *Comm.*, pp. 174–5. Accepted by Moffat, *BoC*, p. 82.
237 For example, extensively illustrated in the so-called *Maciejowski Bible* of *c.*1250.
238 λογχοδρέπανον: *De Cer*, 669.20.
239 Grotowski, pp. 304–5.
240 AlTartusi, in Claude Cahen, 'Un Traité d'Armurerie Compose pour Saladin', *Bulletin d'Études orientales de l'Institut Français de Damas*, 12, 1947/8, p. 139.
241 Vesey Norman, *Arms and Armour*, Weidenfeld and Nicholson, London, 1970, p. 118.
242 *De Cer.* 574.11.
243 Wlodzimierz Baldowski, *Militaria Z Dawnej Kolekcji Wilanowski*, Wydawnictwa Geologiezne, Warsaw, 1990, figs 94, 95.
244 Hilâl al-Sâbi', pp. 65, 73.
245 LSJ, p. 437. The Greek *Chronicon Cassinense* explicitly explains *dextralis* as an 'axe of only one part' (τὸ ἐκ τοῦ ἑνὸς μόνον μέρους ἔχον ἀκμὴν, ὃ καὶ δεξτράλιον καλοῦσι.); Du Cange, *Gloss. Lat.*, vol. 3, p. 92.
246 *De Cer.* 148.15.
247 *De Cer.* 575.6.
248 *De Cer.* 576.3.
249 *Taktika* ch. V §3: *PG* 107, col. 717; Dennis (tr.), p. 74.
250 *De Cer.* 7.5.
251 For more extensive discussion of this term see under *romfaiokrators* in chapter 5.
252 *De Cer.* 506.12.
253 *Smyrna Octateuch*, Vat. Gr. 746 ff. 469v, 447v, 453r, *Homilies Gregory of Nazianzos*, (BNP, Gr. 510) f. 440; *Joshua Roll* (Vat. Pal. Gr. 431), Joshua Casket, Metropolitan Museum, inv. 17.190.137 (Evans and Wixom, pp. 228–9) and numerous other places for pictures of oval *scuta*.
254 θυρεός: *Taktika*, ch. 6 §116 (*PG* 107, col. 728; Dennis (tr.), pp. 90–1), ch. 20, §183 (*PG* 107, col. 1061; Dennis (tr.), p.

600) and elsewhere. Leo's descriptions of this are quite clear: ἐπίμηκες, μέγα, ὃ καλεῖται θυρεός, πάντως στρογγύλον τέλειον – 'rectangular (oblong), large, and entirely curved' and σκουτάρων τετραγώνων ἐπίμηκῶν τῶν λεγομένων θυρεῶν – 'shields, four sided, oblong, called thureos'. Dennis's translation largely agrees. Grotowski evidently overlooked the second description: Grotowski, pp. 211, 231.

255 John F. Haldon, 'Some Aspects of Byzantine Military Technology from the Sixth to the Tenth Centuries', *Byzantine and Modern Greek Studies*, I, 1975, p. 34, for tenth-century types; European use is most famously illustrated in the Bayeaux Tapestry.

256 Ivory triptych, Museo Sacro inv. 2441 (Evans and Wixom, p. 132); ivory of St Dêmêtrios MMA 1970.324.3 (Evans and Wixom, p. 134); enamelled *enkolpion* of two military saints CMA 72.94 (Evans and Wixom, p. 164); Vat. Gr. 746, f. 153r (Nicolle, *Arms and Armour of the Crusading Era*, p. 650, no. 85i.). These citations are only to pictures which show the shields in profile.

257 *De Cer.* 576.2–3. Polished iron shields are corroborated by Leo, *Taktika*, ch. XX §188, *PG* 107, col. 1064; Dennis (tr.), p. 602.

258 *De Cer.* 640.12–15.

259 BNP, Gr. 510, f. 215v; Elizabeth Piltz, 'Middle Byzantine Court Costume', in Henry Maguire (ed.), *Byzantine Court Culture from 829 to 1204*, Dumbarton Oaks, Washington, DC, 1997, plate 15.

260 *De Cer.* 579.2, 6, 12, 14, 17. This is plural in the accusative case, and is the only form in which the word occurs. The nominative might be *dorka*, *dorkê* or *dorkês*, but there is no certainty as to which.

261 David Nicolle, *The Medieval Warfare Sourcebook: Christian Europe and its Neighbours*, Brockhampton Press, London, 1996, p. 76.

262 Lynda Garland, *Byzantine Empresses*, Routledge, London, 1999, p. 113.

263 Judith Herrin, 'Theophano: The Education of a Byzantine Princess', in Adelbert Davids (ed.), *The Empress Theophano: Byzantium and the West at the Turn of the First Millennium*, Cambridge University Press, Cambridge, 1995, pp. 72–3.

264 Nicholas, *Letters*, no. 32, lines 76–85, pp. 218–21.

265 Herrin, pp. 76–7.

266 V. Minorsky, 'Marvazi on the Byzantines', *Melanges Henri Gregoire*, Brusselles, 1950, pp. 459–60.

267 Theofanês, AM 6211: de Boor (ed.), p. 400; Mango and Scott (tr.), pp. 551–2.

268 Theofanês, AM 6261: de Boor (ed.), p. 444; Mango and Scott (tr.), p. 613.

269 Noting only one occurrence per ceremony: *De Cer.* 65.11, 69.25, 72.6, 110.7, 134.1, 136.13, 143.9, 149.2, 159.18, 22, 171.21, 181.4, 194.9, 202.6, 231.11, 244.5, 255.11, 263.10, 277.7, 284.11, 298.7, 303.2, 304.2, 308.10, 327.15, 330.13 (a case when 'the rulers' are present but only the emperor acts), 342.5, 360.15, 364.17, 374.3, 388.7, 389.6, 394.17, 395.17, 397.3, 400.6, 408.8, 414.7, 432.16, 434.18, 441.6, 519.17, 523.1, 525.20, 528.5, 530.9, 533.14 (another case when 'the rulers' are present but only the emperor acts at this point), 541.14, 546.21, 552.20, 564.19, 583.13, 607.19, 621.6, 624.22, 629.17, 633.18.

270 οἱ δεσπόται ἅμα τῶν καισάρων: *De Cer.* 226.20.

271 *De Cer.* 257.10ff.

272 *De Cer.* 619.18–19; Theofanês, AM 6211: de Boor (ed.), p. 400; Mango and Scott (tr.), pp. 551–2.

273 *De Cer.* 620.20–1.

274 *De Cer.* 622–3.

275 For example, *De Cer.* 188.101–2.

276 Timothy Dawson, 'Propriety, Practicality and Pleasure: the Parameters of Women's Dress' in Lynda Garland (ed.) *Byzantine Women: Varieties of Experience 800–1200*, Ashgate, Aldershot, 2006, pp. 41–75.

277 Kazhdan and McCormick, pp. 182–3.

278 *De Cer.* 711.12.

279 Kazhdan and McCormick, p. 183.

280 τὸ σέκρετον τῶν γυναικῶν: *De Cer.* 203.7

281 τὸ σέκρετον τῶν πατρικιῶν: *De Cer.* 259.8.

282 τὸ σέκρετον τῶν συγκλητικῶν: *De Cer.* 616.10.

283 The reception of Princess Olga was held in the *Triklinion* of Justinian: *De Cer.* 595.12.

284 *De Cer.* 596.1–5, 618.12–14.

285 Josef Deer, *Die Heilige Krone Ungarns*, Österreichischen Akademie der Wissenschaften, Vienna, 1966, p. 53, and plates 68–80; Whitting, passim for fine examples of the eighth- and ninth-century coins particularly. Hugh Goodacre, *A Handbook of the Coinage of the Byzantine Empire*, Spink and Son Ltd, London, 1967, p. 197 for a solidus of Constantine VII and Zôê; Éva Kovács and Zsuzsa Lovag, *The Hungarian Crown and Other Regalia*, Korvina Kiadó, Budapest, 1980. p. 37.

286 Archaeological Museum of Istanbul, no. 4309: Evans and Wixom, p. 42.

287 Reiske, *Comm.*, p. 688.

288 *De Cer.* 209.1–6.

289 Achmet, *Oneirocriticon*, p. 202.

290 *De Cer.* 208.13.

291 *De Cer.* pp. 207–16.

292 Alexandra Croom, *Roman Clothing and Fashion*, Tempus Publishing, Stroud, 2002, p. 112.

293 Usamah ibn Munqid, *An Arab-Syrian Gentleman and*

Warrior in the Period of the Crusades, tr. Philip Khouri Hitti, Columbia University Press, New York, 2000, p. 76.

294 North apse of the Pigeon House Church, at Çavusin in Kappadokhia.

295 Otto Demus, *Byzantine Art and the West*, Weidenfeld and Nicolson, London, 1970, fig. 80, p. 82; discussed Jacqueline Lafontaine-Dosogne, 'The Art of Byzantium and its relation to the Germany', in Adelbert Davids (ed.), *The Empress Theophano: Byzantium and the West at the Turn of the First Millenium*, Cambridge University Press, Cambridge, 1995, pp. 212–13.

296 H. Westermann-Angerhausen, 'Did Theophano Leave her Mark on the Ottonian Arts?', in Adelbert Davids (ed.), *The Empress Theophano: Byzantium and the West at the Turn of the First Millenium*, Cambridge University Press, Cambridge, 1995, pp. 255–60.

297 Ebersolt regarded this type as a distinct 'badge of oval form resembling a shield' ('une écusson de forme oval, ressemblant à un bouclier', Ebersolt, *Melanges*, p. 65). De Jerphanion recognised this as an error, and suggested rather that it was in fact a 'piece of a garment or the extremity of a type of sash taken from the back to the front and fastened to the belt' ('un pan du vêtement ou l'extrémité d'une manier d'écharpe ramenée d'arrière en avant et accrochée à la ceinture'), De Jerphanion, pp. 71–79, p. 78. Apparently, however, De Jerphanion failed to take the next step, which was obvious to Hendy (Hendy, *Coinage and Money*, p. 66), of connecting this 'piece of a garment' with the *lôros* with which it invariably occurs, and whose pattern of decoration it invariably continues.

298 De Jerphanion, pp. 71–8; Sharon Gerstel, 'Saint Eudokia and the Imperial household of Leo VI', *Art Bulletin*, 69, 1997, pp. 701–4 for discussion of the dating of this panel and other tenth-century examples.

299 *De Cer.* 208.17, 23, 24, 580.19.

300 *De Cer.* 9.10.

301 *De Cer.* 279.19.

302 *De Cer.* 229.1, 414.9.

303 *De Cer.* 181.5.

304 *De Cer.* 583.17, 593.19.

305 ὁ τάων: *De Cer.* 581.4.

306 τὸ τάωνιον: *De Cer.* 581.6.

307 Du Cange, *Gloss. Graec.*, col. 866, citing Hesukhius, Evstathios and the lexicon of Cyril.

308 Lampe, pp. 825, 826; Sophocles, p. 731.

309 Very conspicuous on the tribute bearers in the mosaics of the Church of Saint Appolaire Nuovo at Ravenna, but also visible in manuscripts such as Vat. Gr. 1613, f. 98 and elsewhere.

310 Ierusalimskaja and Borkopp, p. 84, catalogue items 97 and 98. Another fragment on page 71, catalogue 82 is much more likely also to be a peacock, rather than the pheasant stated, in view of the important place of peacocks in Persian iconography. On this see Victoria and Albert Museum, *A Brief Guide to Persian Woven Fabrics*, Her Majesty's Stationary Office, London, 1950, pp. 5–6.

311 Toby Falk (ed.), *Treasures of Islam*, Wellfleet Press, Secaucus, New Jersey, 1985, pp. 202 and 209 for patterned clothing on pottery; Volbach, p. 148 and plates 70 and 71 for Byzantine fabrics with similar patterns.

312 ἠπλησίον: *De Cer.* 581.3.

313 ἱππηλάσιον: Moffat (tr.), *BoC*, p. 581, n. 3.

314 *De Cer.* 582.10-16

315 Empress Zôê mosaic of the south gallery in Hagia Sofia: Beckwith, pp. 233, 1028–34; a particularly fine illustration of Empress Irene, again in Hagia Sofia: Talbot Rice, *Art of the Byzantine Era*, pp. 120, 1118.

316 Reiske, *Comm.*, p. 687.

317 LSJ, p. 744; Lampe, p. 702.

318 Sophocles, p. 629.

319 Du Cange, *Gloss. Lat.*, vol. 2, pp. 157–8.

320 Lewis and Short, p. 290.

321 Staatliche Museum, Berlin, Antikensammlung, inv. 30219,505. Weitzmann, *Spirituality*, p. 310. Cormack and Vassilaki, p. 168, n. 121.

322 Ernst Hartwig Kantorowicz, 'On the Golden Marriage Belt and the Marriage Rings of the Dumbarton Oaks Collection', *Dumbarton Oaks Studies*, 14, 1960, pp. 3–4.

323 *De Cer.* 582.10.

324 This conclusion is based upon a systematic statistical study of manuscripts in the Vatican Library, and more sporadic notes on manuscripts in other collections.

325 Philip Grierson, *A Catalogue of the Byzantine Coins in the Dumbarton Oaks Collection and the Whitmore Collection*, Dumbarton Oaks, Washington, DC, 1993, vol. 3.i, p. 139.

326 Grierson, vol. 3.i, p. 141; Lynda Garland, 'The "βέργιν τρικλῶνον" of Belthandros and Chrysantza: A Note on a Popular Verse Romance and its Sources', *Byzantinische Zeitschrift*, 82, 1989, p. 87–95.

327 Oikonomidès, p. 47.

328 Oikonomidès, pp. 243–5.

329 Oikonomidès, p. 263.

330 Guilland, 'Contribution à l'Histoire Administrative de l'Empire Byzantin: La Patricienne à Ceinture', *Byzantinoslavica*, 32, 1971, p. 271.

331 *De Cer.* 618.13.

332 Vat. Gr. 1851, f.3v. Evans and Wixom, p. 191.

333 *De Cer.* 258.5, 8.

334 *De Cer.* 214.12–13, 218.18–19, 623.11–12.

335 *De Cer.* 596.1.

336 Sophocles, p. 936.

337 Piltz, 'Court Costume', p. 46; Sayre, p. 233.

338 Reiske, *Comm.*, pp. 584–6; Ebersolt, *Melanges*, p. 74, n. 1; Vogt, *Comm.*, pp. 21, 22, n. 1 and 26.

339 Melita Emmanuel, 'Hairstyles and Headdresses of Empresses, Princesses and Ladies of the Aristocracy in Byzantium', Δελτιο της Χριστιανικης Αρχαιολογικης Εταιρειας, 17, 1993–4, pp. 118–19; *De Cer.* 259.8–10; Dawson, 'Propriety, Practicality and Pleasure', pp. 47–8.

340 *De Cer.* 258.5–6.

341 Guilland, 'Patricienne', p. 269.

342 Achmet, *Oneirocriticon*, ch. 256, p. 210, ll. 8–9.

343 *De Cer.* 623.5–7.

344 Sophocles, p. 1161.

345 Achmet, *Oneirocriticon*, p. 205.15.

346 *De Cer.* 258.18, 259.8.

347 *De Cer.* 624.5–6.

348 *De Cer.* 623.8, 624.3.

349 Vat. Gr. 752, f. 449v.

350 *De Cer.* 433–440.

351 According to Kedrenos: Diehl, 'Proedros', pp. 105–8.

352 *De Cer,* 440.14ff.

353 *De Cer.* 442.22–3.

354 Numerous pictures show *sagia* with multiple gold fastenings running down from the throat. The finest example is that of the donor portraits of the Bible of Leo the Sakellarios (Vat. Reg. gr. 1B) from around the turn of the tenth century.

355 Psellos, *Chronographie*, bk. 1, §XIX–XXII: Renauld (ed.), vol. I, pp. 12–14, Michael Psellos, *Fourteen Byzantine Rulers*, tr. Edgar Robert Ashton Sewter, Penguin Books, Harmondsworth, 1966, pp. 37–40.

356 Monastery of San Lazzaro, Venice, M.S. 887, *Adrianople Gospels*, f.8r; Evans and Wixom, p. 357.

357 Dionysou Monastery codex 587, f. 113r: *Athos 1*, p. 187; Athens codex 93, f. 138, Hetherington and Forman, p. 96.

358 *Homilies of Gregory the Theologian*: St Panteleimon Monastery codex 6, f. 140v: *Athos 2*, p. 182.

359 Madrid Skylitzes, f. 43r: Evans and Wixom, p. 7; André Grabar and M. Manoussakas, *L'Illustration du Manuscrit de Skylitzès de la Bibliothèque Nationale de Madrid*, Bibliothèque de l'Institute Hellénique d'Études Byzantines de Venise, Venice, 1979, fig. 35.

360 πέδιλα κιρρά, σφòρα λαμπρà τὴν χρóαν,: note 73 in chapter 2 above.

CHAPTER 4

1 Oikonomidès, p. 25.

2 Alan Harvey, *Economic Expansion in the Byzantine Empire: 900-1204*, Cambridge University Press, Cambridge, 1989, p. 244; Alexander Kazhdan and Anne Wharton Epstein, *Change in Byzantine Culture in the Eleventh and Twelfth Centuries*, University of California Press, Berkeley, 1985, pp. 25–6, 46–50.

3 Horrocks, p. 80. From then on it becomes a recurrent theme in this fascinating study.

4 H. Hunger 'On the imitation (ΜΙΜΗΣΙΣ) of Antiquity', *Dumbarton Oaks Papers*, 23–24, 1969–70; For a particular case see Timothy Dawson 'The Varangian Rhomphaia: A Cautionary Tale', *Varangian Voice*, 22, May 1992, pp. 28–31.

5 Psellos, *Chronographie*, bk 6, ch. XXIX, Renauld (ed.), vol. I, p. 132, and bk 7, ch. I, Renauld (ed.), vol. II, p. 83–4; Cheynet, pp. 453–77.

6 Komnênê, bk. 3, ch. 4, §3; Komnênê, *The Alexiad of Anna Comnena*, pp. 111–12.

7 Tougher, p. 172.

8 *Actes d'Iviron*, no. 44 (Pakourianos), pp. 150–6 and 47 (Pakourianê) pp. 170–83; Sumbatios Pakourianos, and Basiliakos, the father of Kalê Pakourianê, who was also a *kouropalatês* are both missing from Guilland's list: Rodolphe Guilland, 'Etudes sur l'Histoire Administrative de l'Empire Byzantine: Le Curopalate', *Byzantina*, 2, 1970, pp. 201–6.

9 *De Cer.* 711.13–15; Oikonomidès, p. 97.

10 *De Cer.* 230.7–8.

11 Manganeios Prodromos' poems 56 and 57 on a golden Antiochene *himation*. Text provided by Prof. Michael Jeffreys to accompany his paper, 'Lady Eirene's New Party Dress', delivered at the Australian Association for Byzantine Studies Tenth Conference 1997.

12 Nigel G. Wilson, 'The Madrid Skylitzes', *Scrittura e Civilita*, 2, 1978, pp. 209–19.

13 Ihor Sevçenko, 'The Madrid Manuscript of the Chronicle of Skylitzes in the Light of its New Dating', in Irmgard Hutter (ed.), *Byzanz und der Westen*, Osterreichischen Akademie der Wissenschaft, Vienna, 1984, pp. 117–30.

14 A clear illustration of this is the very strong similarity in the military scenes of the Paris 'Book of Kings' (Bib. Nat. Paris, Gr. 333) of the eleventh century (Jean Lassus, *L'illustration byzantine du Livre des Rois: Par. Gr. 333*, Klincksieck, Paris, 1973). The proposition is further supported by the details of military equipment and the resemblance Madrid Skylitzes depictions bear to descriptions in later tenth-century military manuals. For some details of how military equipment changed in the tenth to twelfth century, see Dawson, 'Kremasmata, Kabbadion, Klibanion: Some Aspects of Middle Byzantine Military Equipment Reconsidered', *Byzantine and Modern Greek Studies*, 22, 1998, and more extensively *Suntagma Hoplôn*.

There are other reasons for doubting the suggestion that it was copied from a single Constantinopolitan prototype: see Sevçenko, 'Skylitzes', pp. 127–8.

15 Spatharakis, p. 230; Michael Jeffreys, 'The Vernacular â0óéôÞéïé for Agnes of France', *Byzantine Papers*, AABS, Canberra, 1981, p. 101.

16 Spatharakis, p. 230; Jeffreys, p. 103. The attempt to redate the manuscript to the fourteenth century made by Cecily Hennessy fails on all counts relating to the regalia, in part due to her failure to appreciate patterns of stylisation in the later artwork, partly as result of her lack of sensitivity to variations in the form of dress and accessories, and more significantly due to an insufficiently wide familiarity with the sources for dress, both written and artistic. Cecily Hennessy, 'A Child Bride and her Representation in the Vatican Epithalamion, Cod. Gr. 1851', *Byzantine and Modern Greek Studies*, 30:2, 2006, pp. 115–50.

17 *De Cer.* 502.6; *Imp. Exp.*, p. 144 (*divêtêsion*); 80.11 and 86.4 (the *votrus*).

18 *De Cer.* 184.5, 188.21, 442.1, 576.11–12, 576.15, 576.17, 661.16, 661.18–19.

19 Vat. Gr. 1613, p. 420.

20 There are a few late Byzantine pictures of imperial *persikomanikion* garments which have been rendered as plain red, presumably in conformity with the imperial *roukhon* of the Palaiologan era: Stylianos Pelekanides, P. C. Christou, Ch. Psioumis, and S. N. Kadas, *The Treasures of Mount Athos, Vol. I: The Illuminated Manuscripts*, Patriarchal Institute for Patristic Studies, Athens, 1973, p. 120.

21 Volbach, pp. 145–51, pl. 70.

22 *Die Gedichte des Christophoros Mitylenaios*, no. 30, pp. 17–18.

23 Khoniatês, p. 271.36. The use of an adverb here is inexplicable, and there seems to be no other course but to treat it as a quasi-adjective. Magoulias does likewise: Nikêtas Choniatês, *O City of Byzantium: The Annals of Nicetas Choniates*, tr. Harry J. Magoulias, Wayne State University Press, Detroit, 1984, p. 150.

24 See the discussion of padded caps in chapter 3. There is also a sewn fabric hat from early medieval Egypt held in the Textile Museum of Canada, inv. no. T88.0043.

25 *Encyclopedia of Islam*, vol. v, p. 747; Steingass, p. 1041.

26 Bib. Marc. 479, f. 33r.

27 Dionysou codex 61, f. 28v: *Athos I*, p. 107.

28 Madrid Skylitzes, ff. 104r, 106v.

29 Madrid Skylitzes, ff. 110, 158, 173v, 178v, 180v.

30 Steingass, p. 823.

31 Steingass, p. 1041.

32 Jacques Brosse, Paul Chaland, and Jacques Ostier, *100,000 Years of Daily Life: A Visual History*, The Bodley Head, London, 1960, p. 89. No details of the manuscript or foliation are given, and communication with BNP went unanswered.

33 *Suda*, vol. 3, p. 81.

34 Bib. Marc. 479, f. 33r.

35 Madrid Skylitzes, ff. 215; 216.

36 Vat. Gr. 1651, f7r.

37 Madrid Skylitzes, ff. 109, 109v, 141v.

38 Particularly fine examples are depicted on a fourth-century ivory showing the women at the tomb of Christ held in the Museum of Art, Milan: Kitzinger, fig. 77.

39 Vegetius, *Epitome de Re Militari*, p. 42.

40 D'Amato and Sumner, pp. 218 and 220.

41 Madrid Skylitzes, ff. 10v, 11, 42, 42v.

42 This is indicated by the way the late pictures show vertical striping on the body of the hat or a roped texture along the top edge, entirely unlike the Middle Byzantine pictures. See the mosaics of the Khora Church particularly, but an array of other fourteenth- and fifteenth-century art in similar vein. In attempting to use headgear to undermine the twelfth-century date of the *Eisitêrioi for Agnes of France*, Cecily Hennessy show herself to be insufficiently sensitive both to artistic stylisation and to morphological differences. 'A Child Bride', pp. 135–6.

43 Eustathios of Thessaloniki, *The Capture of Thessaloniki*, tr. John R. Melville-Jones, AABS, Canberra, 1988, pp. 50–1.

44 Eustathios, p. 68.

45 τὸ ἄνω καὶ πρὸς τῇ πυραμίδι τῆς ἐπιφανείας χῦμα ... τὴν κάτω καὶ κοίλην ἐπιφάνειαν ... λείαν τελέως: Verpeaux, Gregoras, *Historia Rômana*, 1, p. 170. Noted by Verpeaux, *Treatise*, p. 141, note 1.

46 Lydos, *On Powers*, pp. 102–4.

47 βδέλλια: *De Cer.*, 470.6; *Imp. Exp.*, p. 110.

48 *Treatise*, 153.18–154.1.

49 Ivy leaves cover both the *divêtêsion* and cloak of the emperor on Paris Coislin 79, f.1r, droplets appear on many enamels of this era, such as the crown of Constantine Monomachos, palms feature on the tunics of John II and Kaisar Alexios: Vat. Urb. Gr. 2, f. 10v and upon the *khlamus* of the Archangel Michael in Coislin 79, f. 2v.

50 'videlicet bisantos sex milia et mantum pretiosum holosericum auroque textum, quod erat preclara vestis honoris sui, que amplius valere ferebatur quam centum libras argenti purissimi': André Guillou, 'Production and Profits in the Byzantine Province of Italy (Tenth to Eleventh Centuries): An Expanding Society', *Dumbarton Oaks Papers*, 28, 1974, p. 109.

51 Guillou, p. 100.

52 *Actes d'Iviron*, pp. 170–183.
53 *Actes d'Iviron*, p. 179.
54 *Actes d'Iviron*, p. 176.
55 Kouloumousiou codex 60, f. 1v: *Athos I*, p. 240.
56 Lavra codex A 103, f. 3v: Spatharakis, pl. 45, and p. 79 for dating.
57 τῶν κατὰ νώτου κεχυμενῶν λευκολίνων: Khoniatês, p. 271.2; *O City of Byzantium, Annals of Niketas Khoniatês*, tr., p. 150.
58 Spatharakis, p. 60.
59 Kouloumousiou codex 60, f. 1v: Spatharakis, p. 83; Athos I, p. 240, 451.
60 Louis Bréhier, *Le Monde Byzantin*, Éditions Albin Michel, Paris, 1949, vol. II, p. 138; Rodolph Guilland, 'Etudes sur l'Histoire Administrative de l'Empire Byzantine: Les Titres Auliques des Eunuches – Le Protospathaire', *Byzantion*, 25–27, 1955–7, p. 676.
61 Vatican Urb, Gr. 2, f. 19v. Parani, *Reality*, pl. 21.
62 Khoniatês, p. 46.
63 Bodleian Library, MS Rowe 6.
64 Πέδιλα, κιρρά σφόδρα λαμπραὰ τὴν χρόαν: ed. Kurtz, p. 17, l. 16.
65 *Homilies of Gregory the Theologian*: St Panteleimon Monastery codex 6, f. 140v: *Athos 2*, p. 182.
66 *Book of Gifts and Rarities*, tr. Ghâda al-Hijjâwî al-Qaddûmî, Harvard University Press, Cambridge, MA, 1996, p. 197.
67 Psellos, *Chronographie*, bk. 6, ch. LVIII, vol. 1, p. 145; Sewter omits the term *Sevastê*: Psellos, *Fourteen Byzantine Rulers*, pp. 183–4; L. Stiernon, 'Notes de Titulaire et de Prosopographie Byzantines: Sébaste et Gambros', *Revue des Études Byzantines*, 23, 1965, p. 226 (*Sevastos*); *Oxford Dictionary of Byzantium*, vol. 3, p. 1747 (*prôtosevastos*).
68 Oikonomidès, p. 293.
69 καὶ πρὸς τὸ τοῦ ὑποουμένου σχῆμα: Khoniatês, p. 46; Magoulias, p. 27.
70 Francis Grew and Margarethe de Neergaard, *Shoes and Pattens: Medieval Finds from London*, HMSO, London 1996, pp. 9–12.
71 Henry Maguire, 'The Heavenly Court', in Henry Maguire (ed.), *Byzantine Court Culture from 829 to 1204*, Dumbarton Oaks, Washington, DC, 1997, p. 253.
72 Kinnamos, bk I, ch. 10; Meinke (ed.), p. 23; Brand (tr.), p. 27.
73 Giorgios Akropolitês, *Georgii Acropolitae Opera*, ed. A. Heisenberg, Leipzig, 1903 (corr. P. Wirth, Stuttgart, 1978), §82, l. 58; Nikêphoros Gregoras, *Historia Romana*, vol. 1, p. 79, ln. 21.
74 Komnênê, bk. 3. ch. 3, §. 5-8; Sewter, *Alexiad*, p. 113.
75 Charles M. Brand, *Byzantium Confronts the West 1180–1204*, Harvard University Press, Cambridge, MA, 1968, p. 84.
76 Khoniatês, p. 507; Magoulias, p. 279.
77 Evstathios, p. 18.
78 Achmet, *Oneirocriticon*, p. 210.
79 Overlooked by Parani, *Reality*, p. 66 n. 55 and Hennessy following her, p. 136.
80 Evstathios, p. 76.
81 Robert Browning, *Byzantium and Bulgaria*, Sidgwick and Jackson, London, 1975, p. 132.
82 *De Cer.* 381.19 – Gothic guardsmen; 640.8 – Koursores; 700.18 – Dekourioi.
83 Ihor Sevçenko, 'The Illuminators of the Menologium of Basil II', *Dumbarton Oaks Papers*, 14, 1962, p. 272. Both this identity of the crowns and the presentation of a spear called by the commonly used term *romfaia* fully undermine Sevçenko's suggestion that the poem does not correlate fully with the picture. Paul Stephenson elaborates the flaws in Sevçenko's theory in 'Images of the Bulgar-slayer: three art historical notes', *Byzantine and Modern Greek Studies*, 25, 2001, p. 46, n. 5.
84 *Book of Gifts and Rarities*, p. 197. Corundum is a general term for stones of the sapphire and ruby family.
85 *De Cer.* 580.17, 581.9, 581.16–22, 586.19–21.
86 Contrary to Piltz, *Kamelaukion*, p. 31.
87 Spatharakis, pp. 30–1, points out that Alexios' crown in Vatican Barberini Gr. 372, f.5v had been retouched to bring it into conformity with the appearance of later crowns.
88 *Chronographia*, bk 7, ch. XXXIII: Renauld (ed.), vol. 2, p. 103; Psellos, *Fourteen Byzantine Rulers*, p. 295.
89 Komnênê, bk. 3, ch. iii, §5; Sewter, *Alexiad*, p. 112.
90 Inventory number BZ.1937.23.
91 Evans and Wixom, p. 200.
92 Vienna, Hist. Gr. 53, f. 291v; Spatharakis, pl. 99.
93 Spatharakis, p. 156.
94 *Book of Gifts and Rarities*, p. 196.
95 Best illustrated in ivories such as the pyxis in the British Museum, M&LA 79,12-20,1, and also in the *Vienna Genesis*, pp. 16, 35, 36.
96 Harvey, especially p. 244.
97 *Book of Gifts and Rarities*, p. 196.
98 In addition to the Madrid Skylizes coronation, another place the *kontomanikion* appears prominently is in pictures of Isaak Komnênos who ruled Cyprus from 1184 to 1191 and had ambitions for the throne in Constantinople.
99 Eustathios, p. 18.
100 Scholarship has not yet fixed a widely accepted date for this piece. The fact that the emperor is shown wearing a *stemma*, with a wide brow band and visible arching superstructure, rather than a *kaisarikion* is one reason for attributing it to the eleventh century rather than the tenth, as Goldschmidt and Weitzmann proposed (Adolph

Goldschmidt and Kurt Weitzmann, *Die Byzantinischen Elfenbeinskulpturen des X-XIII Jahrhunderts*, Berlin, 1934). Whether it should be accepted as depicting Rômanos III Arguros (1028–34) as Maria Parani suggested at the 32nd British Symposium of Byzantine Studies ('Which Eudokia? A Contribution to the Romanos Ivory Debate', *Bulletin of British Byzantine Studies*, 25, 1999, pp. 87–8), or Rômanos VI and Evdokia Makrembolitissa (1068–71), as Ioli Kalavresou-Maxeiner argued ('Dating the Romanos Ivory', *Dumbarton Oaks Papers*, 31, 1977, pp. 307–25) has yet to be firmly established, but my inclination is toward the latter.

101 Princeton Theological Seminary, Robert E. Speer Library, acc. 11.12.1900, f. 1r.

102 Spatharakis, fig. 77; *Athos I*, p. 102.

103 Contrary to Spatharakis who was of the opinion that his clothing was of no assistance. He was misled in this because he was not sufficiently sensitive to the precise detail in which such portraits were rendered. He also did not consider that court regalia could have evolved, for he was willing to make a direct comparison with the portrait of Leo the Sakellarios, donor of Vatican Reg. Gr. 1, despite the fact that it is a century and a half older, and Leo held a very different rank. Spatharakis, pp. 120f.

104 1074–78: Spatharakis, p. 118; 1071–1081: Evans and Wixom, p. 207.

105 Spatharakis, pp. 75, 119–20.

106 Oikonomidès, p. 299.

107 *Oxford Dictionary of Byzantium*, vol. 3, p. 1727.

108 Dumitrescu proposes that the dark panel on the figure's chest is some sort of bib tied around his waist, put on to mute the brocaded opulence of the regalia. The panel is itself brocade, but a plain cloth would surely have been more suitable if an emblem of modesty had been intended. Furthermore, there is no evidence elsewhere for such a practice. Finally, the author claims that this panel is fastened by cords around the waist. The present author has not had Dumitrescu's privilege of examining the original manuscript, but reproductions show clearly enough that any such hypothetical fastening would be entirely concealed by the garment's sleeves. Going to such lengths to account for the presence of a contrasting breast panel is quite unnecessary, for they had been a standard form of decoration on Roman tunics since Late Antiquity.

109 Shown on an array of Sassanian metalware. See, for examples, Harper, pls 19 and 34. This gesture can be seen extensively in the Madrid Skylitzes manuscript. See illustration 46. Carmen-Laura Dumitrescu is quite mistaken in regarding this as a gesture of piety ('Remarques en Marge du Coislin 79: Les Trois Eunuques', *Byzantion*, 57, 1987, pp. 38–9). The comment she cites made by André Grabar on devotion refers to loyalty to the emperor rather than anyone higher (André Grabar, *L'Empereur dans l'Art Byzantine*, Variorum, London, 1971, p. 88).

110 Spatharakis, p. 228.

111 *De Cer.* 301.20–302.6.

112 *Treatise*, pp. 168.3, 176.4.

113 Parani, Reality, p. 66 n. 55.

114 The *dêmes* alone had four *mandatores* each (*De Cer.* 804.8), and we do not how many there were for general court service.

115 Gamber discusses the relationship between the European surcoat and Byzantine military garments in 'Geschichte der mittlealterlichen Bewaffnung (Teil 4)', *Waffen und Kostümkunde*, 37, 1995, pp. 1–26.

116 *Reconstructing the Reality of Images*, p. 119. Parani's suggestion that *staurôton* should mean with crossing lapels is not plausible on linguistic grounds as much as any other.

117 As well as meaning bile or gall in the human medical sense, χολή (*cholê*) also means squid ink and the liquor derived from molluscs used to make tyrian purple dye.

118 Khoniatês, p. 189, Magoulias (tr.), p. 107.

119 Terrence Wise, *Armies of the Crusades*, Osprey Publishing, London, 1978.

120 Ian Heath, *Armies of the Dark Ages*, Wargames Research Group, London, 1980; and *Byzantine Armies: 886-1119*, Osprey Publishing, London, 1979.

121 Stephen Turnbull, *The Walls of Constantinople AD 324–1453*, Osprey Publishing, London, 2004, and still more recent works.

122 Vat. Gr. 1156, f. 194v, 250r, 261r, 283v; Vat. Gr. 1162, f. 95v, 109r (woman), 133v, 142r, 178v, 186r.

123 Guilland, *Curopalate*, p. 191.

124 Vat. gr. 752, f. 449v; Vat. Barb. gr. 372, f. 228v; Smyrna Evangelical college codex. 8, p. 74; Saint Petersburg Public Library gr. 291, f. 3r; Bib. Marc. gr. 454, f. 1v; Bib. Nat. Paris gr. 74, passim.

125 Vatican gr. 752 f. 449v. See Parani, *Reality*, pl. 82, or Evans and Wixom for this picture in colour.

126 These pictures extracted from their original place now form Saint Petersburg Public Library gr. 291, ff. 2v and 3r.

127 Rodolph Guilland, 'Patrices de Theodora aux Comnènes', *Rivista di Studi bizantini e neoellenici*, 8–9 (XVIII–XIX) 1971–2, pp. 15–16.

128 Closer inspection would have shown Hennessy that this item was contiguous with the upper headgear, and so could not be a 'collar', as she says, p. 127.

129 For the identification of this item as *savanion*, see Dawson, 'Propriety, Practicality and Pleasure'.

130 Unusually, the torso of the unicorn-charming virgin of the

Smyrna Octateuch is shown in three-quarter view, thus allowing us to see how the collar runs over the shoulders. See Dawson, 'Propriety, Practicality and Pleasure' for a reconstruction.

131 Inventory number 3.116. See Shepherd, p. 102, fig. 11.

132 *Actes d'Iviron*, p. 181.

133 Mosaic of Constantine Monomachos and Zôê, Hagia Sofia: Talbot Rice, *Art of the Byzantine Era*, p. 104.

134 Noted by Parani, *Reality*, p. 26. G. Zacos, *Byzantine Lead Seals*, vol. 1, G. Zacos, Basel, 1972, nos. 89, 91, 92, 93.

135 Kremlin Museum, inv. MZ 1148: Bank, pl. 203 and p. 308.

136 Hermitage Museum, inv. w 839: Bank, pl. 206 and pp. 308–9.

137 Art Museum of Georgia, inv. 9719: Bank, pl. 185 and p. 305.

138 Grierson, vol. 3, part 1, p. 141.

139 Garland, 'βέργιν', pp. 87–95; Grierson, vol. 3, p. 141, table 15, E.

140 Grierson, vol. 3, p. 141; Bank, pl. 185; Coislin 79, f. 1(2bis) v: Evans and Wixom, p. 182.

141 Grierson, vol. 3, p. 141; Bank, pl. 180.

142 Parani notes that this change must already have taken place in the thirteenth century (Reality, pp. 25–6), thereby negating Hennessy's attempt to use this practice as evidence for a later date for the *Eisitêrioi*, pp. 134, 136.

CHAPTER 5

1 Warren Treadgold, *Byzantium: A History of the State and Society*, Stanford University Press, Stanford, 1997, p. 734; Donald M. Nicol, 'Refugees, Mixed Population and Local Patriotism in Epiros and Western Macedonia after the Fourth Crusade', *XVe Congrès International d'Études Byzantines, Rapports I. Histoire*, Athens, 1976, p. 11.

2 Khoniatês, bk. 9: Van Dieten (ed.), pp. 586–93; Magoulias (tr.), pp. 322–6.

3 Khoniatês, pp. 546–7; Magoulias, p. 299.

4 Donald M. Nicol, '*Kaisersalbung*: The Unction of Emperors in Late Byzantine Coronation Ritual', BMGS, vol. 2, 1976, pp. 37–44; Ruth J. Macrides, 'From the Komnenoi to the Palaiologoi', in Paul Magdalino (ed.), *New Constantines*, Variorum, Aldershot, 1994, p. 280.

5 Witness the enamels on the cuffs of the Byzantine-derived tunic of Roger II of Sicily: Schuette and Müller-Christiansen, p. 40, and a similar reference in *Digenês Akritês*, GRO IV.222: Mavrogordato, p. 80; also the enamelled drop from a *lôros*: Evans and Wixom, p. 212.

6 Michael Angold, *A Byzantine Government in Exile: Government and Society Under the Lascarids of Nikaia (1204–1261)*, Oxford University Press, Oxford, 1975, p. 109.

7 Khludov Psalter, BNP, Gr. 139, f. 6v and the Madrid Skylitzes, f. 10v, to cite representative examples.

8 Nicol, '*Kaisersalbung*', pp. 40–1.

9 Macrides, pp. 280–2.

10 The clearest being a portion of the description of the battle of Dyrrachion in *Alexiad* bk 4, chs 5 and 6.

11 Sigfús Blöndal, *The Varangians of Byzantium*, rev. Benedikt Benedikz, Cambridge University Press, Cambridge, 1978, chapter 7, pp. 166–76; the Varangians still carry axes in the Palaiologian court: *Treatise*, 264.5–6.

12 Psellos, *Chronographie*, bk 5, §27, 2 (vol. I, p. 103); bk 7, §22, 10 (vol. II, p. 95); bk 7, §28, 8 (vol. II, p. 165); bk 7, §28, 11 (vol. II, p. 165); *Alexiad*, bk 1, ch. 5, §7, 8; bk 1, ch. 5, §7, 14; bk 1, ch. 5, §7, 17; bk 1, ch. 5, §9, 8; bk 9, ch. 9, §2, 7; Attaleiatês, *Historia*, p. 30, l. 10; p. 63, l. 7; p. 123, l. 8; p. 157, l. 14; p. 282, l. 24; Bryennios, *Historiae*, bk 1, §20, 1; bk 4, §9, 15; bk 4, §9, 23.

13 ῥομφαία: τὸ μάκρον ἀκόντιον ἢ μαχαίρα: *Suda*, vol. IV, p. 299.

14 Sevçenko, 'Illuminators of the Menologium of Basil II', pp. 245–76. I am grateful to Paul Stephenson for assistance with the sources and helpful discussion on this subject.

15 *Treatise*, p. 35.

16 André Grabar, 'Pseudo-Codinos et les Cerémonies de la Cour Byzantine au XIVe Siécle', in *Art et Société sous les Paléologues*, Institute Hellénique d'Études Byzantines et Postbyzantines de Venise, Venice, 1971, p. 196.

17 *Treatise*, p. 39.

18 *Treatise*, p. 39.

19 *Treatise*, pp. 25–40.

20 *Treatise*, p. 201.11.

21 *Treatise*, pp. 264.3, 267.4, 358.13.

22 *Treatise*, p. 261.2.

23 Louvre Ivoires 100, f. 2r; Würtemberg, cod. Hist. 2° 601, f. 4: Spatharakis, figs 93 and 181.

24 Nicolette S. Trahoulias, *The Greek Alexander Romance: Venice Hellenic Institute Cod. Gr. 5*, Exandas, Athens, 1997, pp. 31–4.

25 *Treatise*, 134.3–4 and 135.

26 *Treatise*, 134.12–18.

27 Spatharakis dated the manuscript to no later than 1344: p. 203, and see pp. 204–6 for the correlations of the portraits with the *Treatise*.

28 This transition discussed by Piltz, *Kamelaukion*, ch. VI, pp. 77–9.

29 Piltz, *Kamelaukion*, pl. 129a

30 στέφει βασιλικῶς ... κεκρυφαλῶς ἡμιτυμβίως, Pachymerês, p. 147, ll. 1–2.

31 *Suda*, vol. 3, p. 90; LSJ, pp. 935, 774.

32 τοῦτο δὲ ἦν βλάτιον μετὰ λίθων καὶ μαργάρων, κατὰ τὸ

τοῦ βασιλέως μέτωπον κείμενον μὲν, δεδεμένον δ'ὄπιθεν περὶ τὸν ἐγκέφαλον. *Treatise*, 199.4–9.

33 Nicol, *Last Centuries*, pp. 30–1.

34 *Suda*, vol. 2, p. 571.

35 Piltz, *Kamelaukion*, pp. 48–9.

36 Donald Nicol, *The Byzantine Lady: Ten Portraits, 1250–1500*, Cambridge University Press, Cambridge, 1994, pp. 89–90; Marino Sanudo, *Vitae Ducum Venetorum: Rerum Italicum Scriptorum*, XXII, Milan, 1733, cols 617–18. Text kindly supplied by Prof. Tom Madden of Saint Louis University.

37 Battista and Alessio, *balascio*: vol. I, p. 411, *rubino*: vol. V, p. 3292; Battaglia, *balascio*: vol. I, p. 950, *rubino*: vol. XVII, p. 202. I also acknowledge the assistance of Dr Franko Leoni, School of Languages, Cultures and Linguistics, University of New England in refining my translation.

38 Spatharakis, pl. 181.

39 Gregoras, vol. 2, p. 788.

40 *Treatise*, p. 199, n. 1.

41 *Treatise*, 225.15–19, 275.5–14, 276.8–15.

42 εἰ δὲ γάμβρος τύχοι ὢν, ἔχον κάμαραν μίκραν ἔμπροσθεν μόνον, *Treatise*, 275.8–14.

43 The dating of the surviving crowns rests primarily upon palaiographic analysis of the inscription. P. A. Drossoyianni, 'A Pair of Byzantine Crowns', *Jahrbuch der Österreichischen Byzantinistik*, 32:3, 1982, pp. 529–38.

44 *Treatise*, p. 200, n. 2; Piltz, *Kamelaukion*, pls 38, 39.

45 Du Cange, *Gloss. Graec.*, col. 33.

46 *Treatise*, p. 142, n. 2.

47 Sophocles, p. 86.

48 *Treatise*, 181.29.

49 Bowl, Walters Gallery, Baltimore, inv. no. 57.625.

50 *Treatise*, 181.19.

51 Du Cange, *Gloss. Graec.*, col. 584. Blemmydês also employs it for the lid of a glass vessel, vol. 2, p. 458, l. 22.

52 Spatharakis, figs 20, 21, 22. Such hats also appear in the *Hippiatrica*, Bib. Nat. Paris, Gr. 2244, f.8v, 36v, 49r.

53 *Treatise*, p. 145, n. 2.

54 *Treatise*, 145.23; Piltz, 'Costume in Life and Death', p. 52.

55 τὸ δὲ σκαράνικον αὐτοῦ ἐνδεδυμένον κόκκινον χάσδεον, ἔχον ἐπὶ κορυφῆς μικρὰν φοῦνταν κοκκίναν. *Treatise*, 163.7–10.

56 The widely accepted tale that the fez was introduced to Istanbul from Morocco in the nineteenth century does not necessarily negate this transmission. It is likely that having been generally adopted in Constantinople after the Ottoman take over, it would naturally disperse to the provinces, where it would be likely to persist in common use after it fell out of favour with the elite, from there to be re-introduced to the capital.

57 σκαράνικον χρυσοχοϊκόν, λιθάρια καὶ μαργαριτάρια ἔχον: *Treatise*, 145.23–146.1.

58 *Treatise*, 147.1.

59 *Treatise*, 155.4–9.

60 *Treatise*, 156.24.

61 Spatharakis, p. 204.

62 Bib. Nat. Fr. 2144, f. 11r.

63 Donor in the left margin of the Theotokos icon in the Tretyakov Gallery, Moscow, inv. 22722. See Bank, pl. 252 and p. 281

64 Donor in the right margin of the Hermitage Museum Pantokratôr icon, inv. I 515. See Bank, pl. 253 and p. 284.

65 Akropolitês, *Annales*, §87, l. 14; For Khoniatês, see pp. 232, 242.

66 *Treatise*, p. 141, n. 1. Elizabeth Piltz attributed this term to the hat of John VIII, which has been linked above with the term *kapasion*: 'Costume in Life and Death', p. 52. The very meaning of the name is sufficient to discount her theory, for the hat referred to is not capable of providing such protection.

67 τὸ ἄνω καὶ πρὸς τῇ πυραμίδι τῆς ἐπιφανείας χῦμα ... τὴν κάτω καὶ κοίλην ἐπιφάνειαν ... λείαν τελέως: Verpeaux, Gregoras, *Historia Rômana*, vol. 1, p. 170. Noted by Verpeaux, *Treatise*, p. 141, n. 1.

68 Oarsmen: Vat. Gr. 1851, f. 2v; also Vat. Gr. 746, f. 61v.

69 Kupferstichkabinet, A78 A9, f. 66v and 214v.

70 BNP, Gr. 1242, f. 5v; Moscow Historical Museum, Synodal Gr. 429, f. 28v: Spatharakis, p. 134, figs 86 and 92.

71 ταῦτα δὲ καλύπτρα λατινικὴ τὸ σχῆμα καὶ μαργάροις πεποικιλμένη καὶ ὑπὲρ κεφαλῆς λιθιδίω κοκκίνῳ: Akropolitês, *Annales*, §87, ll. 14–15.

72 ὁλομάργαρον: *Treatise*, 141.3.

73 χρυσοκόκκινα, συρματέϊνα, ἔχοντα σταυροὺς μαργαριταρεῖνους καὶ γύρους.: *Treatise*, 147.4–8

74 Piltz, *Trois Sakkoi Byzantines*, Almqvist and Wiskell, Stockholm, 1976, pls. 5–7.

75 *Treatise*, 147.10, 148.23.

76 *Treatise*, 155.22–156.13.

77 *Treatise*, 156.21.

78 *Treatise*, 157.5–180.17.

79 BNP, Gr. 1242, f. 2v.

80 *Treatise*, 159.17.

81 *Treatise*, 181.16–19.

82 Sphrantzes, ch. 19, s. 4, ln. 8.

83 Du Cange, *Gloss. Graec.*, cols. 747, 1400.

84 Stillman, pp. 135–6.

85 *Treatise*, p. 143, n. 1.

86 πλὴν τοῦ κόμπου καὶ τῶν φοινικίων: *Treatise*, 142.2, 147.11, 149.2.

87 BNP, Gr, 2244, f. 36v, 37v, 49v.

88 *Treatise*, 200.6.

89 *Treatise*, 227.26.

90 μαργέλλιον συρματέϊνον, *Treatise*, 205.15.

91 LSJ, p. 1080; Du Cange, *Gloss. Graec.*, p. 878, 1491; Sophocles, p. 733.

92 The suggestion made by Elizabeth Piltz ('Costume in Life and Death', pp. 17 and 21) that the headgear of Theodôros Metokhitês in his donor portrait in the Church of the Holy Saviour in the Fields is a regalia turban must be discounted for several reasons. Metôchitês is not represented in the regalia of his recorded rank of *megas logothetês*, which would consist of a dress *kavadion* and *skaranikon* according to the *Treatise on the Offices*. The *kavadion* he is depicted as wearing has loose sleeves rather than the close-fitting type which can be seen to be characteristic of regalia *kavadia*, and, it need hardly be repeated, his headgear is not a *skaranikon*. If Metôchitês did not see fit to be depicted in his proper regalia, as others preferred, it is hardly plausible that he would have himself portrayed in the regalia of some other rank, let alone in a disparate assemblage of regalia items, as Piltz proposed.

93 Piltz, 'Life and Death', p. 158. She repeats this proposition in *Le Costume Officiel*, p. 53.

94 *C.W.*, I.3: McGeer, pp. 12–13. See the discussion in chapter 3.

95 Spectacular examples are held in the Victoria and Albert Museum: such as inv. 127.1896; and the Cleveland Museum of Art, inv. 50.525, 50.510 and others: *Bulletin of the Cleveland Museum of Art*, January 1987, p. 21.

96 Madrid Skylitzes, f. 45r (a soldier), 49v (an official), 78v (musicians); Vat, Gr. 1162, f. 5r; Iveron cod. 463, f. 169r; Bib. Marc. 479, f. 44r; Kupferstichkabinet 78 A9, f. 184v.

97 Hetherington and Forman, p. 119.

98 As with so much of her work, Elizabeth Piltz' *Trois Sakkoi Byzantines* sheds more shade than light, with such mistaken correlations as the notion that *sakkos* can be equated with *sagion*. See also Walter, p. 16; *Oxford Dictionary of Byzantium*, p. 1830.

99 Piltz, *Trois Sakkoi*, pp. 13–14; Walter, p. 17.

100 Talbot Rice, *Art of the Byzantine Era*, pp. 37, 40; Evans and Wixom, pp. 75, 97, 170, 172, 173. The loincloth begins to be shown on Orthodox icons from the tenth century, but does not entirely supplant the *sakkos* until the twelfth century.

101 ἐνδύονται σακκοῦς, προφανῶς μιμνούμενοι πεπόνθοτα, τὸν ὑπὲρ ἡμῶν, σάκκον τε ἐνδυσάμενον παικτίκως καὶ δία σταύρου θάνατον ἐνεγκόντας: *PG* 155, col. 872; Piltz, *Trois Sakkoi*, p. 17.

102 Piltz, *Trois Sakkoi*, p. 17. Some versions of the ecclesiastical *sakkos* with substantial flaps at the shoulder can look somewhat like the Western dalmatic, which is possibly the reason for Alexander Kazhdan's correlation of the two garments: *Oxford Dictionary of Byzantium*, p. 1830. Christopher Walter (p. 17) is mistaken in seeing penitential *sakkoi* in Bib. Nat. Paris Gr. 510, f. 78 (fig. 4). The garments shown are in fact very long *fenolia* of the antique mantle form, distinguished as such by their lack of arm-holes and very characteristic seam down the centre-front.

103 *Oxford Dictionary of Byzantium*, vol. 3, p. 1830.

104 Maguire, 'A murderer amongst the angels'; see above.

105 *Treatise*, p. 143, n. 2; Piltz, *Le Costume Officiel*, p. 13 passim.

106 *C.W.*, 11.74: McGeer, p. 26; Mihaescu, p. 91.

107 Horrocks notes this practice as a feature of Palaiologian literature: pp. 196–200.

108 ῥούχον σχιστὸν ἐκ χρωμάτων δύο. As was discussed in chapter 3, *skhistos/diskhistos* refered to divisions in the skirt of the garment, as opposed to *diakoptos*, which denoted the full division making it a coat.

109 Black and Garland, p. 115; Millia Davenport, *The Book of Costume*, Crown Publishers, New York, 1976, p. 149.

110 For example in the Paris *Hippiatrika*: BNP Gr. 2244, f. 8v, 29v, 36v, 37v and 49v.

111 Sphrantzês, *Chronicon*, ch. 13, §4, ln. 15 and Ioannês Kananos, *De Constantinopolis Obsidione*, ed. Emilio Pinto, Libreria Scientifica, Naples, 1968, l. 553 where both refer to women's dresses; *himation* used in a generic sense in the *Treatise*: 261.2, 271.12, 356.15.

112 Lincoln College, Oxford, Gr. 35, f. 1v: Spatharakis, p. 192.

113 *Alexander Romance*, pp. 58, 61, 62, 87, 91, and numerous other places.

114 *Treatise*, 195.16; 212.21.

115 Notably the donors of the frescos of various churches in Kastoria, and the sepultural frescos of the Church of the Saviour in Khôra; also Sinai gr. 2123, f. 30r: Spatarakis, Portrait, pl. 19.

116 Donna Green, 'Pattern for a period caftan', *The Byzantine World*, http://members.tripod.com/BlackTauna/period-caftan.gif, 2000 (updated 27 November 2000, cited 15 July 2002). Attempts to contact the holding institution received no response. However the resemblance of this pattern to other surviving garments, including the Manazan Caves *esôforion* lend credibility despite the otherwise poor quality of the website.

117 *Treatise*, 146.2.

118 βλάτιον οἷον ἂν βολύοιτο ἀπὸ τῶν συνήθων. *Treatise*, 153.18–154.1; ranks following this generally have some formula indicating the identity of their *kavadia* with the foregoing, save where a version of the phrase given is repeated: 156.22.

119 Spatharakis, pp. 149, n. 20, 154 n. 12, 156, 193, 196–8, 204, 206; Piltz, *Le Costume Officiel*, p. 52; Piltz, 'Life and Death', p. 158.

120 BNP gr. 2144, f. 11r: Spatharakis, fig. 96; Piltz, *Le Costume Officiel*, fig. 57.

121 *Megas primikêrios*, Hermitage, inv. I 515; *megas logothetês*, Tretyakov Gallery, Moscow, inv. 22722: Bank, pls 252–3, 281, 284.

122 Piltz, *Le Costume Officiel*, p. 102.

123 Ms. Vind. Hist. gr. 35, f. 291v: Spatharakis, p. 156 and pl. 99; Piltz mistakenly called it a *kamision*, *Le Costume Officiel*, p. 11.

124 A finely depicted example is to be seen on the royal hunting relief at Taq-i-Bustan: Tamara Talbot Rice, *Ancient Arts of Central Asia*, Thames and Hudson, London, 1965, p. 168.

125 One often-reproduced Armenian example is represented in the reliefs of Saint Shak on the south facade of the Church of the Holy Cross at Aght'amar: Sirarpie Der Nersessian, *Aght'amar: The Church of the Holy Cross*, Harvard University Press, Cambridge, MA, 1965; Lynn Jones, *Between Islam and Byzantium*, Ashgate, Aldershot, London, 2007, p. 93. For an example of the Armenian style in use by Rômiaoi in the Sultanate of Rüm, see Claude Cahen, *Pre-Ottoman Turkey*, Sidgwick and Jackson, London, 1968, pls 66–7. The Turkish style is commonly seen on minai-ware pottery, such as a plate in the Freer Gallery of Art, Washington, inv. no. 43.3-1, and various early thirteenth-century manuscripts. For the Turkish terminology see Gerard Clauson, *Etymological Dictionary of Pre-Thirteenth-Century Turkish*, Clarendon Press, Oxford 1972, p. 929.

126 Du Cange, *Gloss. Graec.*, col. 667.

127 *De Cer.* 578.5; for the fabrics, see Volbach, pl. 66 (p. 138) and p. 133 for other dated fabrics with the same design; Hetherington and Forman, p. 82.

128 GRO III. 255, IV. 115 and VI.736: Mavrogordato, pp. 58, 72, 206.

129 British Library Add. 39627, f. 2v: Spatharakis, pl. 38.

130 *Treatise*, 206.17–19.

131 Grabar, *Art et Société*, p. 198.

132 *Treatise*, 219.12–13.

133 Du Cange, *Gloss. Graec.*, col. 200; LSJ, p. 339; Hemmerdinger, '158 noms', p. 19.

134 *Suda*, vol. I, p. 509.

135 Du Cange, *Gloss. Lat.*, vol. IV, pp. 34–5.

136 For more on cross-cultural transmission of garments and terms see Timothy Dawson, 'There and Back Again – Cross-Cultural Transmission of Clothing and Clothing Terminology', in Stephanie Hathaway and David W. Kim (eds), *Studies in Intercultural Exchange in the Early Medieval Mediterranean*, Continuum Publishing, London, 2012, pp. 203–13.

137 Hemmerdinger, '158 noms', p. 31; Steingass, p. 1117.

138 Du Cange, *Gloss. Lat.*, vol. V, p. 27.

139 Back wall of tomb F: See, for example, Paul Atkins Underwood, *The Kariye Djami*, Bollingen Foundation, New York, 1966, vol. 3, p. 547.

140 Fluck and Vogelsang-Eastwood, fig. 68d.

141 See McGeer, pp. 12–13, 34–5.

142 Jerusalem ms. 2563, f. 380. Fluck and Vogelsang-Eastwood, fig. 10.

143 Kupferstichkabinet, 78 A9, f. 39v.

144 *Sullogê Taktikôn*, ch. 38, §4, ch. 39, §1.

145 Peter of Eboli, *Liber ad Honorem Augusti de Pietro di Eboli*, ed. G. B. Siragusa, Instituto Storico Italiano, Rome, 1905, p. 129.

146 *Treatise*, 199.3–200.1.

147 *Treatise*, 201.8–9.

148 *Treatise*, 200.4, 256.25, 264.4–5.

149 BM Add. 39627, f. 3r; BNP gr. 1242, f. 5v; Louvre Ivoires 100, f. 2r; Vat. Slav. 2, f. 1v; Monac. gr. 442, f. 7v, 174r, 175v; chrysobull of Alexios III; chrysobull of Alexios II of Trebizond; BNP Sup. gr. 309, f. VI; Württemberg cod. hist. 2° 602f. 2: Spatharakis, figs 39, 86, 93, 102, 108, 109, 110, 134, 136, 175, 180.

150 *Treatise*, 261.3.

151 *Treatise*, 283.7.

152 *Treatise*, 264.3, 276.4, 358.13.

153 *Treatise*, 264.3.

154 Du Cange, *Gloss. Gaec.*, p. 1526.

155 Lincoln College, Oxford, Gr. 35, f. 1v: Spatharakis, pp. 192, 204, pl. 143.

156 Du Cange, *Gloss. Gaec.*, 1526; Battista and Alessio, p. 3690; Battaglia, vol. XX, p. 647.

157 *Treatise*, 143.5, 148.1.

158 *Treatise*, 153.1, 153.9.

159 Du Cange, *Gloss. Graec.*, col. 557.

160 *Treatise*, 143.7.

161 *Treatise*, 147.16, 149.5.

162 *Treatise*, 181.19.

163 *Treatise*, 171.11–17.

164 Akropolitês, §87, l. 15; Doukas, *Historia Turkobyzantina*, ch. 6, §2, line 4.

165 This definite statement can be made from the author's first-hand experience.

166 χρώαμτος ὀξέος καὶ λευκοῦ, ἔχοντα ἀετοὺς μαργαριταρεῖνους ἐκ πλαγίων τε καὶ ἐπὶ τῶν ταρσῶν: *Treatise*, 143.7–144.5.

167 Institute Hellénique d'Études Byzantines et Postbyzantines

de Venise, *Art et Société à Byzance sous les Paléologues*, Venice, 1971, fig. 58.

168 ἠεράνεα ... κόκκινον: *Treatise*, 148.3–6.

169 Akropolitês, §82, l. 58; Gregoras, vol. 1, p. 79, l. 21.

170 Khoniatês, p. 507, l. 13.

171 *Treatise*, 227.6–12.

172 Γιαννακοπούλος, p. 510.

173 *Treatise*, 181. 20, 228.15.

174 *Treatise*, 201.13–202.3.

175 *Treatise*, 200.17–201.1, 202.29, 225.1.

176 *Treatise*, 262.21–2.

177 *Treatise*, 200.17, 202.28, 224.28, 355.16; *De Cer.* 62.16, 187.15.

178 *Treatise*, 190.24; *De Cer.* 397.19 (λευκοφόροι), 744.10, 745.1 (χλανιδοφόροι), 101.14.

179 *Treatise*, 151.15, 154.11,154.25, 156.6, 156.15, 157.9, 157.18, 158.2.

180 *Treatise*, 154.2, 158.20, 160.16, 160.29.

181 *Treatise*, 162.17, 164.14.

182 *Treatise*, 166.16, 162.17; Piltz, *Costume Officielle*, p. 78.

183 *Treatise*, 163.20, 166.28.

184 *Treatise*, 166.26.

185 *Treatise*, 162.29.

186 *Treatise*, 184.10–13.

187 *Treatise*, 161.17–20.

188 Verpeaux follows a widespread opinion in this: *Treatise*, p. 161, n. 1.

189 σειρομάστην, ὃν κοινῶς καλοῦσι σαλίβαν: *Treatise*, 161.19–20.

190 σειρομάστης > σιρομάστης: LSJ, 1589 > 1600; σαλίβα: Du Cange, *Gloss. Graec.*, col. 1327.

191 *Treatise*, 182.18–20.

192 Graham Webster, *The Imperial Roman Army of the First and Second Centuries AD*, Adam and Charles Black, London, 1969, p. 129; Roy Davies, *Service in the Roman Army*, Edinburgh University Press, Edinburgh, 1989, pp. 83–5.

193 *Treatise*, 201.2, 202.4, 225.1.

194 *Treatise*, 218.14.

195 *Treatise*, 200.7.

196 *Treatise*, 200.7, 203.5, 225.19.

197 Manuel II, BNP, Gr. 309, f. VI (Spatharakis, fig. 175), also Andronikos III, Württemberg cod, hist. 2° 601, f. 2 (Spatharakis, fig. 180).

198 *Treatise*, 206.2.

199 *Treatise*, 199.20–200.1.

200 *Treatise*, 180.16. Verpeaux is unjustified in thinking this refers only to bows. Since antiquity this plural has been used to denote a full set of equipment, both the bow and its ammunition: LSJ, p. 1805.

201 *Treatise*, 163.88.

202 Du Cange, *Gloss. Graec.*, col. 887; Sophocles, p. 736.

203 *Treatise*, 164.1.

204 *Treatise*, p. 164, n. 1.

205 *Treatise*, 273.1–18. The notion that has been widely publicised in popular militaria literature and discussion that the *romfaia* was a weapon resembling the ancient Dacian *falx* is a fiction created by one author's ignorance of Greek and Greek literature, elaborated by the laziness and circular referencing of those who came after. See Heath, *Armies of the Dark Ages*, p. 73 and *Byzantine Armies*, p. 38 for the genesis of the idea, and for a refutation see Timothy Dawson, 'The Varangian *rhomphaia*', pp. 28–31, and www.levantia.com.au/theory/rhomfaia.html.

206 *Treatise*, 180.7–1.

207 *Treatise*, 168.3, 171.8, 176.4, 176.14, 190.21, 191.8, 203.20, 234.19.

208 *De Cer.* 80.12, 167.9, 188.24.

209 *Treatise*, 183.12, 196.16, 246.25, 337.76; *De Cer.* 640.13.

210 *Treatise*, 255.21, 256.17.

211 *Treatise*, 273.12.

212 *Vardariôtai*, *Oxford Dictionary of Byzantium*, vol. 3, p. 2153; *Treatise*, 181.29.

213 *De Cer.* 524.3.

214 *Treatise*, 287.15.

215 Spatharakis, pp. 192–9, figs. 143–51.

216 Bank, pl. 254.

217 *Treatise*, 260.21–2.

218 φορεῖ δὲ ἔνδυμα μέλαν λεγόμενον ἱμάτιον.

219 See, for example, the testament of Kalê Pakourianê: *Actes d'Iviron*, p. 180.

220 *Treatise*, 190.1, 283.11, 356.15.

221 Württemberg Cod. Hist. 2° 601, f. 4: Spatharakis, fig. 181.

222 Du Cange, *Gloss. Lat.*, vol. X, tab. VI.

223 *Treatise*, 260.12–21. The *spithamê* is a somewhat vague measurement which could be 15.6, 19.5 or 23.4 centimetres. See Erich Schilbach, *Byzantinische Metrologie*, Brücken-Verlag, Düsseldorf, 1970, and Timothy Dawson, '"Fit for the task"', pp. 1–12.

224 Spatharakis, p. 140 and pl. 93.

225 Grierson, vol. 3, p. 141, table 15 D.

226 Garland, βέργιν, p. 87-95; Grierson, vol. 3, p. 141, table 15 E.

227 *Treatise*, 355.22–3 and 262.22.

228 *Treatise*, 260.12.

229 Spatharakis, fig. 136; Piltz, *Kamelaukion*, pl. 108b.

230 BL, Add. 39627, f. 2v abd 3r: Spatharakis, figs. 38 and 39; Piltz, *Kamelaukion*, pl. 106.

TABLES

This is primarily a list of honorific ranks, with functional offices omitted, although the distinction between honorific ranks and functional offices becomes uncertain in the twelfth- to fourteenth-century context. The shaded areas indicate women whose position is noted as having regalia.

* as given by Cheynet, in 'Dévaluation des Dignités'

compiled from references in literary sources. This must lack some ranks which may have continued, such as *prôtospatharios*.

The double border between the lower portion of the twelfth-century column and the *Treatise on the Offices* indicates that no equivalence, even notional, can be established.

1 Combined *Taktika* Across the Period

Klêtôrologion, 899	*Escorial Taktikon*, 975	*Taxis* of c. 1081*	*Taxis* of the later twelfth century#	*Treatise on the Offices*, c.1380
vasileus	*vasileus*	*vasileus*	*vasileus*	*vasileus*
				despotês
		sevastokratôr	*sevastokratôr*	*sevastokratôr*
kaisar	*kaisar*	*kaisar*	*kaisar*	*kaisar*
			megas domestikos	*megas domestikos*
			panhypersevastos	*panhypersevastos*
			prôtovestiarios	*prôtovestiarios*
			megas doux	*megas doux*
			prôtostratôr	*prôtostratôr*
				megas stratopedarkhos
				megas primikêrios
				megas konostaulos
				megas logothetês
			prôtosevastos	*prôtosevastos*
		sevastos	*sevastos*	
		prôtonôvelissimos		*pinkhernês*
nôvelissimos	*nôvelissimos*	*nôvelissimos*		
		prôtokouropalatês		
kouropalatês	*kouropalatês*	*kouropalatês*	*kouropalatês*	*kouropalatês*
vasileopatôr	*vasileopatôr*			*parakoimomenos*
zôstê patrikia	*zôstê patrikia*	*zôstê patrikia*		
		prôtoprôedros		*prôtovestaritês*
prôedros	*prôedros*	*prôedros*	*prôedros*	*domestikos tou trapetzês*
magistros / ~issa	*magistros / ~issa*	*magistros / ~issa*		*epi tês trapetzês*
	patrikios eunoukhos	*prôtovestarchês*		*megas papias*
	vestarchês	*vestarchês*		*eparkhos*
	patrikios praipositos	*prôtovestês*		
	vestês	*vestês*		Ten more functional ranks with no discernible equivalents in earlier hierarchies
anthupatos		*anthupatos*		
patrikios / ~a	*patrikios/ ~a*	*patrikios/ ~a*		
prôtospatharios				
disupatos	*disupatos*	*disupatos*		
	hupatos	*hupatos*		
	prôtospatharios	*prôtospatharios*		*prôtospatharios*
spatharo kandidatos	*spatharo kandidatos*	*spatharo kandidatos*		

2 Summary of the Regalia of the Late Ninth to Early Eleventh Centuries

Men

Rank or Office	Primary Garment	Secondary Garment	Over-Garments	Accessories
vasileus	*divêtêsion*	*kôlovion*	*lôros, khlamus, sagion*	*stemma, kaisarikion, toufa, tzitzakion, thôrakion*
kaisar	*divêtêsion*	*kôlovion*	*lôros, khlamus, sagion*	*kaisarikion*, turban, *thôrakion*
nôvilissimos	*divêtêsion* of rich red		*lôros, khlamus, sagion*	*thôrakion*
kouropalatês	*divêtêsion* of murex purple		*lôros, khlamus, sagion*	*thôrakion*
zôstê patrikia	see below			
proedros	tunic *(khitôn)* of rich red worked with gold		bright white *khlamus* edged with gold embroidery and fitted with two *tavlia* woven with ivy leaves, *sagion*	*valtidion* (red/purple leather belt with precious stones)
magistros	*stikharion*	*kamision*	white *khlamus* with purple *tavlia, sagion*	
raikôr	*kamision*		white *khlamus* with purple *tavlia, sagio*	*raiktôrikion*, sheaf of purple parchment
patrikios	*spekion*	*kamision*	white *khlamus* with purple *tavlia, sagio*	ivory diptych with pages
prôtospatharios	*spekion* of murex purple	*kamision*	white *khlamus* with purple *tavlia, sagio*	solid gold torque with precious stones
disupatos			white *khlamus* with purple *tavlia, sagio*	inscribed scroll
spatharokandidatos			white *khlamus* with purple *tavlia, sagio*	segmented gold torque with white stones
spatharios			white *khlamus* with purple *tavlia, sagio*	sword with gilded fittings
hupatos			white *khlamus* with purple *tavlia, sagio*	inscribed scroll
stratôr (office)			white *khlamus* with purple *tavlia, sagio*	a gilded whip with precious stones
kandidatos			white *khlamus* with purple *tavlia, sagio*	gold collar with three ornaments
mandatôr (office)			white *khlamus* with purple *tavlia, sagio*	red-dyed baton
vestitôr (office)	*fiblatôrion*		white *khlamus* with purple *tavlia, sagio*	
silentarios			white *khlamus* with purple *tavlia, sagio*	gilded baton

Women

Rank or Office	Primary Garment	Secondary Garment	Over-garments	Accessories
augousta	*divêtêsion*	coat (*diakoptês*)	*lôros, khlamus, taôn, aetarion*	*stemma, pniktarion, stêthokarakallon*
kaisarissa	*delmatikion?*		*lôros? aetarion?*	*stefanos?* purple *propolôma?*
zôstê patrikia	*delmatikion*		*lôros*	*propolôma, thôrakion*
koubikoularea (office)	non-regalia *delmatikion*		golden *paragaudion*	*propolôma, maforion, kharzanion*
magisrissa				*propolôma*
patrikia				*propolôma*

3 Summary of the Regalia of the Palaiologian Period

Rank	Primary Garment	Secondary Garment	Over-garments	Accessories
vasileus	*roukhon*: red with decorative hem and military emblems	black *sakkos*	red *tabarion*	*stemma, skiadion, aêr.* *diadêma.* red / purple footwear.
despotês	*roukhon*: red with decorative hem	*kavadion* of purple and red with such pearl embroidery as he prefers	red *tabarion*	*skiadion* entirely covered with pearls. *aêr* embroidered with his name. *skaranikon* of cloth of gold with pearls and gems. red hose. purple and white boots with eagles embroidered in pearls.
sevastokratôr	*roukhon*: red without decorative hem		unspecified *tabarion*	*skiadion* of red brocaded with gold. *aêr* embroidered with his name. hose and boots of sky blue.
kaisar	*roukhon*: red without decorative hem		unspecified *tabarion*	*skiadion* of red woven with gold. *aêr* embroidered with his name. hose and boots of sky blue.
megas domestikos	*kavadion* of two colours (probably red and yellow) with pearled borders			*skiadion* of red woven with gold and with gold bands. *aêr* likewise red embroidered with gold. *skaranikon* of red and gold with portraits of the emperor front and back. baton having a gilded top with a silver chain coiled around it.
panhypersevastos	*kavadion* of two colours (probably yellow and green) with pearled borders		yellow *tabarion* with a border	*skiadion* of yellow woven with gold and with gold bands. *aêr* likewise yellow embroidered with gold. *skaranikon* of yellow and gold with portraits of the emperor front and back. gold and green baton. yellow boots.

prôtovestiarios	*kavadion* of two colours (probably green and yellow) with pearled borders		green *tabarion* with a border	*skiadion* of green woven with gold and with gold bands. *aêr* likewise green embroidered with gold. *skaranikon* of green and gold with portraits of the emperor front and back. baton of gold with green enamel decoration. green boots.

Rank or Office	Garment	Headgear	Accessories
megas doux	*kavadion* of brocade chosen from the regalia patterns	*skiadion* of red brocaded with gold and with gold stripes, no *aêr.* *skaranikon* of red and gold with portraits of the emperor front and back.	baton with engraved gold bosses on one segment and the remainder beeong gold with a silver chain coiled around it
prôtostratôr	as above	*skiadion* and *skaranikon* as above	baton of four parts, three of silver, top of gold
megas logothetês	as above	*skiadion* and *skaranikon* as above	no baton
megas stratopedarkhos	as above	*skiadion* and *skaranikon* as above	baton entirely silvered
megas primikêrios	as above	gold-embroidered *skiadion.* apricot-coloured *skaranikon* with gold embroidery	baton of gilded wood
megas konostaulos	as above	as above	no baton
prôtosevastos	as above	skiadion of gold and green. *skaranikon* like that of the *megas primikêrios*	no baton
pinkernê	as the *megas primikêrios*	as the *megas primikêrios*	no baton
kouropalatês	as above	as above	no baton
parakoimomenos tês sfendonês	as above	as the *kouropalatês*	baton of wood. upper segment is gilded, second with a cord of white-gold, the third gilded, and the fourth again corded
parakoimomenos tou koitônos	as above	as above	baton has the upper quarter gilded and the rest with a cord of white-gold
logothetês tou genikou	kavadion of the regulation silk	*skiadion* of white silk with pearls. *skaranikon* of gold and white silk with portraits of the emperor front and back	no baton
prôtovestiaritês	as above	as above	baton, upper portion gilded, the remainder alternately red and gold
domestikos tou trapetzês	as above	as above	no baton
epi tês trapetzês	as above	as above	baton, segments gold, black, gold, black
megas papias	as above	as above	baton like that of the *parakoimomenos tês sfendonês*

Rank or Office	Garment	Headgear	Accessories
eparkhos	as above	as above	no baton
megas droungarios tês viglas	*kavadion* as above. ranks from here to the *megas domestikos* may choose to wear an *epilôrikion* in place of the *kavadion*	*skiadion* as above. *Skaranikon* of gold and yellow silk with a portrait of the emperor on the front seated on a golden throne and on the back mounted on a horse	baton, gilded on the upper segment, then wound with a red-gold cord
megas hetaireiarkhês	as above	as above	baton, gilded on the upper segment, then wound with a blue-gold cord
megas khartoularios	as above	as above	no baton
logothete tou dromou	*epilôrikion*	*skiadion* like that of the *megas khartoularios.* turban. No *skaranikon*	no baton
prôtasekrêkrêtis	*epilôrikion*	*skiadion* covered in silk brocade of purple and white, having a wide band of gold and pearl embroidery around the top and the edge of the brim. turban. No *skaranikon*	
epi tou stratou	*kavadion* like the *megas khartoularios*	banded *skiadion. skaranikon* like the *megas khartoularios*	
domestikos tôn skholôn	as above	as above	baton, silver with no gilding. one knob at the top, then another at the first interval, then plain
megas domestikos tou stolou	as above	as above	no baton
primikêrios tês aulês	*kavadion* as the *megas droungarios*	*skiadion* and *skaranikon* as the *megas droungarios*	baton, banded in gold and blue in a manner like the gold and red of the *prôtovestiaritês*
prôtospatharios	as above	as above	no baton
megas arkhôn	as above	as above	no baton
tata tês aulês	as above	as above	baton of polished wood
megas tzaousios	as above	as above	grain gauge (*saliba*) carried on the left side of the belt
praitôr tou dêmou	as above	as above	baton of polished wood
logothetês tôn oikeiakôn	*epilôrikion*	turban. No *skaranikon*	
megas logariastês	as above	as above	
prôtokunêgos	*kavadion* like the *praitôr tou dêmou*	*skiadion* and *skaranikon* like the *praitôr tou dêmou*	
skouterios	as above	as above	
amêralios	as above	as above	
epi tôn deêseôn	epilôrikion	turban. No *skaranikon*	
koiaistôr	*kavadion* like the *megas tzaousios*	*skiadion* and *skaranikon* like the *megas tzaousios*	

Rank or Office	Garment	Headgear	Accessories
megas adnoumiastês	as above	as above	baton, silver with no gilding. one knob at the top bearing a dove
logothetês tou stratiôtikou	*epilôrikion*	turban. No *skaranikon*	
prôtoïerakarios	*kavadion* like the *megas adnoumiastês*	*skiadion* and *skaranikon* like the *megas adnoumiastês*	on his belt, a left gauntlet worked with purple eagles and having a band woven with pearls around the edge of the cuff
logothetês tôn agelôn	*epilôrikion* like the *logothetês tou stratiôtikou*	turban like the *logothetês tou stratiôtikou.* No *skaranikon*	
megas diermêneutês	*kavadion* like the *prôtoïerakarios*	*skiadion* like the *prôtoïerakarios. skaranikon* covered in red silk with a small red tassel on top	baton, one side red, the other silver, with painted spots
akolouthos	as above	as above	no baton
mega dioikêtês	as above	as above	baton of polished wood without knobs
kritês tou fossatou	as above	as above	no baton
arkhôn tou allagiou	as above	as above.	baton of polished wood
prôtallagatôr	as above	as above	in place of a baton, he carries a mace with a gilded and silvered head, the shaft wrapped in red silk with a gilded band in the middle, and at the bottom a gilded pommel
orfanotrofos	as above	as above	no baton
prôtonotarios	as above	as above	no baton
epi tôn anamnêseôn	as above	as above	baton, surmounted by a gilded knob, the rest banded in white and red with no gold-work
domestikos tôn teikhôn	as above	as above	baton of polished wood
prokathêmenos tou koitônos	as above	as above	baton of polished wood
prokathêmenos tou vestiariou	as above	as above	as above
epi tou vestiariou	as above	as above	no baton
hetaireiarkhês	as above	as above	baton, like that of the *megas hetaireiarkhês*, but rather than blue and gold, the cord is yellow and gold
logariastês tês aulês	as above	as above	baton of polished wood
stratopedarkhês tôn monokavallôn	as above	as above	as above
stratopedarkhês tôn tzangratorôn	as above	as above	as above

Rank or Office	Garment	Headgear	Accessories
stratopedarkhês tôn mourtatôn	as above	as above	as above
stratopedarkhês tôn tzakônôn	as above	as above	as above
prokathêmenos tôn megalôn palatiôn	as above	as above	baton of polished wood
prokathêmenos tôn vlakhernôn palatiôn	as above	as above	as above
domestikos tôn thematôn	as above	as above	as above
domestikos tôn anatolikôn thematôn	as above	as above	as above
domestikos tôn dusikôn thematôn	as above	as above	as above
megas murtaïtês	*kavadion* as above	*skiadion* and red *skaranikon* as above	baton, silver dusted with gold with a γ on top
prôtokomês	as above	as above	no baton
droungarios	[as above?]	[as above?]	baton of polished wood
sevastos	[as above?]	[as above?]	no baton
murtaïtês	[as above?]	[as above?]	no baton
prokathêmenos tôn entimôn poleôn	[as above?]	[as above?]	baton of white wood
papias	[as above?]	[as above?]	baton of wood, no knobs

CHARTS

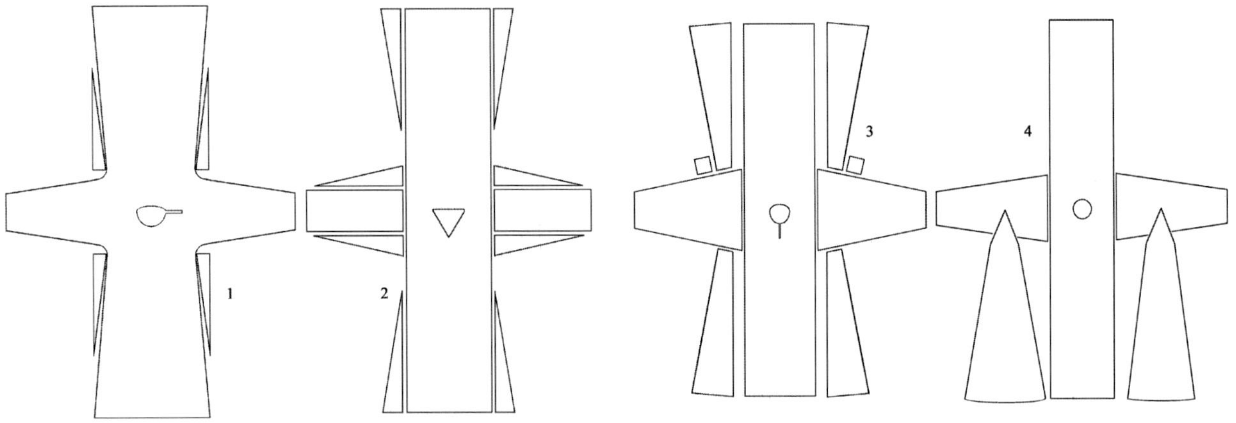

Chart 1
The patterns of main torso garments based upon surviving examples:
1. modified 'Coptic' one-piece construction. Egypt, fifth century (Metropolitan Museum, New York);
2. a shirt forming a part of the so-called 'Persian Horsemen's Outfits', Egypt, sixth century? (Staatliche Museum, Berlin);
3. Egypt (?), eighth–twelfth centuries (Victoria and Albert Museum);
4. main elements of a thirteenth century *esôforion* (Karaman Museum, Turkey).

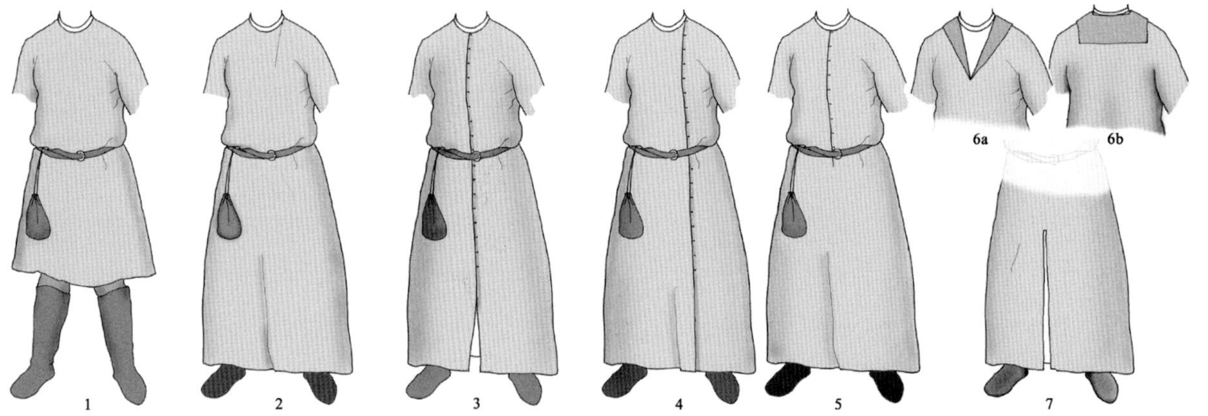

Chart 2
Definitive garment body forms:
1. common or military man's form to the knee (*paganos*);
2. women's/aristocratic male length;
3. ubiquitous coat form (*diakoptês/kavadion*);
4. Persian coat form;
5. *sfinktourion*;
6. eleventh-century development from the *sfinktourion*, a-front, b-back;
7. divided skirt (*diskhistos*).

1 and 7 are purely male forms; others are all genders.

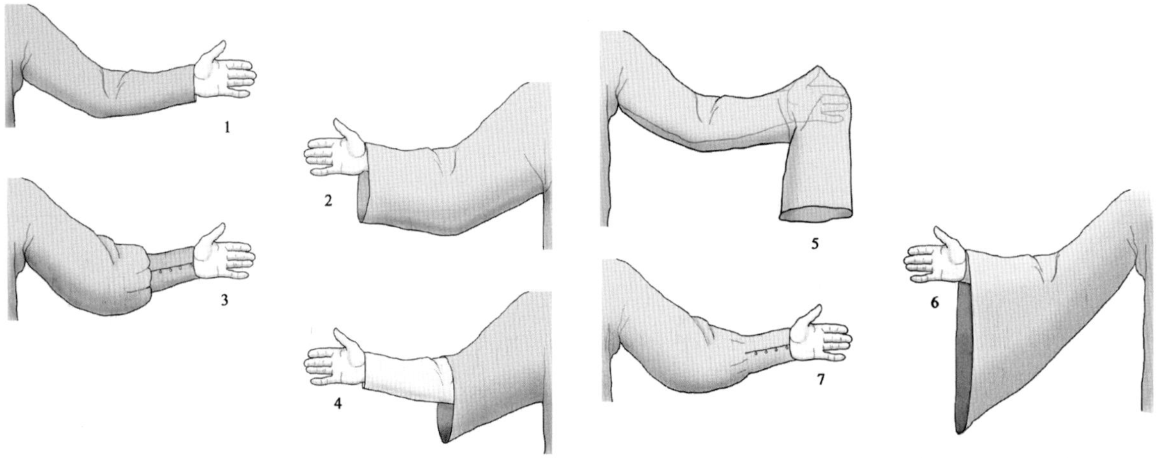

Chart 3
Definitive sleeve forms:
1. *roukhon*;
2. middle Byzantine *kôlovion* and Palaiologian secular *sakkos*;
3. *persikomanikion*;
4. *kontomanikion*;
5. *skaramangion*, *granatza* and *lapatza*;
6. *delmatikion*;
7. simplified form of the *persikomanikion* used from the twelfth century.

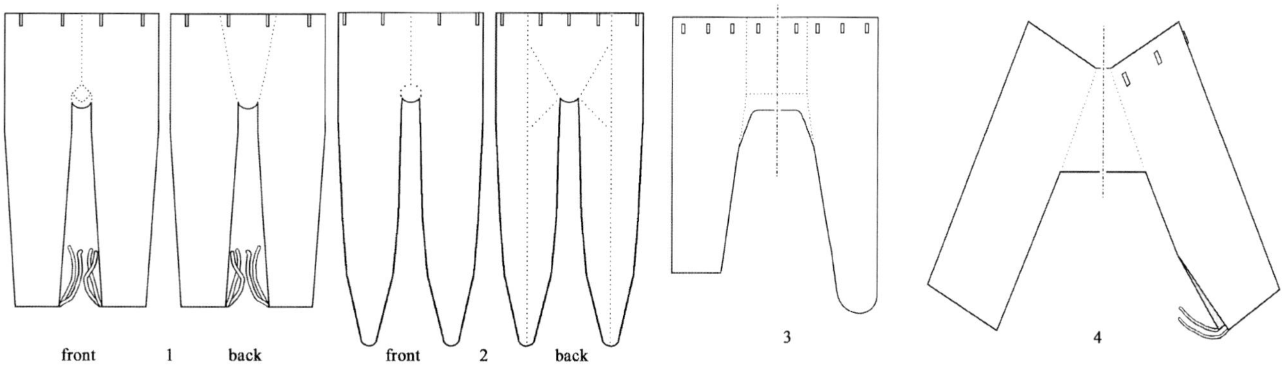

CHART 4

Trousers and breeches, Late Antiquity to modern times:

1. Egypt, sixth century. (Louvre);
2. Halabiye, Syria, early seventh century. (Pfister Collection);
3. vernacular forms related to the Thorsberg trousers (second century) in use in the Near East to the present;
4. various sites, second to ninth century, and onwards.

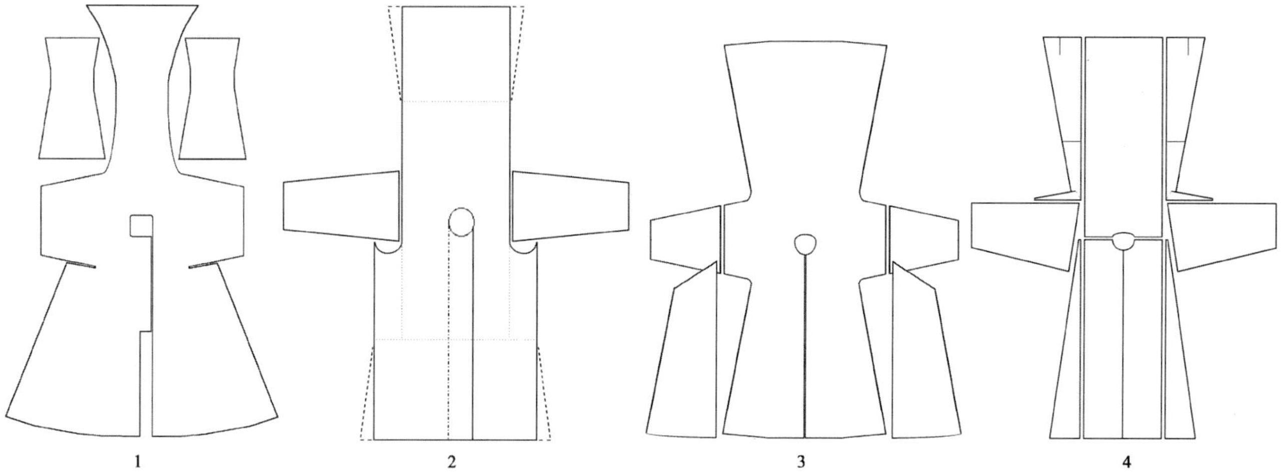

CHART 5

Patterns of coats based upon various surviving examples:

1. a Late Antique *fiblatôrion* from Egypt;
2. *senmurv* coat from Moschevaya Balka, eighth–ninth century. A long panel is attached to the left side to lie under the front right in order to make the garment double-breasted;
3. construction of Turkic coats such as the Seljuk *yalma*;
4. Palaiologian era coat held in the Museum of Art, Bucharest.

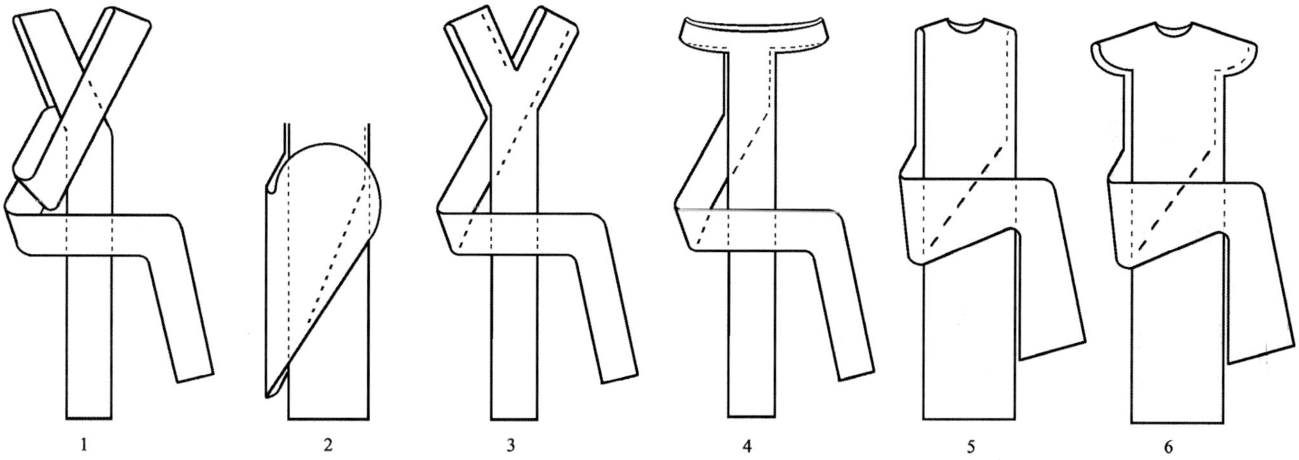

CHART 6

Forms of the *lôros* (later called *diadêma*) across the period:

1. generic form depicted throughout;
2. empress' *lôros* tail, tenth to twelfth centuries;
3. *lôros* of Constantine Porfurogennêtos, tenth–eleventh centuries;
4. 'T' form, tenth century;
5. 'tabard' style, eleventh and twelfth centuries;
6. 'yoke' or 'epaulette' form, twelfth to fifteenth centuries.

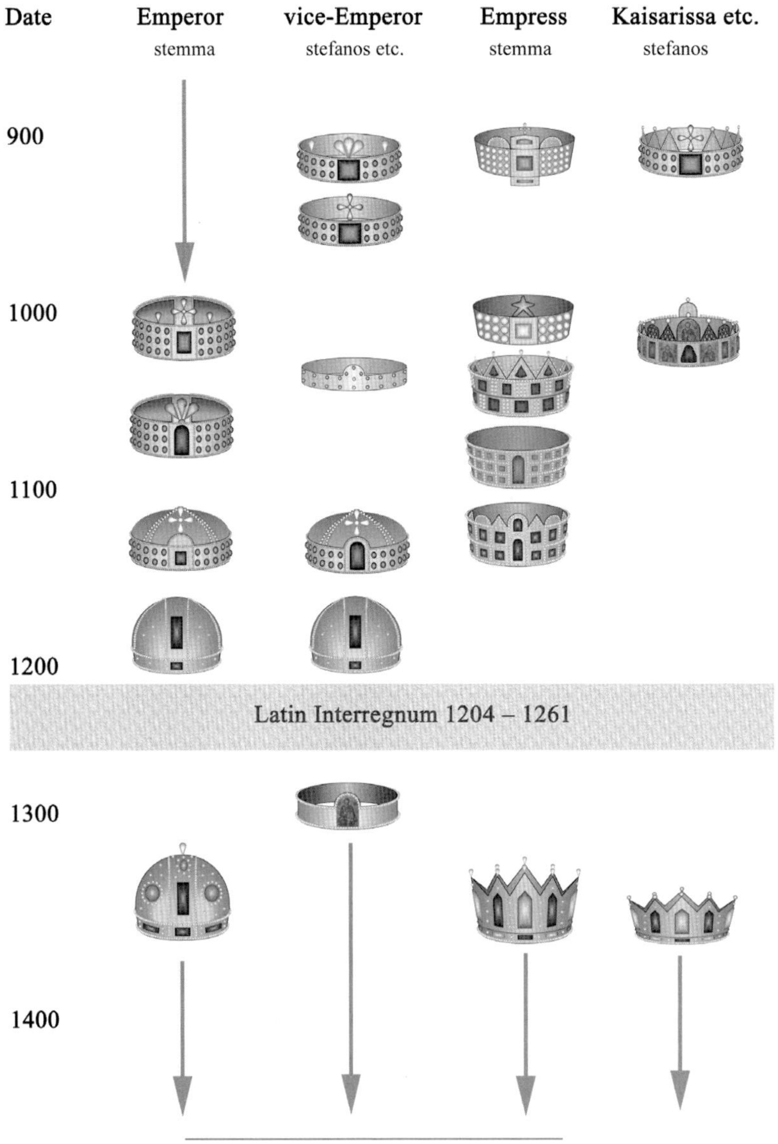

CHART 7: Evolution of crowns and coronets.

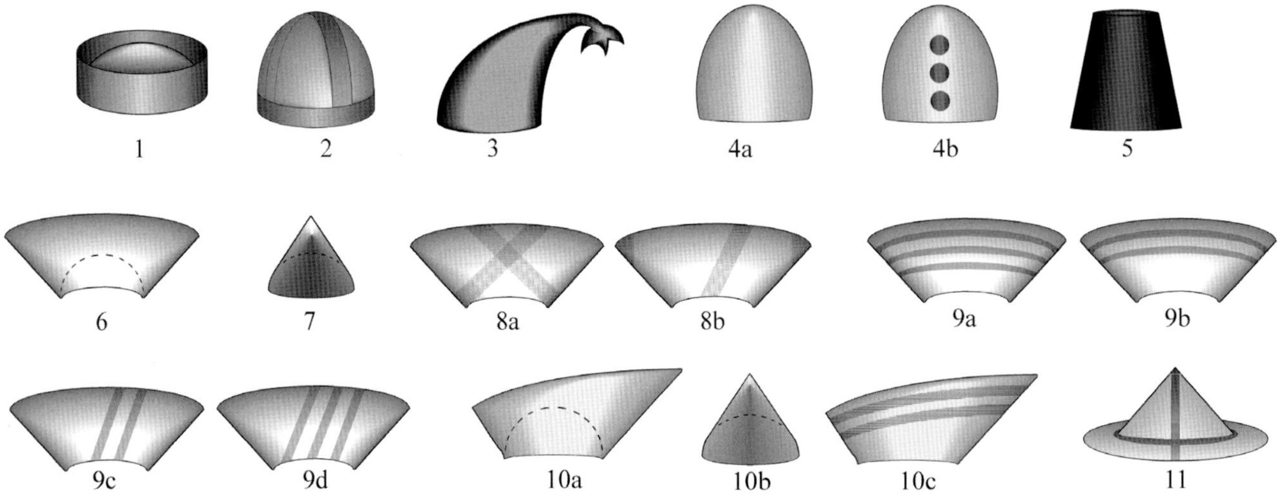

CHART 8
Varieties of hat across the period:

1. Pannonian;
2. Persian;
3. Bulgarian;
4. *kausia*, b- with rank buttons;
5. *kulah*;
6. plain *propolôma*;
7. side view of all *propolômata*;
8. c. eleventh-century *propolôma* decoration;
9. c. twelfth-century *propolômata* with rank bands;
10. *kapasion*, a- plain, b- front view, c. twelfth century with rank bands;
11. *skiadion*.

APPENDIX

THE REGALIA LISTS TO THE *BOOK OF CEREMONIES*

In various places in the *Book of Ceremonies* there are references to a wide variety of regalia which was issued to selected people for specific ceremonies. Sometimes is is stated as to what item they were and where they came from, while at others they are just said to be 'demotic' or 'state' (*dêmosios*) garments.

In the Chapel of St Theodore attached to the Khrusotriklinos

The Staff of Moses; four gilded batons (*ravdia*) for *ostiarioi* with pearls and gems; four silver-gilt batons (*ravdia*) for *silentarioi*; four silver-gilt batons (*ravdia*) with *fengia*[1] for the honour guard[2] and four without *fengia* and one with a key[3]; gold prôto-spathariate collars; all-gold and silver-gilt spatharokandidate collars; gold-embellished spathariate swords, gilded crops of the grooms, a gilded and enamelled shield with pearls; another gilded and enamelled shield with pearls and gems; two silvered and gilded spears.

In the Church of St Stephen in the Palace of Dafnê

The great cross of Constantine the Great; three sceptres; seven ivory plaques; gold collars for *kandidatoi.*

In the Church of the Lord

Twelve sceptres; five drill master's batons; five *lavara;* twelve banner staffs; twelve dragon standards; eight banners; eighteen chests.

The Varieties of Regalia (in the Church of the Lord)

Fifteen gold-woven *lôroi*; twelve *kontomanikia* with gold woven in for those *lôroi*; twelve *thôrakia* to accompany them; six silver embroidered *khlamudes*; gold embroidered *spekia*; fifteen silver embroidered purple and blue *kontomanikia*; twenty-nine variegated mauve *kontomanikia*; eighteen purple and blue variegated *kontomanikia*; twenty-five coloured gold-edged *khlamudes* with gold *tavlia* for *magistoi*, *anthupatoi* and *patrikioi*; thirty gold-edged *khlamudes* with purple *tavlia* for officers of the civil service; six panelled *khlamudes* for the *khartoularioi* of the civil service; gold-edged *khlamudes* with purple *tavlia* called 'the Tyrians' for the men of the imperial chambers; thirty-three black (*atravatika*) *khlanidia.*

---

1 Possibly crescents, as Moffat chooses to regard them.

2 The term used for these men is *koursôres* which in the military manuals of the tenth century (Leo *Taktika*, constitution 4.22) means a class of troops who served as advance skirmishers. In the civil context, these men would presumably precede a dignitary to clear the way, so Moffat's decision to call them 'footmen' might be another fair approximation.

3 It is unclear why Moffat believes that one staff should have a case.

GLOSSARY

A Note on Orthography and Pronunciation

Please refer to the section on terminological and orthographical conventions at the beginning of the volume. The nouns given in this glossary are in the nominative case, and normally singular, except where items come in pairs or groups, such as 'boots' or '*klavoi*' or when a plural is natural, such as 'trousers'. The most common plurals are as follows:

~a > ~ai, except when neuter (n) then ~a > ~ata; ~ê > ~ai; ~ês > ~es; ~on > ~a; ~os > ~oi. Less common plurals will be noted in the respective entries. Adjectives are given in the nominative, masculine singular.

The entries are arranged in Latin alphabetical order according to the phonetic transliteration conventions set out in the introduction.

aetos (αἔτος), also ***aetarion*** (αἐτάριον), minor regalia cape, probably decorated with eagles. *De Cer.*

aêr (ἀήρ, pl. *aeres*), rectangular flap of cloth hung from the back of a *skiadion* to shade the neck. Highly decorated *aêres* were suspended from the *skiadia* of high dignitaries of the Palaiologian court. *Treatise.*

akakia (ἀκάκια), also ***anexikakia*** (ἀνεξικακία), cylindrical bag of silk containing soil carried by emperors as a symbol of mortality. *De Cer., Treatise.*

akromanikion (ἀκρομανίκιον), cuff of a sleeve. See also ***kheiridion***.

anavolos (ἀναβόλος), also ***anavolion*** (ἀναβόλιον), short apron, often hooded, worn by Eastern Orthodox monks and nuns.

anexikakia (ἀνεξικακία), see ***akakia***.

angourôton (ἀγγουρώτον), headgear with yellow band of cloth tied around, worn by the city police (*vardariotai*) in the fourteenth century; probably a dome hat. *Treatise.*

apokomvion (ἀποκόμβιον), also ***komvion*** (κόμβιον), imperial alms purse. *De Cer.* Also ***valantion***.

armelausion (ἀρμελαύσιον), from Latin *armelausa* (*Etymologies*), Late Antique tunic assembled with sleeves sewn on (and sometimes with godets in the skirt), rather than being woven in a piece in the 'Coptic' manner. *Stratêgikon.*

avdion (ἄβδιον), sleeveless, unshaped mantle open down the front without fastenings, commonly made of light linen or cotton. Derived from the Arabic *abeyah*. *De Cer.*

boots, fully enclosing footwear extending beyond the ankle and sometimes as far as the thigh. See ***mouzakia, tzangia, hupodêmata***.

breeches, light pants of varying length worn as underpants or with hose. See ***periskelisma, hupokamisovrakhia***.

cape, shorter top garment of unshaped cloth worn hung from the shoulders. See ***manduas, mandion, mantion, savanion, sagion***.

chemise, a woman's undergarment covering the whole body. Equivalent to the male **shirt**.

cloak, larger top garment of unshaped cloth worn hung from the shoulders. See ***khlamus, khlanidion, fainôlês, felônion***.

coat, tailored torso garment opening in various ways down the full length of the front. Sleeves may be arranged in various ways. See ***diakoptês, fiblatôrion, kavvadês, kavadion, kandus, kontomanikion, zôstarion***.

coronet, lighter or smaller royal or non-royal ceremonial headgear made of precious metal. May not fully enclose the head. See ***stemmatoguron***.

crown, substantial royal headgear fully enclosing the head. Usually made of precious metal. See ***stemma***.

delmatikê (δελματίκη), Hellenised version of the Latin *dalmatica*. See ***delmatikion***.

delmatikion (δελματίκιον), 1: originally, as the *dalmatica*, a loose woollen over-tunic with wide, straight sleeves ranging from three-quarter to wrist length worn by all genders. 2: from the fourth century onwards this form became the male ***kôlovion*** in ecclesiastical and court use. 3: with flaring sleeves, a woman's dress in the middle and late Byzantine periods. *De Cer.*

diadêma (διαδήμα, pl. *diadêmata*), 1: in the middle Byzantine era, the junior crown, a low, open cylinder. *De Cer.* See ***kaisarikion, modiolos, stefanos***. Contrast ***stemma, tiara, toufa***. 2: in the Palaiologian period *diadêma* was the name for the ***lôros***, then worn only by the emperor and empress. *Treatise.*

diaitêsion (διαιτήσιον), synonymous with ***divitêsion***. Vernacular.

diakoptês (διακόπτης), in the tenth century, a **coat** belonging to the empress. *De Cer.*

divikion (διβίκιον), synonymous with ***divitêsion***. Giorgios Monakhos.

divitêsion (διβιτήσιον), fifth to twelfth centuries, a **tunic** with voluminous sleeves pleated into long, ornate cuffs (see ***persikomanikia***). Restricted to royalty and certain high court ranks on certain occasions. Also spelled διβητήσιον and διβιτίσιον. *De Cer.* Also called ***diaitêsion*** and ***divikion***.

divlattion (διβλάττιον), figured fabric woven with two colours on the base tincture. *De Cer., Imp. Exp.* See ***trivlattion***.

dikanikon (δικάνικον), in the Palaiologian period, a ceremonial baton. *Treatise.*

distralion (διστράλιον), single-edged axe. *De Cer.* Contrast ***tzikourion***.

dress, a woman's main garment put on over the head, as distinct from varieties of **coat**.

enkheirion *(ἐγχειρίον)*, napkin or handkerchief (***mandulion***). *De Cer.*

epanoklivanon (ἐπανοκλίβανον), synonymous with ***epilôrikion***. *Treatise.* See ***klivanion***.

epikoutzdoulon *(ἐπικουτζούλον)*, equivalent to ***koutzdoulon*** and ***kamision***. *DAI.* Psellos, *Poemata.*

epilôrikion *(ἐπιλωρίκιον)*, by the tenth century, a heavily padded military surcoat, with openings in the armpits, or at the elbow, to pass the arms through. In combat, the empty portion of the sleeve was buttoned back to the shoulder. *C.W.*, *D.A.*

In the later twelfth and thirteenth centuries the sleeves became short and vestigial, and by the fourteenth century disappeared entirely. In the fourteenth and fifteenth centuries the *epilôrikion* was used as court regalia. *Treatise.*

epirriptarion (ἐπιρριπτάριον), an item worn by some religious functionaries in the Palaiologan court. *Treatise.* Possibly similar to ***ômoforion*** 2.

esôforion (ἐσωφόριον), light **tunic** worn as an undergarment, an indoor garment, or main garment in warm weather. See **shirt**. *De Cer.*, *Imp. Exp.*

esôforokolovion (ἐσωφοροκολόβιον), **shirt** (***esôforion***) of ***kôlovion*** form worn as an outer garment in summer. *De Cer.*

fainôlês (φαινώλης), from the Latin *paenula*, later *fainolion*, *fenôlion*, *felônion*. 1: in antiquity, a closed mantle like a poncho, sometimes with a hood. Originally worn by all genders, in Late Antiquity only by women and religious functionaries routinely, although it survived in consular ceremonial use into the sixth century.

By the middle Byzantine era the early form had evolved in two divergent directions.

2: ecclesiastical use preserves the hoodless poncho form, like the Western chasuble. *De Cer.*

3: in court regalia the garment had diminished to a hood. Particularly worn by the *Eparkhos tês Poleôs* (Governor of Constantinople) and legal functionaries. *De Cer.*

fakeolion (φακεόλιον), also ***fakeôlion***, (φακεώλιον), **turban**. *Imp. Exp.*, *D.A.*

fakeôlitzin (φακεώλιτζιν), diminutive of **φακεόλιον**, light **turban**. *D.A.*

fialion (φιάλιον), also ***fualion***, decorative yoke woven into or embroidered onto a garment. Often with spurs of decoration running down the shoulders. See ***raiktôrikion***. *De Cer.*, *Treatise.*

fiblatôrion (φιβλατώριον), from the third century, a buttonless **coat** with long sleeves which might be vestigial or functional, and which was fastened at the throat with a brooch (*fiblon*). *Edict.* Superseded in common use in the seventh or eighth century by coats with buttons (see ***kavadion***), it survived up to the tenth century as regalia for the rank of *vestitôr*. *Klêt.* See ***zôstarion***.

fillet, decorated metal band worn on the hair or over a headscarf by women.

foinix (φοίνιξ), palm. A decorative motif representing a stylised palm tree, commonly used on regalia textiles of the tenth to twelfth centuries. *Imp. Exp.*

foundatos (φούνδατος), adjective, having a gold border. *De Cer.* See ***khrusoperikleistos***.

fualion (φυάλιον), see ***fialion***.

gauna (γαύνα), see ***gaunakê***.

gaunakê (γαυνάκη), from the ancient Akkadian, *gônakka*. Garment of unknown ancient form, but used in Atticising literature for an outer garment such as a **mantle** or **coat**.

girdle, cloth or cord belt. See ***zônarion***.

gonateia (γονατεία), decorative patches applied to garments at knee level. See ***sêmenta***, ***raiktôrion***. *De Cer.*

gouna (γούνα), also *gounion*, robust outer garment, commonly a voluminous **coat**. Sometimes a military arming coat. *De Cer.*

gounoepilôrikion (γουνοεπιλωρίκιον), military greatcoat designed to protect weapons and armour from inclement weather. *Taktika.*

granatza (γράνατζα), in the Palaiologian period, a dress coat with very long sleeves and openings at the elbows. *Treatise.* Contrast ***lapatza***.

headscarf, cloth worn draped over the head, but not covering the face. See ***vêlarion***, ***kaluptra***, ***maforion***, ***othonê***, **veil**.

hood, a shaped cloth head covering which may or may not be attached to another garment. See ***maforion***, ***koukoulion***.

hose, full-length leg coverings cut and sewn from woven cloth. See ***kampotouva***, ***housia***, ***touvia***.

himation (ἱμάτιον), ancient generic term for any main garment. In the Palaiologan period a particular dress of the empress. *Treatise.* See ***khitôn***, ***stolê***.

housia *(οὔσια)*, from the tenth century, hose, knitted, as distinct from sewn from woven cloth. Achmet. Contrast ***kampotouva*** and ***touvia***.

hupodêmata (ὑποδήματα), in ancient times, **sandals** (literally 'tied underneath'), then a generic term for footwear, with a tendency to mean long boots in the middle and late Byzantine eras. *De Cer.*, *C.W.*, *Treatise.*

hupokamisovrakhia (ὑποκαμισοβράχια), underpants or **breeches**. Literally 'under-shirt-pants'. *De Cer.* Also ***periskelismata***. Contrast ***vrakha***.

hupokamision (ὑποκαμίσιον), tenth century or earlier onwards, a general term for a main torso garment or **tunic**. Achmet.

hupolourikion (ὑπολουρίκιον), padded military garment worn either under armour, as its name suggests, or as stand-alone protection. *D.A.* See ***perisêthidion***.

iustineianeion (ἰουστινειανείον), the late Byzantine triumphal crown. Also ***tropareioukhian***. *Treatise*. Its designation as the 'Justinian crown' suggests it was crested in the manner shown on Justinian's equestrian statue. See also ***tiara***.

jacket, short divided garment opening down the centre front. See ***zoupa***.

kavadion (καβάδιον), eighth to fifteenth centuries, a **coat** opening down the centre front fastened with buttons. *De Cer.*, *Treatise*. A padded arming **coat** worn as sole protection by some troops. C.W. Compare ***epilôrikion***. Also spelled καββάδιον. See also ***diakoptês***, ***kavvadês***, ***kandus***. Contrast ***fiblatôrion***, ***zôstarion***.

kavadês (καββᾶδης), an antiquarian term used in middle Byzantine literature for **coat**.

kaisarikion (*καισαρίκιον*), 1: In the middle Byzantine era, the junior crown, worn by the *kaisar* (vice-emperor) routinely, and the emperor on less formal occasions. *De Cer.* See ***diadêma***, ***modiolos***, ***stefanos***. Contrast ***stemma***, ***tiara***, ***toufa***. 2: In the middle Byzantine era, also a minor regalia cape of the *kaisar*. *De Cer.* 3: In the Palaiologan era, court regalia garment of the emperor symbolising his position as anointed by God. *Treatise*.

kaligia (καλίγια), footwear. In the early Roman period this denoted the **sandals** worn by legionaries (Latin *caligae*). By the middle Byzantine era it referred to stylised **sandals** still worn as part of regalia by members of the Senate. *De Cer.* These ceremonial **sandals** disappeared in the early eleventh century. Also called ***kampagia***.

kaltzai (κάλτζαι), fourteenth century term for **hose** or **leggings**. *Treatise*.

kaluptra (κάλυπτρα), **veil** and a general term for headwear. *De Cer.*

kamêlavkion (καμηλαύκιον), 1: an awning. *De Cer.* 2: headgear. Often applied to quilted caps worn under turbans. *De Obs.*, *C.W.*, *D.A.*

kamision (καμίσιον), from the Latin *camisa*, 1: in Late Antiquity, any **tunic**. The term was supplanted by ***roukhon*** for main outer garments early in the medieval period. 2: in the middle Byzantine era, the least ornate form of male regalia tunic, with ***persikomanikia***, but with little or no decoration. *De Cer.*

kampagia (*καμπάγια*), see under ***kaligia***. *De Cer.*

kampotuva (καμπότουβα), padded leggings. Compare ***housia*** and ***touvia***.

kandus (κανδύς, pl. *kandues*), the earliest recorded name for a **coat**, in use from the fourth century BCE to at least the twelfth century CE. Xenofon, Kinnamos et al. In its early use it referred to the long-sleeved, buttonless Persian coat also called ***fiblatôrion*** and ***zôstarion*** in Late Antique Greek.

kapasion (καπάσιον), type of hat worn in the Palaiologian court. *Treatise*.

kataseista (κατασείστα), alternative term for ***praipendoulia***.

kaunakês (καυνάκης), over-garment, particularly for outdoor wear, often in the form of a **coat**. Related to ***gaunakê***. See ***kaunauges***.

kaunauges (*καυναύγες*), an over-garment particularly for outdoor wear, often in the form of a **coat**. Cognate with ***gaunakê***. Related to ***gauna***, ***gouna***, ***gounion***. Kinnamos.

kausia (καύσια), in the middle Byzantine period, a domical, or semiconical hat derived from the Persian *kalansuwa*. In the eleventh and twelfth centuries the rounded form was white and the conical form black. These evolved into the late Byzantine ***skaranikon***.

kissofulon (*κισσοφύλον*), ivy leaf. A decorative motif resembling the spade of a modern pack of cards, commonly used on regalia textiles of the eleventh and twelfth centuries. *De Cer.*, *Imp. Exp.*

kharzanion (χαρζάνιον), 1: type of whip or flail. 2: an ornament consisting of a strap with triple gemmed terminations worn draped over the head under the ***propolôma*** by tenth- to twelfth-century ladies in waiting. *De Cer.*

khasdion (*χάσδιον*), a fine silk fabric. *De Cer.* Borrowed from Arabic.

kheiridion (*χειρίδιον*), edge of a sleeve or cuff. Komnênê. See ***akromanikion***.

kheiropsella (χειρόψελλα), armour for the lower arms. *Taktika*, etc.

kheirôrtion (*χειρώρτιον*), gauntlet. A left-hand gauntlet was carried by the chief falconer of the fourteenth-century court. *Treatise*.

khitôn (*χιτῶν*), ancient general term for a main torso garment. Used in the *Book of Ceremonies* to designate regalia tunics with ***persikomanikia***. See ***kamision***, ***roukhon***, **shirt**, **tunic**.

khlamus (*χλάμυς*), from antiquity to the fourteenth century, a man's cloak worn pinned on the right shoulder, and decorated with contrasting panels (***tavlia***) appearing on the open edges. In antiquity, the *khlamus* was oval and worn folded along the long axis. In the eleventh century it was simplified to a semicircular shape, and could have an edging instead of, or as well as, the ***tavlia***. *De Cer.* See ***tabarion***.

khlanidion (χλανίδιον), diminutive of ***khlamus***, but with no difference in meaning in the middle Byzantine period. *De Cer.*

khrusoklavos (*χρυσόκλαβος*), in middle Byzantine use, an adjective denoting decorative gold strips, generally of keyhole shape, running up from the hem of a **tunic**. *De Cer.* From Latin *clavus*.

khrusomaniakion (χρυσομανιάκιον), golden torque. *D.A.* See ***maniakion***.

khrusoperikleistos (χρυσοπερικλείστος), adjective, having a gold border all around. Applied to **cape**. See also ***foundatos***.

khrusosôlênokentêtos (χρυσοσωληνοκεντήτος), a decorative technique used on imperial regalia whereby the garment is embroidered with small gold cylinders. *De Cer.*

khrusoun vaion (χρυσοῦν βαίον), 'golden bough', sceptre of the empress used in the eleventh century, and in the fourteenth and fifteenth centuries, and perhaps in between. *Treatise.*

klavoi (κλάβοι), broad bands of decoration running part-way up from the hem, or down from the neck of a garment. From the Latin *clavii*. This style disappeared rapidly with the end of Late Antiquity, surviving only in some regalia tunics. See ***khrusoklavos***. Contrast ***potamoi*** and ***stikhoi***.

klivanion (κλιβάνιον), 1: armour fabric made of modestly-sized solid plates (metal, horn, leather) fixed together in rows, which overlap upward and are suspended by cords. 2: A corselet made of such armour. *Imp. Exp.*, *Taktika.*

kloios (κλοίος), ceremonial collar or torque. Synonymous with ***maniakion***. *De Cer.*

kôlovion (κολόβιον), also *kôlovion* (κωλόβιον), from Latin *colobium*. In antiquity, a sleeveless main garment. By the fourth century, the term was becoming conflated with *delmatikê*, in male and ecclesiastical wear. As a result of this process, in the middle Byzantine period, it was for men, a tunic with wrist-length loose sleeves, identical to the antique *dalmatica*. Certain forms were court regalia in the tenth century. By the late twelfth century, this form supplanted tunics with ***persikomanikia*** as the dominant form of court regalia. *De Cer.* See also ***esôforokolovion***.

kontomanikion (*κοντομανίκιον*), also *kondomanikion*, main garment with elbow-length sleeves. May be made as a **tunic** or **coat**. *De Cer.*

koukoulion (κουκούλιον), **hood** worn as part of monastic dress.

koutzdoulion (*κουτζούλιον*), **tunic**.

lapatza (λάπατζα), in the Palaiologian period, a dress **coat** with very long sleeves and openings in the armpits. *Treatise.* Contrast ***granatza***.

lamellar, armour. See ***klivanion***.

lavouron (λαβούρον), from the Latin *labarum*, stylised rectangular banner carried on occasion by the emperor. Commonly a portrait of Christ painted on a board with gold and gem mounts. *De Cer.*

leggings, heavy protective leg coverings, often padded or made of thick felt. May just cover the calves and shins or extend up over the thighs. See ***housia***, ***kampotouva***, ***touvia***.

leontarion (λεοντάριον), cape or cloak worn on occasion by court functionaries called *praipositoi*. Possibly decorated with lions. Described as 'gold panelled' (***khrusotavlos***). *De Cer.*

leukoleôn (λευκολέων), 'white lion'. A minor imperial regalia cape made of purple silk figured with white lions. *De Cer.*

loupênariôn (λουπηναρίων), ceremonial **hood** (***maforion***) belonging to the rank of *raiktôr*. *De Cer.*

lôrikion (λωρίκιον), from the Latin *lorica*, a general term for armour. If unqualified, usually a **mail** shirt (See ***zava***). *lôrikion halusidôton*, λωρίκιον ἁλυσιδωτόν, chain armour, i.e. **mail**. *lôrikion folidôton*, λωρίκιον φολιδώτον, a corselet of plates, either scales or **lamellar**.

lôros (λώρος), long, ornate drape descended from the old Roman *toga*. In Late Antiquity confined to consular regalia. In the middle Byzantine era, worn by the emperor, empress and *zôstê patrikia* on many ceremonial occasions, and a few other senior court ranks less often. *De Cer.* See ***diadêma***, ***trevenna***, ***zônê***.

lôrôtos (*λωρώτος*), of fabric, striped. Numerous narrow stripes (routinely alternating red and blue) rather than the few broader ones called ***stikhoi*** or ***potamoi***.

mail, armour made of metal rings woven together. See ***lôrikion***, ***zava***.

manklavion (*μαγκλάβιον*), whip carried by the chief of police (*droungarios tês viglas*) in the tenth century. *De Cer.*

mandion (*μάνδιον*), later version of ***manduas***.

manduas (*μανδύας*), semicircular cloak, brooched centre front. Worn by women and by religious functionaries of both sexes. *De Cer.* Also ***mandion***, ***mantion***. See also ***sagion***, ***savanion***.

mandulion (*μανδύλιον*), kerchief or napkin. *Treatise.*

mantion (*μάντιον*), later version of ***manduas***. Also used for the male ***sagion***. *De Cer.*

maniakion (μανιάκιον), ceremonial metal collar, or torque, worn in Late Antiquity as part of the emperor's military regalia, and in later periods by some guardsmen and dignitaries. *De Cer.* See ***kloios***, ***strepton***.

mantle, an all-covering top garment which may be flat or have some simple shaping.

matzouka (ματζούκα), mace. *Treatise.*

maforion (*μαφόριον*), hood. Specific stylised forms were worn by both sexes as part of court regalia in the ninth to early eleventh centuries. *De Cer.* See ***fainôlês***, ***loupênarôon***.

mafortodelmatikion (*μαφορτοδελματίκιον*), *delmatikê* with an attached hood (***maforion***). *Edict.*

makhaira (μαχαίρα), ancient term for a knife. In middle Byzantine military sources a substantial single-edged sidearm carried by some light troops. *Taktika.* Sometimes synonymous with ***paramêrion***.

makhlamion (μαχλάμιον), also *mokhlovion*, μοχλόβιον, twelfth century or later term for a style of tunic opening from throat to waist or lower abdomen and fastened with multiple buttons. *D.A.* Previously called ***sfingktêr*** and ***sfinktourion***.

modiolos (*μοδιόλος*), 1: cylindrical grain measure. 2: in the middle Byzantine period, the junior crown in the form of an open cylinder. *De Cer.* See ***diadêma, kaisarikion***. Contrast ***stemma, tiara, toufa***. Probably also the low cylindrical hat worn from the fourth century.

mokhlovion (μοχλόβιον), see ***makhlamion***.

molkhamion (*μολχάμιον*), sometimes simply *molkham*. From the Arabic, *mulḥam*. Fabric woven with a warp of one fibre and a weft of another, such as silk with linen or cotton. *De Cer., A.I.*

mouzakia (*μουζάκια*), in the tenth century, a man's calf-length boots. *C.W.*

neurikon (νευρίκον), see ***noveronikion***. Maurikios.

noveronikion (νοβερονίκιον), 'cloud-vanquisher' (referring back to the Latin *nubes*). A military greatcoat designed to be water-resistant. Also contracted as ***neurikon***. Maurikios.

ômoforion (ὠμοφόριον), 1: woman's shawl worn around the shoulders. Komnêna. 2: long band decorated with crosses worn draped around the shoulders by Orthodox bishops.

opsimaros (ὀψιμάρος), of the ***khlamus*** of the empress, bearing a portrait of the emperor on the ***tavlia***. *De Cer.*

othonê (*ὀθόνη*), linen cloth. In common use for a woman's **head-scarf** or **veil**. *D.A.*

paganos (πάγανος), adjective denoting the shorter, knee-length garments of common men rather than the ankle-length dress of gentlemen. *Ta pagana*, 'the rustic outfit', a set of regalia comprising a shorter than normal (i.e. knee-length) tunic and *khlamus*. *De Cer.*

papoutzia (παπούτζια), from the beginning of the fourteenth century or earlier to modern times, **shoes**. *Treatise*.

paragavdês (παραγαύδης), later *paragavdion*. 1: in antiquity, a man's white tunic with gold figures. Lydos. 2: sixth to tenth centuries or later, an ornate woman's shawl following Persian fashion draped from left shoulder to right hip. Possibly, like 3, gold with a purple edging. In the tenth century worn as regalia by *koubikoulariai* (ladies-in-waiting). *De Cer.* 3: in the tenth century, a man's regalia cape of cloth of gold with a purple edging. *De Cer.*

paramêrion (παραμήριον), single-edged sword, usually slightly curved. *De Cer., Taktika*. See ***makhaira***.

pektorarion (πεκτοράριον), cloth band tied around the chest to indicate military officer's rank. *De Cer.*

periskelismata (*περισκέλισματα*), underpants or **breeches**. Achmet. See also ***hupokamisovrakhia***.

peristêthidion (περιστηθίδιον), padded garment worn under armour. See ***hupolourikion***.

persikon (*περσίκον*), purse. As common dress accessories, these were either the familiar draw-string type suspended from the draw-string, or a flat, flap type in a fabric and decoration matching the garment with which they were to be worn. *Imp. Exp.* Achmet. See also ***apokomvion, komvion valantion***.

persikomanikia (*περσικομανίκια*), from the fifth century, voluminous sleeves pleated into long cuffs fastened with buttons. Adopted from Persia by Roman women from the early fifth century, and employed on male regalia garments from the late fifth century (*De Cer.*) to the later twelfth century. Achmet. See ***diaitêsion, divikion, divitêsion, kamision, raiktôrikion, spekion*** and ***stikharion*** for garments with this sleeve style.

pilatakia (πιλατάκια), in the Palaiologian era, two embroidered bands worn at the throats of judges to represent their office. *Treatise*.

pniktarion (πνικτάριον), jewelled choker belonging to the empress. *De Cer.*

podopsella (ποδόψελλα), armour for the lower legs, greaves. *Taktika*, etc.

potamoi (ποτάμοι), decorative bands running the full vertical length of a garment. Also called ***stikhoi***. See ***stikharion***.

praipendoulia (πραιπενδούλια), paired ornaments hung from crowns framing the wearer's face, consisting of a string of pearls ending in a cluster of three. *De Cer.*

propolôma (προπόλομα), in the tenth to twelfth centuries, a noblewoman's hat of inverted cone shape flattened at the top. *De Cer.*

ravdion (ῥάβδιον), also *ravdon* and *ravdos*, ceremonial staff carried by various tenth-century courtiers. *De Cer.* See ***dikanikon, vaktêrion, verga***.

raiktôrikion (ῥαικτωρίκιον), tenth-century regalia **tunic** with ***perisikomanikia*** belonging to the rank of *raiktôr* (Latin *rector*) with very specific decoration including a ***fialion*** (φιάλιον) and ***sêmenta*** (σημέντα) setting it apart from other regalia tunics. *De Cer.*

romfaia (ῥομφαία), ancient term for a weapon, most commonly a spear. Gilded spears were carried by the *romfaiokratôres*, a ceremonial guard unit of the fourteenth century. *Treatise*.

roukhon (ῥούχον), by the tenth century a well-established vernacular term for a main garment, a **tunic** or **dress**. In use to the end of the empire and beyond. *C.W.*, Kananos. Used as the title of one regalia garment of the highest court ranks in the late Byzantine era. *Treatise*.

savanion (σαβάνιον), also *savanon*, and *sôvarion*. 1: light, semicircular **cape** of linen or cotton, worn as regalia by certain eunuch court ranks in the ninth to eleventh century, if not a somewhat wider period. *De Cer.* 2: cylindrical, woman's headdress in use by the eleventh century. 3: towel.

sagion (σάγιον), from the Latin *sagum*. Originally a rustic, heavy, rectangular military cape which could double as a blanket. Conflated in court use from Late Antiquity with ***mantion*** and its cognates, and thereafter entering the civil regalia wardrobe. *De Cer.* In middle Byzantine military parade dress is retained its rectangular form.

sakkos (σάκκος), from ancient times, a sack, then, with holes cut for the head and arms, a garment of penitence resembling the ancient ***kôlovion***. Hence later a church vestment, and then a Palaiologian-cra court regalia garment of the emperor symbolising his position as anointed by God. *Treatise*.

saliba (σάλιβα), a spear-like measuring device for determining the depth of stock in grain stores. Carried as an emblem by the imperial provisioning officer (*megas tzaousios*) in the fourteenth century. *Treatise*.

sandals, footwear with a largely open upper. Not to be confused with ***sandalia***. See ***kampagia***.

sandalia (σανδάλια), low **shoes**, often laced. *C.W.*, Achmet.

sea-wool, the fine beard of a bivalve, *pinna maritima*, gathered, spun and woven into a highly precious shimmering fabric. See ***thalassa***.

seia (σεία), ornamental pendant hung from the regalia headgear of several very high court ranks in late Byzantium. *Treatise*. Contrast ***praipendoulia***.

servoulia (σερβούλια), also ***tzervoulia***, low, poorer-quality **shoes**. *DAI*.

sêmenta (σημέντα), decorative patches applied to garments, generally on the shoulders and skirt. Derived from the Latin *segmenta*. See ***gonateia***.

sfinktêr *(σφίγγτηρ)*, earlier name for a style of tunic opening from throat to waist or lower abdomen and fastened with multiple buttons. Supplanted by ***sfinktourion***. See ***makhlamion***.

sfinktourion *(σφιγγτούριον)*, see ***sfinktêr***.

shirt, light torso garment worn as an inner layer, or as informal indoor wear, or alone as a outer garment in warm weather. See ***esôforion***, ***esôforokolovion***.

shoes, footwear encompassing the whole foot but not extending beyond the ankle. See ***papoutzia***, ***sandalia***, ***servoulia***.

sideroravdion (σιδεροράβδιον), mace made entirely of metal. Probably synonymous with ***spathovaklion***.

skaramangion (σκαραμάγγιον), nobleman's dress garment, usually a **tunic**, but sometimes a **coat**, having extremely long sleeves. *De Cer.*, Liutprand, Theophanes, Giorgios Monakhos, Achmet.

skiadion (σκιάδιον), hat, normally white, with a conical crown and broad brim, originating in Georgia around the twelfth century. Evstathios. In the fourteenth century, the version used as regalia came in a variety of colours and decorative schemes. *Treatise*.

skaranikon (σκαράνικον), tall hat derived from the Persian *kalansuwa* or *kulâh*. There were two forms – rounded and truncated cone. In the eleventh and twelfth centuries the rounded form was white and the conical form black. By the fourteenth century this hat become court regalia. The elite form was extensively embroidered. The junior form, only in conical shape, was red with a tassel, and so the precursor to the Ottoman fez. *Treatise*. Late Byzantine name for ***kausia***.

skêpiôn (σκηπίων), the imperial sceptre. From the Latin *scipio*. In antiquity surmounted by an eagle, from the fourth century surmounted by a cross. *De Cer.* See also ***skêptron***.

skêptron (σκήπτρον), the imperial sceptre. *De Cer.* See also ***skêpiôn***.

skoufia (σκούφια), male ceremonial headscarf worn by the staff of the imperial tent in the fourteenth century. *Treatise*. Derived from the Arabic *kufiyyah*.

sôvarion *(σωβάριον)*, see ***savanion***. Achmet.

spathê (σπάθη), from the Latin *spatha*, later most commonly *spathion*, straight, double-edged sword. If unqualified, hung from a shoulder strap. Otherwise, *spathion zôstikion* (σπάθιον ζωστίκιον), such a sword hung from a waist belt. *Imp. Exp.* Contrast ***makhaira***, ***paramêrion***.

spathovaklion (σπαθοβάκλιον), mace with a handle having fittings like a sword hilt (guard and pommel). *De Cer.* Probably made entirely of iron and synonymous with ***sideroravdion***.

spekion (σπέκιον), regalia tunic with ***persikomanikia*** worn routinely by the rank of *prôtospatharios*, and occasionally by higher ranks. *De Cer.*

stemma (στέμμα), the senior crown. For the Emperor in the middle Byzantine period: gold (metal) with gems and pearls, enclosed above with a cruciform structure, and lined in one of four colours – white, red, blue and green. *De Cer.* In the late Byzantine period: a bulbous textile structure decorated with gold embroidery, gems and pearls. For the Empress in the middle Byzantine period: an inverted cone shape of gold (metal) with gems and pearls, often surmounted with vertical projections. In the late Byzantine period: an inverted cone shape of uncertain construction with gems and pearls surmounted with triangular vertical projections. Contrast ***diadêma***, ***kaisarikion***, ***modiolos***, ***stefanos***, ***stemmatoguron***.

stemmatoguron (στεμματόγυρον), junior crown in the Palaiologian period having a single arch on the front. *Treatise*.

stefanos *(στέφανος)*, any type of crown or crown-like item. In *De Cer.* the junior crown. See ***diadêma***, ***kaisarikion***, ***modiolos***.

stêthokarakallon *(στηθοκαρακάλλον)*, wide, flat, jewelled collar worn by the empress since Late Antiquity. *De Cer.*

stikharion *(στιχάριον)*, also *stoikharion*, garment decorated with two broad stripes or pairs of broad stripes (called ***stikhoi*** or ***potamoi***) down the length of the garment. A fairly common motif in Late Antiquity, this design was confined to two secular regalia garments and some religious vestments in the tenth century. *Klêt.*, *De Cer.*

stikhoi *(στίχοι)*, decorative bands running the full vertical length of a garment. Also called ***potamoi***. See ***stikharion***.

stolê *(στόλη)*, ancient generic term for an untailored outer garment. See **cape**, **cloak**, ***khlamus***, ***manduas***, ***sagion***.

strepton (στρέπτον), ceremonial collar or torque. See ***kloios***, ***maniakion***. *Klêt.*, *Treatise.*

strikta (στρίκτα), a name for the imperial ***kampagia***.

surcoat, originally a military garment worn over armour. Later civilianised versions were worn, sometimes as regalia. Usually a divided garment. See **coat**, ***epanoklivanon***, ***epilôrikion***, ***gounoepilôrikion***, ***noveronikion***.

tabarion (ταμπάριον), from Italian *tabarro*, semicircular cloak. Fourteenth-century term for ***khlamus***. Worn in that period only by the emperor, *despotês* and *kaisar*. *Treatise.*

taôn (τάων, pl. *taones*), also *taônion*, 'peacock', a **cape** (***mandion***) used by the empress. *De Cer.* Probably patterned with a curvilinear tessellation resembling the eyes of a peacock's tail.

tavlia (ταβλία), rectilinear decorative panels worked into a ***khlamus***. In the full oval *khlamus* of Late Antiquity *tavlia* were inserted across the long axis centre line. In the semicircular *khlamus* of the eleventh century onwards, they were set on the straight edge. *De Cer.*

thalassa (θάλασσα), minor imperial regalia cape. *De Cer.* Probably made of **sea-wool** or shot silk.

thôrakion *(θωράκιον),* harness of four chains of pierced metal discs linking two larger discs worn over the shoulders and around the chest by women in Late Antiquity. By the tenth century, a golden *thôrakion* was part of court regalia, particularly of a *zôstê patrikia*. *De Cer.*

tiara (τίαρα), originally a type of Persian hat. Later, the crested crown used in triumphal ceremonies. Also ***toufa***, ***toga***. Lydos, *De Cer.* See ***iustineianeion***, ***tropareioukhian***.

toga (τόγα), see ***tiara***. Not to be confused with the Latin garment *toga.*

toufa (τούφα), see ***tiara***. Lydos.

touvia (τούβια), up to tenth century, hose made of cloth, thereafter commonly padded **leggings**. Achmet, *D.A.* See ***kamptouva***. Contrast ***housia***.

travaia (τραβαία), from the Latin *trabea*, Late Antique term for the reduced *toga* used as consular and then royal regalia, and later called ***lôros***. Lydos. See ***trevenna***.

trevenna (τρέβεννα), also ***tervenna***, from the Latin *trabea*, Late Antique term for the long, narrow strip of ornate fabric descended from the ancient Roman *toga* used as consular and then imperial regalia. Called ***lôros*** in the middle Byzantine era, and ***diadêma*** in the Palaiologan period.

trivlattion (τριβλάττιον), figured fabric woven with three colours on the base tincture. *De Cer.*, *Imp. Exp.* See ***divlattion***.

tropareioukhian (τροπαριουχίαν), the late Byzantine triumphal crown. Also ***iustineianeion***. *Treatise.* See ***tiara***, ***toufa***.

trousers, lower garment covering the buttocks, groin and legs, made of robust material and designed to be worn without other leg-wear. See ***vrakha***. Compare **breeches**.

tunic, main or outer torso garment drawn on over the head. See ***divitêsion***, ***epikoutzdoulon***, ***esôforion***, ***kamision***, ***khitôn***, ***koutzdoulon***, ***makhlamion***, ***raiktôrion***, ***roukhon***, ***hupokamision***.

turban, originally a long strip of cloth wound around the head, or over various types of hat or cap. See ***fakeolion***.

tzangia (τζάγγια), also *tzankia*, in Late Antiquity and thereafter, the imperial red or purple **boots**. From the tenth century used generally for boots. *De Cer*, *De Obs.* Etc. In the Palaiologan era once again only used for imperial boots. *Treatise.*

tzervoulia (τζερβούλια), see ***servoulia***.

tzikourion (τζικούριον), double-bladed battle axe. *De Cer.*, *Taktika.* Contrast ***distralion***.

tzitzakion (τζιτζάκιον), ninth- to tenth-century imperial regalia item of unknown type but very probably a form of headgear. Said to have originated with the Khazars. *De Cer.*

vaktêrion (βακτήριον), staff of office carried by public advocates (*ekdikoi*). *De Cer.*

valantion (βαλάντιον), imperial alms purse. *De Cer.* Also ***apokomvion***.

valtidion (βαλτίδιον), an ornate belt of red leather decorated with gems used as regalia in the ninth and tenth centuries. *Klêt.* Probably from the Latin *balteum*.

vamvakêros (βαμβάκηρος), adjective, made of cotton (as cloth). *A.I.*

vamvakion (βαμβάκιον), cotton as a fibre or raw material. *De Obs.*

vdellion (βδέλλιον), droplet. Decorative motif resembling an inverted heart, commonly used on textiles of the eleventh and twelfth centuries. *Imp. Exp.*

veil, cloth worn across the face, which may be distinct from a headscarf. See ***othonê***.

vêlarion (βηλάριον), 1: headscarf. *De Cer.*, *A.I.* 2: awning. Achmet.

verga (βέργα), also *vergion*, ceremonial staff. ***verga triklônon*** (βέργιον τρικλώνον), a sceptre of the empress with a three-lobed head. See also ***ravdion***, ***skêptron***. *De Cer.*

vrakha (βράχα), **trousers**. Also *vrakhia*. Compare **breeches**, ***periskelismata***, ***hupokamisovrakhia***.

zava (ζάβα), 1: in the early medieval period, a garment of flexible armour, either **mail** (see ***lôrikion***) or padding (see ***kavadion***, etc.). Maurikios. 2: in the tenth century, a mail facing on padded limb pieces. *C.W.*

zônarion *(ζωνάριον), textile belts used for both sexes. D.A.*

zonê (ζώνη), general term for a belt. Very occasionally synonymous with ***lôros***.

zôstarion *(ζωστάριον),* in Late Antiquity, an early form of **coat** without buttons and secured with a belt (***zôstêr***). *Stratêgikon.*

zôstêr (ζώστηρ), belt or girdle.

zoupa (ζούπα), waist- or hip-length **jacket**, normally with full-length sleeves. May be padded for warmth or for wearing under armour. Achmet. Cognate with Arabic *djubba*.

BIBLIOGRAPHY

Abbreviations for Most Commonly Cited Works

A.I.	*Actes d'Iviron II.*
BoC	Constantine Porfurogennêtos, *The Book of Ceremonies.*
BMGS	*Byzantine and Modern Greek Studies.*
C.W.	Nikêforos Fôkas, *Composition on Warfare.*
D.A.	*Digenês Akritas.*
DAI	Constantine Porfurogennêtos, *De Administrando Imperio.*
De Cer.	Constantine Porfurogennêtos, *De Cerimoniis Aulae Byzantinae.*
De Obs.	Anonymous, *De Obsidione Toleranda.*
Edict	Diocletian, *Edict on Prices.*
Imp. Exp.	Constantine Porfurogennêtos, *Three Treatises on Imperial Military Expeditions.*
Klêt.	Filotheos, *Klêtôrologion.*
LSJ	Liddell, Henry George, Scott, Robert, and Jones, Henry Stuart, *A Greek-English Lexicon*, Clarendon Press, Oxford, 1963.
PG	*Patrologia Graeca.*
Taktika	Leo VI, *The Taktika of Leo VI.*
Treatise	Pseudo-Kodinos, *Traité des Offices.*

Manuscripts Examined in the Original or Facsimile

Vatican Library, Rome

Barberini. Gr. 372	Psalter
Gr. 394	Klimakos
Smyrna Octateuch, Gr. 746	Gospels
Gr. 749	Book of Job
Gr. 699	Kosmas Indikopleustês
Gr. 1156	Lectionary
Gr. 1162	Homilies
Gr. 1613	*Menologion of Basil II*
Gr. 1947	Gospels
Reg. Gr. 1B	Bible
Urb. Gr. 2	Tetraevangelion
Slav. 2	Manasses Chronicle

Saint Mark's Library, Venice

Z 402 (=1031)	Annals of Glykas
Z 454 (=882)	Homer, Iliad
Z 479 (=881)	Kynegetua of Oppidian
Z 538 (=540)	Book of Job

Biblioteca Nacional, Madrid

Vitr. 26-2	Skylitzes Chronicle

Bibliothèque Nationale, Paris

Gr. 74	Gospels
Gr. 134	Commentary on the Book of Job
Gr. 510	Homilies of Gregory of Nanzianzos
Gr. 543	Gospels
Gr. 923	Sacra Parallela
Gr. 2144	Hippokratês
Gr. 2244	Hippiatrika

Kupferstichkabinet, Berlin

78 A9	Gospels

National Library, Vienna

Theol. Gr. 31	Genesis

Literary and Historical Sources

Achmet, *Achmetis Oneirocriticon*, ed. Francis Drexl, B. G. Teubner, Leipzig, 1925.

— *The Oneirocriticon of Achmet*, tr. Steven Michael Oberhelman, Texas Tech University Press, Lubbock, 1991.

Actes d'Iviron II, ed. Jacques Lefort, Nicholas Oikonomides and Denise Papachryssanthou, P. Lethielleux, Paris, 1990.

Anna Komnênê, *Alexiade*, ed. Bernard Leib, Société d'Édition Les Belles Lettres, Paris, 1976 (1937).

— *The Alexiad of Anna Comnena*, tr. Edgar Robert Ashton Sewter, Penguin Books, Harmondsworth, 1986 (1969).

Anonymous, *De Obsidione Toleranda*, ed. Hilda Van Den Berg, E. J. Brill, Leiden, 1947.

Anonymous, *Digenês Akritas*, ed. and tr. John Mavrogordato, Clarendon Books, Oxford, 1963 (1956).

Anonymous, *Book of the Eparch*, in Johannes Koder (ed.), *Das Eparchenbuch Leons des Weisen*, Verlag der Österreichischen Akademie der Wissenschaften, Wien, 1991.

Anonymous, *Book of Gifts and Rarities*, tr. Ghâda al-Hijjâwî al-Qaddûmî, Harvard University Press, Cambridge, MA, 1996.

Anonymous, *Chronicon Paschale*, ed. L. Dindorf, Corpus Scriptorum Historiae Byzantinae, Bonn, 1832.

Anonymous, *Peri Strategias*, in G. T. Dennis (ed. and tr.), *Three Byzantine Military Treatises*, Dumbarton Oaks, Washington, DC, 1985.

Christopher of Mitylênê, *Die Gedichte des Christophoros Mitylenaios*, ed. Eduard Kurtz, August Neumans Verlag, Leipzig, 1903.

Constantine Porfurogennêtos, *De Cerimoniis Aulae Byzantinae*, ed. Johannes Jacob Reiske, E. Weber, Bonn, 1839.

— *De Administrando Imperio*, ed. Gyula Moravcsik, tr. Romilly James Heald Jenkins, Dumbarton Oaks, Washington, DC, 1967.

— *Le Livre des Cérémonies*, ed. and tr. Albert Vogt, Société d'Édition Les Belles Lettres, Paris, 1967.

— *Three Treatises on Imperial Military Expeditions*, ed. and tr. John F. Haldon, Verlag der Österreichischen Akademie der Wissenschaften, Wien, 1990.

— *The Book of Ceremonies*, tr. Ann Moffat and Maxine Tall, Australian Association for Byzantine Studies, Canberra, 2012.

Diocletian, *Edict on Prices*, in Tenney Frank, *An Economic Survey of Ancient Rome*, Pageant Books, Princeton, 1959.

Evstathios of Thessaloniki, *The Capture of Thessaloniki*, ed. Stilpon Kyriakides, tr. John Melville-Jones, Australian Association for Byzantine Studies, Canberra, 1988.

Flavius Vegetius Renatus, *Epitome de Re Militari*, ed. and tr. Leo F. Stelton, Peter Lang, New York, 1990.

Filotheos, *Klêtôrologion*, in Nicholas Oikonomidès (ed. and tr.), *Les Listes de Préséance Byzantines des IXe et Xe Siècles*, Éditions du Centre National de la Recherche Scientifique, Paris, 1972.

Giorgios Akropolitês, *Georgii Acropolitae Opera*, ed. A. Heisenberg, Leipzig, 1903 (corr. P. Wirth, Stuttgart, 1978).

Giorgios Monachos, *Chronikon*, ed. John Classen, B. G. Teubner, Stuttgart, 1978 (1834).

Giorgios Pachymerês, *Georgii Pachymeris de Michaele et Andronico Palaeologi Libri tredecim*, vol. 2, ed. I. Bekker, E. Weber, Bonn, 1835.

— *Georges Pachymérès: Relations Historiques*, ed. A. Failler and V. Laurent, 2 vols, Société d'Édition Les Belles Lettres, Paris, 1984.

Hilâl al-Sâbi', *The Rules and Regulations of the Abbâsid Court*, tr. Elie Salem, American University Press, Beirut, 1977.

Ibn Yahya, Harun, 'Harun ibn Yahya and His Description of Constantinople', tr. Alexei Vasiliev, *Seminarum Kondakovum*, 5, 1932.

Isidore of Seville, *The Etymologies of Isidore of Seville*, tr. Stephen A. Barney et al., Cambridge University Press, Cambridge, 2006.

Iôannês Kinnamos, *Epitome Rerum ab Ioanne et Alexio* [=Manuel] *Comnenis Gestarum*, ed. Augustus Meinke, Edward Weber, Bonn, 1836.

— *Deeds of John and Manuel Comnenus*, tr. Charles M. Brand, Columbia University Press, New York, 1976.

Iôannês Lydos, *De Mensibus*, B. G. Teubner, Stuttgart, 1967

— *On Powers or The Magistracies of the Roman State*, ed. and tr. Anastasius C. Bandy, American Philosophical Society, Philadelphia, 1983.

Iôannês Malalas, *Ioannis Malalae Chronographia*, ed. L. Dindorf, E. Weber, Bonn, 1831.

— *The Chronicle of John Malalas*, Elizabeth Jeffreys, tr. Michael Jeffreys and Roger Scott, Australian Association for Byzantine Studies, Melbourne, 1986.

Iôannês Zonaras, *Epitomê Historiarum*, ed. L. Dindorf, B. G. Teubuer, Liepzig, 1868–75.

Justinian I, *The Civil Law*, tr. Samuel Parsons Scott, Central Trust Company, Cincinatti, 1932.

Leo IV, *The Taktika of Leo VI*, ed. and tr. George T. Dennis, Dumbarton Oaks, Washington, DC, 2010.

Leo Grammatikos, *Chronographia*, ed. Immanuel Bekker, E. Weber, Bonn, 1842.

Liutprand of Cremona, *Die Werke Liudprands von Cremona*, ed. Joseph Becker, Hahn, Hannover, 1915.

— *The Embassy to Constantinople and Other Writings*, tr. F. A. Wright, J. M. Dent, London, 1993 (1930).

Maurikios, *Das Strategikon des Maurikios*, ed. George T. Dennis, tr. Ernst Gamillscheg, Verlag der Österreichischen Akademie der Wissenschaften, Wien, 1981.

Michael Attaliatês, *Historia*, ed. Immanuel Bekker, E. Weber, Bonn, 1853.

Michael Doukas, *Decline and Fall of Byzantium to the Ottoman Turks: An Annotated Translation of "Historia Turco-Byzantina" 1341-1462*, tr. Harry J. Magoulias, Wayne State University Press, Detroit, 1975.

Michael Psellos, *Fourteen Byzantine Rulers*, tr. E. R. A. Sewter, Penguin Books, Harmondsworth, 1966 (1953).

— *Chronographie*, ed. and tr. Emile Renauld, 2 vols, Société d'Édition Les Belles Lettres, Paris, 1967.

— *Michaeli Pselli Poemata*, ed. L. G. Westerink, Stuttgart, 1992.

Nicholas I, Patriarch of Constantinople, *Letters*, ed. L. G. Westerink, tr. Romilly James Heald Jenkins, Dumbarton Oaks, Washington, DC, 1973.

Nikêforos Bryennios, *Commentarii*, ed. and tr. Paul Gautier, Byzantion, Brussels, 1975.

Nikêforos Fôkas, *Composition on Warfare*, in Eric McGeer

(ed. and tr.), *Sowing the Dragon's Teeth*, Dumbarton Oaks, Washington, DC, 1995.

Nikêtas Choniatês, *Historia*, ed. Jan-Louis Van Dieten, de Gruyter, Berlin, 1975.

— *O City of Byzantium: The Annals of Nicetas Choniates*, tr. Harry J. Magoulias, Wayne State University Press, Detroit, 1984.

Peter of Eboli, *Liber ad Honorem Augusti de Pietro di Eboli*, ed. G. B. Siragusa, Instituto Storico Italiano, Rome, 1905.

Pseudo-Kodinos, *Traité des Offices*, ed. and tr. Jean Verpeaux, Centre National de la Recherche Scientifique, Paris, 1966.

— *Suidae Lexicon*, ed. Ada Adler, 5 vols, B. G. Teubner, Stuttgart, 1971.

Sanudo, Marino, *Vitae Ducum Venetorum: Rerum Italicum Scriptorum*, XXII, Milan, 1733.

Theophanês, *Chronographia*, ed. Charles de Boor, B. G. Teubner, Leipzig, 1980 (1883–5).

— *The Chronicle of Theophanes Confessor*, tr. Cyril Mango and Roger Scott with Geoffrey Greatrex, Clarendon Press, Oxford, 1997.

— *Continuatus*, ed. I. Bekker, E. Weber, Bonn, 1838.

Theophilus, *De Diversis Artibus*, tr. Charles Reginald Dodwell, Thomas Nelson and Sons, London, 1961.

Usamah ibn Munqid, *An Arab-Syrian Gentleman and Warrior in the Period of the Crusades*, tr. Philip Khouri Hitti, Columbia University Press, New York, 2000.

Xenofon, *Cyropaedia*, ed. T. E. Page and W. H. D. Rouse, Loeb Classical Library, London, 1914.

Secondary Sources Cited

Alexander, Paul Julius, 'Religious Persecution and Resistance in the Byzantine Empire of the Eighth and Ninth Centuries: Methods and Justifications', *Speculum*, 52, 1977, pp. 238–64.

Alföldi, Andreas, *Die Monarchische Repräesentation im* Römischen Kaiserreiche, Wissenschaftliche Buchgesselschaft, Darmstadt, 1980.

Anastos, Milton, 'Leo III's Edict against the images in the year 726–27', *Byzantinische Forschungen*, 3, 1968, pp. 5–41.

Baginski, Alisa, and Tidhar, Amalia, *Textiles from Egypt: 4th to 13th Centuries CE*, Mayer Institute, Jerusalem, 1980.

Baker, Joseph M., 'Tyrian Purple and its Precursors from Australian Molluscs', unpublished dissertation, University of Queensland, 1967.

Baldowski, Wlodzimierz, *Militaria Z Dawnej Kolekcji Wilanowski*, Wydawnictwa Geologiezne, Warsaw, 1990.

Ball, Jennifer, *Byzantine Dress: Representations of Secular Dress in Eighth to Twelfth-Century Painting*, Palgrave-Macmillan, New York, 2005.

Bank, Alice, *Byzantine Art in the Collections of Soviet Museums*, Aurora Art Publishers, Leningrad, 1985.

Battaglia, Salvatore, *Grande Dizionario della Lingua Italiana*, 22 vols, Unione tipografico-editrice torinese, Turin *c.*1961–2000.

Battisti, Carlo, and Alessio, Giovanni, *Dizionario Etimologico Italiano*, Università Degli Studi, Florence, 1950–7.

Baumann, Gerd, 'Ritual Implicates 'Others': Rereading Durkheim in a Plural Society', in Daniel De Coppet (ed.), *Understanding Rituals*, Routledge, London, 1992.

Beckwith, John, *Early Christian and Byzantine Art*, Penguin Books, Harmondsworth, 1970.

Bellinger, Louisa, 'Patterned Stockings: Possibly Indian, Found in Egypt', *Textile Museum Workshop Notes*, Paper 10, December 1954.

Bénazeth, Dominique, and Dal-pra, Patricia, 'Quelques Remarques à Propos d'un Ensemble de Vêtements de Cavaliers Découverts dans Tombes Égyptiennes', in *L'Armée Romaine et Barbares du Troisème au Quatrième Siècle*, L'Association Francaise d'Archéologie Mérovingienne, Saint-Germain-en-Laye, 1993, pp. 367–82.

Bishop, Michael C., and Coulston, John C. N., *Roman Military Equipment from the Punic Wars to the Fall of Rome*, Batsford Books, London, 1993.

Black, J. Anderson, and Garland, Madge, *A History of Fashion*, Orbis Publishing, London, 1978.

Blair, Sheila S., Bloom, Jonathan, and Wardwell, Anne, 'Re-evaluating the Date of the 'Buyid' Silks by Epigraphic and Radiocarbon Analysis', *Ars Orientalis*, 22, 1992, pp. 1–41.

Blöndal, Sigfús, *The Varangians of Byzantium*, rev. Benedikt Benedikz, Cambridge University Press, Cambridge, 1978.

Bocock, Robert, *Ritual in Industrial Society*, Allen and Unwin, London, 1974.

Boucher, François, *A History of Costume in the West*, Thames and Hudson, London, 1987.

Brand, Charles M., *Byzantium Confronts the West 1180–1204*, Harvard University Press, Cambridge, MA, 1968.

Bréhier, Louis, *Le Monde Byzantin*, Éditions Albin Michel, Paris, 1949.

Brooks, Sarah T., *Byzantium, Faith and Power (1261–1557): Perspectives on Late Byzantine Art and Culture*, Metropolitan Museum of Art, New York, 2007.

Brosse, Jacques, Chaland, Paul, and Ostier, Jacques, *100,000 Years of Daily Life: A Visual History*, The Bodley Head, London, 1960.

Browning, Robert, *Medieval and Modern Greek*, Hutchinson,

London, 1969.

— *Byzantium and Bulgaria*, Sidgwick and Jackson, London, 1975.

Brownlee, Marina, Brownlee, Kevin, and Nichols, Stephen S. (eds), *The New Medievalism*, Johns Hopkins University Press, Baltimore, 1991.

Bulletin of the Cleveland Museum of Art, January 1987.

Burnham, Dorothy, *Cut my Cote*, McKinnon-Moncur, Ontario, 1973.

Bury, John Bagnell, *A History of the Later Roman Empire*, Dover Books, New York, 1958.

Cahen, Claude, 'Un Traité d'Armurerie Compose pour Saladin', *Bulletin d'Études Orientales de l'Institut Français de Damas*, 12, 1947/8.

— *Pre-Ottoman Turkey*, Sidgwick and Jackson, London, 1968.

Cameron, Averil, 'The Construction of Court Ritual: The Byzantine Book of Ceremonies', in David Cannadine and Simon Price (eds), *Rituals of Royalty: Power and Ceremonial in Traditional Societies*, Cambridge University Press, Cambridge, 1987, pp. 106–36.

Cameron, Alan, *Circus Factions: Blues and Greens at Rome and Byzantium*, Clarendon Press, Oxford, 1976.

Canta, Antonietta Amanti, 'Bridal Gifts in Bari', *Medieval Clothing and Textiles*, 9, 2013.

Cardon, Dominique, 'A Mysterious Group of Textiles, Probably Medieval, Found in the Caves of Manazan, Near Tazkale, Karaman Province, Turkey', *Bulletin du CIETA*, 7 1993, pp. 183–4.

Chatzidakis, Manoulis, and Grabar, André, *Byzantine and Early Medieval Painting*, Weidenfeld and Nicholson, London, 1965.

— and Stylianos Pelekanides, *Kastoria*, Athens, 1985.

Cheynet, Jean-Claude, 'Dévaluation des Dignités et Dévaluation Monétaire dans la Seconde Moitié du XIme Siècle', *Byzantion*, 53, 1983, pp. 453–77.

Clauson, Gerard, *Etymological Dictionary of Pre-Thirteenth-Century Turkish*, Clarendon Press, Oxford, 1972.

Collingwood, Peter, *The Technique of Sprang*, Watson-Guptill Publications, London, 1974.

— *The Techniques of Tablet-Weaving*, Faber and Faber, London, 1982.

Contini, Mila, *5000 Years of Fashion*, Chartwell Books Inc., Secaucus, NJ, 1979.

Cormack, Robin, and Vassilaki, Maria (eds), *Byzantium: 330–1453*, Royal Academy of Arts, London, 2008.

Croom, Alexandra, *Roman Clothing and Fashion*, Tempus Publishing, Stroud, 2002.

Cubberly, Anthony L., Lloyd, J. A., and Roberts, Paul C., '*Testa* and *Clibani*: The Baking Covers of Classical Italy', *Papers of the British School at Rome*, 56, 1988, pp. 98–119.

Dalton, Ormonde Maddock, *Byzantine Art and Archaeology*, Dover, New York, 1961.

D'Amato, Rafaele, *Roman Military Clothing (3) 400–640*, Osprey Publishing, Oxford, 2005.

— and Sumner, Graham, *Arms and Armour of the Imperial Roman Soldier: From Marius to Commodus, 112 BC–AD 192*, Frontline Books, London, 2009.

Dark, Ken, *Byzantine Pottery*, Tempus, Stroud, 2001.

Davenport, Millia, *The Book of Costume*, Crown Publishers, New York, 1976.

Davids, Adelbert (ed.), *The Empress Theophano: Byzantium and the West at the Turn of the First Millenium*, Cambridge University Press, Cambridge, 1995.

Davidson, Gladys R., *Corinth: Results of Excavations Conducted by the American School of Classical Studies at Athens. Vol XIII: The Minor Objects*, American School of Classical Studies at Athens, Princeton, 1952.

Davies, Roy, *Service in the Roman Army*, Edinburgh University Press, Edinburgh, 1989.

Dawson, Timothy, 'The Varangian Rhomphaia: A Cautionary Tale', in *Varangian Voice*, 22, May 1992, pp. 28–31.

— 'Kremasmata, Kabbadion, Klibanion: Some Aspects of Middle Byzantine Military Equipment Reconsidered', *Byzantine and Modern Greek Studies*, 22, 1998, pp. 38–50.

— 'Suntagma Hoplôn: The Equipment of Regular Byzantine Troops, c.950–c.1204', in David Nicolle (ed.), *Companion to Medieval Arms and Armour*, Boydell & Brewer, London, 2002, pp. 81–90.

— 'Concerning an Unrecognised Tunic from Eastern Anatolia', *Byzantion*, 73:1, 2003, pp. 201–10.

— 'Oriental Costumes in the Byzantine Court Reconsidered', *Byzantion*, 75, 2005.

— 'Propriety, Practicality and Pleasure: The Parameters of Women's Dress', in Lynda Garland (ed.), *Byzantine Women: Varieties of Experience 800–1200*, Ashgate, Aldershot, 2006, pp. 41–75.

— '"Fit for the Task": Equipment Sizes and the Transmission of Military Lore, Sixth to Tenth Centuries', *Byzantine and Modern Greek Studies*, 31:1, 2007, pp. 1–12.

— *Byzantine Infantryman: Eastern Roman Empire, c.900–1204*, Warrior Series, Osprey Publishing, Oxford, 2007.

— 'The Monomakhos Crown – Towards a Resolution', ΒΥΖΑΝΤΙΝΑ ΣΥΜΜΕΙΚΤΑ, 19, 2009, pp. 183–93.

— *Byzantine Cavalryman: Eastern Roman Empire, c.900–1204*, Warrior Series, Osprey Publishing, Oxford, 2009

— 'There and Back Again: Cross-cultural Transmission of Clothing and Clothing Terminology', in Stephanie Hathaway and David W. Kim (eds), *Studies in Intercultural Exchange in the Early Medieval*

Mediterranean, Continuum Publishing, London, 2012, pp. 203–13.

— *Armour Never Wearies: A History of Scale and Lamellar Armour in the West from the Bronze Age to the Nineteenth Century*, The History Press, Stroud, 2013.

De Coppet, Daniel (ed.), *Understanding Rituals*, Routledge, London, 1992.

Deer, Josef, *Die Heilige Krone Ungarns*, Österreichischen Akademie der Wissenschaften, Vienna, 1966.

De Jerphanion, Guillaume, 'Le "Thorakion" Caracteristique Iconographie du XIe Siècle', *Melanges Charles Diehl*, 2, 1930, pp. 71–9.

Demus, Otto, *Byzantine Art and the West*, Weidenfeld and Nicolson, London, 1970.

Dennis, George T. (tr.), *Maurice's Strategicon*, University of Pennsylvania Press, Philadelphia, 1984."

Der Nersessian, Sirarpie, *Aght'amar: The Church of the Holy Cross*, Harvard University Press, Cambridge, MA, 1965.

De Waha, M., 'Review of *Kamelaukion et Mitra* by Elizabeth Piltz', *Byzantion*, 48, 1978, pp. 523–31.

Diehl, Charles, 'La Signification du Titre de "Proèdros" a Byzance', *Melanges G. Schlumberger*, 1, 1924, pp. 105–17.

Donovan, Frank R., *The Vikings*, Harpercollins, London, 1964.

Drossoyianni, P. A., 'A Pair of Byzantine Crowns', *Jahrbuch der Österreichischen Byzantinistik*, 32:3, 1982, pp. 529–38.

Du Bourget, Pierre, *Musee National du Louvre: Catalogue des Etoffes Copts*, Éditions des Musées Nationaux, Paris, 1964.

— *Early Christian Art*, Weidenfeld and Nicolson, London, 1972.

— and Pascale Gremont, *Tissus Coptes*, Musée d'Angers, Angers, 1977.

Du Cange, Charles du Fresne, *Glossarium ad Scriptores Mediae et Infimiae Graecitatis*, Akademische Druck-U. Verlagsanstalt, Graz, 1958.

— *Glossarium Mediae et Infimiae Latinitatis*, Akademische Druck-U. Verlagsanstalt, Graz, 1954.

Dumitrescu, Carmen-Laura, 'Remarques en Marge du *Coilin 79*: Les Trois Eunuques', *Byzantion*, 57, 1987, pp. 32–46.

Eastwood, Anthony, 'An Intentional Error? Imperial Art and 'Mis'-Interpretation under Andronikos I Komnenos', *Art Bulletin*, 76:1, March 1994, pp. 502–10.

Ebersolt, Jean, *Les Arts Somptuaires de Byzance*, E. Leroux, Paris, 1923.

— *Melanges d'Histoire et d'Archéologie Byzantines*, E. Leroux, Paris, 1951.

Emmanuel, Melita, 'Hairstyles and Headdresses of Empresses, Princesses and Ladies of the Aristocracy in Byzantium', Δελτιο της Χριστιανικης Αρχαιολογικης Εταιρειας, 17, 1993–4, pp. 113–20.

Encyclopedia of Islam, E. J. Brill, Leiden, 2000.

Evans, G. Roger, *Corinth: Results of Excavations Conducted by the American School of Classical Studies at Athens: Vol VII, Part III: Hellenistic Pottery*, American School of Classical Studies, Princeton, 1975.

Evans, Helen, and Wixom, William D., *The Glory of Byzantium: Art and Culture of the Byzantine Era A.D. 843–1261*, Metropolitan Museum of Art, New York, 1997.

Ewing, Thor, *Viking Clothing*, Tempus Books, Stroud, 2006.

Falk, Toby (ed.), *Treasures of Islam*, Wellfleet Press, Secaucus, NJ, 1985.

Featherstone, Michael, 'Preliminary Remarks on the Leipzig Manuscript of *De Cerimoniis*', *Byzantinische Zeitschrift*, 95, 2002, pp. 457–79.

— 'Further remarks on the *De Cerimoniis*', *Byzantinische Zeitschrift*, 95, 2002, pp. 113–21.

Frauberger, Heinrich, *Antike und Fruhmittelalterlich Fussbekleidungen aus Achmim-Panopolis* (publisher unknown), Dusseldorf, 1895.

Frese, Pamela R., *Celebrations of Identity; Multiple Voices in American Ritual Performances*, Bergin and Garvey, Westport, 1993.

Fluck, Cäcilia, and Vogelsang-Eastwood, Gillian (eds), *Riding Costume in Egypt: Origin and Appearance*, E. J. Brill, Leiden, 2004.

Gabrielli, Francesco, *Arab Historians of the Crusades*, Routlege & Keegan Paul, London, 1969.

Galavaris, George P., *The Symbolism of Imperial Costume as Displayed on Byzantine Coins*, museum notes of the American Numismatic Society, 8, 1958, pp. 99–117.

Garland, Lynda, *Byzantine Empresses*, Routledge, London, 1999.

— 'The "βέργιν τρικλῶνον" of Belthandros and Chryzantza: A Note on a Popular Verse Romance and its Sources', *Byzantinische Zeitschrift*, 82, 1989, pp. 87–95.

Geanakoplos, Deno John, *Byzantium: Church, Society and Civilisation Seen Through Contemporary Eyes*, University of Chicago Press, Chicago, 1984.

Gerstel, Sharon, 'Saint Eudokia and the Imperial Household of Leo VI', *Art Bulletin*, 69, 1997, pp. 698–707.

Gervers, Veronika (as Gervers-Molnár), *The Hungarian Szur: An Archaic Mantle of Eurasian Origin*, Royal Ontario Museum, Toronto, 1973.

— (ed.) *Studies in Textile History*, Royal Ontario Museum, Toronto, 1977.

— 'Medieval Garments in the Mediterranean World', in Negley P. Harte, and Kenneth G. Ponting (eds), *Cloth and Clothing in Medieval Europe*, Heinemann, London,

1983, pp. 279–315.
— Γιαννακοπουλος, Γ. Σαιρενος, Ε. Αριστον Ελλενοαγγελικον Λεξικον, Π. Κουτσουμπος, Αθενα, 1971.
Goddard, Eunice Rathbone, *Women's Costume in French Texts of the Eleventh and Twelfth Centuries*, Johnson Reprint Corporation, New York, 1973 (1927).
Golombek, Lisa and Gervers, Veronika, 'Tiraz Fabrics in the Royal Ontario Museum', in Veronika Gervers (ed.), *Studies in Textile History*, Royal Ontario Museum, Toronto, 1977, pp. 82–125.
Goodacre, Hugh, *A Handbook of the Coinage of the Byzantine Empire*, Spink and Son Ltd, London, 1967.
Gordon, Stewart (ed.), *Robes and Honour: The Medieval World of Investiture*, Palgrave, Basingstoke, 2001.
Grabar, André, *L'Empereur dans l'Art Byzantine*, Variorum, London, 1971.
— and Manoussacas, M., *L'Illustration du Manuscrit de Skylitzès de la Bibliothèque Nationale de Madrid*, Bibliothèque de l'Institute Hellénique d'Études Byzantines de Venise, Venice, 1979.
Grabar, Oleg, 'The Shared Culture of Objects', in Henry Maguire (ed.), *Byzantine Court Culture from 829 to 1204*, Dumbarton Oaks, Washington, DC, 1997, pp. 115–29.
Granger-Taylor, Hero, 'Weaving Clothes to Shape in the Ancient World', *Textile History*, 13, 1982, pp. 3–25.
Gregorietti, Guido, *Jewelry Through the Ages*, American Heritage Press, New York, 1969.
Grew, Francis, and de Neergaard, Margarethe, *Shoes and Pattens: Medieval Finds from London*, HMSO, London, 1996.
Grierson, Philip, *A Catalogue of the Byzantine Coins in the Dumbarton Oaks Collection and the Whitmore Collection*, Dumbarton Oaks, Washington, DC, 1993 (1973).
Griffith, Ross, Potter, M. David, and Corbman, Bernard, *Textiles: Fiber to Fabric*, McGraw-Hill Book Company, Sydney, 1967 (1954).
Grotowski, Piotr Ł., *Arms and Armour of the Warrior Saints*, E. J. Brill, Leiden, 2010.
Guilland, Rodolphe, 'Sur Quelque Terms du Livre des Cérémonies du Constantine VII Porphyrogénète', *Revue des Études Grecques*, 58, 1945, pp. 197–211.
— 'Sur Quelque Terms du Livre des Cérémonies du Constantine VII Porphyrogénète', *Revue des Études Grecques*, 62, 1949, pp. 328–50.
— 'Etudes sur l'Histoire Administrative de l'Empire Byzantine: Les Titres Auliques des Eunuches – Le Protospataire', *Byzantion*, 25–7, 1955–7, pp. 650–96.
— 'Etudes sur l'Histoire Administrative de l'Empire Byzantine: Le Curopalate', *Byzantina*, 2, 1970, pp. 187–249.
— 'Contribution à l'Histoire Administrative de l'Empire Byzantin: La Patricienne à Ceinture', *Byzantinoslavica*, 32, 1971, pp. 269–75.
— 'Patrices de Theodora aux Comnènes', *Rivista di Studi bizantini e neoellenici*, 8–9 (XVIII–XIX), 1971–2, pp. 7–23.
— *Titres et Fonctions de l'Empire Byzantine*, Variorum Reprints, London, 1976.
Guillou, André, 'Production and Profits in the Byzantine Province of Italy (Tenth to Eleventh Centuries): An Expanding Society', *Dumbarton Oaks Papers*, 28, 1974, pp. 102–10.
Haldon, John F., 'Some Aspects of Byzantine Military Technology from the Sixth to the Tenth Centuries', *Byzantine and Modern Greek Studies*, 1, 1975, pp. 11–47.
Harper, Prudence Oliver, *Silver Vessels of the Sassanian Period*, Metropolitan Museum, New York, 1981.
Harvey, Alan, *Economic Expansion in the Byzantine Empire: 900–1204*, Cambridge University Press, Cambridge, 1989.
Haussig, Hans Wilhelm, *A History of Byzantine Civilization*, Praeger Publishers, New York, 1971.
Heath, Ian, *Armies of the Dark Ages*, Wargames Research Group, Oxford, 1980.
— *Byzantine Armies: 886–1119*, Osprey Publishing, Oxford, 1979.
Hemmerdinger, Bertrand, '158 Noms Communs Grecs d'Origine Iranienne', *Byzantinoslavica*, 30, 1969, pp. 18–41.
— '173 Noms Communs Grecs d'Origine Iranienne', *Byzantinoslavica*, 32, 1971, pp. 52–5.
Hendy, Michael F., *Coinage and Money in the Byzantine Empire: Dumbarton Oaks Studies*, 12, Dumbarton Oaks, Washington, DC, 1969.
Hennessy, Cecily. 'A Child Bride and her Representation in the Vatican *Epithalamion*, Cod. Gr. 1851', *Byzantine and Modern Greek Studies*, 30:2, 2006, pp. 115–50.
Herrin, Judith, 'Theophano: The Education of a Byzantine Princess', in Adelbert Davids (ed.), *The Empress Theophano: Byzantium and the West at the Turn of the First Millennium*, Cambridge University Press, Cambridge, 1995, pp. 64–85.
Hetherington, Paul, and Forman, Werner, *Byzantium: City of Gold, City of Faith*, Orbis Publishing, London, 1983.
Holum, Kenneth G., *Theodosian Empresses*, University of California Press, Berkeley, 1982.
Horrocks, Geoffrey, *Greek: A History of the Language and its Speakers*, Longman, London, 1997.

Houston, Mary G., *Ancient Greek, Roman and Byzantine Costume and Decoration*, Adam and Charles Black, London, 1966 (1947).

Hubert, Jean, Porcher, Jean, and Volbach, W. F., *The Arts of Mankind: Europe in the Dark Ages*, Thames and Hudson, London, 1969.

Hunger, Herbert, 'On the Imitation (ΜΙΜΗΣΙΣ) of Antiquity', *Dumbarton Oaks Papers*, 23–24, 1969–70, pp. 15–38.

Huyghe, René, *The Larousse Encyclopedia of Byzantine and Medieval Art*, Paul Hamlyn, London, 1963.

Ierusalimskaja, Anna, and Borkopp, Birgitt, *Von China nach Byzanz*, Bayerischen Museum, Munich, 1996.

Innemée, Karel, *Ecclesiastical Dress in the Medieval Near East*, E. J. Brill, Leiden, 1992.

James, Liz, *Light and Colour in Byzantine Art*, Clarendon Press, Oxford, 1996.

Jeffreys, Michael, 'The Vernacular εἰσιτήριοι for Agnes of France', *Byzantine Papers*, Australian Association for Byzantine Studies, Canberra, 1981, pp. 101–15.

Jenkins, Romilly James Heald, 'The Emperor Alexander and the Saracen Prisoners', *Studi Bizantini e Neoelleniki*, 7, 1953, pp. 389–93.

— 'Three Documents on Tetragamy', *Dumbaron Oaks Papers*, 16, 1962, pp. 231–41.

— 'The Chronolgical Accuracy of the "Logothete" for the Years A.D. 867–913', *Dumbarton Oaks Papers*, 19, 1965, pp. 91–112.

— and Basil Laourdas, 'Eight Letters of Arethas on the Fourth Marriage of Leo the Wise', *Hellenika*, 14, 1956, pp. 293–372.

Jensen, Lloyd B., 'The Royal Purple of Tyre', *Journal of Near Eastern Studies*, 22, 1963, pp. 104–18.

Jones, Lynn, *Between Islam and Byzantium,* Ashgate, Aldershot, 2007.

Kalamara, Paraskévé, *Le Système Vestimentaire à Byzance du IVe Jusqu'*à la *Fin du XIe Siècle*, Presses Universitaires du Septentrion, Villeneuve d'Ascq Cédex, 1995.

Kalavresou-Maxeiner, Ioli, *Byzantine Icons in Steatite*, Österreichischen Akademie der Wissenchaften, Vienna, 1985.

— 'Dating the Romanos Ivory', *Dumbarton Oaks Papers*, 31, 1977, pp. 307–25.

Kantorowicz, Ernst Hartwig, 'On the Golden Marriage Belt and the Marriage Rings of the Dumbarton Oaks Collection', *Dumbarton Oaks Studies*, 14, 1960, pp. 1–16.

Karatzas, Stamatê, 'Byzantinogermanika (κάρανος-σκαράνικον)', *Byzantinische Zeitscrift*, 47, 1954, pp. 320–32.

Kazhdan, Alexander, 'Encore Fois le Term βιρριν', *Jahrbuch der Österreichichen Byzantinistik*, 33, 1983, p. 15.

— and Epstein, Anne Wharton, *Change in Byzantine Culture in the Eleventh and Twelfth centuries*, University of California Press, Berkeley, 1985.

— and Franklin, Simon, *Studies in Byzantine Literature of the Eleventh and Twelfth Centuries*, Cambridge University Press, Cambridge, 1984.

— and McCormick, Michael, 'The Social World of the Byzantine Court', in Henry Maguire (ed.), *Byzantine Court Culture*, Dumbarton Oaks, Washington, DC, 1997, pp. 167–97.

— and Talbot, Alice Mary, Cutler, Anthony, Gregory, Timothy E., and Shevchenko, Nancy P. (eds), *Oxford Dictionary of Byzantium*, 3 vols, Oxford University Press, Oxford, 1991.

King, Donald, 'Roman and Byzantine Dress in Egypt', *Costume*, 30, 1996, pp. 1–15.

Kitzinger, Ernst, *Byzantine Art in the Making*, Faber and Faber, London, 1977.

Kolias, Taxiarchis, *Byzantinische Waffen*, Österreichischen Akademie der Wissenchaften, Wien, 1988.

— 'Kamelaukion', *Jahrbuch der Österreichichen Byzantinistik*, 32:3, 1982, pp. 493–502.

Kondakov, Nikodim Pavlovich, 'Costumes Orientaux à la Cour Byzantine', *Byzantion* 1, 1924, pp. 7–49.

Kovács, Éva, and Lovag, Zsuzsa, *The Hungarian Crown and Other Regalia*, Korvina Kiadó, Budapest, 1980.

Kuhnel, Ernst, and Bellinger, Louisa, *The Textile Museum Catalogue of Dated Tiraz Fabrics*, Textile Museum, Washington, DC, 1952.

Kuhnel, Ernst, and Volbach, Wolfgang Fritz, *Late Antique Coptic and Islamic Textiles of Egypt*, E. Weyhe, New York, 1926.

Kybalova, Ludmila, *Coptic Textiles*, Paul Hamlyn, London, 1967.

Lafontaine-Dosogne, Jacqueline, 'The Art of Byzantium and its Relation to Germany', in Adelbert Davids (ed.), *The Empress Theophano: Byzantium and the West at the Turn of the First Millenium*, Cambridge University Press, Cambridge, 1995, pp. 211–30.

Lampe, Geoffrey William Hugo, *A Patristic Greek Lexicon*, Clarendon Press, Oxford, 1961.

Lane, Christel, *The Rites of Rulers: Ritual in Industrial Society – The Soviet Case*, Cambridge University Press, Cambridge, 1981.

Lane, Edward William, *An Arabic–English Lexicon*, Frederick Ungar, New York, 1955–6 (London, 1885).

Lang, David Marshall, *Armenia: Cradle of Civilisation*, Allen and Unwin, London, 1970.

Lassus, Jean, *L'Illustration Byzantine du Livre des Rois: Vat. Gr. 333*, Klincksieck, Paris, 1973.

Lauffray, J. *Textiles de Halabiye*, **, Paris, 1951.
Le Bohec, Yann, *The Imperial Roman Army*, Batsford Books, London, 1994.
Lerch Patricia, 'Powwows, Parades and Social Drama among the Waccamaw Indians', in Pamela R. Frese (ed.), *Celebrations of Identity: Multiple Voices in American Ritual Performances*, Bergin & Garvey, Westport, 1993.
Levy, Reuben, 'Notes on Costume from Arabic Sources', *Journal of the Royal Asiatic Society*, 1935, pp. 319–38.
Lewis, Charleton T., and Short, Charles, *A Latin Dictionary*, Clarendon Press, Oxford, 1980 (1879).
Liddell, Henry George, Scott, Robert, and Jones, Henry Stuart, *A Greek-English Lexicon*, Clarendon Press, Oxford, 1963 (1843).
Lopez, Robert S., 'The Silk Industry in the Byzantine Empire', *Speculum*, 20, 1945, pp. 1–42.
Lovillo, José Guerrero, *Las Cantigas: Estudio Arqueologio de sus Miniaturas*, Instituto Diego Velasques, Madrid, 1949.
Macrides, Ruth J., 'From the Komnenoi to the Palaiologoi', in Paul Magdalino (ed.), *New Constantines*, Variorum, Aldershot, 1994, pp. 269–82.
Maguire, Henry, 'A Murderer amongst the Angels: The Frontispiece Miniatures of Paris Gr. 510 and the Iconography of the Archangels in Byzantine Art', in Robert Ousterhout and Leslie Brubaker (eds), *The Sacred Image East and West*, University of Illinois Press, Urbana, 1995, pp. 61–71.
— (ed.), *Byzantine Court Culture from 829 to 1204*, Dumbarton Oaks, Washington, DC, 1997.
— 'The Heavenly Court', in H. Maguire (ed.), *Byzantine Court Culture from 829 to 1204*, Dumbarton Oaks, Washington, DC, 1997.
Manafis, Konstantine A., *Sinai: Treasures of the Monastery of Saint Catherine*, Ekdotike Athenon, Athens, 1990.
Mango, Cyril, 'Discontinuity in Byzantium', in M. Mullett and R. Scott (eds), *Byzantium and the Classical Tradition*, Centre for Byzantine Studies, Birmingham, 1981, pp. 48–57.
McCormick, Michael, 'Analyzing Imperial Ceremonies', *Jahrbuch der Österreichichen Byzantinistik*, 35, 1985, pp. 1–20.
— *Eternal Victory*, Cambridge University Press, Cambridge, 1986.
McGeer, Eric (ed. and tr.), *Sowing the Dragon's Teeth*, Dumbarton Oaks, Washington, DC, 1995
Migne, Jacques-Paul, *Lexicon Manuale ad Scriptores Mediae et Infimiae Latinitatis*, ed. J.-P. Migne, Petit Montrouge, Paris, 1858.
Mihaescu, Harlambie, 'La Terminologie d'Origine Latine des Vêtements dans la Littérature Byzantine', *Byzantion Aphieroma ston Andrea N. Strato*, 2, 1986, pp. 587–99.
— 'Les Terms Byzantines birrov, birroς "Casaque, Tunique d'Hommes" et Gouna "Fourrures"', *Revue des Études Sud-Est Européenes*, 19, 1981, pp. 425–32.
Morgan, G., 'A Byzantine Satirical Song?', *Byzantinische Zeitschrift*, 47, 1954, pp. 292–7.
Müller-Christiansen, Sigrid, 'Examples of Medieval Tablet-Woven Braids', in Veronika Gervers (ed.), *Studies in Textile History*, Royal Ontario Museum, Toronto, 1977, pp. 232–7.
Muthesius, Anna, 'From Seed to Samite: Aspects of Byzantine Silk Production', *Textile History*, 20:2, 1989, pp. 135–49.
— 'Crossing Traditional Boundaries: Grub to Glamour in Byzantine Silk Weaving', *Byzantine and Modern Greek Studies*, 15, 1991, pp. 326–59.
— *Studies in Byzantine and Islamic Silk Weaving*, Pindar Press, London, 1995.
— *Byzantine Silk Weaving, AD 400 to AD 1200*, Verlag Fassbaender, Vienna, 1997.
Nicol, Donald M.*The last centuries of Byzantium*, 1261-1453, Hart-Davis, London, 1972.
— 'Refugees, Mixed Population and Local Patriotism in Epiros and Western Macedonia after the Fourth Crusade', *XVe Congrès international d'études byzantines, Rapports I. Histoire*, Athens, 1976.
— '*Kaisersalbung*: The Unction of Emperors in Late Byzantine Coronation Ritual', *Byzantine and Modern Greek Studies*, 2, 1976, pp. 37–44.
— *The Byzantine Lady: Ten Portraits, 1250-1500*, Cambridge University Press, Cambridge, 1994.
Nicolle, David, *Arms and Armour of the Crusading Era*, Kraus International Publications, White Plains, NY, 1988.
— *The Medieval Warfare Sourcebook: Christian Europe and its Neighbours*, Brockhampton Press, London, 1996.
— (ed.), *Companion to Medieval Arms and Armour*, Boydell & Brewer, London, 2002.
Nichols, Stephen G., 'The New Medievalism: Tradition and Discontinuity in Medieval Culture', in M. Brownlee, K. Brownlee, and S. G. Nichols (eds), *The New Medievalism*, Johns Hopkins University Press, Baltimore, 1991.
Niermeyer, J. F., *Mediae Latinitatis Lexicon Minus*, E. J. Brill, Leiden, 1976.
Norman, Vesey, *Arms and Armour*, Weidenfeld and Nicholson, London, 1970.
Oberhelman, Steven Michael, 'Oneirocritic Literature of the Late Roman and Byzantine periods', PhD thesis, 1981, University of Minnesota.
Oikonomidès, Nicholas (ed. and tr.), *Les Listes de Préséance Byzantines des IXe et Xe Siècles*, Éditions du Centre National de la Recherche Scientifique, Paris, 1972.

Omont, Henri Auguste, *Fac-similés des Manuscrits Grecs Datés de la Bibliothèque Nationale du IXe au XIVe Siècle (Des Plus Anciens Manuscrits Grecs en Onciale et en Miniscule du IVe au XIIe Siècle)*, Paris, 1891–2.

Önder, Mehmet, 'Mevlâna Müsesinde Bulunan Mevlâna'nin Elbiseleri Üzerinde Bir Arastirma', *Turk Etnografia Dergisi*, 5, 1974, pp. 5–14.

Ousterhout, Robert, and Brubaker, Leslie, *The Sacred Image, East and West*, University of Illinois Press, Urbana, 1995.

Oxford Latin Dictionary, 2 vols, Clarendon Press, Oxford, 1968–76.

Parani, Maria, 'Which Eudokia? A Contribution to the Romanos Ivory debate', *Bulletin of British Byzantine Studies*, 25, 1999, pp. 87–8.

— *Reconstructing the Reality of Images: Byzantine Material Culture and Religious Iconography*, E. J. Brill, Leiden, 2003.

Payne, Blanche, *A History of Costume*, Harper and Row, New York, 1965.

Pelekanides, Stylianos, Christou, P. C., Psioumis, Ch., and Kadas, S. N., *The Treasures of Mount Athos: The Illuminated Manuscripts*, Patriarchal Institute for Patristic Studies, Athens, 1973.

Piltz, Elizabeth, *Trois Sakkoi Byzantines,* Almqvist and Wiskell, Stockholm, 1976.

— *Kamelaukion et Mitra: Insignes Byzantines Impériaux et Ecclésiastiques*, Almqvist and Wiskell, Stockholm, 1977.

— 'Costume in Life and Death in Byzantium', *Byzantium and the North: Transactions of the Nordic Research Course in Byzantine Art History*, Almqvist and Wiskell, Uppsala, 1989, pp. 153–65.

— *Le Costume Officiel des Dignitaires Byzantins à l'Époque Paléologue*, Acta Universitatis Upsaliensis, Uppsala, 1994.

— 'Middle Byzantine Court Costume', in Henry Maguire (ed.), *Byzantine Court Culture from 829 to 1204*, Dumbarton Oaks, Washington, DC, 1997, pp. 37–51.

Reinhold, Meyer, *The History of Purple as a Status Symbol in Antiquity*, Latomus, Brussels, 1970.

Reiske, Johannes Jacob, *Commentarii ad Constantine Porphyrogennetos De Cerimoniis Aulae Byzantinae*, E. Weber, Bonn, 1839.

Rodley, Lyn, 'The Pigeon House Church, Çavusin', *Jahrbuch Österreisches Byzantinistik*, 33, 1983.

Rutschowskaya, Marie-Helene, *Tissus Coptes*, A. Biro, Paris, 1990.

Romanin, S., *Storia Documentata de Venezia*, Venezia, 1853.

Sayre, Pamela G., 'The Mistress of Robes – Who was She?', *Byzantine Studies*, 13:2, 1986, pp. 229–39.

Santangelo, Antonio, *A Treasury of Great Italian Textiles*, Harry N. Abrams, New York, [1964].

Serjeant, Robert Bertram, *Islamic Textiles: Material for a History up to the Mongol Conquest*, Librairie du Liban, Beirut, 1972.

Schilbach, Erich, *Byzantinische Metrologie*, Brücken-Verlag, Düsseldorf, 1970.

Schuette, Marie, and Müller-Christiansen, Sigrid, *The Art of Embroidery*, Thames and Hudson, London, 1964.

Schug-Willie, Christine, *Art of the Byzantine World*, Harry N. Abrams, New York, 1969.

Sevçenko, Ihor, 'The Illuminators of the Menologium of Basil II', *Dumbarton Oaks Papers*, 14, 1962, pp. 245–76.

— 'The Madrid Manuscript of the Chronicle of Skylitzes in the Light of its New Dating', in Irmgard Hutter (ed.), *Byzanz und der Westen*, Osterreichischen Akademie der Wissenschaften, Vienna, 1984, pp. 117–30.

Shepard, Jonathan, 'Silks, Skill and Opportunities in Byzantium: Some Reflections', *Byzantine and Modern Greek Studies*, 21, 1997, pp. 246–57.

Shepherd, Dorothy, 'Medieval Persian Silks in Fact and Fancy', *Bulletin de Liaison de la Centre Internationale d'Études des Textiles Anciennes*, 39/40, Lyon, 1974, pp. 1–240.

Sherrard, Philip, *Byzantium*, Time-Life Books, New York, 1966.

Smyth, Herbert Weir, *Greek Grammar*, Harvard University Press, Cambridge, MA, 1959.

Sophocles, Evangelinus Apostolides, *A Greek Lexicon of the Roman and Byzantine Periods,* Frederick Ungar, New York, (undated).

Sotiriou, M. 'Le Vêtement des Imperatrices Byzantines Appélé "Thorakion"', Επετηρις Εταιρειας Βυζαντινων Σπουδων, 23, 1953, pp. 524–30.

Spatharakis, Ioannes, *The Portrait in Byzantine Illuminated Manuscripts*, E. J. Brill, Leiden, 1976.

Staniland, Kay, *Medieval Craftsmen: Embroiderers*, British Museum Press, London, 1991.

Steingass, Francis Joseph, *Persian–English Dictionary*, Routledge, London, 1977 (1892).

Stephenson, Paul, 'Images of the Bulgar-slayer: Three Art Historical Notes', *Byzantine and Modern Greek Studies*, 25, 2001, pp. 44–68.

Stiernon, L. 'Notes de Titulaire et de Prosopographie Byzantines: Sébaste et Gambros', *Revue des Études Byzantines*, 23, 1965.

Stillman, Yedida Kalfon, 'Female Attire of Medieval Egypt: According to the Trousseau Lists and Cognate Material from the Cairo Geniza', unpublished PhD thesis, University of Pennsylvania, 1972.

Stillwell, Agnes Newhall, *Corinth: Results of Excavations Conducted by the American School of Classical Studies at Athens: Vol. XV, Part III: The Potters' Quarter, The Pottery*, American School of Classical Studies, Princeton, 1984.

Talbot Rice, David, *Art of Byzantium*, Harry N. Abrams, New York, 1959.

— *Art of the Byzantine Era*, Thames and Hudson, London, 1963.

Talbot Rice, Tamara, *Ancient Arts of Central Asia*, Thames and Hudson, London, 1965.

Thierry, Nicole, and Thierry, Michel, *Nouvelles Églises Rupestres de Cappadoce*, Librairie C. Khinosieck, Paris, 1963.

Tilke, Max, *Costume Patterns and Designs*, A. Zwemmer, London, 1956.

Tougher, Shaun F., 'Byzantine Eunuchs: An Overview, with Special Reference to their Creation and Origin', in Liz James (ed.), *Women, Men and Eunuchs: Gender in Byzantium*, Routledge, London, 1997, pp. 168–84.

Toynbee, Arnold, *Constantine Porphyrogenitos and His World*, Oxford University Press, London, 1973.

Trahoulias, Nicolette S. *The Greek Alexander Romance: Venice Hellenic Institute Cod. Gr. 5*, Exandas, Athens, 1997.

Treadgold, Warren, *Byzantium: A History of the State and Society*, Stanford University Press, Stanford, 1997.

Turnau, Irena, 'The Diffusion of Knitting in Medieval Europe', in Negley B. Harte, and Kenneth G. Ponting (eds), *Cloth and Clothing in Medieval Europe*, Heinemann, London, 1983, pp. 368–89.

Turnbull, Stephen, *The Walls of Constantinople AD 324–1453*, Osprey Publishing, Oxford, 2004.

Underwood, Paul Atkins, *The Kariye Djami*, Bollingen Foundation, New York, 1966.

Victoria and Albert Museum, *A Brief Guide to Persian Woven Fabrics*, Her Majesty's Stationary Office, London, 1950.

Vogt, Albert, *Constantin Porphyrogénète: Le Livre des Cérémonies, Commentaire*, Société d'Édition Les Belles Lettres, Paris, 1967.

Volbach, Wolfgang Fritz, *Early Decorative Textiles*, Paul Hamlyn, London, 1969.

Walter, Christopher, *Art and Ritual of the Byzantine Church*, Variorum Publications, London, 1982.

Webster, Graham, *The Imperial Roman Army of the First and Second Centuries AD*, Adam and Charles Black, London, 1969.

Weitzmann, Kurt, *Studies in Classical and Byzantine Manuscript Illumination*, University of Chicago Press, Chicago, 1971.

— *The Place of Book Illumination in Byzantine Art*, Art Museum of Princeton University, Princeton, 1975.

— *The Age of Spirituality*, Metropolitan Museum, New York, 1979.

— Chatzidakis, Manolis, Krsto, Miatev, and Radojic, Svetoar, *Icons from South Eastern Europe and Sinai*, Alpine Fine Art Collection, New York, 1974 (London, 1968).

Wessel, Klaus, and Restle, Marcel, *Reallexicon zur Byzantinische Kunst*, A. Hiersemann, Stuttgart, 1978.

Westermann-Angerhausen, H., 'Did Theophano Leave her Mark on the Ottonian Arts?', in Adelbert Davids (ed.), *The Empress Theophano: Byzantium and the West at the Turn of the First Millenium*, Cambridge University Press, Cambridge, 1995, pp. 244–64.

Whitting, Philip D., *Byzantine Coins*, Barrie and Jenkins, London, 1973.

Wilcox, Peter, *Rome's Enemies 3: Parthians and Sassanid Persians*, Osprey Publishing, Oxford, 1999 (1986).

Wilcox, R. Turner, *The Dictionary of Costume*, Batsford Books, London, 1979 (1970).

Wilson, Nigel G., 'The Madrid Skylitzes', *Scrittura e Civilita*, 2, 1978, pp. 209–19.

Wise, Terrence, *Armies of the Crusades*, Osprey Publishing, Oxford, 1978.

Zacos, G., and Veglery, A., *Byzantine Lead Seals*, vol. 1, G. Zacos, Basel, 1972.

— and Nesbitt, J. W., *Byzantine Lead Seals*, vol. 2, Benteli, Berne, 1984.

Zuppan, Jo (ed.), *Bulletin of the Cleveland Museum of Art*, vol. 74, no. 1, Cleveland Museum of Art, Cleveland, 1987.

PICTURE CREDITS

1 Dionysiou Monastery, codex 587, f. 19v. After *Treasures of Mount Athos*, vol. 1.
2 Archaeological Museum, Istanbul. Author photograph.
3 Author photograph.
4 Emperor Constantine IV (668–685) gives privileges to the Church of Ravenna. Mosaic, St Apollinare in Classe, Ravenna. Apse, window area, left. Photo: akg-images / Cameraphoto.
5 Reproduced through the courtesy of the Michigan-Alexandria Expedition to Mount Sinai.
6 Staatliche Museum, Berlin. © BPK images.
7 Author photograph.
8 Bargello Museum, Florence, Bruneld-Denon 19c. © Kornbluth photography.
9 Reproduced through the courtesy of the Michigan-Alexandria Expedition to Mount Sinai.
10 Monastery of St Panteleimon, Athos, codex 2, f. 243r. After *Treasures of Mount Athos*, vol. 2.
11 After Heinrich Frauberger, *Antike und fruhmittelalterlich Fussbekleidungen aus Achmim–Panopolis*, Dusseldorf, 1895, pl. XXV.
12 After Heinrich Frauberger, *Antike und fruhmittelalterlich Fussbekleidungen aus Achmim–Panopolis*, Dusseldorf, 1895, pl. XXIII.
13 Bibliothèque Nationale, France, ms. Gr. 510. After Ludwig von Sybel, *Christliche Antike*, vol. 2, Marburg, 1909.
14 After Henri Omont, *Fac-similés des Manuscrits Grecs Datés de la Bibliothèque Nationale*, Paris, 1891–2.
15 Procession of the virgins and martyrs. Church St Maria in Valle, Cividale del Friuli. Langobardic, first half of the eighth century, interior view: west wall of the auditorium. Photo: akg-images / Cameraphoto.
16 Hagia Sofia, Istanbul. Author photograph.
17 Victoria and Albert Museum. Author photograph.
18 Author artwork.
19 Schatzkammer, Vienna. Author photograph.
21 Sion Collection. Author photograph.
22 Church of Nea Moni, Khios. *c.*1049. Photograph courtesy of Piotr Grotowski.
23 Victoria and Albert Museum. Author photograph.
24 Courtesy Pushkin Museum, Moscow.
25 Karaman Museum, Tashkale Province, Turkey. Author photograph.
26 Dionysiou Monastery, Mount Athos, codex 587, f. 44v. After *Treasures of Mount Athos*, vol. 1.
27 Cabinet des Médailles, Bibliothèque Nationale, Paris. Author photograph.
28 Photograph courtesy of Marcel Restle.
29 After Antonio Santangelo, *A Treasury of Great Italian Textiles.*
30 British Library, additional manuscript 19352, f. 19v. © British Library.
31 Author artwork.
32 British Library, additional manuscript 19352, f. 33v. © British Library.
33 *Adrianople Gospels.* Monastery of San Lazzaro, Venice. After Evans and Wixom, *The Glory of Byzantium.*
34 Dionysiou Monastery, Athos, codex 587, f. 113r. After *Treasures of Mount Athos*, vol. 1.
35 Victoria and Albert Museum. Author photograph.
36 Tokali Kilese Church, Kappadokhia. © Dumbarton Oaks Archive.
37 From *Liber ad Honorem Augusti* of Peter of Eboli, *c.*1225. Author artwork.
38 Syria, eleventh–twelfth century. Lampas weave. 22 x 22 x 22 cm. Cleveland Museum of Art, John L. Severance Fund 1950.525.
39 Wikimedia Commons. Photograph courtesy of Yelkrokoyade.
40 Church of Nea Moni, Khios, *c.*1049. Photograph courtesy of Piotr Grotowski.
41 Author photograph.
42 Victoria and Albert Museum. Author photograph.
43 Istanbul Archaeological Museum. Author photograph.
44 St Mark's Library, Venice, ms Z454 (822) f. 1v. © St Mark's Library.
45 Hagia Sofia, Istanbul. Author photograph.
46 Mosaic, Monastery of Xenofon, Athos. After *Treasures of Mount Athos*, vol. 4.
47 Hagia Sofia, Istanbul. Author photograph.
48 St Mark's Library, Venice, ms 479, *Kunegetika*, f. 33r. © St Mark's Library.
49 Biblioteca Nacional de España, Vitr. 26-2, f. 10v.
50 Great Lavra, Athos, codex. 1.1., f. 114v. After *Treasures of Mount Athos*, vol. 3.
51 Author artwork.
52 Dionysiou Monastery, Athos, codex 61, f. 1v. After *Treasures of Mount Athos*, vol. 1.
53 Koutloumousiou Monastery, Athos, codex 60, f. 1v. After *Treasures of Mount Athos*, vol. 1.
54 Dionysiou Monastery, Athos, codex 61, f. 28v. After *Treasures of Mount Athos*, vol. 1.
55 Dionysiou Monastery, Athos, codex 587, f. 129r. After *Treasures of Mount Athos*, vol. 1.
56 Mosaic, Church of Nea Moni, Khios. Photograph courtesy of Gryffindor via Wikimedia Commons.
57 Vatican Library, ms Gr. 1851, f. 6r. By permission of Biblioteca Apostolica Vaticana.
58 © British Library. BL Add. 19352, f. 29v.
59 Byzantine Museum, Athens.
60 Lincoln College, Oxford, Ms Gr. 35, fol.6r. © Lincoln College.
61 Photograph courtesy of Petar Milošević via Wikimedia Commons.
62 Church of the Holy Saviour in the Fields (Khôra). Author photograph.
63 Khrusobul, Dionysiou Monastery, Mount Athos. After *Treasures of Mount Athos*, vol. 1.
64 Church of the Holy Saviour in the Fields (Khôra). Author photograph.
65 Church of the Holy Saviour in the Fields (Khôra). Author photograph.

INDEX

Note on transliteration: For Greek words beginning in β, look under the Koinê to modern phonetic equivalent, v. For words beginning in φ, look under f. χ is transliterated kh.
Key to numbers: plain text = text references; italic text = figures